# THE BONDAGE OF LOVE
*A Life of Mrs Samuel Taylor Coleridge*

By the same author


FICTION (CHILDREN'S NOVELS)

SCRATCH AND CO:
*The Great Cat Expedition*

THE HUNTING OF WILBERFORCE PIKE

THE LOONA BALLOONA


NON FICTION

EVIDENCE FOR THE CROWN

MURDER WITH A DIFFERENCE

THE ENGLISH LAKE DISTRICT

CUMBERLAND HERITAGE

CUMBRIAN DISCOVERY

SAMUEL TAYLOR COLERIDGE:
*A Bondage of Opium*


AS MARY BLANDY

RAZOR EDGE
*The Story of a Youth Club*

HARVEST FROM ROTTEN APPLES:
*Experimental work with detached youth*

Mrs Sara Coleridge, aged thirty-nine: a miniature portrait painted by
Matilda Betham in 1809 (see Notes to Illustrations 1)
(*Reproduced by permission of Mrs A.H.B. Coleridge*)

# THE BONDAGE OF LOVE

*A Life of Mrs Samuel Taylor Coleridge*

by

## MOLLY LEFEBURE

W · W · NORTON & COMPANY
NEW YORK    LONDON

Printed in the United States of America.


Library of Congress Cataloging-in-Publication Data

Lefebure, Molly.
  The bondage of love.

  Reprint. Originally published: London: Gollancz,
1986.
  Bibliography: p.
  Includes index.
  1. Coleridge, Sara Fricker, d. 1845. 2. Coleridge,
Samuel Taylor, 1772-1834—Biography—Marriage.
3. Poets, English—19th century—Biography. 4. Wives—
England—Biography. I. Title.
PR4483.L38  1987  821'.7 [B]  86–23881

ISBN  0-393-02443-1

W. W. Norton & Company, Inc., 500 Fifth Avenue, New York, N. Y. 10110
W. W. Norton & Company Ltd., 37 Great Russell Street, London WC1B 3NU

1 2 3 4 5 6 7 8 9 0

TO THE MEMORY OF A. H. B. COLERIDGE
Great great grandson of
Mrs Samuel Taylor Coleridge

# CONTENTS

page

PREFACE     15

### PART ONE: SANGUINE SEASON OF YOUTH!
### (1770–September 1798)

1 An Angry Young Man and a Disappointed Young Woman     21
2 Sarah Enchanted by a Meteor from the Clouds     34
3 Ebullience and Duty     44
4 The Glowing Gorgeous Poetry of Courtship     52
5 The Fair Electric Flame     65
6 Domestic Bliss     69
7 The Rock of Reality     76
8 Domestic Bliss Continued     86
9 Farewell, Sweet Youth!     91

### PART TWO: A SOMETHING TO CONTEND WITH
### (September 1798–May 1812)

10 Calamity     101
11 Decoy'd     118
12 Farewell to Happiness     129
13 The Pains of Opium     133
14 The Advent of Asra     142
15 Constancy to an Ideal Object     152
16 Constancy to an Ideal Object — Variation on the Theme     164
17 "The Best Friends in the World" (1)     170
18 "The Best Friends in the World" (2)     178
19 "The Best Friends in the World" (3)     186
20 The Best of Friends — "On His Side Quite"     197

### PART THREE: SNOUTERUMPATER
### (May 1812–June 1834)

21 A Case of Desertion     209
22 Snouterumpater in Full Confabulumpatus     216
23 "Without Hope or Heart"     224
24 House of Bondage     234
25 Domestic Bliss — Reprise     247

ENVOI                                    257

Notes and References                     261
Notes to Illustrations                   276
Selected Bibliography                    277
Index                                    280

# LIST OF ILLUSTRATIONS

*Frontispiece*

Mrs Sara Coleridge, aged thirty-nine: a miniature portrait painted by Matilda Betham in 1809. (*By permission of Mrs A. H. B. Coleridge*)

*Following page 80*

Samuel Taylor Coleridge in 1796. Sketch in pen and chalk by R. Hancock. (*Courtesy National Portrait Gallery, London*)

Thomas Poole (1765–1837); the only known portrait of him, artist unidentified, and used by Mrs Sandford in her book, *Thomas Poole & his friends* (1880)

Robert Southey in his study at Greta Hall in 1804, by H. Eldridge. Note the view of Derwent Water through the window. (*Courtesy National Portrait Gallery, London*)

Mrs Edith Southey, aged thirty-five: a miniature portrait painted by Matilda Betham in 1809. (*Courtesy Fitz Park Museum, Keswick*)

Miniature portrait by unknown artist of young woman thought to be Dorothy Wordsworth. (*By permission of Mrs A. H. B. Coleridge*)

Miniature portrait of William Wordsworth, attributed to D. B. Murphy. (*Courtesy National Gallery of Ireland, Dublin*)

Sara *fille*, six and a half years old; not long after her first wide-eyed visit to Allan Bank with her father. Miniature portrait by Matilda Betham.

*Following page 240*

Sarah Hutchinson, *circa* 1815. Silhouette portrait by artist unknown. (*Courtesy Dove Cottage Trustees*)

Daguerreotype portrait of Hartley Coleridge, *circa* 1845. (*By permission of Mrs A. H. B. Coleridge*)

Derwent Coleridge in 1819 or 1820, by E. Nash, sketched at Greta Hall. (*Humanities Research Center, The University of Texas at Austin, Austin, Texas*)

Engraving of the grounds of Greta Hall, with ladies of the Laureate's household, and a view of Crosthwaite church and Bassenthwaite Water beyond, *circa* 1820, drawn and engraved by W. Westall.

Sara Coleridge *fille* with her cousin Edith May Southey, painted at Greta Hall in 1820 by E. Nash. (*Courtesy National Portrait Gallery, London*)

# ACKNOWLEDGMENTS

I would like especially to thank Mrs A. H. B. Coleridge and the late Mr A. H. B. Coleridge for their extensive co-operation and help with the material, information and illustrations for this book.

I must also thank the Humanities Research Centre, The University of Texas at Austin, for their generous permission to use the original manuscript letters of Mrs Samuel Taylor Coleridge, and also the Nash portrait of Derwent Coleridge.

For permission to use copyright material I thank Sir Charles Cave; the late Mr A. H. B. Coleridge and Mrs A. H. B. Coleridge; Dove Cottage Trustees; Mrs Priscilla Coleridge Needham.

I am deeply indebted to Mrs Mary Wedd, who read the entire first draft of the book and made many valuable and practical comments. I greatly appreciate this kindness. Any errors in these pages are mine and not hers.

Also I would like to thank David V. Erdman for generously putting at my disposal his own notes and erudition on republican activity in London and Bristol in the 1790s. I also much appreciate the help given me on these same matters by Nicholas Roe.

I should like to express my thanks to the Arts Council of Great Britain for assistance with research and library expenses. Also I must thank the staff of the Keswick branch of the Cumbrian County Library for their unfailing help, and the staff of Dove Cottage Library and Museum, Grasmere. My thanks are due also to Mary Burkett and the Abbot Hall Art Gallery, Kendal; the Cumbrian County Archivist; Fitz Park Museum, Keswick; London Library; National Gallery of Ireland; National Portrait Gallery, London; Victoria and Albert Museum.

I thank Mrs Sue French and Mrs Joan Piercey for their expert typing. I would also like to thank Richard and Sylvia Wordsworth for kindness and help in innumerable ways.

M.L.

"Love is not a hot potato that you can throw out of the window."

*Old Russian proverb*

# *Preface*

Mrs Samuel Taylor Coleridge must surely rank among the most maligned of great men's wives. Three great writers have given us a combined, surviving, portrait of her which far exceeds prejudice; it is a positive arraignment, pronounced in the first instance by Coleridge, taken up by Dorothy Wordsworth and, subsequently, by De Quincey — an outstanding case of what Hartley Coleridge would have called "Destruction by pen and ink".

It was Coleridge himself who sedulously cultivated the theme that his wife's explosive irritability and total lack of sympathy with him in his habits and feelings as a man of genius drove him to opium and thus brought about his downfall. Dorothy Wordsworth, William Wordsworth's sister, into whose sympathetic ears Coleridge chiefly poured his marital woes, knew nothing of the effects and characteristics of morphine addiction (if we are to believe the addict it is never his own fault that he has become reliant upon the drug). The classic excuse of the victim is to blame his predicament upon those nearest to him; lack of love and understanding at home is the stock cry, couched in terms of guilty virulence. The innocent and kind-hearted Dorothy, together with her future sisters-in-law, Mary and Sarah Hutchinson, accepted every word that Coleridge told them. Dorothy in conversation and letters to her friends disclosed without restraint the sorry story of poor S.T.C. and his loveless marriage. Grasmere gossip spread abroad.

Dove Cottage, Grasmere, the home of Wordsworth, has received far more attention than has Greta Hall, Keswick, the shared home of Coleridge and Southey. Dove Cottage is open to the public, Greta Hall is not. The Wordsworth *ménage* at Grasmere has been subjected to the closest possible study; a public image has been built of life at Dove Cottage. Greta Hall has remained private, in every sense.

Above all Robert Southey, who wrote so warmly and generously about his sister-in-law, Mrs Coleridge, has sunk in estimation as a literary figure and is now rarely, if ever, read. Hartley and Sara Coleridge, who likewise wrote tenderly and truly of their mother, are but minor figures on the literary scene. But the reputation of Dorothy Wordsworth as a writer increases steadily with the passage of time; her Grasmere journal and the Wordsworth letters have made her voice well known. A personality not given to reticence, she poured out her thoughts, feelings and opinions. Mrs Coleridge figures frequently in Dorothy's portrait gallery, though in the case of "Mrs C" it is not so much portraiture as caricature, since Dorothy was faithfully repeating the opium-distorted Coleridge.

Southey, the Coleridge children, family friends such as Thomas Poole, even Coleridge himself in his happier hours, have left us sufficient writing about Mrs Coleridge for us to see how distorted was the picture that her husband drew of her in his dark periods of "dwelling upon his supposed afflictions". Some two hundred of her own letters have survived; of these forty-two, written by her to Thomas Poole between 1799 and 1834, have been published; the rest have hitherto remained unpublished. A selected number of these, together with excerpts and material from those not quoted in full, provide much of the substance of this book.

Following Coleridge's death sensational journalism, led by De Quincey in *Tait's Edinburgh Magazine* in a series of articles during 1834–5, fell upon the scurrilous details of the dead man's opium-impregnated life, resulting in a spate of "recollections" and "reminiscences" which smeared not only the name of Samuel Taylor Coleridge but, by repeating all the malicious things said by him about his wife, gravely misrepresented her.

It was expected that her firstborn, Hartley Coleridge (himself a poet and author of distinction), would pick up his pen in defence of his parents, and this he vowed to do; but nothing came from him. It was left to his brilliantly scholastic sister, Sara, and her husband Henry Nelson Coleridge (who was also her first cousin) to refute the accusations of plagiarism which had been levelled against Coleridge: but the matter of opium was discreetly ignored by them; his addiction had been too widely known during his lifetime for there to be any possibility of refutation. Henry, though infuriated by the mean insults heaped upon his mother-in-law, was persuaded to refrain from writing a defence of her. Naturally reticent by nature, Mrs Coleridge thought that discreet silence would be more dignified and, in the final count, more effective as a protection for her own reputation: people would soon forget what had been said.

On one occasion only did she commit to paper her own reminiscences of Samuel Taylor Coleridge. This was following the death of Robert Southey, poet laureate and figure of the Establishment, in 1843; naturally it was deemed proper to produce a *Life and Letters* of Southey, and Henry Taylor,[*] the intending author of the work, asked Mrs Coleridge for material concerning Southey's early years, when he and she had been young Bristolians together.

Mrs Coleridge, hiding behind a pseudonym, "Mrs Codian", dictated

*Notes and references begin on p. 261.

her reminiscences to her daughter. As it was impossible for her to recall her youth without having Coleridge soon erupt upon the scene, these recollections were headed; "Mrs Codian. Remembrancies of R.S. and S.T.C." It was common practice in those days for intimates to refer to one another by their initials, but it was at Coleridge's own insistence that the world knew him as "S.T.C."; Samuel was a name that he detested and he did all he could do to discourage its use:

> from my earliest years I have had a feeling of Dislike & Disgust connected with my own Christian Name; such a vile short plumpness, such a dull abortive smartness in the first Syllable, & this so harshly contrasted by the obscurity & indefiniteness of the syllable Vowel, and the feebleness of the uncovered liquid, with which it ends — the wabble it makes, & staggering . . . the whole name sounding as if you were abeeceeing. S.M.U.L.[2]

By the age of sixteen he always referred to himself by his initials, which he often wrote phonetically as Esteese, Esteesee or Esteesi. Only his immediate family called him Samuel, or Sam; his wife was allowed to call him Samuel in the early years, but gradually for her too (and in due course for his own children) he became S.T.C.

"Mrs Codian" remained a fragmentary, unused manuscript; the projected Southey *Life and Letters* ran into problems; when at last the work appeared Mrs Coleridge's artless reminiscences were not included. Her chief effort at protecting her husband's reputation consisted of burning all the old letters that had accumulated over the years. At the time of his death she had had in her possession "loads" of his letters to her (as she had informed an autograph-seeking friend — who nonetheless had been sent away empty-handed because of the private nature of the material). Within the space of a few years almost all of his correspondence, covering a period of forty years, had been burned. Not only letters from S.T.C. to her, or from her to him, had been destroyed; all intimate letters that had any bearing on the Coleridge, Southey and Wordsworth families (for the Wordsworths had come to be regarded virtually as family) were sent to the holocaust; "sackfuls and sackfuls" we are told (many of the surviving letters have "To be burned" or "Burn" scrawled on the outside, but by one chance or another have escaped destruction).

This holocaust was carried out in order that damaging "secrets" should remain secret for ever. As it transpired the family had no chance of preventing posterity from learning the most intimate truths about S.T.C. There were many revealing letters written by him to persons

other than his wife and family. The six-volume *Collected Letters* give us
a portrait of Coleridge which is indeed full-dimensional, while
publication of his notebooks has exposed what might be described as his
entire cerebral and visceral contents, not to mention the very essence of
his Esteesian spirit. With such material as this at our disposal the
destruction of his letters to his wife can scarcely have afforded him more
than the skeleton of a figleaf, if that, in the way of protection.

The injustice of Mrs Coleridge's fate has been that, by this wholesale
destruction of revealing correspondence she robbed herself of evidence
that might well have entirely altered the way in which posterity has
viewed her; a view based upon morphine distortion, sour Grasmere
gossip and the sensation-seeking "revelations" of journalism.

"Lie loud enough and long enough and some of the mud will stick" as
Coleridge was given to saying in self-defence in the face of his own
critics. Such has certainly proved the case with Mrs Coleridge. Mud-
encoated, she has become a symbol of the unloved, unloving and
unlovable wife; ungenerous in spirit, small in mind. Indeed, more than
mud-caked, Mrs Coleridge has become silted up and lost to view. The
time has come to restore her to light; to make true acquaintance with
one of whom even Dorothy Wordsworth was obliged to admit (albeit in
baffled tones), "Mrs Coleridge is a most extraordinary character — "

# PART ONE

*Sanguine Season of Youth!*

(1770–SEPTEMBER 1798)

# An Angry Young Man and
# a Disappointed Young Woman

I

On a September day in 1821 Robert Southey sat in his study at Greta
Hall, Keswick, in the Lake Country, writing a letter to his lifelong
friend Grosvenor Charles Bedford,

Dear Stumparumper,
   Don't rub your eyes at that word, Bedford, as if you were slopy. The
purport of this letter . . . is to give you some account (though but an
imperfect one) of the language spoken in this house by Mrs Coleridge,
and invented by her. I have carefully composed a vocabulary of it by the
help of her daughter and mine, having my ivory tablets always ready
when she is red-raggifying in full confabulumpatus. True it is that she has
called us persecutorums, and great improprietors for performing this
meritorious task, and has often told me not to be such a stuposity;
threatening us sometimes that she will never say anything that ends in
lumpatus again; and sometimes that she will play the very dunder; and
sometimes bidding us get away with our toadymidjerings. And she asks
me, how I can be such a Tomnoddycum (though my name, as she knows,
is Robert), and calls me detesty, a maffrum, a goffrum, a chatterpye, a
sillycum, and a great mawkinfort.
   But when she speaks of you it is with a kinder meaning. You are not a
vulgarum, not a great ovverum govverum. The appellations which she
has in store for you are either words of direct endearment, or of that sort
of objurgation which is the playfullest mood of kindness. Thus you are a
stumparumper, because you are a shortycum; and you are a wattlykin, a
tendrum, a detestabumpus, and a figurumpus. These are the words
which came from her chapset when she speaks of you, and you need not
be told what they signifump.
   I dare say you have set up a whickerandus at this, and I hope you will
not be dollatory in expressing the satisfaction which you derive from
knowing you are thus decidedly in her good graces. Perhaps you may
attempt an answer in the same strain, and show yourself none of the little
blunderums who deserve to be bungated, but an apt pupolion, which if
you do, you will deserve to be called as clever as De Diggle.
   . . . It is much to be regretted that Mrs Coleridge's new language is
not . . . investigated by some profound philologist. Coleridge, perhaps,
by the application of Kant's philosophy, might analyze and discover the

principles of its construction. I, though a diligent and faithful observer, must confess that I have but little insight into it. I can indeed partly guess why donkeys are in the language called jacks, and why peck is a nose; why some part of an elephant's trunk is a griper, but not why it is a snipe; why nog is a lump, bungay a bundle, and why trottlykins should stand for children's feet; but not why my feet and yours should be opprobriously termed hocksen and hormangorgs. So, too, when I hear needles called nowgurs, ladies laduls, whispering twistering, vinegar wiganar, and a mist fogogrum, or fogrogrum, I have some glimpse, though but a glimpse, of the principle upon which these mologisms are fabricated . . . but I should in vain seek to discover the *rationale* of other parts of this speech . . . P.S. I forgot to say that apple-dumple-dogs are apple dumplings, and that Dogroggarum is a word of reproach for a dog.[1]

Mrs Coleridge's "Lingo Grande" as the family called it, was in frequent usage at Greta Hall; smatterings of it are to be found peppering the more intimate correspondence and lighthearted writings of Southey and the Coleridge progeny, Hartley, Derwent and Sara. The etymology of the lingo is subtle, the sources far-ranging and varied. This kaleidoscopic compression of verbal impressions and fancies reveals a dazzling expertise in the invention of portmanteau words and an exploitation of the subconscious pre-dating Lewis Carroll by a good half-century. It would be no great exaggeration to claim Mrs Samuel Taylor Coleridge as the mother of Surrealism; certainly she deserves to be recognized as a pioneer in this art form!

Of course she herself would never have viewed her Lingo Grande in that pompous light. Nor did her family attach any serious implication to it, seeing it purely as an expression of her fundamentally laughter-loving nature, her "dancing, frisking high spirits";[2] one of what Hartley called her "FUNNY THINGS".[3] Neither age nor sad experience could quench Sara Coleridge's propensity for jokes and laughter; a characteristic which she shared with Southey: in middle age they still joked and teased one another as they had done when boy and girl together. A letter written to the eleven-year-old Hartley, in 1807, by Southey speaks volumes on his relationship with Sara:

"Your friend Dapper [Southey's old dog] grows every summer graver than the last. This is the natural effect of time, which, as you know, has made me the serious man I am. I hope it will have the same effect upon you and your mother, and that . . . she will [leave] off that evil habit of quizzing me, and calling me names: it is not decorous in a woman of her years."[4]

Southey was to say that he had been "partly educated" with the little Fricker girls (Sarah, Mary and Edith); but gave no details of when or where. It would certainly have been in Bristol, probably when he (born in 1774) was a child of six. It was scarcely surprising that Southey and the Frickers got on so well together, for there was a close resemblance between the backgrounds and fortunes of the two families. Both came from good Somersetshire country stock; Sarah Fricker's paternal grandfather having been "a farmer and maltster in a thriving way"[5] near Wells, who had left a good patrimony to each member of his large family upon his death, while Southey's forebears had been, down the centuries, substantial woollens manufacturers of Taunton. The fathers of the Fricker sisters and Robert Southey, alike, had been second sons who had deserted the countryside for commerce in the city of Bristol; Robert Southey senior being a linen draper, while Stephen Fricker[5] had become a wine and spirit merchant. From the first he had kept a foreman, thinking himself "too much of a gentleman for business". The histories of both Robert Southey senior and Stephen Fricker were records of lamentable business failure, chiefly due, it would seem in each case, to lack of committed personal involvement in their respective trades.

Stephen Fricker's first marriage, (as we learn from "Mrs Codian") had been to a local beauty, Lucinda Voles, who died in childbed, the infant perishing too. His second marriage was to Martha Rowles, aged twenty; "very pretty, but little", and bringing him not only a dowry[6] but the advantage of "genteel connections", the Perkinses: "Perkins was a great iron founder". Stephen and Martha had ten children of whom six survived infancy: Sarah, born 10th September 1770; Mary, born in 1771; Edith, born 20th May 1774; Martha, born 12th January 1777; Elizabeth (Eliza), born 1778 and George, born last, in 1785.

Over the course of these years of prolific paternity Stephen Fricker failed in a succession of business ventures: as landlord of The Fountain Tavern in Bristol High Street; as partner with his brother in a large pottery at Westbury,* two miles outside Bristol, and as proprietor of a coal yard and spirit vaults in Bath. Throughout all these disastrous enterprises Stephen Fricker continued to maintain the life style of a gentleman with ample private means; at Westbury he built himself a country villa with "kitchen, nursery and dairies off at a distance" (that is, in a distant wing of the residence) and sizeable gardens; while at Bath the Frickers lived in what Mrs Coleridge was to term a "smartish way". This period covered the years of her girlhood between the ages of ten

---

*A factor in his failure here was the cessation of the transatlantic trade in chimney pots and sugar moulds as a result of the American War of Independence.

and sixteen and goes far to explain her life-long interest in other people's houses, drawing-rooms, furniture and equipages; an interest that was natural to her, brought up as she was during her most impressionable years in Bath in its fashionable heyday; one of the most elegant and sophisticated spas in Europe, where everyone vied to dazzle with all the latest refinements of *bon ton*. Sarah was very much a daughter of Bath.

On the other hand the background of her mother was that of Bristol, rather than of Bath. Although the two cities lay within a few miles of each other they were entirely different in character. Bristol, a major sea port and mercantile centre, city of wealth and enterprise, in constant touch through its seafaring population with all quarters of the globe, was historically of a thrusting and enquiring spirit, forever throwing up opportunities for the radical and venturesome (including opportunities to emigrate) and encouraging dissenters and democrats. Iron masters, ship builders, merchant tradesmen, potters, tanners, industrialists across a broad spectrum of activity: it was from this class that the dissenting, forward-minded movement of the period came (for instance the very strong influence of the Society of Friends in Bristol and the county of Somerset resulted in regional support for the abolition of the slave trade, the second petition presented to Parliament in 1785 coming from Bridgwater).

Forward thinking was already veering towards improved standards of education for women. Mrs Martha Fricker was herself an educated woman according to the standards of her day, having been "to a smart boarding school" as a girl (though this in itself did not necessarily guarantee what we today would think of as education). But the education which Mrs Fricker was at pains to bestow on her own daughters reveals that she had a sound idea of what education meant. Sarah, for example, was quick and reliable with figures, fluent and graceful with her pen, priding herself on being strong on grammar and punctuation (the weak points of many a so-called educated young lady in those days); knew her history and geography, and was a voracious reader, including books in French. Mary, similarly well taught, in addition had knowledge of both Latin and Greek; indeed, in later years Coleridge at one point contemplated recommending her to the Wedgwood family as a governess. The Fricker girls were also skilled needlewomen.

Thus the Frickers enjoyed comfortable early years; happy and well cared for and well reared. Then, in 1786, Stephen Fricker went bankrupt. The house and furniture were seized; Mrs Fricker took refuge with her two youngest children in the home of a friend. The other girls were quartered on other friends who proved willing to help at this time of crisis; the sixteen-year-old Sarah was sent to stay at Chewton Keynsham, the country residence of a Mr Kirby, a Bristol attorney. Here too came Stephen Fricker for refuge, a sick and broken man. Within months he had died, aged forty-eight: a distressed and distressing failure.

The widowed Mrs Fricker found herself virtually destitute with a family of six on her hands, ranging in age between sixteen and one year. The family had never known poverty before, indeed quite the reverse; now, abruptly, they were confronted with penury. Mrs Fricker took lodgings on Redcliffe Hill, Bristol, and there opened a small dame school. In order to augment the family income Sarah and Mary, and in due course Edith, were sent out to do needlework. (There would seem to have been a marked disinclination on the part of prosperous Rowles and Fricker connections to have come forward with financial assistance; very possibly the extravagantly smart life style of the Stephen Frickers and the manner in which he had romped through his wife's inherited money coupled with his constant failure to make good in any of the enterprises he had embarked upon, despite active assistance from relatives and friends who had always ended up out of pocket for their pains,[7] had exhausted the patience of those who might otherwise have been readier with help when his widow and children fell on hard times.)

Sarah and her sisters (with the exception of Edith) all revealed strong characters; they were all possessors of a proper pride and natural dignity; and all shared hot tempers, quickly provoked, but as quickly subsiding. Their transition from a "smartish" style of living in Bath to scraping a subsistence as needlewomen in Bristol, returning home to cheap lodgings at night, with no male presence in their household to protect them or buttress them in a society and era which held poor and unprotected women in contempt, the entire neighbourhood aware of their miserably reduced circumstances and inevitable loss of social standing, not unnaturally resulted in the sisters becoming touchy about slights; quick to scent condescension; strongly resentful of being ignored. Their pride grew prickly; their independence of spirit verged on the fierce. All this was inherent in their plight. It speaks volumes for Sarah's inborn generosity of nature and kindness of heart that she never, as a result of her harsh experiences, became unfair or spiteful in her opinion of others. Malice of any sort was not in her: she was prone to hotly indignant outbursts, sometimes approaching rages, but she was always ready to apologize and to make amends. She was given to gentle irony, but nowhere in her letters do we find a single spark of shrewish criticism or so-called sharp wit.

But she did have strong feelings (never was Dorothy Wordsworth herself more unfeeling than in her constant reiterations that Sara Coleridge had "no feelings") and these strong feelings prompted her to equally strong reactions. Hers was not a smooth or soothing personality: her spirited response to everything and everyone, her intense interest in every detail of everyday life, coupled with an energy and practicality which prompted her not only to put her finger into every pie but (conscious of her superior powers of efficiency and dispatch) to attempt to assume complete management of the said pie, ensured that anyone who became involved with her could be certain of a stimulating, not to say at moments an exasperating, time. She had gusto, zest, a keen sense of humour, but she did not, certainly as a young woman, believe in the saying, "Anything for a quiet life." She was born a great participator. Moreover she learned early that life was a battle, and her instinct was to come out fighting, with all her guns blazing.

## II

Among those for whom the Fricker sisters did sewing was Mrs Margaret Southey, mother of their childhood friend, Robert. Through her the Fricker girls met Robert's formidable aunt, Miss Elizabeth Tyler, half-sister of Mrs Southey, twelve years her senior and with absolute domination over her. Between the ages of two and six Robert had lived most of the time with this aunt; Miss Tyler having decided that she wanted little Robert: an exquisite infant with big dark eyes and a head of glossy curls. Accordingly she had carried him off to dwell with her in Bath, from time to time taking him home to Wine Street, Bristol, where the Southeys lived above their linen drapery shop. It was on one of these occasions that Sarah Fricker saw him for the first time: "a little boy in frocks" — possibly in the incredible garment his aunt Tyler garbed him in for high days and holidays — a costume that Southey could not recall without a shudder: "A fantastic costume of nankeen . . . trimmed with green fringe; a vest and tunic outfit known as a *jam*."[8]

Miss Tyler was beautiful, "Remarkably beautiful, as far as any face can be called beautiful in which the indications of a violent temper are strongly marked",[9] wrote Robert. As a young woman one of her close friends had been Lady Bateman, from whom Miss Tyler acquired "the manners of high life, and . . . many of its habits and notions".[10] The death of an uncle left her with ample private income; she travelled to Portugal and then returned to England to enjoy the pleasures of all the fashionable watering places, after which, somewhat depleted in pocket but firmly committed to living beyond her means, she settled in Bath and bore away Robert and dressed him in his *jam*.

At the age of six Southey returned home to live with his parents, that he might go to school in Bristol. Eight years later, in 1788, his uncle, the Reverend Herbert Hill, sent him to London, to become a boarder at Westminster school, but even so he continued to spend his holidays with the simultaneously "tyrannical and indulgent"[11] Miss Tyler, who by now had moved from Bath to Bristol. Yet, impossible as she was, and little as Robert loved her, or even much cared for her, she made a powerful and lasting impression upon him. Her temper, her beauty, her domineering manner, her love of society, her love of dressing up, her energy, her undoubted cleverness, her sheer gusto for life — these characteristics of an extraordinary woman, together with memories of the *jam* of his infancy, became steel-engraved upon his mind.

Almost certainly it was a form of reaction against the domination of Miss Tyler which prompted Southey, as an adolescent, to assume a strongly rebellious stance while at Westminster school. This stance was buttressed by the political climate of the time, arising from the revolution raging upon the other side of the Channel. Southey himself was to write retrospectively, "Few persons but those who have lived in it can conceive or comprehend what the memory of the French Revolution was, nor what a visionary world seemed to open upon those who were just entering it. Old things seemed passing away, and nothing was dreamt of but the regeneration of the human race".[12] Revolutionary France, for the radical British young, held all their wishes and expectations. The universities were in an uproar of debate; the excitement percolated to the public schools.

At Westminster Southey, together with a group of friends, started a radical newssheet, *The Flagellant*, modelled upon the Eton newsheet, *The Microcosm*. The fifth number of *The Flagellant* contained an essay by Southey condemning flogging; this was seen as seriously subversive and Southey was expelled. As a result the Dean of Christ Church, Oxford, refused to admit Southey to that college, for which he had been entered; Balliol, however, was prepared to accept him, taking a more tolerant view of the youth's behaviour.

By the close of 1792 France had made clear her policy of spreading revolution to her neighbour states and had offered help to all peoples prepared to fight for their liberty. The British government responded to this with alarm. When, in February 1793, France declared war on Britain there was, among British radicals, a burning sense of betrayal at their government's opposition to the forces of international liberation.

Sympathy was entirely with France, seen as the embodiment of all that "enlightenment" stood for.

Southey proclaimed himself a republican. Massacres and regicide in no way deterred him from voicing his wholehearted support of France. He rapidly found himself in a difficult personal predicament. "My principles and practice are . . . democratic," he announced, but this, when thought through, produced problems. His uncle was financing his education on the understanding that Southey would enter the Church; yet Southey's radical democratic principles meant that he must declare himself opposed to established religion; indeed "the very existence of a priest is wrong. To obtain future support — to return the benefits I have received — I must become contemptible . . . and perjured,"[3] he mused, miserably. It was an uncomfortable moral dilemma.

To add to Southey's distress of mind, in 1792, the year in which he went up to Balliol, Robert Southey senior became bankrupt and was sent to debtor's prison. His brothers, though of ample means, showed an indifference amounting to hostility towards him and his unfortunate family. However Miss Tyler, appalled to learn that she had a brother-in-law in so low a place as gaol, was propelled by sheer horror to hasten to the Southeys' assistance. Robert senior's release from imprisonment was secured and money was advanced by Miss Tyler to Mrs Southey for the purpose of taking and furnishing a house in Bath: 9 Duke Street, which Mrs Southey then conducted as a lodging and boarding establishment (Miss Tyler temporarily installing herself there). Mr Southey never recovered from the shock of his failure and imprisonment; he went into a rapid decline and died, in Duke Street, in early December of that same year. Mrs Southey found herself a widow with four sons on her hands, the youngest of whom, Herbert and Edward, were still mere children.

Young Robert raged against the blow which Fate had dealt his sweet, gentle-hearted mother; he saw it as rank injustice that she should have had to suffer so grievously. The imprisonment and death of his father, the cruel refusal of the paternal uncles to give assistance, reduced Southey to impotent rage. Moreover there was the knowledge that other families, up and down the country, suffered equal, indeed even worse, hardship and deprivation, without a finger being lifted by society to help them. His radicalism, his republicanism, his disgust with Establishment mounted to fiery intensity; it became increasingly impossible for him to sanction any thought of the priesthood as his destiny. Instead he dreamed of pioneering "an island peopled by men who should be Xtians and Philosophers and where Vice only should be contemptible". On such an island a man "might be truly happy in himself and his happiness would be increased by communicating it to others. He might introduce the advantages and yet avoid the vices of cultivated society."[4]

He discussed his politics, his problems, particularly his moral dilemma over priesthood, at interminable length with his two closest friends at Oxford: his old school crony, Charles Watkin Williams Wynn who was at Christ Church, and George Burnett, a Balliol man, a west country farmer's son and, like Southey, intended by his family for the Church. Southey also sent long brooding letters upon the subject to Grosvenor Charles Bedford and his brother Horace, both great friends from days at Westminster.[15] In holiday times, back with his mother and Miss Tyler, Southey was unable to unburden himself, for obvious reasons. However there were the Fricker sisters to confide in: they were always receptive listeners to all his troubles. Significantly he was "corresponding" with Sarah Fricker and indeed had been doing so for some time past; "corresponding" in that era was seen as a virtual declaration of a serious interest.

But, then, Southey met and fell headlong in love with a girl named Augusta Roberts. "I was lost," he was to confess.[16] To his despair Augusta was not for him; she had already formed an attachment elsewhere.

He now passed through a period of profound dejection: the result of losing Augusta and having to struggle to put her from his mind, together with concern over his family. His mother was showing signs of following her late husband into a decline and Southey had distracting visions of himself burdened with the care of his two youngest brothers. He returned home for Christmas, but Duke Street he could not abide: he found his mother's lodgers "condescending fools". Bristol was equally a city without congenial society: it was peopled with "rich fools". The only persons whose company he wished for were the Fricker sisters. Unfortunately Miss Tyler was now forbidding this: the Fricker girls were charming young women when they kept their place, but she was not allowing her cherished nephew to throw himself away on a Fricker. Southey dismissed her dark suspicions as "ill grounded fears"[17] (he was still struggling to forget Augusta).

Through working in Duke Street for Mrs Southey the Fricker girls had become well acquainted with Miss Tyler and resultantly under her influence. They admired her for being "elegant, handsome and fashionable", and though admittedly she was "very haughty" she was "civil and even complimentary" to them (though drawing the line at

the thought of them becoming seriously interesting to young Robert —
she had no suspicion that he corresponded with Sarah).

The Fricker sisters were certainly girls to win compliments, even
from Miss Tyler. They were all pretty (Sarah and Mary were reckoned
beautiful), accomplished, well-mannered. Poor as they had now
become they always kept themselves smart (their cleverness in making
their own gowns and bonnets must have been of great help to them).
Indeed there is evidence that they contrived to cut quite a dash in their
style of dress and continued to do so, when occasion demanded, for the
greater course of their respective lives; Bath upbringing told (the
Betham portraits of them in middle age show Sara in a romantic veil,
Mary wearing pearls twined in her hair, and even the far less exuberant
Edith sporting a species of Turkish turban).

Mary, whose accomplishments included a pleasing singing voice,
particularly impressed Miss Tyler, who, through her theatrical contacts, was able to get Mary into the Bath-Bristol repertory company.
Influential as Miss Tyler was in shaping Mary's life she was also to play
a salient role in Edith's destiny while, less obviously but with lasting
impact, the Tyler influence upon Sarah was equally significant. From
girlhood onward Sarah (when not irresistibly provoked to fiery
reaction) affected a polished, calculatedly light style, the throwaway
phrases and gestures of elegant society of her youth: Bath society. She
had, in Miss Tyler, an estimable example of manners *à la mode*. Sarah
never became haughty (she could not have been haughty had she tried)
but she did become noted for her wit touched with delicate irony, her
panache in dress, her "high spirits of a gay woman of fashion".[18] There
is evidence that she followed the Bath style of dropping her aitches (one
of her favourite phrases was that such and such, or so and so, bestowed
kindnesses or favours "with no niggard 'and")[19] and she was given to
scattering French elegancies throughout her speech; "entre nous", "en
passant", "outré", "au courant", "au fait", "au fond", "à discrétion", and
the like.

Her Bath style was distrusted and misconstrued by her contemporary
critics and has been consistently misunderstood by posterity (Potter,[20]
for example, sees her delicately satirical exclamation, concerning a
youth blessed with an influential relative, "'Tis a glorious thing to have
a bishop for an uncle!" as an instance of "her ethic prudence and
respectability"). Others have accused her of mindless frivolity. Poor
Sarah! she whom Fate was to place among the leading exponents of the
school of Romantic sensibility had modelled herself upon a polished
exponent of the Bath school. The mode of her choice insisted upon
lightness of touch as its hallmark; the other demanded *soulful*

*earnestness*. Sarah, having adopted the Bath style and made it hers, remained true to it for life. This did not indicate that she was shallow or silly; it was simply her chosen way of presenting herself. Her later letters demonstrate this perfectly; their contents all too often deal with calamity, but we find them sealed (not invariably, for she enjoyed a choice of seals, but often enough to show that it was her favourite) with an elegant little seal depicting a chirpy cricket and bearing the motto, "*Toujours gai*". Bath would have approved.

### III

As it turned out Miss Tyler's ban on the Fricker girls as companions for Southey did not signify much. She had now removed from Bath back to Bristol and Sarah and Southey were soon seeing each other in Duke Street. Sarah was full of the news that Mary was on the point of marrying a highly romantic figure, one Robert Lovell, whose father, a rich Bristol Quaker, was against his son wedding an actress. But Robert, twenty-two years of age, a poet and democrat, and much in love, was used to displeasing his father and was going ahead with the marriage in spite of parental threats that he would be cut off with the proverbial shilling (threats which subsequently were to prove true).

Sarah introduced Southey to Robert Lovell; they immediately formed an enthusiastic friendship. Southey returned to Bristol and Miss Tyler in a less dejected condition. Edith Fricker was now working for Miss Tyler and Southey had good opportunity to admire the "beautiful figure" which Sarah tells us was her sister's outstanding attraction. Southey formed the habit of escorting Edith home at the close of her day's work, "to Miss Tyler's annoyance". Very possibly this was the reason why Southey did it: annoying the older generation afforded him intense gratification since they were all rich (or condescending) fools who symbolized for him the conventional order of society which he, as a Jacobin, sought to abolish.

Balliol in the New Year of 1794 found Southey writing republican poetry and determined to abandon priesthood and self-perjury; instead he would study medicine. He was still on the rebound from Augusta; moreover he soon discovered that he had no bent for medicine, nor was his uncle, Herbert Hill, prepared to be supportive if Southey abandoned the Church for physic and anatomy. Holy Orders again loomed for Southey; once again he found himself confronted with the problem of how to square the priesthood with his republican principles. Yet, if he didn't go into the Church, how to earn a living? Not to mention the possible responsibility of two small brothers? Robert became, as he confided to Grosvenor Bedford, "Worn out with anxiety and sensibly impaired by the ceaseless agitation that preys upon me".[21]

In these circumstances it was not altogether unnatural that he should toy with dreams of finding repose in domestic tranquillity with some devotedly affectionate young woman whose figure held promise, as Eliot puts it, of "pneumatic bliss" while her general demeanour threatened no jolts. Edith Fricker seemed to be the answer. He described her to Grosvenor as, "My own age. Her face expresses the mildness of her disposition — and if her calm affection cannot render me happy I deserve to be wretched. She is mild and affectionate." She was like "the lily of the valley lovely in humility".[22] To himself he painted visions of, "Calm Contentment's woodbind cot" with Edith as soothing companion; his "dearest Friend". Her destiny was bound up in his, he had now definitely decided.

Apart from the four-year gap between himself and the twenty-three-year-old Sarah Fricker (at nineteen four years appears as a marked discrepancy of age) it must have seemed to Southey that the salient characteristics of Sarah herself might well make her an uneasy life partner for him. "Know your own mind"; Southey's favourite precept. In choosing Edith, Robert objectively put his conscious mind to the problem of how to ensure himself a haven of repose in a restless world. But subconscious memories may have dictated his choice even more decisively. Beauty, energy, cleverness; a fondness for dressing up and being a woman of fashion; strength of personality allied to a hasty temper: these were characteristics in Sarah Fricker which may well have reminded him of his Aunt Tyler and that distant childhood spent with her in Bath, garbed in a green fringed nankeen *jam*. He was not going to tie himself for life to any woman likely to force him into any species of metaphorical *jam*.

Miss Tyler refused to believe that Robert could be serious in his courting of Edith. Mrs Southey voiced her surprise at her son's choice; she thought Sarah much the prettier and cleverer. It was a surprise which Sarah obviously shared — and still showed fifty years later when she was dictating her remembrances to her daughter Sara, transcribing in third person: "R.S. . . . corresponded with mama before his marriage . . . He had a friendship with mama first . . . [Edith] was an exceedingly fine girl but very unanimated."

IV

Southey spent the Trinity term of 1794 determining that he would not return to Oxford after the summer. He had definitely decided against the Church; as an alternative he would try to find some steady job in London. If he could not find this he would quit England for America.

Grosvenor Bedford and Wynn agreed to try to procure Southey a situation; the former in the Exchequer, the latter through Lord Grenville (Wynn's maternal uncle), the then Foreign Secretary. But because of Southey's reputation as a republican and Jacobin there was slender hope. If these offers of help did not result in a situation, he would try his pen as a means of support. If this failed, as he proclaimed with dramatic despair, the alternative was "obscurity and emigration, a solitary life embittered by remembrance — and a premature death unalleviated by one comfortable reflection".[23]

The above jeremiad was sent to Grosvenor Bedford from Balliol on 1st June, followed eleven days later by yet another letter of despair. In addition to dejection, or perhaps because of it, Southey now had a stomach upset, "My poor trillibubs are empty. A dose of salts yesterday and another this morning has been scouring out my tripes. This may possibly remove indisposition for a while, but I am not fool enough to hope it will remove the cause. Continual anxiety will wear out a stronger frame than mine — oh, that gripe."

Here the letter broke off, to resume, "One week has elapsed since my letter was so unpleasantly interrupted. In the interim the salts have worked and your last arrived. . . . I am delaying the pickling of my tripes again till the departure of a Cantab; one whom I very much esteem and admire."[24] The Cantab was Samuel Taylor Coleridge.

# CHAPTER TWO

# Sarah Enchanted by a Meteor
## from the Clouds

I

According to Southey it was on 5th June 1794 that Robert Allen,[1] a University College man and a friend from anatomy school days, first brought Samuel Taylor Coleridge to his rooms at Balliol. Coleridge, accompanied by his friend Joseph Hucks, was on the preliminary lap of a pedestrian tour of Wales; the two Cantabs stopped at Oxford to visit Allen, who had been a school friend of Coleridge's at Christ's Hospital. As Coleridge, like Southey, was a rising poet and strong democrat, Allen felt that the two should be acquainted.

Coleridge, throughout his life, possessed an instant, irresistible charm. Indeed it was more than mere charm, it was the power of enchantment: of "leading all hearts captive", as Lamb put it.[2]

> And all should cry, Beware! Beware!
> His flashing eyes, his floating hair!
> Weave a circle round him thrice,
> And close your eyes with holy dread,
> For he on honey-dew hath fed,
> And drunk the milk of Paradise.

These lines, from Coleridge's *Kubla Khan*, must be seen as self-portraiture, even if of a subconscious kind: the youth of the flashing and unforgettable eyes — "large and full . . . such an eye as . . . speaks every emotion of his animated mind", exclaimed Dorothy Wordsworth; "the heaven-eyed creature", wrote Wordsworth. Dorothy further spoke of Coleridge's "longish loose-growing half-curling rough black hair"; hair that had an untamed aspect.[3] But Coleridge, aware that all should beware of him, was not considering himself simply as a youth with exceptionally fine eyes, wild unkempt hair and uncanny personal charm, but as a whirling dervish weaving the convoluted magic of his spells as he twirled ceaselessly, arms outspread, eyes shining, hair flying: impossible to watch without becoming dizzy, yet himself never dizzified though spinning and spinning like a top; a *sufi*; pantheistic, mystic; fed on honey-dew and the milk of Paradise. And therefore "weave a circle round him thrice", as a necessary counter-magic to hold him and his dangerous mysteries enclosed: a talisman to contain the genie that must be prevented from breaking out of his magical whirling pattern; for, once out, he could never be crammed, fitted, coaxed or cajoled back in again but must whizz at uncontrolled tangents, causing fearful havoc.

Coleridge was perfectly aware of his own powers of capturing people and holding them. He was also aware that he whirled, and that his balance was a matter of the utmost nicety. One disturbing movement, one unsympathetic gesture, one breath of adverse criticism from his audience and his concentration and therefore his miraculous spiral of progress into the infinite universal Oneness would be broken. For it was universal Oneness that was his goal,

> that eternal language, which thy God
> Utters, who from eternity doth teach
> Himself in all, and all things in himself.[4]

He knew that, left to himself, he could attain this goal by intense concentration; but his friends would never leave him in peace to concentrate to the degree required. Not understanding, they failed to apply counter-magic by weaving a circle round him thrice and letting him be, to perfect his spiralling and fly. Instead they hung on to his coat tails and bawled, "Pull yourself together!" When he was most near to achieving what he knew to be perfect balance, then his onlookers concluded that he was most perilously unbalanced; thereby setting up doubts in himself, disrupting his concentration and his spiralling and bringing his down.

But at this point in time all is going well: S.T.C. is spiralling blithely across the floor of Southey's rooms at Balliol, to cast his spell over Southey and George Burnett (Allen was already under it) and carry them off to the heady realm of Pantisocracy and Aspheterism,

> Where Virtue calm with careless step may stray,
> And dancing to the moonlight roundelay,
> The wizard Passions weave an holy spell . . . [5]

## II

Southey's first impression of S.T.C. was of being swept away by a great torrent of talk, mainly "disputing on metaphysical subjects".[6] Metaphysics and politics lay closely akin for the visionary radicals of that era; politics were truly seen as "the art of the possible". The fundamental aims of the French Revolution in its early stages were to establish a fraternal system which would set all men free in universal equality; a Oneness of nations that would be an effective expression of Spinozistic Pantheism that saw the human mind as part of Nature and Nature as One with God (which gave the Revolution particular appeal for Coleridge).

During the course of their talk Southey doubtless spoke of his island community where man might enjoy "the advantages and yet avoid the vices of cultivated society". S.T.C. was equally enthusiastic for a society where individual property was abolished (for which he invented the name "Aspheterism") and liberty, equality and fraternity were observed under a participatory government by all and for all (which he called "Pantisocracy").

S.T.C. and Hucks had arrived in Oxford proposing a brief stay of three or four days; they remained instead for three, almost four weeks. During this time the leading features of a Pantisocracy were thrashed out. As it was agreed that finding a suitable island for the experiment might prove difficult, the decision for America was taken; Kentucky being the first choice for the place of settlement. A party of ladies and gentlemen (twelve of each sex, it was ideally envisaged) were to depart for America the following April; previous to leaving they were to get to know one another as well as possible and they were firmly to settle every regulation for the government of their future conduct. They would support their colony by their own labour and the produce of their industry would be property common to them all. They would assemble a good library of books and their leisure hours were to be spent in study, liberal discussion and the education of their children. The women were to take care of the infants and to perform tasks suited to their strength; attention was to be paid to the cultivation of their minds. Everyone was to enjoy his own religious and political opinions provided that these did not encroach upon the rules previously laid down, which rules, of course, would in some measure be regulated by the laws of the state and the district in which the Pantisocrats settled. It was calculated that if each gentleman provided £125 this would be sufficient to carry the scheme into execution. Every individual would be at liberty to withdraw from the society whenever he wished to do so.

In the manner of all advanced liberals the Pantisocrats were exceedingly keen on drawing up regulations; they wished to leave nothing to chance and the weakness of human foible. Vice was to have no opportunity of raising its head in their community, but was to be well clamped down from the start; rules must be formulated for every possible contingency. The chief stumbling block to the perfection of this man-made ideal society lay, as usual, in the women. Eve deprived Adam of his garden of Eden and, unless immense care were taken, she would doubtless do so again. Thomas Poole, in subsequent discussion of Pantisocracy and the male Pantisocrats observed that, "The regulations relating to the females strike them as the most difficult".[7]

The "regulations relating to the females" were worked out by these young males without the slightest consultation with the said females themselves. Some readers may feel that the founding fathers of Pantisocracy had no real notion as to whom the founding mothers might be: they would turn up spontaneously, as homely items of household furniture tend to do. But in fact there is evidence that, in the process of drawing up at least tentative plans for the Pantisocratic distaff side, the Fricker sisters, from the first, were given prominent roles; though, again, no attempt was made to consult them.

The Pantisocratic project was almost invariably referred to by Coleridge and Southey as "the Scheme of Pantisocracy" and S.T.C., when later ruminating glumly upon his involvement with Sarah Fricker, would observe that he had mistaken "the ebullience of schematism for affection".[8] Coleridge was, he confided to Southey, recovering from losing Mary Evans, the sonsy little sister of a Christ's Hospital school fellow. It may well have seemed to Southey that if his own bruised heart could find "calm contentment" with Edith Fricker, Coleridge might equally well find solace in Sarah. Moreover choice of Sarah for Coleridge would mean that the Pantisocratic females would contain a firm nucleus of Fricker sisters; all well known to Southey so that he could vouch for their strength of character and loyalty to one another as a family group; all democratic in their sympathies. He would have his Edith; Robert Lovell, if he joined the emigrants, would be accompanied by his Mary; Coleridge would have Sarah and George Burnett would have Martha — for, further to buttress the contention that Coleridge's courtship of Sarah had its origins in a definite scheme, there is the fact that at the time when he was making his whirlwind proposal to Sarah, Burnett was proposing to the fourth sister, Martha Fricker, who, significantly, "refused him scornfully, saying that he only wanted *a wife in a hurry*, not her individually of all the world".[9]


### III

But, of course, it was not the object of the Pantisocrats to marry for sentimental or emotional reasons. Their haven was to be founded principally upon Hartleian ideology[10] (at that time exerting powerful influence upon radical intellectuals). Both Coleridge and Southey were profoundly impressed by Hartley's theory of "benevolence", which maintained that the necessary functioning of the associational mechanism must inevitably transform subjective interest into objective benevolence; thus the personal and domestic sympathies of each individual must equally inevitably become transformed into universal brotherly love, leaving no place in society for vice. Coleridge was to repeat the theme cogently in conversation, letters, lectures and pamphlets:

> The searcher after Truth must love and be beloved; for general Benevolence is begotten and rendered permanent by social and domestic affections. . . . The paternal and filial duties discipline the Heart and prepare it for the love of all Mankind. The intensity of private attachments encourages, not prevents, universal Benevolence.

From this concept rose further concepts: of Motivism, Optimism, Progression and Necessitarianism. Quoth Coleridge:

> So shall we find through all Nature that Pain* is intended as a stimulus to Man in order that he may remove moral Evil. . . . In morals as in Science our Wisdom is the effect of repeated Errors. . . . It was therefore necessary that Man should run through the Course of Vice and Mischief since by Experience alone his Virtue and Happiness can acquire Permanence and Security. And this is a new proof of Wisdom and Benevolence . . . the Sum of Happiness is twice as great to a Being who has arrived at a certain point by gradual progressiveness as it would be to him who was placed there in the first step of his Existence.[11]

In short, as S.T.C. put it less formally, and retrospectively, to Southey, "However wickedly you might act, God would make it ULTIMATELY the best", adding, "Such expressions applied to bad actions had become a habit of my Conversation".[12] Youth, as Sarah was to observe, is "a sanguine season"[13] and to have one's worse excesses of behaviour supported by Hartleian "pious confidence of Optimism" and indeed seen as necessary steps along the path of virtue and happiness made the springtide of life particularly joyous for their generation.

Two other salient influences upon the scheming Pantisocrats were Dr Joseph Priestley[14] and William Godwin.[15] Priestley, theologian, philosopher, scientist and reformist, firmly preached the doctrines of

---

*"Instead of evil, a disputable word, let us use Pain" — S.T.C. introducing this passage.

Necessitarianism and the perfectibility of man: virtue as a natural instinctive response, vice as the product of circumstance, the subordination of individual to public good, and equality of rights. His unorthodoxy and republicanism had forced him to emigrate to America. The Pantisocrats, particularly Coleridge, revered him as saint and sage. As for Godwin, his *Enquiry Concerning Political Justice*, which had appeared the previous year, had become a virtual bible for radicals (with its emphasis on philosophic anarchy which would make government unnecessary and a firm belief in the possibility of human perfectibility).

Coleridge, with his fundamental "reticulative need and . . . refusal to compartmentalize his interests",[16] when he came to marriage had to see that, too, as naturally part of the grand scheme; the "true System of Philosophy". Marriage, viewed from this predominantly intellectual stance need not involve any excitement of the passions, any falling in love with one who was wanted "individually of all the world". To quote from Godwin, "A consequence of the doctrine of necessity is its tendency to make us survey all events with a tranquil and placid temper . . . to be superior to the tumult of passion . . . to reflect upon the moral concerns of mankind with the same clearness of perception, the same unalterable firmness of judgment and the same tranquillity as we are accustomed to do upon the truths of geometry".[17]

Certainly Southey felt like this over his projected passionless union with Edith Fricker and S.T.C., in this elevated summer of 1794, was perfectly in harmony with the view that domestic bliss might be attained by using, as it were, a smattering of geometrical method; that science of relations of bodies in space. He had never set eyes on Miss Sarah Fricker in his life; but what did that matter? It was the concept of marriage that was important; the philosophical concept. Marriage was the epitome of Rousseauist retirement into the simple joys and virtuous satisfactions of "Love pure and spotless" with a "meek eyed maiden mild".[18]

Like Southey, S.T.C. was insistent that the "beloved woman" must possess humility; emancipated females battling for their rights were excellent in radical theory, but might not be relied upon to promote "domestic peace". A wife should be "a compassionate Comforter . . . innocent and full of love".[19] Indeed S.T.C. was given to citing Shakespeare to the effect that it was "the perfection of every woman to be characterless".[20] We do not know how Southey depicted Sarah, or if he described her at all in much detail, apart from assuring S.T.C. that she was beautiful, with "polished manners". In all probability S.T.C.

was left to assume that if one sister was "the mild and retired kind"[21] then the other sister would naturally be so too.

Necessitarianism meant that he and Miss Fricker *must* unite and that it *must* be for the best; domestic bliss would follow spontaneously and necessarily; serenely he would love Miss Fricker and serenely would he be loved: in the "pious confidence of Optimism" he would woo her and wed her and make her his partner in some log cabin, hand-hewn by himself, in distant Kentucky.

The intending emigrants had only the wildest notions of what America was like; romantic travellers' tales of Indians, forests and buffaloes mingled in their imagination with scenes of rural country life such as they knew in England. Southey dreamed of how: "When Coleridge and I are sawing down a tree we shall discuss metaphysics; criticise poetry when hunting a buffalo, and write sonnets whilst following the plough. Our society will be of the most polished order." He saw himself living in a house that was "simple and convenient" and enjoying "spruce beer, brown bread, a good fire";[22] attended, of course, by a meek wife.

At last the scheme for this paradisiacal life was drawn up as fully as was possible at that point in time. Three major tasks now lay ahead for the months between the birth of the Pantisocratic idea among the colleges and quadrangles of Oxford drowsing in the July sunshine and departure in a "storm tossed bark" next spring. The first was to find recruits. The second was to raise the necessary money. Thirdly, none of the intending Pantisocrats being drawn from labouring ranks, but all being polished, it would be necessary to put in a little practice in the use of spade, hatchet, hammer and nails, and to harden their hands and bodies.

The party of schemers now broke up. Coleridge and Hucks resumed their tramp into Wales; Southey and Burnett set their faces towards Bristol, Allen departed for London. The Balliol rooms lay deserted and silent. Pantisocratic exuberance had removed itself elsewhere. The two prime movers in the venture were positively euphoric as they faced the future: "My mind is never at rest," declared Southey, "not even for a moment. One grand object has fully possessed my soul."[23] While Coleridge, looking back on that hour, was to say, "America really inspired Hope, & I became an exalted Being".[24]

It was some measure of their exalted state that they seriously contemplated raising money for the Pantisocratic venture by poetry. Southey now put in train attempts to sell his *Joan of Arc*; the proceeds to help him purchase "a few acres, a spade and a plough"[25] to start off the colony. There were also his *Botany Bay Eclogues* and a projected slim volume of verse by himself and Robert Lovell. As for Coleridge, his head was crammed with literary schemes of which he spoke as if they were already accomplished. He was, he assured Southey, virtually in the act of having published, by subscription, translations of classical verse; he could ensure more than two hundred subscribers (in actual fact he had been talking about these translations for the past two years and would speak of them for many months to come: they were purely a brain child).

In Bath Southey's sailor brother Tom, home on leave, proved enthusiastically receptive to the Pantisocratic idea and Mrs Southey too, much to her son's delight, announced that she and the two young Southey boys would join the party. Southey, in joyous mood, left Bath for Bristol on 21st July, to attempt to win Robert Lovell and Mary over to the scheme. Lovell at first was opposed to the principles of Pantisocracy but after Southey had preached the doctrine to him for the best part of a week Lovell changed his opinion, or perhaps simply capitulated, and said that he would join the venture. The decision of course included Mary.

During this time Southey never stopped raving about his marvellous fellow Pantisocrat, Coleridge: "He is of most uncommon merit — of the strongest genius, the clearest judgment, the best heart."[26] Then, suddenly, Coleridge appeared in Bristol, utterly unexpectedly. Southey, at the time of this arrival, was supping with the Lovells and Sarah too was present. Nothing could have been more fortuitous! The wonderful young man of whom they had all heard so much was here!

We will let "Mrs Codian" take up the tale of this Bristol supper party and what happened after: "S.T.C. was brown as a berry. Robert Lovell said, 'He can have prog here — but he must sleep elsewhere'." Sarah thought S.T.C., "Plain, but eloquent and clever. His clothes were worn out; his hair wanted cutting. He was a dreadful figure." She remarked upon this, in a quiet aside, to Southey, who replied, "Yes; he is a diamond set in lead." Southey himself was, of course, most elegantly polished: "very neat, gay and smart".

S.T.C. got "righted up a little in Bristol" and was then taken by Robert to Bath to be introduced to Mrs Southey. After he had been there a few days Mrs Southey begged Robert to write to Sarah asking her to come to Bath, to "spend a week or fortnight with her, to talk over the American affair". Sarah accordingly went to Bath. "There was a great deal of conversation about the Pantisocratic scheme." After a few days S.T.C. said that he must soon return to Cambridge and asked Sarah if she would write to him. "This brought on a proposal of marriage." S.T.C. asked Sarah if she would accompany him to

America. The match was agreed on and they were to correspond and "he was, after his time at Cambridge, to come to Bath again".

Thus everything had gone according to plan. S.T.C., at the crucial moment, was sufficiently carried away by the ebullience of schematism to seem sincerely whole-hearted in his advances, while as for Sarah, she, poor young woman, had fallen under his spell and was totally enchanted by him.

## IV

The actual date on which S.T.C. proposed to Sarah Fricker is not known, but evidence provided by Southey establishes that it could not have been after 22nd August at the latest. So, when she accepted this extraordinary young man, she had been acquainted with him for little more than a fortnight.

She knew nothing about him apart from what he himself chose to tell his new circle of Bristolian friends. He was, he said, twenty four* years of age, the son of an eccentric but scholarly clergyman, long since dead, who had been rector and schoolmaster at Ottery St Mary in Devonshire. S.T.C. had a large number of older brothers, the eldest of whom was now himself rector and schoolmaster at Ottery. These brothers, he said, were perfectly unfeeling and had treated him most unkindly. His mother lived with his brothers at Ottery; to her S.T.C. made merely the slightest, disinterested allusion, saying that she had cruelly let him be sent away from home to become a poor charity boy at Christ's Hospital, at a tender age. Later, due to debts, he had run away from Cambridge and, having no one to turn to, had joined the Dragoons under a ridiculous name, Silas Tomkyn Comberbache. Totally unfitted to be an equestrian he had been bolted with, or thrown, or both, every time he had mounted his horse (when he recounted this Comberbache episode he made it so hilarious that his hearers literally rolled about utterly helpless with laughter and with tears streaming down their faces). He had at last been discharged from the army and had returned to Cambridge; but could expect no help or sympathy from his brothers, either with his debts or his path in life: his only hope lay in America. He admitted, with engaging frankness, that his "aberrations from prudence" had been great; but he now vowed to be as sober and rational as his most sober friends could wish.

For the rest he was a Cantab; a shining classical scholar; had gained the prize for the Greek verses; and was now "engaged in publishing a

*In fact he was twenty-three; throughout his life he always added an extra year to his age.

selection of the best modern Latin poems with a poetical translation". In religion he was a Unitarian; in politics a "Democrat to the utmost extent of the word".[27] This was the compass of anyone's knowledge of him. As Tom Poole was so succinctly to say of him, Providence had been pleased to drop him on this globe "as a meteor from the clouds".[28] With this meteor Sarah was now proposing to sail away to the New World and "find repose in an Indian wig-wam".[29]

The truth behind S.T.C.'s dark remarks about his brothers made during that summer of 1794, at Bath and Bristol, was that he was riddled with guilty feelings concerning them. He knew that his brothers, who were far from being wealthy men, had made sacrifices to help him and had treated him uncommonly well. He was indeed a brilliant scholar, but through "sloth" he had failed to live up to his promise and had not gained the Craven scholarship that everyone had anticipated would be his; he had offered a spate of excuses for this failure but it is clear that his heart was full of self-reproach. He was aware that he had let his family down badly. His stupid bolt into the Dragoons had only made matters worse. Yet his brothers had shown the deepest concern for him and had afforded him generous help and support. He had promised to mend his ways; to make a glittering success of his remaining time at Cambridge. Instead here he now was in the west country, preaching the newly invented faith of Pantisocracy, planning to emigrate, getting himself engaged to be married; and all without a word to his family. He had put himself entirely in the wrong with them once again and was now desperately attempting to excuse himself by throwing the blame on them.

"My whole life has been a series of Blunders!"[30]

# CHAPTER THREE

# Ebullience and Duty

## I

So vociferous were Southey and Coleridge upon the twin themes of Pantisocracy and Aspheterism that by mid-August Southey could claim that these words were "well understood now in the city of Bristol".[1] The city's mood, as already noted, was sympathetic to radicalism: by 1794 it boasted a flourishing Constitutional Society; the atmosphere was receptive to ideas for political change and social improvement, further stimulated by regional unemployment and dissatisfaction. The cumulative effect was that Bristol and Somerset were considered by officialdom to be among the most gravely disaffected parts of the entire country.

Not only was Bristol made well-acquainted with the creed preached by the Pantisocrats, but the far less sympathetic Bath, too, was soon repeating (with ill-repressed shudders) the utterances of these two young men so "shamefully hot with Democratic rage".[2] Their gospel was now carried further afield, into the countryside. On 15th August the pair set off from Bath, on foot, for Huntspill, there to see George Burnett before going on to visit Thomas Poole of Nether-Stowey.

Tom Poole, owner of an old-established tannery in which he had succeeded his father, had a reputation as an active democrat; allegedly Government considered him to be the chief instigator of disaffection in Somerset. His correspondence had been intercepted and opened by security officials; friends earnestly cautioned him to be careful in his speaking and writing. To this Poole, typically, had retorted that it had formerly been

> the boast an Englishman was wont to make that he could think, speak, and write whatever he thought proper, provided he violated no law, nor injured any individual. But now an absolute control exists . . . and if . . . speaking is to be checked, the soul is as much enslaved as the body in the cell of a Bastile [sic]. . . . With respect to my future conduct: as I have done no more than every man ought to do, I shall continue to act as before . . . give my opinion if I choose it, and ever will, on every subject, as long as I live. I would fight to the last drop for this privilege. . . . Is this sedition? I glory in it.[3]

Poole's stance as a democrat and his evolving attitudes to the revolution in France as he contemplated its progress well typified the stance and attitudes of thoughtful, radical, mature Englishmen of that period (as opposed to the headlong vociferation of undergraduates). Poole wrote of "the glowing spirit of liberty, which, I thank God, pervades the world, and which, I am persuaded, all the powers on earth cannot destroy". He called for reform, rather than revolution in Britain. The excesses of the French revolution must at all costs be avoided.[4]

It was to this decent, humane, reflective man that Southey and Coleridge introduced themselves on August 18 and over whom they spilled a confusion of Jacobin inflammation including a eulogy of Robespierre. Poole, somewhat injudiciously, took his visitors to meet his nephew John Poole who was made "extremely indignant" by their conversation as was a neighbour of his who was "very indignant over the odious and detestable ill-feeling of those two young men".[5]

During the Stowey visit the Pantisocratic scheme had been fully outlined to Poole in the hope that he might join the venture. He was seriously contemplating emigrating to America but felt that he would do better there by not becoming a fully fledged Pantisocrat, though "I should like well to accompany them and see what progress they make," he confided to an acquaintance. Could the Pantisocrats achieve their aims "they would, indeed, realize the age of reason; but, however perfectible human nature may be, I fear it is not yet perfect enough".[6]

Southey and S.T.C. returned to Bristol: their Nether-Stowey sortie was to have repercussions of a long-lasting and far-reaching nature that would leave Sarah, among others, not untouched.

## II

That Sara Fricker (the *h* now having disappeared for ever at S.T.C.'s insistence) and her sisters sympathized with democratic politics may only be seen as in keeping with their family background of industry and commerce, based in a radical-minded city, at a time when industrial revolution and political independence impregnated the national climate. The least politically minded developed strong feelings, if not active opinions, in the 1790s: Charlotte Poole's journal for 1792 says that interest in French politics had become so intense (even in the quiet countryside of the Quantock foothills) that people who held opposing views could no longer converse without temper.[7] That the Fricker girls, as they grew up, came to reckon themselves democrats and republicans is amply borne out by events; commencing with Southey's stated preference for their sympathetic society and buttressed by S.T.C.'s observation that, in Bristol, he had found "love and kindness" with "democrats" (below, p. 77); best evidence of all is the fact that, when it came to marriage, the sisters all chose partners with strong radical views; Mary wedding the democrat son of a Quaker family, while Edith and Sara became betrothed to young men with notorious reputations as Jacobins.

No discrepancy was noticed between Fricker Bath elegancies and style, and democratic allegiances and aspirations. Quite the reverse, in fact; Southey boasted of his Pantisocrats that, "Our society will be of the most polished order . . . Our females are beautiful amiable and accomplished";[8] manifestly suited for pioneering in some "delightful part of the new back settlements".[9]

Sara, it seems, was all eagerness for the venture; Edith, on the other hand, had qualms. Despite Southey's frequently voiced confidence that she would be accompanying him as Mrs Robert Southey, she herself had so far failed to make up her mind on the matter. However at last she consented to marry; chiefly, it seems, in order not to be separated from Mary and Sara. Edith sighed to Southey, "I cannot leave my Mother without being unhappy — yet I will go with you — staying or going I must be miserable."[10] And with this unenthusiastic response he had to be content.

A party of some twelve men, women and children, had now been recruited for Pantisocracy. The schemers had abandoned the idea of Kentucky as the birthplace of their experiment to "regenerate mankind" and were proposing to settle at "a convenient distance from Cooper's Town on the banks of the Susquehannah".[11] Here they would purchase a thousand acres and hire labourers to assist in clearing the land and building houses. The date of departure was fixed for the following March.

In later years S.T.C. was fond of demonstrating the harmless naïveté of the Pantisocrats by saying that the Susquehannah had been chosen in preference to Kentucky because of the prettiness of the name (the ladies especially liking it). In fact the naïveté went deeper than that: the Pantisocrats, in their touchingly "pious confidence of Optimism", their faith in "benevolence", had fallen prey to the soundly capitalist instincts of Dr Priestley who, though firmly protesting his belief in equality of rights and fraternity, strongly denied the obligation of Christians to practise equality of material possessions: the benevolent "saint and sage", in "the virtuous spirit of commerse", had become a speculator in land, acquiring more than 700,000 virgin acres of Pennsylvania; this area being fulsomely advertised by an agent, Thomas Cooper (after whom a new settlement, Cooper's Town, had been named) in a prospectus, *Some Information Respecting America* (1794),[12] designed to exploit the ignorance and gullibility of would-be pioneer back-woodsmen; assuring them of the temperance of the climate, the convenience of the neighbourhood, the benevolence of the Indians, and the ease with which labour might be hired to do all the dirty and hard work; thence Pantisocratic interest — they were among those who read the prospectus.

"Everything smiles upon the undertaking . . . " announced Southey on 22nd August; the happy prospect being "only clouded by some slight shadows — my Aunt knows nothing of it and we have money to raise".[13] Leaving Miss Tyler to repose for a little longer in blissful ignorance of the scheme, Southey addressed himself once more to his poetic muse in order to obtain funds. With Coleridge, a tragedy in blank verse, *The Fall of Robespierre*, was written within a matter of two days. The authors were delighted with their work and anticipated ample repayment.

It was now decided that S.T.C. should travel back to Cambridge via London, where he would recruit further Pantisocrats, sell *The Fall of Robespierre*, make contact with an agent for land in the Susquehan-nah region and, at record speed, write and see through the press and distribute a handbook about Pantisocracy which he and Southey had drafted. After this he would hasten to Cambridge. He would keep in touch with Bristol through weekly parcels of letters, leaflets and documents pertaining to the Cause. In these parcels there would also be letters for Sara.

Final farewells were made; S.T.C. departed on 2nd September. Bristol was left in breathless anticipation of news of Pantisocratic developments in the metropolis and Cambridge. But no weekly parcels materialized; not even one letter, one line, for Sara. Instead there ensued a profound and baffling silence.

At last a scrappy note, dated 11th September, arrived for Southey. S.T.C. was ensconced at the Cat and Salutation Inn, Blood Alley, Newgate Market, an address which worried Southey, as did the note, which ended on an extraordinary key, "To Lovell, and Mary, the wife of Lovell . . . say all the friendly things for me — to &c — all the *tender* things". "&c" was Sara. Southey (and doubtless Sara also) was of the opinion that Samuel should have written the tender things in a letter direct to her: it was anticipated that this would quickly follow. But a week passed without further word. Finally, on 17th September, Southey sent S.T.C. a severe reprimand for neglecting his brothers and sisters in Pantisocracy and above all for neglect of Sara; it was being suspected that his intentions towards her might not be truly serious.

But no sooner had this letter been committed to the post than there arrived in Bristol the long overdue promised parcel of letters from S.T.C. (now back in Cambridge), containing a sentimental note for Edith on the theme of sisterhood; another for Mrs Southey, extolling the virtues of maternal love; a letter for Southey on the theme of Sara, "I certainly love her. I *think* of her incessantly"; and for Sara herself a passionate love letter in which he "poured forth the Heart".

Hot on the heels of this parcel came another letter for Southey, in reply to his letter of reprimand. S.T.C. reeled off a string of excuses for not having written earlier and concluded, in an injured tone, "I ought not to have been *suspected*".[14]

S.T.C. wrote a further letter to Sara, repeating the excuses. After which he ceased writing to her.

The truth was that Southey's strictures had disturbed his whirling, had drawn him up short, dispelling his ecstatic dreams of a Pantisocracy on the wizard banks of the Susquehannah. Now, in a "calmer moment" he recognized his Balliol scheming and whirlwind courtship of Sarah Fricker and the talk that had "brought on a proposal of marriage" for exactly what it had all been: a fatal combination of an "ebullient Fancy, a flowing Utterance, a light & dancing Heart, & a disposition to catch fire by the very rapidity of [his] own motion, & to speak vehemently from mere verbal associations, choosing sentiments" that now made him recoil with "Horror from the actions expressed in such sentences & sentiments".[15] To become a backwoodsman sawing logs, hunting buffalo and following the plough, with a log cabin to crawl into at night with Miss Fricker for company was a prospect which, judged coolly, filled him with a sense of unspeakable doom. No, he would not do it! So commenced the first recorded instance of that game he was to play so often during the course of his life, of maintaining the stance of being exceedingly enthusiastic over a certain course of action while running away from it with all the desperate energy he could summon.

Brother George Coleridge, getting wind of the current Esteesian escapade, desperately tried to save Samuel from Pantisocracy as he had previously saved him from the Dragoons; it was hinted that the family might have to have Samuel restrained in a private lunatic asylum (the army had finally discharged him as "being Insane" and though this had been a convenience at the time it had left the senior Coleridge brothers and especially George with a horrid lurking suspicion that young Sam might genuinely be a case of Reason tottering on its throne). S.T.C., to take his mind off his troubles, embarked upon an ardent flirtation with a young actress, Elizabeth Brunton, while simultaneously pursuing her pretty sister, Ann; George, meanwhile, persuaded S.T.C.'s former sweetheart, Mary Evans, to write to him urging him to abandon the "Plan [of Pantisocracy] so absurd and extravagant". George and Ottery made a "liberal Proposal" embodying the suggestion that S.T.C. should, with the assistance of his family, enter the Temple after leaving Cambridge and read for the Bar; S.T.C. seized upon the idea and also attempted to resume his courtship of Mary but failed because she (persuaded of his total unsuitability as a husband) had become betrothed to another.

Meantime Southey kept up his exhortations of "Duty" to Pantisocracy and Sara Fricker. Not that Southey was fully informed of the extent to which S.T.C. had turned renegade — he wasn't; but he could scent desertion. It would seem that Sara, for her part, never lost faith in her swain's constancy. When he ceased writing to her she discreetly refrained from writing to him: Southey had reported to her the Coleridge family threats to have Samuel "restrained". We are told that Sara decided not to aggravate the situation by attempting further correspondence with him. We know that she remained sublimely convinced of his attachment to her.

## III

But in Bristol there were other matters to worry about. Miss Tyler had so far been kept in ignorance both of the Pantisocratic scheme and Southey's engagement to Edith. At last the news reached her. The result was instantaneous drama; announcing that she would never see Robert Southey again, nor open a letter from him (and she was as good as her word), she forthwith turned him out of her house; penniless, without an overcoat, on a pitch-black stormy night.

This event had serious and far-reaching repercussions. Not only Southey himself had been dependent upon his aunt for financial help, the rest of his family had also been receiving substantial assistance from her and this was now withdrawn. Mrs Southey soon saw it as her duty to withdraw from the Pantisocratic scheme of emigration. Mrs Fricker, who had only agreed to go with her younger children if Mrs Southey went with hers, withdrew likewise. Southey's heart strings were "sadly jarred" by this; he had depended upon his mother's going. "Ariste" (his name now for Edith) was similarly shaken by her mother's decision to stay in England. After considerable hesitation Edith said that she would still go to America with Robert, but a gloom had been thrown over the enterprise.

With the Pantisocratic scheme literally eroding under his feet it became essential for Southey that S.T.C. should reveal himself as still firmly committed to the project. Accordingly Southey wrote anxiously to Cambridge, demanding to know when S.T.C. would be returning to Bristol; there was no reply.

Both Southey and Sara succumbed to renewed consternation. They decided that S.T.C.'s brothers must have carried out their threats and had placed him somewhere in confinement. At last Robert in desperation wrote to a mutual acquaintance who provided the information that S.T.C. was back in his old haunts in the neighbourhood of Newgate Street. Southey, like some relentless Hound of Heaven, posted off a fresh spate of correspondence stiff with cries of "Duty!", stimulating S.T.C. to unconvincing protestations that his Duty he would do (Duty invariably spelt with a doomlike capital D) and lacing these protestations with admissions that the bethrothal to Sara had been an error: that he had mistaken "the ebullience of schematism for affection. . . . A moment's reflection might have told me, Love is not a plant of so mushroom a growth". As for the fatal love letter, written on his return to Cambridge, that he described as "the most criminal action of my life . . . I had worked myself to such a pitch, that I scarcely knew I was writing like an hypocrite".[16]

Probably Coleridge hoped that Southey would pass all this on to Sara who would then resultantly write to break off the engagement. But Southey did not, would not, do his dirty work for him: S.T.C. must do the manly thing and face up to Sara himself, or at least write direct to her telling her of his change of heart. But this S.T.C. could not steel himself to do.

In the New Year Southey redoubled his demands that S.T.C. should return to Bristol. S.T.C , secretly committed to his family's plans for his career at the Bar and still hoping to wriggle out of his betrothal to Sara, repeated his increasingly unconvincing assurances that he would shortly be reappearing in Bristol to do his Duty. "Think you I wish to stay in Town? I am all eagerness to leave it."[17]

Now came a pantomime sequence of events. In a letter postmarked 29th December Coleridge informed Southey that "whatever the consequence" he was resolved to be in Bath by Saturday, 3rd January. On 2nd January came another letter from Coleridge, still in London, saying that he now intended setting off from London on Sunday night, travelling by waggon, and expected to be with Southey by Wednesday (waggon, at two miles an hour, was the slowest form of transport available). Accordingly Southey and Lovell walked to Marlborough to meet the waggon but no Coleridge was on it. More promises of further arrivals were made and Southey was kept in exercise walking to meet coaches and waggons from which no Coleridge ever emerged. The fearful truth dawned on Southey that, unless he went to London to collect Coleridge in person, the renegade would never appear at Bristol again.

So up to London went the fuming Southey, to return with an inwardly groaning S.T.C., gripped in the remorseless clutch of Duty: "Resolved — but wretched!"[18]

# CHAPTER FOUR

# The Glowing Gorgeous Poetry of Courtship

## I

It is generally believed that Coleridge was virtually frog-marched to the altar by Robert Southey and forced into union with an unloved and unloving partner. S.T.C., it is true, himself gave birth to this distortion of the truth by his later loud and long lamentations, "I played the fool, and cut the throat of my Happiness, of my genius, of my utility, in compliment to the merest phantom of overstrained Honour! O Southey! Southey! an unthinking man were you!"[1]

In fact there had been no way in which Southey could have prevented S.T.C., upon his return to Bristol, from confessing to Sara, had he so wished, that in proposing to her he had simply been over-influenced by Pantisocratic scheming and now asked, as much for her future happiness as for his own, to be released from an engagement which could only result in disaster for them both. Sara, an honest and decent young woman, would surely have understood and complied with such a request.

But this request was not made (though there are indications that Southey rather expected that it might be voiced). Instead S.T.C. fell dramatically in love with Sara and a true courtship commenced which was to remain for long after a byword in Bristol for its romantic intensity and unprecedented poetic raptures. Says De Quincey, "Coleridge . . . assured me that his marriage was . . . forced upon his sense of honour by the scrupulous Southey. . . . On the other hand, a neutral spectator of the parties protested to me, that, if ever in his life he had seen a man under deep fascination, and what he would have called desperately in love, Coleridge, in relation to Miss F., was that man."[2]

That Coleridge fell in love with Sara Fricker and as a result became, for a considerable length of time, a joyously happy man, is abundantly evident from well-recorded facts. Indeed S.T.C. himself was to testify that his had been a love match, though this testimony was given in a series of, as it were, back-to-front avowals, made a quarter of a century after the event. He then jotted dourly in his notebook, "Marriage, the meagre prose comment on the glowing gorgeous poetry of Courtship".[3] By 1819 he had concluded that the basic threat to marital happiness arose from the wretched initial business of falling love:

My experience as well as my insight into human Nature . . . authorizes, *compels* me to hold it not merely possible but highly probable that the sexual impulse, acting not openly in the excitement of conscious desire . . . but acting covertly and unconsciously in the imagination, and in that form contracting a temporary alliance with the best moral Feelings, may assume and counterfeit the appearance of exclusive *Love*. . . . How else could it be that what are called Love-matches are so proverbially unhappy . . . and the consequent disappointment acute & alienating in exact proportion to the degree in which the self-deluded Husband is by nature & education susceptible of domestic Bliss, if only he had chosen *wisely* and with his eyes free from Film and Fever?[4]

Sara might equally well have sighed that her eyes, too, had been distorted in their vision when she had chosen S.T.C. as her future husband. It was really quite astonishing that such a fundamentally sensible young woman should burn to marry a wild poet intending to settle in the American backwoods, there to pioneer Pantisocracy. But Sara had fallen completely under the Esteesian spell; lost to any vestige of clear-sighted prudence. In her middle age she allowed herself occasional wry comments about those lucky enough "to have drawn a prize in the matrimonial lottery".[5]

## II

Upon his return to Bristol in those first weeks of 1795, Sara received S.T.C. with an unfeigned warmth which totally disarmed him, displaying "an affection to the ardour of which my Deserts bear no proportion" as he, in almost shame-faced modesty mingled with pride, informed his friends. She disclosed to him that she had received two offers of marriage during his absence; one of a particularly advantageous nature from a man of wealth. This proposal her family had urged her to accept; strenuously advising her to forget the penniless Coleridge who seemed to have forgotten her. But Sara had remained faithful to Samuel, believing that, against all appearances to the contrary, he would return.

The discovery that Sara was so demonstrably head-over-heels in love with him, preferring the prospect of hardship with him to guaranteed security with another, set S.T.C. aglow; prompting him to feel gratitude to her as well as a marvellously flattered ego. Moreover, opposition brought to the fore his strong streak of perversity; as he observed of himself to himself: "You have some small portion of pig-nature in your moral idiosyncrasy, and, like these amiable creatures, must occasionally be pulled backward from the boat in order to make you enter it."[6] Had all been plain sailing, with everyone keen that he should marry the girl, he would doubtless have held back and found reasons for escaping her. Instead, spurred on by adversity, he looked at Sara with eyes no longer bespectacled with schematism and saw her, as it were, anew; beautiful, accomplished and alluring; courted and admired by several suitors yet pulsating with love and loyalty for him alone; sensitive, sympathetic, devoted, trusting; a combination of delectable charms and invaluable virtues. And he was betrothed to this priceless jewel; this ravishing bloom of young womanhood! He must have been insane to have lingered in London, wrapping himself in imaginary woes! Truly, he was the luckiest man in the world! And he began proclaiming ecstatically from the rooftops: "I love and I am beloved, and I am happy!"[7]

Coleridge was trapped in the initial stages of morphine addiction by the time he was an undergraduate.[8] His case history as an addict was tragically typical of his day; laudanum (the alcoholic tincture of opium) was then widely used for a variety of complaints; as commonly resorted to, and as easily obtainable, as aspirin in our era. Furthermore for many afflictions and complaints laudanum was the only known effective, or even remotely effective, medication; used by the medical profession in almost every ailment, from trivial indisposition to severe contagion. S.T.C., at the age of eighteen, while a pupil of Christ's Hospital, had been seriously ill with rheumatic fever for which he had been administered (perfectly properly, within the context of medical treatment of that day) large doses of laudanum; his body's chemistry first adapting itself to become tolerant of the drug (a process which, in the case of morphine, is literally impossible to reverse) and then, inevitably, becoming reliant upon it, or, to use the popular phrase, addicted.

During these early years of addiction S.T.C. was experiencing the pleasurable "honeymoon" period of the drug. Opium elated, stimulated him; promoted delicious day dreams and fantasies. However strenuously he was later to protest to the contrary, there is no doubt that at Cambridge and in the west country years to follow S.T.C. was using opium for pleasure (of course, had he tried to abandon use of the drug entirely he would have discovered that already he could not wean himself from it. It was established in his bloodstream, part of his pattern of life).

In S.T.C.'s day none of this was understood, though some observers comprehended better than others the hopeless tragedy of the addict's dilemma (it took fifteen years of witnessing S.T.C.'s struggles, relapses, collapses and catastrophes before Southey could begin to understand and extend charity towards him in the matter).

Clearly, in that spring of 1795 S.T.C., carried away by the sheer euphoria of being in love, gave himself up to delicious sessions when, with his almost-too-much-for-him-to-bear exquisite happiness lulled and yet simultaneously fortified by opium, he lay, lost to the outside world, spinning delectable daydreams of domestic bliss with Sara. To what extent, at this stage, such behaviour was recognized by his intimates as opium-induced, or simply ascribed by them to common indolence, it is impossible to say: it seems highly unlikely that Southey and Burnett, sharing with S.T.C. the lodgings at 25 College Street, Bristol, and the closely associated, worldly wise Robert Lovell, should not have detected the laudanum bottle underlying the languor; indeed it is virtually certain that such was the case, though probably, at this juncture, it was Lovell alone who grasped the full implications of the situation.

Furthermore he must have alerted the Frickers to the "indolence" of Sara's betrothed; even if they were kept in ignorance, at this stage, of the root cause of the "indolence" (it is impossible to say precisely when the Bristol circle became fully cognizant of Coleridge's "laudanum habit", because "indolence", the euphemism then used for laudanum addiction, was simultaneously being used in its ordinary sense too). What we do know for certain, is that the Fricker family renewed pressure upon Sara to give up Coleridge in favour of her more substantial suitor, while Robert Lovell, in every likelihood prompted by the family, warned S.T.C. not to be "impatient for marriage" with Sara; S.T.C. being given to understand, by Lovell, that the Frickers considered him too indolent to make Sara a good husband.

The criticism was a just one; S.T.C. subsequently conceded that, following his return to Bristol, he had been "criminally indolent".[9] But the very justice of the accusation had the effect of producing a furiously indignant reaction in him at the time; he stormed about Bristol vehemently telling anyone who would listen to him that Lovell was a "Villain". Joseph Cottle, a printer and bookseller friend of the Pantisocrats, pressed for details. S.T.C. responded, "Lovell, who at first, did all in his power to promote my connexion with Miss Fricker, now opposes our union".[10] Southey, unlike the Lovells, at this stage stood staunchly by S.T.C., while Sara's ardour was only heightened, if such a thing were possible, by her family's opposition (she as yet knew nothing of the "pains of opium").

Some kind of ultimatum was now issued by the Fricker forces: either

S.T.C. must start earning money, without delay, and prove himself the kind of man capable of supporting a wife, or he must relinquish Sara to the rival suitor. American backwoodsmanship no longer offered an escape route: Southey was now firmly wedded to the notion that Pantisocracy should be given a preliminary trial in Wales, once enough money had been raised jointly to buy a farm. S.T.C. remained strongly opposed to this Welsh variation on the Pantisocratic theme but he was outnumbered; the Lovells, Burnett, Mrs Southey, all supported the Welsh project. Apparently acquiescing, S.T.C. privately worked upon an alternative strategy for himself and Sara.

Before leaving London Coleridge had discussed with Southey the possibility of professional work, such as tutoring or journalism, to tide over the period before departure could be made, as originally intended, for America. George Dyer[11] had offered to help Coleridge procure a tutorship with the family of the Earl of Buchan. Late February 1795 found S.T.C. writing from Bristol to Dyer in London, enquiring if it might be possible to obtain lodgings as a married man while tutoring in Scotland?

In other words, S.T.C. and Sara were preparing to elope together, prompted by the "commanding . . . requests of her relations" that she must take the sensible step of discarding Coleridge for her wealthy suitor. Only a runaway marriage with Coleridge seemed likely to save her from this fate. "A short time must decide whether she marries me whom she loves . . . or a man whom she strongly dislikes in spite of his fortune and solicitous attentions to her," Coleridge confided to Dyer. In order to make money as quickly as possible (doubtless to finance the envisaged journey to Scotland with Sara) Coleridge, without delay, delivered three political lectures.

By mid-March it was clear that there was to be no tutorship in Scotland. Coleridge held a fresh council of war with Southey. It was decided that if, by lecturing and writing, they could jointly raise a sum of one hundred and fifty pounds per annum, they would respectively marry Sara and Edith, retire into the country and there carry on their literary business and practise agriculture until they had saved enough money "for America — still the grand object in view".[12] Accordingly, Southey proposed giving twelve historical lectures, two a week, each lasting an hour, "Teaching what is right by showing what is wrong".[13] Coleridge assisted in preparing these. Southey's lectures were concluded by 9th May; he delivered thirteen instead of the advertised twelve; the final lecture being "a flaming panegyric of Tom Paine" written by Coleridge.[14] The latter, in his anxiety to build up "a provision for his speedy marriage" (as Cottle expressed it in his

*Reminiscences*) planned a further series of his own; a projected fourteen on varied religious and political subjects; but these, it would seem, were never delivered: Coleridge's rapidly acquired reputation, not to say notoriety, as a fiery radical obliged him to discontinue his political lecturing; principally because innkeepers and other landlords of public rooms refused to lease them to anti-Government speakers, for fear of having their licences withdrawn.

However, there still remained literary endeavour to yield income: Southey's *Joan of Arc* had yet to appear; Cottle voiced the intention of publishing volumes of new poems by both R.S. and S.T.C.; John Scott promised Southey a guinea and a half a week for writing in a projected radical periodical to be called *The Citizen*; Coleridge's three political lectures were to be published (they appeared in November of that year).[15] Coleridge also spoke loudly and confidently of his subscription work of translations of classical verse which, he forecast, would clear well over a hundred pounds; the long dreamed-about project which had so far remained nothing but a dream and continued to remain so: at the present time S.T.C. was absorbed chiefly in writing verses to Sara.

He showered her with effusions extolling her charms and accomplishments. He contemplated her with delight, "Akin to the delight in a beautiful flower".[16] Nonetheless at the same time he recognized her qualities of strength and integrity; her earthy genuineness, "A lovely Female no Bird of Paradise to feed on dews and Flower-fragrance . . . but a Flower that must fix its roots in the rich genial Soil, thence suck up nutriment, to bloom strong & healthy — not to droop and fade mid sunshine & Zephyrs on a soilless rock".[17]

## III

Against his favourite later lament that there was no way in which a man might discover, before marriage, that his partner was the possessor of a hot temper should be placed Coleridge's reflective observation (again of 1819) that: "Temper . . . may disturb and interrupt, but it will not be likely to subvert the happiness of domestic life"; it was "the soft Moonlight of Love's first phantasies"[18] which was the true cause of all the trouble: together with certain flaws of personality in the woman such as indocility and a mind of her own and her lack of appreciation that she was of the inferior sex. An intending husband should ask himself, concerning the object of his choice, "Does she sincerely adopt my opinions upon all important subjects? Has she at least that known *docility* of nature which, uniting with true wifely love, will dispose her so to do?"[19]

So wrote Coleridge in 1819. But in 1795 he had (at least overtly) entertained decidedly different opinions upon the subject of woman, her place in society and her rights: opinions which had coincided with Sara's own views upon this all-important subject.

Despite the natural inclinations of Southey and Coleridge for docile, meek brides who would prove "compassionate comforters", the Dawn of Reason and the principles of Liberty, Equality and Fraternity made it quite impossible for women to be kept in their traditional place on a humble rung of society's ladder. When peasants, slaves and convicts were being set free and greeted with cries of fraternal acceptance it was no longer possible to deny basic rights to that serf of serfs, Woman.

In revolutionary France women were playing active roles: the mob knew no sex discrimination when violence erupted on the streets; women turned out to demonstrate alongside the men. When the popular and fraternal societies of the *petit bourgeoisie* appeared in 1791 women were unrestrictedly admitted as members and together with their male counterparts were educated in revolutionary doctrine. This open inclusion of women in fraternal comradeship had a profound effect upon patterns of social behaviour; progressive young women abandoned chaperones and appeared boldly in places of public entertainment, as well as public meetings.

Mary Wollstonecraft's *A Vindication of the Rights of Woman* had been published in 1792, a work which caused a furore and was given pride of place on the lists of the radical book societies, coming a close second to Tom Paine as inflammable reading (it was the first choice put forward by Thomas Poole as a suggestion for the Stowey Book Society, when this was formed at his instigation). Questions relating to women became fashionable subjects with the debating societies. Suddenly everyone was voluble upon the necessity of according women freedom and equality, of recognizing their problems and of promoting them to a respected place in society as individuals as well as mere slaves in a household.

Mary Wollstonecraft,[20] who wrote her powerfully seminal work in six weeks in a rush of strong feeling ("Enthusiasm is the all in all") combined with intense thinking, was a true daughter of the Age inasmuch as she entertained the deepest regard for the doctrines and writings of Rousseau; but it was a regard tempered by one strong reservation: Rousseau, she emphatically stated, was the enemy of women, maintaining as he did that woman's role, intended by nature, was to please men; to be useful to them, to win their love and esteem; to advise, console and in general render the lives of men easy and agreeable.

This theme had in turn been taken up by Dr James Fordyce in his *Sermons to Young Women*, which, appearing in 1765, had been widely read, rapidly going into three editions. In this he had recommended "the retiring graces"; women should be meek, timid, yielding, complacent, benign, tender, with a "propensity to melt into affectionate sorrow". Mary Wollstonecraft rejected this; declaring roundly of Rousseau (and by implication of good Dr Fordyce also): "I war . . . with the sensibility that led him to degrade woman by making her the slave of love."

*Rights of Woman* is not about "rights" in the fundamentally combative sense in which we use that word today, but about the desirability of an equal participation by both sexes in a society oriented upon a two-sex and not a single-sex axis. It is not about sexual equality as we popularly construe that greatly abused ideal; as Wollstonecraft correctly saw it, a demand for equality of women with men assumes the superiority of the masculine standard. She was urging the equality of men and women *with each other* (she did not fall into the trap of maintaining that women should merely be imitation men). She upheld a view of women's rights within the moral and social concept of a regenerated, revolutionized society where there would be equal participation in common rights and duties; a concept immeasurably more radical, intellectually subtle and seriously challenging than is our purely materialistic approach to the question today. "I have thrown down my gauntlet, and deny the existence of sexual virtues, not excepting modesty. For man and woman, truth, if I understand the meaning of the word, must be the same . . . Women, I allow, may have different duties to fulfill; but they are *human* duties, and the principles that should regulate the discharge of them I sturdily maintain, must be the same."[21]

To bring about this change, women *must* be educated: herein lay the answer to the condemnation, by men, that women were incapable of playing an equal role in society: education through learning, through knowledge, through experience. "Contending for the rights of woman, my main argument is built on this simple principle, that if she be not prepared to become the companion of man, she will stop the progress of knowledge and virtue; for truth must be common to all, or it will be inefficacious with respect to its influence on general practice." "Can she rest supinely dependent on man for reason, when she ought to mount with him the arduous steeps of knowledge?" The battle cry to women became, "Wisdom is the principal thing: therefore get wisdom".

The sexes should associate together in every pursuit; this, of course, implied that there must be co-education in schools. Even though women, in maturity, would chiefly be faced with duties of wives and mothers this did not mean that they did not require education: indeed the reverse was the case. Mary Wollstonecraft was in complete agreement with her distinguished predecessor in the feminist field, the anonymous "Sophia, A Person of Quality" (generally thought to have been Lady Mary Wortley Montagu) whose *Woman not Inferior to Man*; "or, a Short and Modest Vindication of the Natural Right of the *Fair-Sex* to a perfect Equality of Power, Dignity, and Esteem, with the Men" had appeared in 1739: in this "Sophia" had demolished the specious allegation that women were "fit only to breed and nurse children" with a splendid and scornful *"Only*!" and had gone on to point out the importance of child bearing and rearing in comparison with the fundamentally useless roles of many men in positions of authority.

In support of the contention that woman's basic role is as vital a human duty as any other and indeed of far greater importance than most, Wollstonecraft maintained that, "To be a good mother a woman must have an independent mind. Meek wives make foolish mothers". Likewise, "Marriage will never be held sacred till women by being brought up with men are prepared to be their companions rather than their mistresses". Marriage should be a matter of friendship; "The most sublime of all affections, because it is founded on principle, and cemented by time. The very reverse may be said of love." Marriage should be founded on "esteem"; "after marriage calmly let passion subside into friendship — into that tender intimacy, which is the best refuge from care".

Nonetheless, and all this said, no motive on earth (declared Wollstonecraft) should make a man and wife live together a moment after mutual tenderness and esteem were gone.

"Let women share the rights and she will emulate the virtues of man", became the most famous and oft-quoted contention from *Rights of Woman* (as Sims points out, this presupposed a degree of morality that did not generally exist in either sex, but Wollstonecraft had to be harder on women because she was addressing herself to them rather than to men). If woman failed to "grow more perfect when emancipated" then her subjugation to man would stand as justified.

The essence of the *Rights of Woman* is, of course, that men and women corrupt each other; but have it in them to improve each other. Wollstonecraft's vindication was of women in relation to men, to the rest of the world; the world about them that was there to be shared by both women and men. The liberation of woman was intrinsic in that of man.

*Rights of Woman* was read and enthused over by the Pantisocrats and their intending brides: Southey declared that "most of [Woll-stonecraft's] remarks" were "wise and true"; S.T.C. was subsequently to say that Godwin, following his marriage to her, was "in heart and manner . . . all the better for having been her husband".[22] Certainly S.T.C. during the early years of his marriage endeavoured to put Wollstonecraft precepts into enthusiastic practise, albeit ebullience prompted him to do so, rather than any genuine conviction that men and women were equal. Equality of the sexes, on the other hand, was definitely no mere hypothetic proposition for the Fricker sisters, who were proving themselves dangerously emancipated in their behaviour (even Edith was revealing a remarkable capacity for what conventional Bristol saw as "Immodest behaviour").

It was really not all that surprising therefore that Sara and Edith discovered that, "People are talking strangely of us". Southey had been too confident in his statement that Bristol understood Pantisocracy and Aspheterism; there had been — in both Bristol and Bath — some serious midunderstanding; encouraging a general impression that, "Pantisocracy meant a system of things which dispensed with the marriage tie",[23] while Aspheterism, under which all property would be shared, surely suggested that the women might be shared likewise? The behaviour of the Misses Fricker who were constantly seen, brazenly unchaperoned, in the company of young men popularly regarded as "vile Jacobin villains" (who would certainly harbour no respect for female virtue!) buttressed this popular impression. Southey calmly counselled Sara and Edith to ignore the malicious talk, "Can you not smile at the envy and absurdity of the many?" But it was not so easily a smiling matter for the sisters. Society could insult women with an impunity it did not dare, or care, to extend to men. Even Southey stopped smiling when he grasped the extent of the humiliation which other women, in the role of pillars of respectability, were prepared to inflict upon Edith and Sara.[24]

Almost certainly it was some random echo, surviving in stale Bath gossip, that percolated into London literary circles at the time of the much-discussed Coleridge "separation" and subsequently inspired Byron's well-known jibe that Southey and Coleridge had married "two milliners from Bath": a jibe that is largely lost on us today because we are no longer aware of the euphemism entailed, and have to read De Quincey to discover what Byron was really implying: "Everybody knows what is *meant* to be conveyed in that expression," wrote De

Quincey.[25] It was a way of suggesting that Sara and Edith had been a little "too obliging".

The sisters ignored the scurrilous tittle-tattle and continued to be seen, unchaperoned, in the dangerous company of the Pantisocrats. (All this, of course, makes nonsense of the theory that Sara Fricker was "too conventional" for Coleridge. The truth was rather the reverse; subsequently he was to be found complaining that paramountly Sara lacked a capacity for "Conformity").[26]

Some time during that rapturous spring of 1795 (probably in April) Cottle invited Southey and Coleridge, together with Edith and Sara, on a two-day excursion to the Wye Valley and Tintern Abbey. An unchaperoned jaunt into the country with three gentlemen, not one of them in any way even a relative or family connection of the young ladies concerned, was emancipated behaviour indeed; the addition of an overnight stay at an inn as part of the itinerary was calculated to suggest, to conventional minds at least, that the sisters had flung to the winds all concern for their reputations. The sisters would have replied, of course, that they were following the new convention of social freedom for their sex.

The outing was intended by Cottle to be one of the happiest entertainments in the world, but unbeknown to him (he was never the most perceptive of men) uncomfortable tides and cross-currents were already disturbingly at work beneath the apparently tranquil surface of the Pantisocratic lagoon: those dreamy blue shallows protected by romantic reefs against the wild surf of reality breaking beyond.

Southey, though he had stood stoutly by Coleridge during Lovell's attack, was becoming increasingly aware, as the weeks passed and his acquaintance with Samuel developed into close intimacy, that between himself and his future brother-in-law there yawned formidable differences.[27] It was all very well to attribute Coleridge's often (for Southey) incomprehensible behaviour to his genius and the eccentricity which that genius naturally promoted, but there were some things done by S.T.C. which turned Southey ("the man of virtue" as *The Observer* some time that spring or summer called him)[28] hot and cold with horror. For example, the Esteesian absence of mind and general disregard for keeping appointments was becoming a byword in Bristol society. Especially unpardonable was S.T.C.'s latest lapse of memory. Southey had been advertised to lecture on the rise, progress and decline of the Roman empire; S.T.C. had begged to be allowed to give this lecture, saying it was a subject to which he had devoted much attention. Southey had generously acquiesced; the announcement had been made that Coleridge would deliver the lecture. However when the time came he had failed to appear on the platform, having entirely forgotten the engagement.

There can be little doubt that Southey's disturbed reactions in that spring of 1795 stemmed from the certainty now forced upon him that S.T.C.'s lapses of memory and general disregard for obligations, as well as his "indolence" arose (as Lovell had already suspected, if not actually suggested) from opium. Southey was jolted into the realization that here was no sound comrade with whom to hunt buffalo or fight redskins. His discovery of S.T.C.'s opium as an established fact explains why Southey suddenly assumed, as he did, "a Mantle of self centering *Resolve*"; abandoning the fraternal and Pantisocratic "we" for an aloof and poker-faced "I will do so and so".[29] It also explains his grim comment (made to Grosvenor Bedford on 12th May), "I am grown an acute observer of men, and agree with Burns that 'they are an ugly squad' . . . I could say very much".[30]

The business of the Roman empire lecture brought all Southey's feelings of indignation and distress to a head. The next day was fixed for the Tintern Abbey excursion;[31] the party of five crossed the Severn and made for Chepstow, where they dined at the Beaufort Arms. Here, after dinner, Southey and S.T.C. had a lively altercation; arising, superficially, out of the topic of the missed lecture but, of course, in fact dealing fundamentally with matters of much deeper import. It might well be said that this quarrel at the Beaufort Arms was to send its echoes reverberating down the long years that were to follow.

Southey accused S.T.C. of a gross inability to keep engagements and he must have said something about this lack of responsibility being a danger to the Pantisocratic future — however we do know that he made no allusion, on this occasion, to indolence and certainly not to opium. S.T.C. responded by accusing Southey of having abandoned his Pantisocratic principles; even of planning to abandon the Pantisocratic experiment entirely. Tempers rose; hot words were exchanged. Eventually the young ladies joined the controversy; each siding with her respective *fiancé*. S.T.C. became desperately agitated and much to everyone's alarm (and Cottle's acute embarrassment) burst into floods of tears — although no mention had been made of opium no doubt a certain guilt tormented him.

At length tranquillity was restored; all made a decent pretence of recovered good spirits and the party set out for the then popular beauty spot known as Piercefield (Percifield) Walks. Cottle, who suffered from an old leg injury, was travelling on horseback; a betrothed couple walked on either side of his mount.

Some time was spent in the extensive walks of Piercefield: the young ladies strolled and rapturized with Cottle over the "enchanting scenes", while Robert and S.T.C. disappeared together and had a long heart-to-heart conversation which resulted (so it seemed at the time) in their mutual suspicions being dismissed as groundless and their trust in one another being reaffirmed.

The party then directed their steps towards Tintern Abbey; but they had been so delayed by altercation and agitation at Chepstow and the intimate talk and delicious walks of Piercefield that they became benighted and, in the thickening dusk, lost their road to Tintern. S.T.C., the former Dragoon, mounted Cottle's horse and rode in wide circles searching for the true path; Southey "marched on like a pillar of strength, with a lady pressing on each arm" (how symbolic, if the quartet had but known it, of the road that lay ahead of them in life!) while Cottle, quite forgotten, limpingly brought up the rear. At first they were able to see the funny side of the adventure (a particularly stony stretch of track, along which they floundered in the gloom, was hailed as Bowling Green Alley) but then it ceased to be funny and the merry comments and laughter subsided into the glum silence of exhaustion.

At length they reached Tintern and put up for the night at the inn. After supper Cottle reminded them that there was a foundry nearby which all true devotees of the Picturesque went to gaze at in the dark; the virtuous Southey therefore braced himself, rose to his feet and announced himself ready to set forth. He and Cottle accordingly went out, but S.T.C., sprawled before the fire, vowed he would stir for no man. The young ladies, scarcely able to stand in their weariness, begged to be excused from further sightseeing and retired upstairs. One can imagine their conversation (Jane Austen alone could do credit to it) as they donned their nightgowns and nightcaps and clambered into bed.

Next day the party explored the abbey and afterwards returned to Bristol. The excursion, which seemed to them to be concluded, was in truth only just beginning. They were not returning home, but setting forth.

# CHAPTER FIVE

# The Fair Electric Flame

The break-up of the Pantisocrats, having first surfaced at Chepstow, next threatened some six weeks later at a strawberry party: when Southey informed George Burnett that Wynn had announced his intention of giving Southey an annuity of one hundred and sixty pounds, to be first payable in the final quarter of 1796, when Wynn would come of age. Southey added the bombshell rider that, in spite of Pantisocracy and Aspheterism, he would consider this annuity as a private resource of his own and would not be putting it at the disposal of either S.T.C. or Burnett. This information Burnett passed on to S.T.C., who received it "With Indignation and Loathings of unutterable Contempt".[1]

It must be conceded that Southey had a point in not wishing to sink all his assets in an enterprise shared with two opium addicts, for Burnett was now also freely taking laudanum.

It seems that, to his own family, Southey explained that he was abandoning the Pantisocratic venture with Coleridge because of his "indolence". When the news of these allegations reached Coleridge he exploded with indignation.[2] The point was reached where Southey and Coleridge no longer recognized one another when they met on the street. The quarrel became the foremost topic of gossip in Bristol. One unfortunate and inevitable result was that the Fricker sisters became estranged in their turn.

There is no evidence that Southey, having become convinced of Coleridge's addiction to opium, at any time suggested to Sara that he might not prove the best of husbands for her; since Southey had initially made the choice for her, it would perhaps have been asking too much of him that he should now admit how wrong he had been. He doubtless recognized that she was too hopelessly in love to heed his advice, any more than she had paid attention to other admonitions and warnings. "I could say very much. . . . " But Southey didn't say it: Sara, more justly than Coleridge, was to have the right to exclaim, "O Southey! Southey! an unthinking man were you!"

Sara's family had had a change of mind about the marriage; she had so damaged her reputation by her emancipated behaviour that Mrs Fricker was by now anxious that her daughter should retrieve her good name by marrying S.T.C. as soon as possible. Mrs Sandford,

Thomas Poole's biographer, with her Poole family and Stowey connections, knew enough handed-down gossip to be able to write with authority that the "marriage was believed to have been rather hurried on, in consequence of some hostile breath of rumour that had arisen in connection with the Misses Fricker, caused partly by the unconventional manner in which they were constantly to be seen walking about Bristol with two such remarkable and well-known young men as Coleridge and Southey, and partly from the impression that Pantisocracy meant a system of things that dispensed with the marriage-tie".[3]

Hostile rumour at work or no, it is doubtful if S.T.C. and Sara would have delayed their nuptials any longer; impatience had them aflame. S.T.C., his Pantisocratic future lost to him, showed commendable buoyancy; he was full of high hopes for his success as a breadwinner. Cottle had entered into an engagement to give him a guinea and a half for every hundred lines of poetry he wrote; "which will be perfectly sufficient to my maintenance", even with the addition of a wife to feed, as S.T.C. assured his friends. Moreover in the course of the next six months or so he intended returning to Cambridge and taking lodgings there for himself and Sara while he finished his projected subscription work of transliterations of classical verse, or "Imitations in 2 vols". After which, he would open his own school.[4]

Thus, presumably secure in financial prospects, and buttressed by belief in Optimism and Necessitarianism, Sara and Samuel faced their future without qualms; they *knew* that they must enjoy total bliss.

At some time in July, S.T.C. and Sara set about house-hunting in the countryside around Bristol, and before long S.T.C. had discovered a cottage in the little village of Clevedon on the Bristol Channel. As a place of bliss for a honeymoon couple anxious to escape from the world it was perfect: set at the edge of the village in a gentle wooded landscape; the cottage and its little garden smothered in flowers, the sea crooning in the distance; the air perfumed with the scent of roses and jasmine and a nearby bean-field:

> Low was our pretty Cot; our tallest Rose
> Peep'd at the chamber-window. We could hear
> At silent noon, and eve, and early morn,
> The Sea's faint murmur. In the open air
> Our Myrtles blossom'd; and across the porch
> Thick Jasmins twined: the little landscape round
> Was green and woody, and refresh'd the eye.
> It was a spot which you might aptly call
> The Valley of Seclusion![5]

It was paradise; and the rent was a mere five pounds per annum, cheap even in those days. S.T.C. became its tenant with the least possible delay.

Sara was taken to see it. An Eolian harp* was, it would seem, the first item of furniture that the couple installed in their new home; probably on their first visit, or at all events one of their earliest:

> My Pensive Sara! thy soft Cheek reclin'd
> Thus on my arm, how soothing sweet it is
> Beside our Cot to sit . . .
> And watch the Clouds, that late were rich with light,
> Slow-sad'ning round, and mark the star of eve
> Serenely brilliant, like thy polish'd Sense,
> Shine opposite! . . .
> . . . and behold, my love!
> In the half-closed window we will place the Harp,
> Which by the desultory Breeze caress'd,
> Like some coy maid half willing to be woo'd,
> Utters such sweet upbraidings as, perforce
> Tempt to repeat the wrong![6]

The summer wore on and turned to autumn, with the wedding ever drawing closer. But this period, which should have been one of unalloyed happiness, was marred by the Coleridge-Southey quarrel, resulting in an exchange of angry letters: Southey, even if he did not reach the point of cutting Sara, looked at her with "Chill'd Friendship's dark disliking eye". This caused Sara much distress. A week before the wedding, while S.T.C. was staying at Shurton Bars (on the Bristol Channel and not far from Clevedon) he received a letter from Sara describing her sorrow. He responded with *Ode to Sara*,

> . . . I see you all oppressed with gloom
> Sit lonely in that cheerless room —
> Ah me! You are in tears!

And he burst into impassioned verse: poignantly naïve, hot from the mint of feeling; no working into further, polished drafts before sending it off to Sara, whose soul he felt hovering round his head, he declared, as he wrote. He began with gloomy enthusiasm (as a romantic poet should), plunged into a mood of the Sublime and Terrible, envisaging a

---

*All the rage at the time: placed at a window, or suspended in a tree so that breezes might pluck random Ossian-like notes from the strings.

shipwrecked vessel foundering on a stormy night near their Clevedon
cottage; then moved on to happier visions,

> The tears that tremble down your cheek,
> Shall bathe my kisses chaste and meek
>     In Pity's dew divine;
> And from your heart the sighs that steal
> Shall make your rising bosom feel
>     The answering swell of mine!
>
> How oft, my Love! with shapings sweet
> I paint the moment, we shall meet!
>     With eager speed I dart —
> I seize you in the vacant air,
> And fancy, with a husband's care
>     I press you to my heart!
>
> 'Tis said, in Summer's evening hour
> Flashes the golden-colour'd flower
>     A fair electric flame:
> And so shall flash my love-charg'd eye
> When all the heart's big ecstasy
>     Shoots rapid through the frame!

In 1796 and 1797 these lines, when they appeared in publication,
carried a note:

LIGHT *from plants*. In Sweden a very curious phenomenon has been
observed on certain flowers, by M. Haggern, lecturer in natural history.
One evening he perceived a faint flash of light repeatedly dart from a
marigold. . . . The flash was frequently seen on the same flower two or
three times in quick succession . . . and when several flowers in the same
place emitted their light together, it could be observed at a considerable
distance. . . . This phenomenon was remarked in the months of July and
August at sun-set. . . . The following flowers emitted flashes, more or
less vivid. . . .
>     1. The marigold, *galendula [sic] officinalis*,
>     2. Monk's-hood, *tropaelum [sic] majus*.
>     3. The orange-lily, *lilium bulbiferum*.
>     4. The Indian pink, *tagetes patula et erecta*.

From the rapidity of the flash, and other circumstances, it may be
conjectured that there is something of electricity in this phenomenon.

So the love-charged Sara and Samuel flashed their electric
flames to one another, oblivious of all else as they conducted their
dialogue of passion.

# CHAPTER SIX

## *Domestic Bliss*

### I

The wedding took place at St Mary Redcliffe, Bristol, on Sunday, 4th October 1795. Benjamin Spry, the vicar, officiated. The witnesses were the bride's mother and Josiah Wade, a Bristolian tradesman and radical who had become one of S.T.C.'s firmest friends. The bridal pair then departed to Clevedon for a honeymoon which, by every available account, was as romantically blissful as any honeymoon might be.

So impatiently had they precipitated themselves towards the moment of consummation that they had furnished the cottage with little more, it would seem, than an Eolian harp, a bed, and a pair of old prints. This was sufficient for the first forty-eight hours; after which S.T.C. sent Cottle a note requesting him to dispatch to Clevedon an assortment of further basic necessities, ranging from a kettle, a carpet brush, mats, candlesticks and a bible, to a pair of slippers, a keg of porter and an assortment of spices, raisins, currants, a flour dredge, and catsup. This the obliging Cottle did, adding "a few pieces of sprightly wallpaper" for the parlour-dining-room to cover the "dirty old white-wash" which had offended his eye when he visited[1] — the Coleridges themselves probably never even noticed it, so deeply enraptured were they with one another. "Mrs Coleridge — Mrs COLERIDGE!" exclaimed the ecstatic bridegroom, rolling the former Sara Fricker's new name round his mouth like some miraculous lollipop. And, from Sara, "My adored, my divine husband. . . ."[2]

### II

Once the first few weeks were over, Clevedon proved to have defects. It was too far from Bristol; Coleridge, whose poverty obliged him to walk everywhere, could not get to Bristol City library and back all in one day, and this Sara disliked as she found herself "lonely and uneasy" during his overnight absences. A remote cottage within earshot of a gently murmuring summer sea was a very different place on stormy nights with winter closing in. Moreover (and this perhaps was the worst defect of all) the neighbours (to quote Cottle) were "a little too tattling and inquisitive" in an unfriendly sort of way; Clevedon did not welcome a young Jacobin and his bride, about whom so many tongues had wagged, and were still wagging. Yet, despite these drawbacks, the honeymoon home was "a Blessed Place/And we were blessed".[3]

Political developments all too soon constrained the Coleridges to quit Clevedon. By mid-November they were back in Bristol,[4] lodging, as a temporary measure, with Sara's mother on Redcliffe Hill. On 26th October a mass meeting had been held in Islington, demanding universal suffrage, annual parliaments and the cessation of the war against France. The meeting, though large, had never got out of hand, but when, three days later, the King had been attacked on his way to open Parliament the government had connected this outrage with the Islington mass meeting. On 4th November a Royal Proclamation against seditious assemblies and the circulation of treasonable papers was issued. On 6th November Grenville introduced into the Lords an Act for the Safety and Preservation of His Majesty's Person and Government against Treasonable and Seditious Practices and Attempts — this becoming known as Lord Grenville's Bill or the Treason Bill. On 10th November Pitt introduced into the Commons an Act for the More Effectually Preventing Seditious Meetings and Assemblies (referred to as Pitt's Bill or the Convention Bill); the two measures together becoming notorious as "the Gagging Acts", since they were levelled in particular against the "patriotic" associations; the fraternal and debating societies and reformist groups.*

No sooner were the two bills introduced than there was public outcry, up and down the country. Two meetings of protest were held at Bristol, on 17th and 20th November, in the Guildhall; Coleridge was among the speakers. On 26th November, at seven in the evening in the "Great Room at the Pelican Inn, Thomas-Street" he delivered a well-received public address in further protest against the two bills.[5]

On 18th December, the day on which the bills were passed and became law, the Whig Club met to propose the formation of an association devoted solely to the purpose of securing the repeal of the new measures. Hitherto Coleridge had never joined any of the "patriotic" societies; but by the close of that year he was an active supporter, if not a member, of the newly formed association, and as a result embarked upon the project of producing a weekly political publication, to be called *The Watchman*. He flung himself into the task of issuing a prospectus[6] and obtaining subscribers.

This political involvement meant that Sara was now seeing but little of him. In any case their honeymoon bliss had deteriorated sharply in

*The Government was suspected of plotting a fabricated riot, to justify introducing even stronger repressive legislation.

the face of the discomforts and exasperations of a shared existence with Mrs Fricker and her younger children in pent-up rooms.

S.T.C. never hesitated to confide his woes to his friends and one to whom he now lamented his Redcliffe Hill hardships was Thomas Poole, with whom, since the rupture with Southey, he had become warmly friendly. Poole, a man of keenly perceptive intelligence, profoundly good heart and marked delicacy of feeling, quickly came to realize how nicely Coleridge was balanced between abnormality of endowment and abnormality of susceptibility to weakness of will, dejection, and real or imagined lack of response in others; how violently he over-reacted to any kind of agitation or emotional or physical strain; in short, how dangerously vulnerable he was to stresses which those of less uncommon clay barely detected: Coleridge could be damaged, wounded by the world without the world even having noticed that it had wounded him.

It became Poole's self-appointed role to act as Coleridge's guardian; to protect him from such injury and, by encouragement and praise, a little careful admonition when necessary, a little spurring here and restraining there, enable him to exercise his astounding gifts to the full and perform as only he could perform. Poole also did his best to provide an element of business-like commonsense, Coleridge being so singularly devoid of this faculty. Observed Poole, "People of genius ought imperiously to command themselves to think *without* genius of the common concerns of life. If this be impossible — happy is the genius who has a friend ever near of *good sense*."[7] Poole made it his duty (but he loved it) of being such a friend to S.T.C.

Poole had not objected to the Coleridge-Fricker marriage (which to others had seemed so unwise a step). The marriage appealed to Poole as one more indication of the "disinterested traits" in Coleridge's character. "He has united himself to her he loves, regardless of every other consideration. It is thus that, lifted above the cupidity almost interwoven in the hearts of all who live in a society such as ours, he presents in himself an object which awakens every tender and noble sensation of the soul."[8]

When, shortly after his marriage, S.T.C. wrote an ecstatic letter to Poole, "On Sunday morning I was *married* . . . united to the woman, whom I love best of all created Beings . . . Mrs Coleridge — MRS COLERIDGE!! — I like to *write* the name — well — as I was saying — Mrs Coleridge desires her affectionate regards to you", Poole, (who had never yet met Sara) replied with unfeigned warmth, "I do congratulate you — most heartily I do. I wish I knew Mrs Coleridge — remember me most kindly to her. May you both long, long be happy."[9]

Now, in late autumn of 1795, Poole and Sara met. Moved by
S.T.C.'s complaints of the strain of life with a mother-in-law, Poole
invited the young couple to stay for a few weeks at Nether-Stowey,
where he, a bachelor, lived with his widowed mother ("a dee-ar old
soul"). The Coleridges accepted the invitation gratefully and soon felt
at home in the "commonplace, comfortable brown house, with the
tanyard at the back, and the long garden, from which there was a view of
the hills".[10] S.T.C. spent hours with Poole in his book-room-cum-den
and Sara was among the privileged few who were shown the lock of
Washington's hair, given Poole by American friends from Mas-
sachusetts; this Poole "regarded as a sacred treasure and kept in a
special casket placed within the precious copy of the Barberini Vase
presented to him by the Wedgwoods".[11]

In short the Stowey visit was an immense success: Sara liked Stowey
and loved Thomas Poole and his mother who in turn loved her.[12]
Indeed over the years Poole was to prove, next to Robert Southey,
Sara's most trusted friend. "My dear, dear Mr Poole!"

During that eventful November Southey had departed to stay in
Portugal for six months with his uncle, the Reverend Mr Hill. Although
Robert did not know it when this trip was being arranged (ostensibly to
give him a chance to refresh his mind and reorient himself before turning
to law studies), his uncle and mother intended the sojourn overseas to
wean Southey from what they now thought of as a "foolish attachment":
Edith Fricker no longer being seen as a suitable bride for him, her
reputation having become as tarnished as her sister's. However Mr Hill
and Mrs Southey were balked in their designs: Robert married Edith in
secret on the morning of Saturday 13th November, at St Mary Redcliffe.
She returned home as usual that night, wearing her wedding ring on a
cord round her neck and concealed from view. The marriage was not
consummated; next day Robert and Edith met simply to press hands and
part in silence. Robert went to Bath to inform his mother of his marriage;
Edith, still using her maiden name, went to lodge with the Misses Cottle.
Robert felt it best that Edith should keep her own name: "It may not be
convenient for us to live together immediately upon my return," he
explained to Grosvenor Bedford. Here was a very different bridegroom
from the impatiently passionate S.T.C., who had hardly been able to
wait to get Sara to bed!

Southey's sole reason for marrying Edith at this juncture had been (as
again he confided to Bedford) to prevent "the tongue of malice" from
whispering that he had forsaken her: a girl of damaged name, finally
forsaken by her lover, would have been doomed to a dark future
indeed.[13] He had therefore done the right thing by Edith, as he was able

to congratulate himself; he had acted in obedience to honour (it is an interesting reflection that ultimately it was Southey, not S.T.C., whose marriage was prompted by a sense of duty).

The news of Southey's marriage leaked and became public early in 1796. Edith thereafter used her legal name. She remained estranged from the Coleridges.

S.T.C., in his final correspondence with Southey, had directed at him a last Parthian shot, "I neither have or could deign to have an hundred a year" (this was directed against the Wynn annuity of course) — "Yet by my own exertions I will struggle hard to maintain myself, and my Wife, and my Wife's Mother, and my associate [George Burnett]."[4] Towards the end of that momentous year, 1795, S.T.C. and Sara returned to Redcliffe Hill from Stowey and S.T.C. began twelve months of brave endeavour to keep his word; watched over by Thomas Poole, a guardian angel who advised, encouraged and solaced him, propped him up when things turned out badly, picked him up when he fell, and in every respect proved a friend of loyalty and "good sense". Being a husband and breadwinner was a rough ride, as S.T.C. rapidly discovered; it would have been a far rougher one without Poole.

Meanwhile Sara learned the inexorable Necessitarianism of Woman. In the New Year she realized that she was pregnant and, as a result of this joyous circumstance, began to feel horribly ill.

## III

Coleridge had returned to Bristol to plunge himself enthusiastically into launching *The Watchman*. Having produced and circulated a prospectus, he whirled away on a subscription-raising tour of the Midlands and the north west. During his absence Sara and her mother succumbed to some contagion described as "a fever"; Sara threatened a miscarriage, becoming so ill that her husband was finally summoned home. Though he had had to cut his tour short he had raised nearly a thousand subscribers; *The Watchman* accordingly went into production without delay. Coleridge was also busy finishing his volume of collected early poems. Working almost round the clock in a burst of frenetic energy he brought out the first issue of *The Watchman* on 1st March (1796). Meanwhile Sara remained "dangerously ill"; in considerable pain and "expected hourly to miscarry". He suffered from her sufferings, finding it hard to "write the high flights of poetic enthusiasm, when every minute I am hearing a groan of pain . . . groans, and complaints & sickness!" as he put it to Cottle.[15]

Once again the "regulations relating to the females" struck S.T.C. as "difficult"; this time within the context of how to fit the bare physiological facts of woman's lot into an enlightened philosophy. The Golden Age of Mankind, upon the threshold of which humanity assuredly now stood, promised universal release from hardship, suffering, injustice in its many and various guises. Yet here was an entire sex apparently doomed to almost constant indisposition, danger and not infrequently premature death, simply as part of the normal, inescapable function of perpetuating the species; while males continued on their way through life wholly untrammelled by such afflictions. What greater inequality could there be than this? How might the so-called Dawn of Reason be expected to redress this enormity of discrimination?

The more S.T.C. contemplated pregnancy the more he found that it "seems coercive against Immaterialism — it starts uneasy doubts respecting Immortality, & the pangs which the Woman suffers, seem inexplicable in the system of optimism".[16] Meanwhile Sara, lost to philosophizing, retched and groaned. Finally, on 19th March, her condition convinced her that she had had a miscarriage. From thereon she recovered her health.

Some time that same month the young Coleridges removed from Redcliffe Hill to Oxford Street (Bristol) in the neighbourhood known as Kingsdown; George Burnett going with them as lodger and assistant in the production of *The Watchman*, though, thanks to his ever-deepening laudanum habit, he was not particularly effective in this capacity. S.T.C. himself worked at *The Watchman* in a state at times approaching frenzy, composed partly of ebullience (the professional writer in him enjoyed productive hard work), partly because he believed that he was serving the democratic cause, and partly through sheer economic necessity. Marriage: "taught me the wonderful uses of that vulgar article, yclept BREAD. . . . Formerly I could select a fine morning, chuse my road, and take an airing upon my Pegasus right leisurely — but now I am in stirrups all day, yea, and sleep in my Spurs."[17]

But despite all Coleridge's hard work *The Watchman*, from the point of view of financial reward, never yielded more than "a bread-and-cheesish profit",[18] while its role as a democratic voice was eroded by events: as early as that February, 1796, an increasing popular fear of the French, together with a mistrust in the popular mind of English Jacobinism as an ally of the French, markedly reduced support for *The Watchman*'s causes. S.T.C. struggled to keep his publication alive; but it was a losing battle.

Fortunately Sara was now revealing remarkable expertise as a "domestic oeconomist", able to make ends meet where others would have had to admit defeat. But she had been wrong about the miscarriage: by mid-April her expanding waistline put her pregnant condition beyond doubt. Another mouth to feed was on its way.

During the whole of that spring Mrs Fricker had been ill; so ill indeed that S.T.C. and Sara had nursed gloomy apprehensions concerning funeral expenses. Now, with improving weather, Mrs Fricker began to recover; anxiety over how to find money for an undertaker was replaced by concern about finding money for baby linen. Life had become a grinding non-stop succession of "privations, anxieties and embarrassments".[19] Then came the final, inevitable blow: *The Watchman* folded. The last number appeared on 13th May. S.T.C. and Sara now found themselves without any immediate means of livelihood. Under the strain tempers frayed; S.T.C., for relief from tension, resorted to laudanum with increasing frequency.[20]

A mere ten months previously, with his nuptials approaching, S.T.C. had written to Southey in ecstatic anticipation, "Domestic Happiness is the greatest of things sublunary".[21] Now the honeymoon period was definitely over: "The surly Overbrowing frowning Rock of Reality cast the dusky shadow of this Earth on the soft Moonlight of Love's first phantasies."[22]

# CHAPTER SEVEN

## *The Rock of Reality*

I

Coleridge was not suited, either by temperament or experience, to deal with the realities of this earth, neither in the guise of money matters and what Poole called "the common concerns of life", nor in the shape of the emotional vicissitudes which are an integral part of day-to-day living, and especially part of family circumstance. His emotional predicament was one of particular difficulty: by nature his was a deeply loving and responsive personality, but his early experiences had been of a most damaging kind. Having been the youngest child of a very large family, his "Mother's darling" and "the Benjamin" of his ageing father, he had been hopelessly spoiled throughout those first seven years which are said to be pre-eminently formative in the shaping of character and emotional response. Any thwarting brought from little Samuel reactions of violent resentment. There was the highly significant episode of his childhood knife attack upon his brother and S.T.C.'s subsequent bolt from home and staying out all night "thinking . . . with inward & gloomy satisfaction, how miserable my Mother must be!"[1] In his tenth year came the sudden death of his father, resulting in S.T.C. being sent as a boarder to a large and impersonal public school, where enforced homosexual incidents were a nightly torment to the smaller boys — a commonplace feature of public school life in those days.[2] All in all it was a bad start, resulting in the adult Coleridge having great difficulty in sustaining closely intimate relationships and being the victim of that neurosis which results in the sufferer feeling obliged to destroy everything dear to him because his sense of insecurity prompts the instinct to knock the house down before it collapses around him.

S.T.C. feared, above all, the intrusion of harsh realities within the context of the affections. As with all of us, his early experiences in terms of affection and personal encounter had imprinted him with certain expectancies: in his case sharply conflicting ones. Initially he had learned to take it for granted that he was the beloved object of everyone who set eyes on him; then had followed a violently disillusioning series of incidents; of abrupt deprivation, disruption, bewilderment and fracas. This, for him in childhood, had been the dreadful face of reality; reality which was synonymous henceforth, for him, with evil, which in turn he equated with pain ("Instead of evil, a disputable word, let us use pain" — above, p. 38).

It was a resultant life-long obsession with him to prefer to savour affection in some domestic environment other than his own. For example, as a Christ's Hospital schoolboy he had been drawn towards Mary Evans and her family because he had been able to play-act that this was his *own* domestic circle; that the Miss Evanses were his sisters, Mrs Evans his mother.[3] Similarly, when his bolt from Cambridge and the incident of the Dragoons followed by a second bolt had not unnaturally reduced him to a state when he couldn't get himself to look his brothers in the eye, he had found refuge in the Southey-Fricker circle: "Democrats [who] alone had shown him love and kindness".[4] And so it continued. Barely out of infancy when he had first learned to distrust the reliability of happiness in his own home circle, he had gone on to conclude that, when everything that you had supposed real and lasting had fallen apart, was it not safer henceforth to seek happiness in a make-believe; the evaporation of which would distress you no more than a transformation scene at a pantomime?

"The social and domestic affections" held a profound significance for Coleridge, but for obvious reasons he required them to be steeped in tranquillity — exacting no traumatic emotional exertion on his part. He loved, as it were, to lie on his bed like a baby while devoted smiles were showered upon him.[5] In order to place a barrier between himself and pain he not only favoured make-believe family situations, and enactments of an infantile basking in love, but further distanced himself from the risk of trauma through the pressure of reality by resorting to objectivity; for him the affections had to be intellectualized, elevated on to a metaphysical plane. If love for a wife, child, friend, could not be exalted into something of profound metaphysical significance not only for himself but for society ("mankind") in general, if it could not be given an interpretation which made it a vitally integral part of some grandiose overall scheme of "universal Benevolence", a Spinozistic Oneness, then he ceased to be receptive to it and dismissed it as "unworthy".

"The paternal and filial duties . . . prepare [the Heart] for the love of all Mankind" (above, p. 38). As for marriage, that was one of those "private attachments" "the intensity of which encourages, not prevents, universal Benevolence". As it turned out, Coleridge's record as a parent was to prove a tragic one, while his filial history (owing to circumstances for which he was not initially to blame) was fragmented and unfulfilling. Marriage was to prove the most difficult relationship of all, necessitating as it did attachment to a real woman; which automatically meant that it could never be pleasingly sublimated into a smoothly fitting component part of Hartleian ideology (or any other ideology for that matter). How prophetic that warning which Coleridge, canvassing for Pantisocracy in Cambridge, had received from a fellow Democrat,* "Your System, Coleridge! appears strong to the head and lovely to the Heart — but depend upon it . . . your women . . . *They* will spoil it!"[6] The eternal Eve, forever depriving Adam of his Eden.

## II

*The Watchman*, formerly a living voice weekly proclaiming its message of liberty and right of suffrage, and anticipated by Sara (if not S.T.C.) to support the Coleridge ménage for some time to come, transmogrified into piles of unsold copies taking up valuable space in the Coleridges' Oxford Street abode: gradually mildewing bundles, which, as time passed, mysteriously began to dwindle. At last the mystery was solved when S.T.C. discovered their little servant girl "putting an extravagant quantity of paper into the grate" in order to light the fire. He remonstrated with her for her wastefulness, and received the reply, "La, sir, it is only Watchman".[7]

S.T.C. was now, in that summer of 1796, thinking up fresh ways of earning a living; he spoke of travelling to Jena, there to perfect his German and meet Schiller, whose works he would then translate into English and sell. While at Jena he would also study anatomy and chemistry and on his return home he would open an expensive and exclusive academy for young men of particular promise. Alternatively he would become "a Dissenting Parson & abjure Politics & carnal literature".[8]

Poole, that man of unerring loyalty, now came to Coleridge's aid by organizing a group of the latter's Bristol friends and admirers to contribute a small annuity (tactfully disguised as a testimonial) to be paid Coleridge throughout the next six years. George Dyer also came forward with a sum to help tide over the period of unemployment and a further donation, of ten guineas, came from the Royal Literary Fund. Attempts were made to get Coleridge a newspaper job in London. While he was glumly debating whether or not to accept a post on the *Morning Chronicle* there came an invitation from a widowed Mrs Evans of Darley,[9] near Derby, asking Coleridge to visit her with a view to becoming tutor to her two sons. The Coleridges donned their best clothes and travelled to Darley.

*Lushington, a university counsellor of "Briaréan intellect" (CCL L 68).

Mrs Evans was delighted with Coleridge, who had taken unusual pains with his appearance, reported Sara: "He was handsomely drest . . . Mrs Evans admired him greatly — even thought him personable and said he reminded her of Abelard."[10] Details of the tutorship were arranged; the matter settled upon, to the intense satisfaction of both Mrs Evans and the Coleridges. Sara was in seventh heaven. Mrs Evans was kindness herself and so was her amiable daughter Bessy; the house was immensely comfortable; the future suddenly looked secure and bright.

Presently Coleridge returned to the west country alone, leaving the happy Sara with "kind Mrs Evans and Bessy". While in the west he visited his mother and brothers; the result was complete reconciliation. This news further delighted Sara, who privately had nursed strong misgivings over his estrangement from his family. But this good news was immediately followed by bad: the uncles (and guardians) of Mrs Evans' sons totally opposed her plans, insisting that the proposed tutor was out of the question. Coleridge returned to Darley to collect Sara; there was intense disappointment voiced by all parties (except the uncles). The Coleridges remained another ten days with Mrs Evans leaving her with exchanges of lively affection. Indeed with the Evans family Sara was to maintain a lasting friendship. "We spent five weeks at her home — a sunny spot in our life!"[11]

Now came a new plan that Coleridge should open a school in Derby. While considering this he and Sara stayed as guests with Thomas Hawkes of Moseley, near Birmingham; it was there that Charles Lloyd, the twenty-one-year-old epileptic son of the Quaker banking family, developed an extravagant admiration for Coleridge, becoming determined to domicile with him and be tutored by him; moreover Lloyd would pay a generous fee for these privileges: eighty pounds a year, inclusive of board, lodging and tuition.

While this proposal underwent further consideration S.T.C. and Sara returned to Bristol. Without delay S.T.C. hurried to Stowey to discuss his future with Poole, who was still seething with indignation over Mrs Evans and her submission to the ruling of her boys' guardians: "I am now convinced of what I doubted before, that woman is inferior to man," spluttered Poole. "Woman, thou wast destined to be governed. Let us then bow to destiny."[12]

On 17th September S.T.C. returned to Birmingham to finalize arrangements with the Lloyds. Sara's lying-in was approaching but she assured her husband that she might safely be left as she was not due to be confined for a good three weeks to come. Sara, however, had "strangely miscalculated" (yet there was nothing truly strange about it;

she was all her life hopelessly at odds with dates). At half past two in the morning, two days after S.T.C.'s departure and while she was alone in the house, Sara was suddenly seized with labour pains; she gave birth before either the surgeon or the nurse could reach her and was obliged to deliver herself — "the Nurse just came in time to take away the after-birth". Sara, throughout, behaved with great coolness and presence of mind and had (as S.T.C. put it) "God be praised — a wonderfully favorable time". Within a few hours of the birth "she was, excepting weakness, perfectly well".[13] S.T.C. rushed back to her, bringing Charles Lloyd with him. The child was named David Hartley Coleridge, "in honour of the great Master of Christian Philosophy" as S.T.C. told everyone: his doubts, raised by Sara's earlier suffering, were now dispelled by the triumphant birth; he reavowed himself "a compleat Necessitarian".[14]

## III

From this it will be gathered that the Rock of Reality had another face in addition to its surly frowning aspect. True, the first twelve months of the Coleridge marriage had been packed with vicissitude, but the couple themselves had survived well, in terms of their relationship: love's first phantasies were undergoing the steady process of being metamorphosed into a married partnership. True, S.T.C. grumbled a lot during those first twelve months; but these were the grumbles of "a happy man".[15] As for Sara's groans and complaints, these had been merely part and parcel of early pregnancy and morning sickness and were now wholly behind her.

The Wollstonecraft precept, that marriage should be a matter of friendship, caused the young Coleridges no fundamental trouble. Sara was S.T.C.'s "dearest friend" in terms of fraternity, equality and marriage; but S.T.C. being S.T.C., with his boyhood roots firmly implanted in London's Christ's Hospital and the cockney haunts of Newgate Street, he naturally hailed a friend as a pal; thus Sara, having become Sally (for democratic reasons, Sally being more a name of the people than Sara) next progressed to Pal, and from there it was a mere versifying step to Sally Pally. So Sally Pally she became for him: a soubriquet which in itself tells much about their marriage in its earlier years.

Of course there were the inevitable minor disharmonies and discomforts of growing to fit one another (a process of adjustment required both in and out of bed and usually more difficult out of it than

Samuel Taylor
Coleridge in 1796.
Sketch in pen and
chalk by R. Hancock
(*National Portrait
Gallery, London*)

Thomas Poole
(1765-1837); the only
known portrait of him,
artist unidentified, and
used by Mrs Sandford
in her book, *Thomas
Poole & his friends*
(1880)

Robert Southey in his study at Greta Hall in 1804, by H. Eldridge. Note the view of Derwent Water through the window (*National Portrait Gallery, London*)

Mrs Edith Southey, aged thirty-five: a miniature portrait painted by Matilda Betham in 1809 (*Courtesy Fitz Park Museum, Keswick*)

Miniature portrait by
unknown artist of young
woman thought to be
Dorothy Wordsworth (see
Notes to Illustrations 2)
*(Reproduced by permission of
Mrs A.H.B. Coleridge)*

Miniature portrait of
William Wordsworth,
attributed to D.B. Murphy
*(Courtesy of the National
Gallery of Ireland, Dublin)*

Sara *fille* six and a half years old; not long after her first wide-eyed visit to Allan
Bank with her father, as described on pp. 191-3. Miniature portrait by
Matilda Betham (*Reproduced by permission of Mrs A.H.B. Coleridge*)

in it; such it certainly proved for the Coleridges). "My wife's every day self and her minor interests, alas, do not at all harmonize with my occupations, my temperament, or my weaknesses"; S.T.C. was "often almost miserable", he self-pityingly complained.[16] The operative word here is "almost". Again, this is the grousing of a basically happy man. Doubtless Sara, too, had her complaints, but she, a housewife and mother of an infant, lacked time to commit them to paper. In later years she would recall how desperately overworked she had been and how tired she had become; how wearisome the strain of the eternal struggle to make ends meet. Above all, how Samuel's bouts of ill-health had preyed on her peace of mind.

S.T.C.'s health first gave her cause for alarm in the autumn of 1796. It was complicated: it wasn't like other people's. He fell ill not through catching cold or mounting a fever or eating something disagreeable, after the manner of ordinary folk; no, Samuel became ill when he was *anxious*. Both Sara and Poole learnt this lesson in the autumn of 1796: it was frightening.

The tenancy of the Oxford Street lodgings was due to terminate on the coming Christmas Day: by mid-October S.T.C. had decided to move into the country; partly because he didn't wish his children to be city-reared, partly because he wanted to escape the tensions arising from the proximity of Fricker family problems, and (chiefly) because the failure of the Dawn of Reason (the French Revolution and its resultant developments on either side of the Channel) had filled him with a genuine despair about the future of mankind. He had decided to heed the "Birds of Warning" and turn his back upon degenerate society (Albion, "Abandoned of Heaven! mad Avarice thy guide");[17] he would shake the dust of the city from his feet and bury himself in a rural life of stark simplicity,

> With daily prayer and daily toil
> Soliciting for food my scanty soil . . .
> Now I recentre my immortal mind
> In the deep sabbath of meek self-content. . . . [18]

In short he had now set his heart on a species of mini-experiment in Pantisocracy : he would till his own plot of ground, harvest his own crops, keep his own livestock. He and his own little family unit would be almost entirely self-supporting.

He did not intend asking anyone else to join him. When Hartley had been a few days old reconcilement had taken place between Southey and Coleridge (Southey having returned to Bristol at the end of May).

"The overture was to come from dear S. to my great joy," Sara recalled.[19] Southey and Edith, cementing the reconciliation, moved to Clarence Place, opposite the Coleridges' house in Oxford Street. An animated discussion of poetry developed between the two brothers-in-law; politics would seem to have been a topic now largely avoided by them. No attempt was made by S.T.C. to tempt Southey to join him in the project. In any case Southey no longer deluded himself that he possessed the least aptitude, or inclination, to wield a spade or follow a plough. Furthermore Edith was needed in Bristol to offer solace and assistance to her sister, Mary Lovell, who had been tragically widowed the previous April and now found herself unprovided for, with an infant son to bring up.

A charming cottage with six acres had been discovered by Poole, on S.T.C.'s behalf, at Adscombe, not far from Stowey. The Coleridges prepared to move there and braced themselves to adopt "a severe process of simplification" in their life style.[20] They drew up a stern daily schedule: "We arranged our time, money and employments." Sara was to devote herself to nursing Hartley and sewing; S.T.C. was to do the rest: they would keep no servant. The washing would be put out. They would eat no meat except on Sundays. There would be no strong liquor in the house. Sara calculated that sixteen shillings a week should cover all their expenses. S.T.C. announced proudly that he was delighted with the way in which she had entered with enthusiasm into the scheme, assisting him to think "much and calmly"; together they "calculated time & money with unexceptionable accuracy" and concluded that if they "managed properly" they should be able to maintain themselves.[21]

S.T.C. went to the lengths of drawing up a list of daily domestic chores, divided between himself, Sara and Betty the nursemaid (who apparently didn't count as a servant. The reader will also notice that the resolution to eschew daily meat would seem to have been abandoned):

> Six o'clock. Light the fires. Clean out the kitchen. Put on the Tea kettle. Clean the Insides of the Boiling Pot. Shoes &c C. and B.
> Eight o'clock. Tea things &c put out &c after cleaned up. Sara.
> One o'clock — spit the meat. B & C.
> Two o'clock Vegetables &c. Sara.
> Three o'clock — Dinner.
> Half past three — 10 minutes for cleaning Dishes — [22]

after which it must be supposed that he proposed to rush outside and dig in the vegetable patch, act the hind and the haymaker, sower and reaper, with an evening of poetry and reviewing to follow. It is scarcely surprising that Poole shook his head. Sara, it would seem, still had total faith in Samuel.

Charles Lloyd insisted upon joining in with the adventure; Mrs Fricker announced that she didn't want to be left behind; little George should be found an apprenticeship in Bristol, leaving her free to come to Adscombe. Though this in some ways would be anything but desirable it was a suggestion that had its advantages, Sara and Samuel decided, since she would bring her furniture with her; without which they could only furnish one bedroom and a kitchen-parlour, which in turn meant that Charles Lloyd and Betty could not be accommodated.

But, while Sara was "enthusiastic" over the scheme, S.T.C.'s excitement grew beyond bounds, until it approached the irrational. He was "interested even to an excess and violence of Hope" as he confided to Poole.[23] As always, when in an agitated state, he became victim to anxiety, anxiety prompted dejection and dejection resulted in opium. He lay sunk in "day-mair dreams" (undoubtedly opium-induced); sadistically torturing himself with phantasies of disappointment over Adscombe. Shortly afterwards he was seized by acute rheumatic pains which nearly drove him frantic. The doctor was called and diagnosed the pain as being of nervous origin, "originating in mental causes".[24] A blister was applied and the patient was prescribed twenty-five drops of laudanum every four hours. S.T.C. buttressed the prescribed laudanum with massive extra doses.[25]

It is impossible to estimate the actual strength of the amounts of opium taken by Coleridge and his fellow addicts, because in their day the extracts varied greatly, never being standardized. One supply of laudanum might differ greatly in pharmaceutical power from another. The reason why Coleridge and De Quincey would seem to have been able to swallow what today would be fatal doses of laudanum was because their laudanum contained so much less opium than now, when the quantity has become standardized. For this reason, to state that they drank this or that quantity of laudanum tells us nothing; apart from the important fact that their high tolerance to such large quantities indicates the extent of their addiction. That Coleridge, in 1796, could swallow these quantities of the drug without poisoning himself indicates that he must have been taking opium regularly and in quantity over a long period).

Sara and Poole were both horribly alarmed by this attack, although its true nature of basic neurosis combined with morphine addiction was not understood by them. How could it be? They had no previous experience to guide them. Had they but been able to recognize it, here was the writing on the wall.

Barely a fortnight after S.T.C.'s attack Charles Lloyd was seized with epileptic fits and mania. He returned to Birmingham for convalescence; his father wrote that he must return to Birmingham for good at the close of one twelvemonth; thereby removing any long-term prospect of his eighty pounds per annum — upon which the Coleridges had been confidently counting to pay their rent at Adscombe and to buy cloth, shoes, agricultural implements and so forth. Nor would anyone take on Sara's young brother George as an apprentice; he was too young, and premiumless. So Mrs Fricker had to change her mind about leaving Bristol. This meant that there would not be enough furniture. Finally, to complete the picture of disappointment, the Adscombe property itself came to nothing.

The only possibility now was a small, dilapidated cottage in Nether-Stowey. At first Poole said that, with certain improvements, this cottage "might do" and that the Coleridges would be happy in it. Thus encouraged they worked up a second wind. But then Poole himself developed doubts about having the Coleridges at Stowey: they were delightful as occasional visitors but as close permanent neighbours they might be an embarrassment. The neighbourhood was strongly anti-Jacobin and Coleridge was notorious locally for his "rascally views". Sara, too, was under a cloud of suspicion: was she, or was she not, a respectably married woman? asked the good people of Stowey.[26] Poole himself had been described as the most dangerous man in the county and had had considerable difficulty in living down this reputation; to establish Coleridge in Stowey would set a fresh flood of rumours afoot and invite further odium all round.

However, rather than confront S.T.C. point blank with these brutal facts (thereby running the risk of inducing a fresh attack of "anxiety") Poole took refuge behind the argument that the Stowey cottage was beyond redemption, and that the Coleridges should seek accommodation nearer Bristol, which would be much more convenient for them. He suggested a cottage at Acton, and gently repeated his doubts over Coleridge's suitability as an agriculturalist.

This, as was to be expected, brought a torrent of wild wailing and gnashing of teeth from S.T.C. "O my God! . . . Disappointment follows Disappointment!" He scrawled page after page of a letter of vehement protest; Sara, seated opposite him as he wrote, observed the workings of his face; finally he flung down his pen and burst into lamentations to her. At eleven next morning, after "an almost Sleepless Night", S.T.C. resumed the letter to Poole, with a passionate account of the shattered Esteesian feelings and a fresh reiteration of the scheme for survival which S.T.C. and Sara had been working on for almost three months and which could not fail to succeed.[27]

And now Charles Lloyd's father retracted the twelve months' threat: Charles could rejoin the Coleridges in the New Year. So keen was the youth that he volunteered to do without a servant and even to "put up on a Press Bed". As for S.T.C., "Literature, tho' I shall never abandon it, will always be a secondary object with me . . . I would rather be an expert, self-maintaining gardener than a Milton, if I could not unite both".[28] Out-talked, if not out-manoeuvred, Poole surrendered and discussion commenced upon how to improve the Stowey cottage by insulating the rooms with green baize and "Rumfordizing" the chimneys.[29]

On 31st December the Coleridges, all Optimism, removed from Bristol to Nether-Stowey. On 6th January of the New Year, 1797, S.T.C. scribbled a note to Cottle, to let him know that the party had arrived safely, that they were all in good health, that the neighbours were most cordial and the Pooles most loving and "from all this you will conclude, *that we are happy*".[30] Well, almost. "We all have a somewhat to encounter in this life . . . " as Sara was given to remarking.

# CHAPTER EIGHT

# *Domestic Bliss Continued*

## I

Coleridge had allowed Optimism to run riot in his note to Cottle. Inspired flights of the imagination were required in order to see the Nether-Stowey cottage as a happy nest for young marrieds. It was an ugly, dilapidated little edifice crouching on the verge of Nether-Stowey's main gutter; the accommodation consisted of two small living-rooms, one on either side of a dark and narrow passage leading from the front door to a small kitchen-scullery in the rear. There were three poky bedrooms upstairs. The back door gave access to a long strip of kitchen garden, with an orchard. There was an earth-closet privy in the garden. The chimneys smoked, the place was incurably damp; of marrow-chilling cold in winter, rich with smells in summer (from the open gutter), plagued by legions of mice within and rowdy urchins sporting without, in the said gutter; (urchins named by Coleridge, "The Poor-house Nightingales", for many came from that institution, situated nearby). In bad weather Lime Street, the gutter overflowing, mud everywhere, became "an impassable Hog-stye, a Slough of Despond."[1]

Poole exerted himself to combat the damp and draughts; Coleridge hardened his heart, stifled his moral principles about luring innocent trusting mice to their deaths, and set cheese-baited traps. The cottage was gradually transformed into "an abode of comparative comfort" (that is to say, compared with what it had been). Nothing could be done about the smells, the urchins or the mud.

S.T.C., in his initial ebullience at having effected the removal to Stowey, wrote enthusiastic letters to his Bristol friends, extolling the charms of his new home, and his prowess as an agriculturalist.[2] Sara, with her "more literal Fricker temperament" saw the place as "miserable".[3] It must be borne in mind that the Coleridges made their move in the dead of winter and it must furthermore be conceded that Sara, by very virtue of her sex, bore the brunt of the hardships. Life as a simple agricultural labourer's wife was far from easy. There was no heating in the house, apart from draughty open fireplaces for which endless fuel had to be fetched and endless kindling chopped; there was no oven or kitchen range: the cooking was done at the open hearth, where heavy cast-iron pots and kettles required lifting and setting on trivets or suspending from hooks. All water had to be fetched from the pump; any hot water required had to be heated over the fire. Wash day was a strenuous undertaking and therefore occurred on an average of once a fortnight; however an infant in the family necessitated more frequent wash-tub exercises. In bad weather wet clothes and an endless succession of diapers had to be dried on clothes horses set round the fire and a drying rack suspended above it; the living-room was a perpetual miasma of damp clouts. Ironing necessitated the use of heavy flat irons, either heated at the fire or containing small hot bricks; in either case the implements were wearisome to wield. Then there were the endless chores entailed by rush lights and oil lamps; the darning and patching and mending of old clothes, the making of new; the scrubbing, scouring and general cleaning about the house: finances tight. It was true that they had the services of "poor Nanny",* as she was invariably called; a consumptive little maiden, slightly soft in the head, loyal, hardworking and devoted; but there was a limit to what Nanny could perform unaided, pound away as she might; Sara found herself likewise involved in hours of wearing drudgery. Samuel, after a frenetic start of hacking in the garden, struggling in the mud, cleaning shoes, trimming wicks, fetching fuel and lighting fires, relapsed into poetic vein and resumed his privileged role of exclusive man of letters, writing a tragedy, *Osorio*, for Sheridan at Drury Lane. Sara and Nanny ran the household together in the sisterhood of domestic slavery.

With one of two notable exceptions the local people were at first suspicious and unfriendly. As S.T.C. glumly observed, a man's bad character follows him long after he has ceased to deserve it. Stowey continued to view him as a dangerous revolutionary. As for Sara, she was treated not infrequently as little better than a scarlet woman: Tom Poole's brother's widow indulged "in more than one instance" in "absolute insult" to her.[4] It was no surprise that Sara would occasionally burst into tears: asked by Samuel what ailed her, she would reply, "I was thinking, my dear! of Mrs Evans and Bessy".[5] The five weeks of kind hospitality in the welcoming house at Darley lingered in Sara's memory as a species of Paradise Lost.

However the Coleridges persevered with their neighbours and gradually Sara's naturally blithe sociability and obvious devotion to her husband coupled with S.T.C.'s "peaceable manners & known attachment to Christianity"[6] allayed suspicions and Stowey accepted them. Poole was a tower of strength throughout all this and his mother behaved to the young Coleridges as if she were in truth their own "kind & tender mother".[7] In due course friends were made among the

*Betty, perhaps not surprisingly, had decided to find herself another "place".

neighbours; the Coleridges, accepted increasingly into Stowey society, found themselves enjoying parties and musical evenings. Life brightened. Even the cottage grew to be more tolerable; it is true that between themselves the couple invariably referred to it as "the old hovel", but nonetheless they did not disguise the attachment they formed for the place; it was their home and, despite the odds, they shared many hours of "domestic bliss" within its walls.

As for David Hartley, he grew "a sweet boy"; all high health and high spirits: "He laughs at us till he makes us weep for very fondness. — You would smile to see my eye rolling up to the ceiling in a lyric fury, and on my knee a Diaper pinned, to warm", a famous self-portrait of S.T.C. in 1797. As part of the lyric fury he composed — and sang — a lullaby, "Did a very little babby make a very great noise?"[8]

Charles Lloyd now rejoined the Coleridge household. He was apparently wholly restored in health and proved remarkably sweet-tempered over the "inconveniences of cottage accommodation" and pleasingly gentle with little Hartley.[9] Thus all seemed set fair for a durable spell of "the deep sabbath of meek self-content" as S.T.C. had written in his *Ode to the Departing Year*. However, in early March, as a result of Lamb's harsh criticism of *The Destiny of Nations*, an epic poem on which S.T.C. had been working for the past several months, a bout of deep dejection set in. S.T.C. had "no heart" for finishing *The Destiny of Nations*, nor, for a while, for working on *Osorio*; he subsided into a fresh trough of depression and opium; a morass of "irresolution aggravated by irrational anxiety" and "day-mairs".[10]

The pattern of the previous November repeated itself; there is little doubt that Coleridge's bouts of dejection unsettled Charles Lloyd's equally perilous equilibrium, for hot on the heels of his host's incapacitation Lloyd succumbed to another bout of fits and frenzy. He recovered sufficiently to return home; but his condition was such that soon afterwards he entered a sanatorium in Lichfield, under the care of Dr Erasmus Darwin. Lloyd's father decently sent the Coleridges ten pounds to cover the expenses involved during the period that Charles had lodged with them. They were now left with a spare room. This was to have profound consequences.

## II

Over the past year Coleridge had made the slight acquaintance of William Wordsworth and had become enthusiastic about the work of this star as yet but little noticed in his ascent. The two poets corresponded intermittently and, shortly after Charles Lloyd had departed for Birmingham following his second attack of illness, Wordsworth visited Coleridge at Stowey; a visit made possible by the spare room. Wordsworth was then on his way from Bristol to Racedown near Lyme Regis, where he was in temporary residence with his sister, Dorothy.

Henceforth Coleridge was ebulliently declaring to anyone who would listen that Wordsworth was the greatest man that he had ever met. Poole was introduced to him on this visit and, probably influenced by Coleridge's enthusiasm, himself formed a glowing first impression of the poet. However an attempt by Wordsworth, through Poole's good offices, to secure the tenancy of Alfoxden House (a manorial residence in a deer park three miles from Stowey) came to nothing.[11]

Nonetheless, despite this disappointment, Coleridge continued to harbour dreams of having Wordsworth in the near neighbourhood and, in early July, Wordsworth again negotiated for Alfoxden and was successful in this second application for a lease. The months of that summer were one whirl of social activity at Nether-Stowey; with Coleridge hospitality as the hub. Among the many guests were Charles Lamb (who noted with amusement a few light skirmishes between the Coleridges, these prompted by disagreement over "the management of little Hartley" — the father was thought to spoil the child),[12] and, in July, John Thelwall,[13] the celebrated seditionist; who talked much of "his Stella and his babies" and rapidly became "a great favourite with Sara".

Thelwall remained at Stowey until the close of the month; he had no sooner departed than Coleridge was inviting Josiah Wade to stay a week at Stowey; mentioning breezily, in passing, that Sara had now suffered a miscarriage, "But in so very early a stage, that it occasioned but little pain, one day's indisposition and no confinement — Indeed, the circumstance is quite unknown, except to me".[14] Doubtless Sara had been working too hard. Nevertheless this did not prevent further guests from being cordially entertained in Lime Street: Cottle and Charles Lloyd now arrived (the latter much recovered in health and apparently the epitome of friendship) and all was once more genial talk and laughter. Cottle has left us a famous passage relating to this visit:

> [Coleridge] took peculiar delight in assuring me . . . how happy he was; exhibiting successively, his house, his garden, his orchard, laden with fruit; and also the contrivance he had made to unite his two neighbours' domains with his own.

After the grand circuit had been accomplished, by hospitable contrivance, we approached the "Jasmine harbour", when to our gratifying surprise, we found the tripod table laden with delicious bread and cheese, surmounted by a brown mug of true Taunton ale. We instinctively took our seats. . . . As we sat in our sylvan hall of splendour, a company of happiest mortals, (T. Poole, C. Lloyd, S. T. Coleridge, and J.C.) . . . elevated in the universal current of our feelings, Mrs Coleridge approached with her fine Hartley; we all smiled, but the father's eye beamed transcendental joy![15]

However no family, however transcendentally joyous, can exist on air; there was no income of any kind being earned by S.T.C. that summer, though high hopes were pinned on *Osorio* as a source of future wealth: S.T.C. anticipated profits of five or six hundred pounds from it and he and Sara had many discussions over whether the sum should be sunk into an annuity for her, or used for financing S.T.C. to study medicine and philosophy in Germany.[16] By early September Sara was pregnant once more and S.T.C. succumbed to a bout of dejection over immediate money problems and the realization that, "It is probable that my children will come fast on me".[17]

He began to consider, with increasing seriousness, the possibility of entering the Unitarian ministry; he was invited to Bristol to discuss the matter with his friend, the Unitarian minister Dr John Prior Estlin.[18] S.T.C.'s penniless condition had reduced his wardrobe to even worse straits than usual, giving rise to some joking at his expense concerning the new Unitarian minister mistaken for a tramp; as part of this joking Poole mentioned that he had an old coat that S.T.C. might care to have, as well as some silk and cotton mixture stockings. S.T.C. accepted, "You shall be my Elijah — & I will most reverentially catch the Mantle, which you have cast off".[19] Poole gave S.T.C. an old uncle's old coat, never supposing that S.T.C. would wear it; but wear it he did, just as it was, not even letting the tailor alter it, much to Sara's mortification. This was the coat in which S.T.C. preached to Unitarian congregations: the coat which Hazlitt was to immortalize in his pen-portrait of the young Coleridge; "a round-faced man, in a short black jacket (like a shooting-jacket) which scarcely seemed to have been made for him";[20] the coat which Sara never forgot, nor how S.T.C. burst "out a-laughing whenever he looked at himself in the glass with it on".[21]

# CHAPTER NINE

# Farewell, Sweet Youth!

The autumn and spring of 1797–98, famous within the context of the Coleridge-Wordsworth poetical partnership resulting in *Lyrical Ballads*, were, for the celebrated trio, S.T.C., William Wordsworth and his sister Dorothy, months of long picturesque walks, enthusiastic talk about the scenery they saw on their rambles and the poems that the two poets planned, and the forging of an extraordinarily close, triangular friendship. For the pregnant Sara, confined by domestic duties and drudgery to the Lime Street cottage, but in any case tacitly excluded from the magic triangle, they were months of mounting anxiety and resentment.

De Quincey was to write, "A young lady [Dorothy] became a neighbour, and a daily companion of Coleridge's walks. . . . Intellectually she was very much superior to Mrs Coleridge. That superiority alone, when made conspicuous by its effects in winning Coleridge's regard and society, could not but be deeply mortifying to a young wife . . . it is a bitter trial to a young married woman to sustain any sort of competition with a female of her own age for any part of her husband's regard, or any share of his company."[1]

It was true that, once the Wordsworths had entered his life, Coleridge never ceased to sing their praise and we know that Sara was not the only one to become distinctly tired of this. But it is doubtful if, at any time, she felt in competition with Dorothy Wordsworth in the everyday sense that De Quincey is describing. Sara never acknowledged Dorothy as an *intellectual* superior; indeed on pure grounds of intellect Sara rather believed herself to be in no way inferior to Dorothy, and S.T.C. would probably have supported his wife in this: Sara Coleridge, he recorded, possessed "an excellent understanding" and was "a woman of considerable intellect"[2] (he was, of course, adhering to the definition of intellect as "the action, or process, of understanding, especially as opposed to *imagination*"). His estimation of her abilities is buttressed by the way in which her mind and learning expanded steadily under the influence of both himself and Southey, gaining a level where she herself was largely able to educate her brilliantly intellectual daughter Sara. However, in praising his wife thus Coleridge was paying her a distinctly backhanded compliment and emphasizing the difference between her and Dorothy. Coleridge, at heart, actively disliked and despised intellectuality and education in women: "bluestockingism" (as he called it) destroyed not only the womanly virtues of tractability and "the desire to please" the male head of a household, but eroded sensibility and sympathy; feeling *for* and *with* the said male. Herein lay the kernel of all the uncomplimentary things which were said about Mrs Coleridge by the Wordsworths and by Coleridge himself; she lacked that spontaneous enthusiasm for the enthusiasms of others which Rousseauists found so immensely more satisfying in a woman than brains and learning.

In short, Wollstonecraft was quickly disavowed by S.T.C. once Dorothy Wordsworth arrived on the scene with her inherently Rousseauist instincts to "give William pleasure". The "absorption of her whole Soul in her Brother's fame and writings" was an example of love and dedication to the male which, hereafter, was always before Coleridge's eyes. He perceived that Dorothy, as "a Woman of Genius, as well as of manifold acquirements" might, albeit in "a different style", perhaps "have been as great a Poet as [William Wordsworth] Himself", had she not thus absorbed herself in his interests; but, having perceived this, S.T.C. could not deplore that this was so: Dorothy's dedication to the promotion of William's happiness and the fostering of his genius were "worth all the rest told 10,000 times".[3]

It was not intellect that S.T.C. admired in Dorothy, but genius; and this not so much her wonderful use of language and skill with descriptive prose but rather herself as tutelary genius of the wild, the natural. "She was", said De Quincey, attempting to put this elusive quality into words, "the very wildest (in the sense of the most natural) person I have ever known"; a wonderful companion to have on a country walk because of "the exceeding sympathy, always ready and always profound, by which she made all that one could tell her, all that one could describe . . . reverberate, as it were *à plusieurs reprises*, to one's own feelings, by the manifest impression it made upon *hers*. The pulses of light are not more quick or more inevitable in their flow and undulation, than were the answering and echoing movements of her sympathetic attention." What Coleridge meant, in short, when he described her as "a perfect electrometer".[4]

Sara *fille* has left us some telling comments upon her mother in comparison with Dorothy Wordsworth. Dorothy had "greater enthusiasm of temperament than my mother possessed," observed Sara *fille*. "*She* never admires anything she doesn't understand." Sara *fille* went on to add that her mother's "very honesty stood in the way".[5]

None of this means, of course, that Mrs Coleridge was an insensible clod, incapable of appreciating the beauties of nature or enjoying poetry. S.T.C., since their days of courtship, had complimented his wife upon her own taste and sensibility, her accomplishments and cultivation; he has recorded discussions with her of poets and poetry and has remarked upon her insights of criticism; it is also on record that she "could read poetry aloud beautifully",[6] which in itself indicates her feeling and fondness for it, and at least a certain degree of imagination. But with the Wordsworths she was, as we would say, in a different league. She was quickly found to be "deficient in organic sensibility" and resultantly was never admitted within the "sacred and privileged pale" of the so-called "Wordsworth circle".[7]

Not only had Sara to put up with the knowledge that she was considered inferior within the context of taste and organic sensibility, not only did she have to stay at home superintending the wash-tub while Samuel and the Wordsworths regaled themselves with picturesque excursions; she further had to contend with what female readers will probably agree was calculated provocation at the hands of Dorothy. De Quincey received the following tale, first-hand, from Dorothy Wordsworth herself. She seems not to have realized that, by telling it, she was giving herself away, though we may well suspect that De Quincey, with his subtle insight, perfectly understood the true implications of the story. To quote him: "Often it would happen that the walking party returned drenched with rain; in which case [Dorothy], with a laughing gaiety, and evidently unconscious of any liberty she was taking . . . would run up to Mrs Coleridge's wardrobe, array herself, without leave asked, in Mrs Coleridge's dresses, and make herself merry with her own unceremoniousness and Mrs Coleridge's gravity." Dorothy was to say that she regarded this merry dressing-up in Mrs Coleridge's clothes as one of "the natural privileges of friendship"; Mrs Coleridge, however, "viewed her freedoms with a far different eye . . . and it barbed the arrow to her womanly feelings, that Coleridge treated any sallies of resentment which might sometimes escape her as narrowmindedness".[8]

To appreciate the full import of this story the reader should remember that Sara Coleridge prided herself on her reputation as a smart and elegant dresser: Dorothy was laughing at Mrs Coleridge's Bath-inspired wardrobe; a wardrobe which had cost its innocently proud owner heaven knows how many hours of needlework, and how many self-denials and frugalities in order to obtain the materials with which to make up the dresses! There is a degree of cruelty here, in Dorothy's behaviour, which tells us a great deal about her private feelings at this time.

A usually kind and generous-spirited woman, Dorothy permitted herself, in conversation, writing and behaviour, to reveal uncharacteristic malice towards Sara Coleridge. The spiteful portrait which Dorothy has left us, for those early years, of a Mrs Coleridge narrowminded and tediously conventional, shallow, complaining, a "sad fiddle-faddler" in domestic matters, with next to no notion of how to feed her children and bring them up, with never a serious thought in her head or feeling in her heart, is a portrait utterly at variance with all that we know of Sara from other undoubtedly dependable sources. Coleridge (writing in opium-untinctured moments) has left us a portrait of his wife radically opposed to that given us by the youthful Dorothy. It is difficult to escape the conclusion that, in Dorothy Wordsworth, we have a young woman who has fallen in love with a married man and is voicing her jealousy of that man's wife: a jealousy made keener for Dorothy because, although she was able to provide S.T.C. with a certain kind of company and stimulation not in Sara's capacity, Coleridge was still in love with his wife and drew "transcendental joy" from his conjugal and domestic bliss.

Sara clearly felt herself secure in S.T.C.'s affections. True, she became more and more concerned over the hold that the Wordsworths increasingly gained upon him, but it was a concern prompted not by mere shafts of commonplace jealousy, but by the attitude which the Wordsworths displayed towards what Poole called S.T.C.'s "unbidden excursions of the mind".

It is plain, from all that Poole had to say on the subject of the danger, to Coleridge, of an over-stimulated imagination, that S.T.C.'s bout of illness at the time of the Adscombe episode and the doctor's diagnosis that this illness had its origin in "mental causes" had signalled to Poole that his beloved Col was placed in jeopardy by the very genius which distinguished him so markedly from his fellow men. Poole recognized the truth of Coleridge's repeated assertion that he had never required opium to stimulate his imagination: but Poole was equally well aware that S.T.C.'s neurotic personality was chronically prone to collapse under pressure and that flights into the "wilder realms of poesy" constituted just as much a form of pressure as did an accumulation of household bills. "The racehorse cannot always be upon the turf" as Poole sagely observed of S.T.C. and, equally, the poet could not always be "in a fine frenzy".[9] Overstimulation by genius must, for Coleridge's own sake, be curbed — all this apart from opium to which S.T.C. invariably had recourse once over-stimulated by his natural inbuilt powers of imagination, rather than the other way round. From this subtle understanding of S.T.C.'s predominant "weakness" arose Poole's incessant admonitions to him upon the dangers of "the unbidden excursions of your mind"; Col must learn to *master* his imagination, rather than to allow it to master *him*.[10]

Poole, in his vigilant care for his "beloved friend", prompted Sara to a like sensitivity on S.T.C.'s behalf; she was constantly receiving cautions from Poole that Col must not be upset, must be kept as far as possible on an even keel. This was not easy for Sara, who had an inborn habit of speaking her mind to her nearest and dearest. However, she did her best to maintain Samuel in as tranquil a state as possible. But now had arrived the Wordsworths. They quickly revealed themselves, in the opinion of Sara and Poole, as dangerous friends for S.T.C.; soon becoming "those persons" who were "the great means of his self-indulgence".[11] What Sara Coleridge and Poole were saying and continued to say, was that the Wordsworths, far from restraining S.T.C. from damaging excursions of the mind, encouraged him; nor, it would seem, did they protest when these excursions were made down the laudanum-impregnated streams of Fancy.[12]

Wordsworthians who balk at the notion of the Wordsworths countenancing Coleridge's indulgence in opium (or more correctly countenancing it during this early period of their friendship — later, of course, they came to hold a tragically different opinion upon the subject) should bear two important points in mind. First, the moral stance of the young William Wordsworth bore no resemblance whatever to the Christian moral stance of the older man: Wordsworth at that stage of his development did not embrace Christianity, "He loves & venerates Christ & Christianity [as part of an overall benevolence of human speculative philosophy] — I wish he did more", S.T.C. confided to a Unitarian friend.[13] Wordsworth, when Coleridge first knew him, was "even to Extravagance a Necessitarian" and "It is his practice & almost his nature to convey all the truth he knows without any attack on what he supposes falsehood, if that falsehood be interwoven with virtues or happiness," Coleridge explained.[14] Thus, even had Wordsworth seen opium as possibly dangerous he would not have proscribed it, since it brought Coleridge pleasure; quite apart from its medicinal value to him as an anodyne — though even the use of opium as a medication was tinctured with voluptuous pleasure, an oasis, "a spot of enchantment, a green spot of fountains, & flowers & trees, in the very heart of a waste of Sands!"[15]

Secondly, the Wordsworths were wholly ignorant of the true hazards of morphine addiction. They had known Coleridge for only a short time and were probably quite unaware of his already established "opium habit" (though acquaintance with Charles Lloyd was soon to feed them with anecdotes of Coleridge's "weakness"). They certainly did not realize — the chemistry of drug addiction was not understood in their day — that it was only through the regular consumption of ever-increasing quantities of opium, over a considerable time, that Coleridge had reached the state where his body could tolerate the large amounts which he now took with impunity, and that the very fact that he had achieved this high tolerance made it inevitable that he must soon enter the appalling bondage of total reliance.

Wordsworth, like Coleridge, at this time was enthusiastic about the possibilities of writing remunerative gothic-style ballads. The two poets were most systematic in their approach to the project: they read, studied and analysed every example of the *genre* that they could lay hands on, from Percy's *Reliques* to M. G. Lewis's most recent spine chillers.[16] Ancient myths and fairy stories, tales of the extraordinary, histories of exploration: "all the tribe of Horror & Mystery . . . even to surfeiting"[17] were devoured. Amongst this reading matter were Samuel Purchas's collections of travel and voyaging in the early seventeenth century: it was from this source that Coleridge took material for *The Ancient Mariner* (begun in this autumn of 1797) and it was in *Purchas His Pilgrimage* that Coleridge was browsing when opium bore him to Xanadu where "did Cublai Chan build a stately Palace".

The Wordsworths fell under the fascination of Coleridge's personality; were captivated by his magic; became engulfed in his genius (as he in theirs); they marvelled at his "capacious Soul". They saw him as a species of enchanted voyager, the Old Navigator himself, bursting into uncharted seas; at other times he was a fantastic spelaeologist fathoming caverns measureless to man: he was a Samuel Purchas of their very own, telling tales of marvels and miracles.

The pursuit of such El Dorados of the imagination would seem to have intoxicated Coleridge and the Wordsworths. Brother and sister (at least so it seemed to Poole and Sara) had no compunction in sending S.T.C. out, in his frail craft, to circumnavigate whole universes; or, suspended by Fancy's fragile strand, to dangle peering into bottomless crevasses; or to vanish, again and again, under the waterfall. Like a Drake, a Shelvocke, a Bartrum, a Dampier and Captain Cook combined he would return with fabulous treasure to spill, spellbinding, before the Wordsworths.

They accepted his booty; their enthusiasm sufficient reward for him in his loyal adulation. In any case, he was a born reckless adventurer; extreme experience laced with peril was his element. He was the supreme existentialist forever hurling himself forward; the sufi of sufis whirling aloft to soar into deeper awareness,

O! the one Life within us and abroad,
Which meets all motion and becomes its soul,
A light in sound, a sound-like power in light,
Rhythm in all thought, and joyance every where —[18]

Poole and Sara, troubled onlookers, trembled on their beloved's behalf; Poole (uttering imploring cries of "Chain yourself down" and warning against "Wordsworth idolatry") made a metaphorical leap to grab S.T.C. by his coat tails and haul him back to earth; but it was too late, S.T.C. was already whirling far beyond reach.

Now came news that Coleridge's drama, *Osorio*, was rejected by Sheridan. Coleridge, daunted by the prospect of continuing financial insecurity as a literary man, was on the brink of entering the Unitarian ministry when he was saved from the said financial insecurity by the offer, from the Wedgwood brothers, Josiah and Thomas, of an annuity for life of a hundred and fifty pounds. With the offer of the annuity the sun emerged from behind its temporary bank of cloud; Benevolence was seen to triumph, the System of Optimism was confirmed.

As we know, one of the dreams which Coleridge had long cherished was that of going to Germany, there to complete his mastery of the language and study at a university, preferably Jena; his family to accompany him. Financial security meant that he might now indulge in making that dream come true. The Wordsworths instantly declared their interest in such a scheme (not entirely to the satisfaction of Sara, Poole and the Wedgwoods, all of whom would have preferred to have seen the Wordsworths and Coleridge separated). A plan was drawn up without delay; the party to leave in late summer, by which time the new Coleridge offspring (expected at the end of April) would be hardy enough to travel.

The spring and early summer of 1798 saw S.T.C. writing Part One of *Christabel* and caught in a whirlpool of quarrelling with Southey, Charles Lloyd and Charles Lamb;[19] the *agent provocateur* in all this being, essentially, Charles Lloyd, who indulged himself in flagrantly slandering his friends behind their backs to one another. At this stage no one realized that Lloyd was a pathological liar and trouble maker; everybody accepted his allegations and tittle-tattle as truth; the results were damaging. Furthermore Sara, who hated it when S.T.C. and Southey quarrelled, became upset in her turn; not a desirable state of affairs, as she was now nearing the time of her lying-in.[20]

On the morning of 14th May she was "safely delivered of a fine boy".[21] The new baby was named Berkeley, in honour of George Berkeley, Bishop of Cloyne, whose theory of the relation of man to nature was at that time greatly esteemed by S.T.C. Berkeley, by all accounts, was an outstanding infant, both in physique and promise of intelligence, "Fine and flourishing". S.T.C., informing Poole of the birth, observed that the new infant, even in his hour of arrival, was "already almost as large as Hartley".[22] From the first Berkeley was a remarkably responsive, aware, noticing infant and as the weeks passed he developed a promise of handsome looks matching his promise of exceptional intelligence. His parents' pride and delight in him knew no bounds.

To quote Sara *fille*, writing many years later, "Mama used to tell me mother's tales, which, however, were confirmed by my Aunt Lovell, of this infant's noble and lovely style of beauty, his large, soft eyes, of a 'London-smoke' colour, exquisite complexion, regular features and goodly size. She said that my father was very proud of him, and one day, when he saw a neighbour approaching his little cottage at Stowey, snatched him away from the nurse half-dressed, and with a broad smile of pride and delight, presented him to be admired. In her lively way, she mimicked the tones of satisfaction with which he uttered, 'This is my second son'. Yet, when the answer was, 'Well, this is something like a child,' he felt affronted on behalf of his little darling Hartley".[23]

As the summer wore on Sara lost much of her enthusiasm for the visit to Germany, deciding that it would be wiser to remain at Stowey with the children; they were too young, both she and Poole felt, to be taken abroad. It was planned that she should join S.T.C. at a later date, if expense would bear it, and his continued residence in Germany to study promised to have advantages.

S.T.C., together with the Wordsworths and a young Stowey neighbour, John Chester, left for Germany in early September; the party sailed from Yarmouth on the sixteenth of that month. In London, before catching the Yarmouth coach, S.T.C. bought himself, for twenty-five shillings, a great-coat: a "weighty, long, high caped, respectable rug",[24] he described it. We hear no more thereafter of Tom Poole's old uncle's coat.

And it was here, with the fading of that summer of 1798 into an autumn of departure, and the disappearance of the young man in the old coat who had "burst out a-laughing whenever he looked at himself in the glass with it on", that the lamb-sappy, flower-flashing, springtide of youth vanished for Sara Coleridge. At the time we do not notice these demarcation lines, but in retrospect they stand out clearly.

# PART TWO

*"A Something to Contend With"*

(SEPTEMBER 1798 — MAY 1812)

# CHAPTER TEN

## *Calamity*

### I

With a fair wind it took travellers forty-eight hours, by pacquet, from Yarmouth to Cuxhaven. Once there, S.T.C. immediately began a letter to Sara, telling her how, "When we lost sight of land, the moment that we quite lost sight of it, & the heavens all round me rested upon the waters, my dear Babies came upon me like a flash of lightning — I saw their faces so distinctly!" He concluded the letter, "Good night, my dear, dear Sara! — 'every night when I go to bed & every morning when I rise' I will think of you with a yearning love, & of my blessed Babies! — Once more, my dear Sara! good night".[1]

S.T.C. had promised that he would write alternately to Poole and Sara, twice a week, during his absence; all letters to be shared (Sara only to keep private to herself those letters, or parts of letters, which were, to use Poole's bluff bachelor expression, "too foolish"). All his letters were to be copied by Poole's seventeen-year-old apprentice Thomas Ward, in the interests of posterity: the more *foolish* passages to be omitted. These omissions proved, in the event, to be frequent. Even after Ward's censoring we are left with constant exclamations from S.T.C. lamenting that he had no Sara with him, "O my love! I wish you were with me!" "O my God! how I wished you to be with me!" "O God! I do languish to be at home!"

His children, too, were yearned for, "Kiss my Hartley, & Bercoo Baby Brodder/Kiss them for their dear Father, whose heart will never be absent from them many hours together!"[2] Hartley's first steps in learning also came under consideration, Sara being told, "I pray you, my Love! read Edgeworth's Essay on Education — read it heart & soul, & if you approve of the mode, teach Hartley his Letters — I am very desirous, that you should begin to teach him to read — & they point out some easy modes".[3]

It had been agreed that letters of a personal and private nature would be augmented by a kind of running journal which would be dispatched at intervals throughout his travels, conveying a detailed picture of German scenes, activities and people and intended for publication upon his return to England.[4]

The travellers proceeded from Cuxhaven to Hamburg ("An ugly City that stinks in every corner"). On 29th September Coleridge and the Wordsworths parted company (news that was received with great satisfaction in Stowey and by the Wedgwoods).[5] Coleridge and Chester removed to Ratzeburg, where S.T.C. planned to stay a few months while perfecting his command of the German tongue, while the Wordsworths, anxious to find cheaper accommodation, went to Goslar.

S.T.C.'s letters followed one after the other at regular intervals of writing; just as he had promised Sara and Poole. But a growing note of consternation gradually made itself heard:[6] though he was keeping his promise of regular and frequent correspondence, to his utter amazement not a word of reply reached him from Sara and Poole.[7] True, he had anticipated that the mail service between Germany and England might be bad, but never so bad as this! By 26th November he was becoming desperate; he burst out, in his letter of that date to Sara,

> Another, and another, and yet another Post day; and still Chester greets me with, "No letters from England"! A Knell, that strikes out regularly four times a week — How is this my Love? Why do you not write to me? — Do you think to shorten my absence by making it insupportable to me? Or perhaps you anticipate that if I received a letter, I should idly turn away from my German to *dream* of you — of you & my beloved babies! — Oh yes! — I should indeed dream of you for hours and hours . . . and of the Infant that sucks at your breast, and of my dear dear Hartley — You would be *present* . . . and . . . with what leaping and exhilarated faculties should I return to the objects & realities of my mission. — But now — nay, I cannot describe to you the gloominess of Thought, the burthen and Sickness of heart, which I experience every day.[8]

Here S.T.C. was, of course, speaking of opium dreams. He knew that Sara would know what he meant (hence the, "Do you anticipate I should idly turn away from my German to dream of you"): Sara, by this stage of their marriage, was only too well acquainted with the S.T.C. who lay languidly on his couch, lost in opium and dreams, when he should have been working. But it would do him good to dream of her! To escape from the realities of here and now, in Ratzeburg and weary exile, into the joys of how he wished things to be!

In any case anxiety over lack of letters from home had already given him the excuse to resort to opium as a tranquillizer against gnawing fears of what might have gone wrong to bring about this mystifying silence of Sara. In these resultant opium dreams he time and again returned to Nether-Stowey and Sara and the beloved babies: that nest of domestic peace which was the nub and epitome of all that lay closest to his heart.

From these dreams of Sara and her children and home came the poem, *The Day-Dream: From an immigrant to his absent wife*: the poem which must be seen as the major statement of the theme which was to haunt him for the rest of his days — married happiness, happiness with Sara, yet Sara not simply Sara but rather the symbol of that ideal object, Domestic Bliss, "Home and Thou art one"* to which he would remain for ever constant — even when the symbol herself was lost and he had been excluded from that sheltered, firelit, tranquil room, that womb of security and peace, with its couch, its gentle caresses, its warmth and tenderness.

THE DAY-DREAM
From an immigrant to his absent wife

If Thou wert here, these Tears were Tears of Light!
— But from as sweet a Day-dream did I start
As ever made these Eyes grow idly bright;
And tho' I weep yet still about the *heart*
A dear and playful Tenderness doth linger
Touching my heart as with a Baby's finger.

2

My Mouth half open like a witless Man,
I saw the Couch, I saw the quiet Room,
The heaving Shadows and the fire-light gloom;
And on my Lips, I know not what then ran,
On my unmoving Lips a subtle Feeling —
I know not what, but had the same been stealing

3

Upon a sleeping Mother's lips I guess
It would have made the loving Mother dream
That she was softly stooping down to kiss
Her Babe, that something more than Babe did seem —
An obscure Presence of its darling Father
Yet still its own sweet Baby self far rather!

4

Across my chest there liv'd a weight so warm
As if some bird had taken shelter there,
And lo! upon the Couch a Woman's Form!
Thine Sara! thine! O Joy, if thine it were!
I gaze'd with anxious hope, and fear'd to stir it —
[A deeper] Trance ne'er wrapt a yearning Spirit!

*Constancy to an Ideal Object* (below, p. 162).

5

And now when I seem'd *sure* my Love to see,
Her very Self in her own quiet Home,
There came an elfish Laugh, and waken'd me!
'Twas Hartley, who behind my chair had clomb,
And with his bright Eyes at my face was peeping —
I bless'd him — try'd to laugh — and fell a weeping.[9]

Although S.T.C. did not know it, he was invoking a paradise already
lost.

II

The reason for the silence from home was that calamity had struck
Nether-Stowey: calamity in the guise of a faulty smallpox vaccine that
had caused havoc among the local infants, including Berkeley Coleridge,
who was soon fighting for his life. Hartley, too, was ill; Sara herself
succumbed to infection, worry and exhaustion. The situation was
desperate, but Tom Poole was determined that Coleridge must be kept in
ignorance of the trouble: anxiety always had a devastating effect upon
Col and devastated he should not be when so far from home and upon an
expedition so important to his intellectual acquirements and future
prospects. On the other hand he could not be left entirely without letters
from home for this in itself would make him miserably anxious.

Sara, immersed in Berkeley's illness, which was now at crisis point,
and under stern instructions from Poole that not a breath of bad news
must reach S.T.C.'s ears, left Poole to write at this juncture: accordingly
the good man heaved a deep sigh and, with tears pouring down his
cheeks, set about penning a cheery letter[10] containing the monstrous lie
that all was well at home. "We are going on at Stowey just as when you left
us. Mrs C. and the children are perfectly well. Mrs C. keeps up her
spirits. . . . The Wordsworths have left you — so there is an end to our
fears about amalgamation, etc. . . . It was right for them to find a
cheaper situation; and it was right for you to avoid the expense of
travelling, provided you are where *pure German* is spoken. . . . One
thing which you must determine to acquire . . . is as perfect a knowledge
of the language as possible". And so on: several close written pages of
sound advice, ending with, "Mrs C. will write you a long letter next".

Poole's letter had reached Coleridge by 20th October; he at once wrote
to Sara begging for the promised "long letter"; "A very, very long letter —
write me all that can cheer me — all that will make my eyes swim & my

heart melt with tenderness!"[1] On 1st November Sara was at last able to take up her pen: Berkeley had turned the corner and seemed on the mend; she could write without too severely endangering S.T.C.'s peace of mind. Her resultant letter was certainly a long one; taking a vast sheet of paper, larger than foolscap. It was addressed to "Mr Coleridge/at the Pastor Unruke/Ratzburg [sic] Germany" (scrawled alongside this address, at a later date, in the hand of Mrs Coleridge, are the words, "These letters kept by the desire of S. T. Coleridge").

November 1 — 1798

My dear Samuel

I received your welcome letter from Hamburgh and, since that, two containing the journal (which gave us all a great deal of pleasure) and should have answered the first but I was at that time struggling under the most severe trial that I had ever had to undergo and when you have heard my account of it I am sure you will pity me.

About three weeks after you left Stowey, Mrs R. Poole proposed to inoculate her child and sent round to the inhabitants. I objected on account of the warm weather; she was not convinced, but very politely delayed it a week when the weather changed: on Saturday her child was inoculated and ours and several others; in a few days I perceived that Berkeley had taken the infection but Hartley had not; he was inoculated again — and again — and at last his arm rose to a great head and turned, but he never had any other sign. This was pretty well, tho' not quite satisfactory and I experienced some anxiety on his account, for he had very little if any of the eruptive fever; but my dear baby [Berkeley] on the eighth day began to droop, on the ninth he was very ill and on the tenth the pustules began to appear in the skin by hundreds.

He lay upon my lap like a dead child, burning like fire and all over he was red as scarlet; after I had counted about two hundred I could almost see them coming out and every one that appeared after that, seemed to me a little ugly messenger come bid me prepare for his death! By the thirteenth day every part of his face and body was covered except the pit of his stomach. I was almost distracted! Lewis [the doctor] was frightened — he came six *or eight times a day* — the ladies of Stowey also visited me and wept over this little victim, affected by my complaints, and the miserable plight of the child! What I felt is impossible to write — I had no husband to comfort me and share my grief — perhaps they boy would die, and he far away! All the responsibility of the infant's life was upon me, and it was a weight that dragged me to the earth! He was blind — his nose was clogged that he could not suck and his dear gums and tongue were covered and he was so hoarse that he could not cry; but he made a *horrid noise in his throat* which when I dozed for a minute I always heard in my dreams.

The night of the turn he was very ill, and Lewis gave him a larger dose of laudanum. Two of us were obliged to sit by him one on each side the cradle to hold his hands for the itching was intolerable and he would kick and beat his head about like any thing mad, and the sight of this threw me into agonies which I was obliged to suppress and which made me ill in the end.

After this critical night he grew better and was never happy but lying with the nipple in his mouth; the consequence of which was, in a few days my nipples were covered with the pustles; they became swelled as big as walnuts and I could not endure him to touch me. I had now a wet nurse to seek — James Cole's wife kindly undertook to suckle him by day, and by night we had recourse to a glass tube through which he sucked cow's milk, tho' very reluctantly, and only when his eyes were shut. My milk which was but little was drawn off by various strategems, with very great torture as you may easily believe. In the midst of all this, to fill my bitter cup the fuller, I was seized with a pain in my eye; it in a few hours became quite closed — my face and neck swollen, my head swimming; in short, I had caught a most violent cold in sitting up at night and sometimes lying on the ground in the smokey parlour.

[The letter now becomes badly damaged by tearing in the neighbourhood of the seals: see Sara's explanation for this in her next letter, of 13th December. The repaired letter continues,]

The child grew . . . and better and I . . . worse and I was very ill for a . . . at the end of which time the pustles were nearly all . . . Child except his head, which is so clogged with the hair . . . yet disengaged it. I suppose his hair must be all cut off . . . trifle.

I know not my dear love if I have . . . clear to you, but I trust you will understand . . . to know that your poor Sara has had nothing but calamity . . . two months absence which I thank God has saved you a worse. . . .

When Mr Poole wrote to you, and piously said, "Your Wife and children are well" the tears started into his eyes and flowed from mine, for the dear Babe was then at the very crisis of his distemper.

Things now begin to wear a brighter appearance, my small-pox are well and yesterday I made my acknowledgements to Mrs Cole who suckled Berkeley for the last time — my milk is returned in great quantity, and I shall soon be able to leave the bandage off my eye. The dear child is getting strength every hour and seems to be in perfect health — but *when you had your last sight of land* and the *faces of your children crossed you like a flash of lightning* you saw *that* face for the *last time* — when you return you will see a face full of little holes, his once beautiful and smooth eyebrows, irregular, and his eyelashes quite gone; however let us be thankful to God! that He has spared his life, his sight, and limbs and senses and endeavour to reconcile ourselves to the loss of his beauty!

True he was fair — [Inset note written by Mrs S.T.C. much later:— He recovered his good looks and was quite lovely when I took him to Bristol where he died many weeks after.] ah! how divinely fair! and his foolish Mother placed some of her happiness upon it, or to speak more properly, it gave me much delight.

You will easily believe, my dear Samuel, that I have been at great expences during this trying time: two nurses, one for the night and the other for the day; I could have no assistance from the neighbours, as all the children was ill at the same time. Mrs R. Poole's child had it very favourable; Buller's — Roskilly's, Cole's, Bastone's etc etc — but some of the poor children had it as bad as mine, and one that Mr Forbes inoculated from Berkeley — died! . . .[12]

Unfortunately Sara, in posting off her letter, had mistakenly paid no inland postage on it, supposing that Samuel should bear the entire cost (it was the recipient, not the sender, who paid postage in Britain of those days): consequently the letter was stopped at Yarmouth, opened (and torn in the process) and returned to her. She patched it up, paid double money and sent it off again; this, of course, badly delayed its arrival at Ratzeburg. Meantime S.T.C. had penned the desperate query, "How is this my Love? Why do you not write to me?"

S.T.C.'s distracted letter reached Sara the weekend of 12th December, by which time further calamity had overtaken her. She replied immediately, on Monday 13th.

In spite of Poole's renewed insistence that S.T.C. must be kept in ignorance of Berkeley's fresh bout of illness Sara, still nervously and physically exhausted from the smallpox catastrophe, decided that she must share with Samuel her renewed heavy burden of anxiety and nursing vigil: more than anything in the world she now needed the comfort of his shoulder to weep upon; this denied her, she must at least be able to confide her troubles to him. Thus she now wrote, with no attempt at either tact or dissembling,

[Monday 13 December 1798]
My dear dear Samuel your letter has kept me awake all night! Good God! what can be the reason that you have not (or that you *had* not) received my letter dated first November? I knew not that I ought to pay the inland postage, so it went to Yarmouth, was opened, torn, and returned: I was frightened and not having time to write another, and the subject being a most disagreeable one, I made shift to patch up the same, paid double Money and sent it on: I hope you have got it long ago, for by the time you receive this it will be more than a month from the date of your last.

So far from wishing to make the time of your absence intolerable to you my poor dear, I sincerely hope, I am sure, that you will have as much pleasure and comfort as your great distance from your family will allow: for that reason now see in my last, that I did not write of my troubles until they were nearly over. What a riddle will this seem to you if you have not received it!

We are all very thankful to you for your entertaining accounts. Poole's letter of the twentieth and mine of the twenty-sixth came at the same time; you of course will write as soon as you receive the letter in question.

And now what shall I say? It seems cruel to vex you after so many inquietudes, but I must either write to you my griefs, or not write at all for alas! my Samuel,

> There's nae gude luck about the house
> Sen my gude Mon's awa.

To keep you no longer in suspense, I believe I closed *my journal* — with a swollen Eye. I resume it labouring under the same malady on the other side of the cheek — but of this in order.

Our dear children were charmingly recovered from the small pox; Hartley's eruption was well, my eye was healed, and Berkeley had the day before taken his last powder and in spite of his red spots and little pit-holes began to look a little like himself, when on the night of the twentieth of November he was taken very ill, a violent suffocation and fever. We arose, and as soon as it was day sent for T.P. and *he* for Lewis. An emetic was given; the dear lamb, it almost strangled him — and I felt — but that was nothing!

We sat up with him that night and the next; finding he was not relieved, Lewis talked of a Blister! I could not hear it: he went to Mrs Poole and she sent him back directly with a prayer and many fears that I would suffer the application of the Blister. This caused the child much pain in rising [viz. in the rising action of the blister], but that is trifling compared to the intolerable itching after; it is near three weeks since this was applied and it is not yet healed.

Well, after the Blister he still grew worse and worse and but for it must have died. After the first week he was seized with a very violent cough; in short, until Saturday the 8th of December we knew not whether he would live or die. On that day however his cough was considerably worse but he looked about, and breathed better, and we discovered many other favourable symptoms. This is Wednesday the 12th and tho' he does not recover as fast as his anxious, frighted mother hopes and wishes, yet (and I am thankful to God for that) he does not go back; Lewis says a relapse would be fatal to him. His complaint is an inflammation on his lungs and I suppose his complaint will end in the hooping-cough, for half the children in the town are dreadfully afflicted with this most grievous malady; our dear little ones will both have it, I fear, unless I can get them to Bristol in time to avoid it.

I am aware that this account of the dear child will very much wound you, my dear love, but the instant that I have a glimpse of comfort I will sit down to impart it to you, and make you a partaker of my pleasures as well as my sorrows. One thing will please you; our dear Hartley is full of health and spirits, and has a sweet tongue; but rather too loud a voice for a sick room. Every now and then he cranes up his neck to look out of the window and with shrill tones, cries, "Boys, you must not make such a noise, to wake my little brother Berkhoo — I horse-whip ye, naughty Boys!" When a stranger comes in he says, "Mama a letter in her *Tocket* from Papa — from Germy; give it." Poor fellow, he is a great enemy to sickness for he makes a great noise with his cart and playthings, that I am obliged to send him out of the house; he goes frequently up to Mrs Poole's and behaves tolerably well.

Now I must give you some little account of myself. Our Parlour is so apt to smoke that I am obliged to live upstairs and having no fireplace in my own room I am forced to sleep in the wainscotted one; which I suppose has given me this dreadful cheek and Eye. This, and the dear child's suffering, together is sometimes too much for my spirits — the child will go to no one but myself — and he is too ill to lie in the cradle so that I am obliged to sit whole hours with him in my lap or in my arms until my whole frame is benumbed; indeed indeed, I have nursed this "wan and sickly one" with "an agony of care" for these last nine weeks until my whole person is so changed by confinement that I look at least ten years older than when you left me. Oh! that I could lay my aching forehead upon your shoulder and weep until I was relieved, for my heart is very full — and I [letter torn here in region of seal] to see you — I will finish presently.

[Further damage by tearing and a clumsy attempt at repair.]

T.P. has been here: he *insists* on my not telling you about the child until he is quite well — I am sorry I let my feelings escape me so — Be assured, my dear, that I am as comfortable as my situation (with respect to the child) will admit, and that I am truly glad that you are not here to witness his sufferings, as you could not possibly do more for the boy than has been already done for him — God bless him!

Edith writes me that her husband bought a very beautiful poem of yours in London, "Fears in Solitude". I thought they were to have been sent here, some of them, for your brother. Martha has removed her lodgings; they now live in a genteel house near Portland Square, which, if I can get to Bristol, will be a good situation for the children.

God almighty bless you my dear Samuel! Pray continue to cherish affection for us; and be assured that tho' I long to see you, I should be much hurt if you were to return before you had attained the end of your going — and I am very proud to hear that you are so forward in the language — and that you are so gay among the Ladies: you may give my respects to them and say that I am not at all jealous, for I *know* my dear Samuel in her affliction will not forget entirely, his most affectionate wife, Sara Coleridge.

I have but one Eye — and scarcely can hold my pen, so pray excuse crooked lines etc etc.

Monday 13 December.

[Scrawled on outside of folded sheet:—]

Mr Chester's family are all well please to remember me to him. Hartley spent yesterday at his mother's.[13]

Clearly, at this stage of Berkeley's further bout of illness, Sara had not grasped its full implications. Nanny had been suffering from a cough for over the past six months or more; a cough which had grown progressively worse, so that during the time of Berkeley's smallpox the girl had been unable to help with night-nursing the infant because her incessant coughing had been a disturbance. Sara was subsequently to inform S.T.C. that the girl was "in a galloping consumption". This, alas, tells us volumes: more than it told poor Sara. Infection was not understood in 1798 (nor for long afterwards).

Sara's first letter, giving details of Berkeley's smallpox and his recovery, reached S.T.C. on 30th November. He wrote back without delay: "When I read of the danger and the agony — My dear Sara! — my love! my Wife! — God bless you & preserve us." He went on to say that he could write nothing but a short note at this juncture, but would write again, at length, within a few days. Meantime, "My Wife, believe and know that I pant to be home & with you."[14]

Sara's letter about Berkeley's new onslaught of sickness arrived at Ratzeburg on 14th January; S.T.C. replied to it that same day: "Ah little Berkley — I have misgivings — but my duty is rather to comfort you, my dear dear Sara! . . . I entreat & entreat you, Sara! take care of yourself — if you are well, I think I could frame my thoughts so that I should not sink under other losses — You do right in writing me the Truth — Poole is kind — but you do right, my dear! In a sense of *reality* there is always comfort — the workings of one's imagination ever go beyond the worst that nature afflicts us with." He then informed her that he hoped, within the next three weeks, to go to Göttingen to do further studying and to write a *Life of Lessing*. The letter concluded, "Once more, my dearest Love, God love & preserve us thro' this long absence! — O my dear Babies! — my Babies! — "[15]

This is a Ward-censored letter: it contained an emotional outburst about the babies which Ward saw proper to omit; it seems likely that it closely resembled a passage sent to Poole at a later date when S.T.C.

blamed himself for the disaster that had overtaken his family, saying that he had a sensation that if he had not left them they would have met with no harm.

The letter reached Stowey on the evening of 23rd January; Sara was by now in Bristol with her children; she had gone there on 31st December. Berkeley was in the final stages of his illness; Sara had taken him to Bristol in the hope that a change of air would promote his recovery, but he was beyond saving. However Poole was determined that Coleridge must be braced, rallied; as we say today, pep-talked into a good British stiff-upper-lip frame of mind. He must be given to understand that he was allowing himself to become unduly emotional; informed that Mrs Coleridge was showing no such weakness; and so on. . . . Therefore, without delay, and regardless of what untruths he was uttering (were they not in an excellent cause and wholly with the interests of Col at heart?) Poole addressed himself to his friend:

Stowey, ye 24th January 1799.

My very dear Col. — We were rejoiced last night by the receipt of your two letters, one for Mrs Coleridge, the other for me. . . . Mrs Coleridge went to Bristol the last day of the old year . . . She arrived safely at Bristol with the little ones, and is very well. Hartley is very well; nothing ails him. He is a most amusing rogue. Berkeley had a cough which prevailed amongst the children here. I find from my sister that the change of air had been of great service to him; but the particulars of the children Mrs C. will inform you of. Let, my dear Col., nothing trouble you. When Berkeley had the small-pox, and gave his mother trouble, I assure you she and all of us rejoiced you were not at home. I forwarded this morning the letter for Mrs C. I did not open it, as she had told me I must not if it was a *small* letter; however, I desired her, after she had had the first view of it, and if it was *not too foolish*, to send it to me. I am delighted to hear of your progress in German. . . .

But once more, my dearly beloved, let me entreat you not to over-interest yourself about your family and friends here; not to incapacitate yourself by idle apprehensions and tender reveries of imagination concerning us. Those things are wrong. . . . Mrs Coleridge has sent me from Bristol the letter you wrote her. Was it well to indulge in, much less express, such feelings concerning *any* circumstances which could relate to two infants? I do not mean to check tenderness, for in the *folly* of tenderness I can sympathise — but be *rational*, I implore you . . . permit no circumstance, of whatever nature, to make you unhappy. *All that depends on you*, you do; therefore you have no cause to be unhappy. Whatever is external — independent of you — *what have you to do with it*? — For ever your affectionate
Thos. Poole[16]

It was not until April that this letter reached S.T.C. in Göttingen: in mid-January the whole of Europe and Britain fell into the grasp of the coldest winter within living memory. The river Elbe was frozen, Hamburg was cut off from Cuxhaven; the pacquets from England ceased to ply. All communication was at a standstill.

Sara remained in Bristol. She had hoped that the change of air and the more comfortable conditions of Newfoundland Street, where her mother and sisters were now living, might improve Berkeley's condition; but by the close of January the doctor, Mr Morris, told her that she must reconcile herself to losing Berkeley as nothing more could be done for the child. Poole, who was kept closely informed of all developments in Bristol, wrote to Sara on the delicate subject of breaking to S.T.C. the now inevitable news of Berkeley's death: S.T.C. was expected home towards the end of April and Poole's first instinct was to delay until then the tragic moment of telling him the truth. It would seem that Sara demurred: he should be told before his return. At length it was decided that, as S.T.C. had said in his last letter to Poole that he would require three solid months of work at Göttingen to complete what he had to do, he should be given these three months without disturbance by harsh realities; therefore, in mid-March, the news might be broken to him. Poole would write first on the subject; delicately paving the way. Until then Sara was to give her husband no hint of "disagreeable subjects". It was indeed a cruel demand to be made of the unhappy young mother; that she should keep her heartbreak to herself for three months lest he should suffer any "violent effects"; but Poole had no hesitation in insisting that Col's well being and peace of mind must be put before all else.

On 12th February in the evening, an undated, hastily scribbled little note was delivered to Poole; it was from Sara and read,

> Monday Noon.
> [11th February, 1799]
> Oh! my dear Mr Poole, I have lost my dear dear child! at one o'clock on Sunday Morning a violent convulsive fit put an end to his painful existence, myself and two of his aunts were watching by his cradle. I wish I had not seen it, for I am sure it will never leave my memory; sweet babe! what will thy Father feel when he shall hear of thy sufferings and death! I am perfectly aware of every thing you have said on the subject in your letter; I shall not yet write to Coleridge, and when I do — I will pass over all disagreeable subjects with the greatest care, for I well know their violent effect on him — but I count myself most unfortunate in being at a distance from him at this time, wanting his consolation as I do, and feeling my griefs almost too much to support with fortitude. Hartley is

better — but still a little feverish towards evening — he is taking some cool physic and I mean to have him carried out every fine day. Southey has undertaken the business of my babe's interment and in a few days we shall remove to his house at Westbury which I shall be rejoiced to do for this house at present is quite hateful to me.

I thank you for the kind letters you sent me and depend on your writing again — I suppose you will have received from Coleridge the promised letter for me. I long for it — for I am very miserable!!!

I wish we were not at such a distance from you and dear Mrs Poole — you will come to Bristol on the first of March I hope; I shall be tranquil by that time if no other misfortune should happen in the interim and I shall be enabled to meet you with the smile of resignation.

I shall go and see Mrs King when I return from Westbury, perhaps she is now at Stowey.

My money is nearly gone; could you supply me untill Samuel makes me some provision? — I do not chuse to be obliged to any one here — perhaps he may think I have enough to last untill his return not knowing my situation. — I suppose we must direct to C — at Gottengen.

Please to remember me most kindly to Mrs Poole — God bless her and you and yours

Sara Coleridge

My kind respects to Mr Ward; I shall be much obliged if he would parcell up the news-papers for me and send them next week by Milton with (I hope) a letter from Coleridge and one from you.[17]

Sara spent the next several weeks with Southey and Edith who were now living in a house of their own at Westbury. They showed Sara the greatest possible kindness. Her own health was now suffering, not surprisingly; her long ordeal having resulted in a combination of nervous and physical exhaustion. She struggled between prostration from grief and a desire to put a brave face on her sufferings — a struggle revealed in her brief, but poignant letter to Tom Poole. But the body evinces distress with silent signals; Sara's formerly luxuriant rich brown hair, one of her beauties, had thinned and lost its colour, falling out in handfuls; she was obliged to have it cut off and she took to wearing a wig in order to conceal what was seen in her day as a disfigurement for a woman: and a wig she wore for the rest of her life, her hair never recovering its former colour or quantity. (This loss of her hair, trivial an affliction as it seemed in comparison with her greater trials, was to prove of considerable significance in the later shaping of events; such, so often, is the way of life.)

Luckily, apart from her hair, she gradually recovered her general good looks; she was blessed with a remarkably strong constitution and unusual resilience of spirits. But the trauma of what she had passed through left its mark upon her; she remained nervous and irritable for a considerable time thereafter.

By the end of February Sara was in better health and back in Bristol, at 17 Newfoundland Street, with her mother and sisters. Nanny, now in the final stage of "galloping consumption" had been obliged to return to her own home. Sara, servantless, found herself once more hard at work; taking care of Hartley and Mrs Fricker, the latter being confined to her chair, having "thrown a barrel on her foot". Sara's life was gradually establishing its pattern as one long chapter of accidents, or close association with accidents. As she wrote to Poole, "I am almost ashamed always to write to you in strains of complaint but I expect you to pity and forgive me".[18] Unreservedly, Poole did both.

No letters had arrived from Germany for the past two months, thanks to the appalling weather, but in the second week of March the Hamburg mail at length arrived in Stowey; including S.T.C.'s letter to Sara dated 14th January in which he had said, "Ah little Berkley — I have misgivings . . . You do right in writing me the Truth"; above, p. 110). The time had now come to send S.T.C. the news of Berkeley's death: this hardest truth of all could be withheld no longer.

Poole accordingly wrote his letter, designed to pave the way for Sara's. He wrote it on 15th March and it was conveyed to Bristol by messenger; Sara read it and then posted it on to Coleridge (the Bristol postmark is 18th March). However, it was not until Sunday 24th March, Easter Sunday, that Sara wrote to her husband. She had taken a week in which to cogitate upon the contents of Poole's letter and to consider what she herself should say; perhaps it had required that length of time for her to gain control of her feelings after reading what Poole had written as consolation to his "ever dear" Col:

March 15, 1799.

My ever dear Col. — The Hamburgh mail at length arrived, but it brought no great weight of pleasure for me. One letter came for Mrs Coleridge, which, as she desired, I opened. . . . I sent it to Mrs C. at Bristol, and desired her not to write to you till I had written, and that I would forward her my letter to read. I have this morning heard from her. . . . She is very well, and I shall send her this letter that she may read it and forward it to you. Perhaps even by reading so far, you *feel the reason* for my wishing to write to you before Mrs Coleridge. I suspect you feel it by the anticipations in your last letter. You say there that you have serious misgivings concerning Berkeley — well — you now, my dear Col., know the worst. I thus give you to understand the catastrophe of the drama, without heightening it by first narrating the circumstances which led to it; but, as you will hear by and by, those circumstances were purely natural, and such as probably no human conduct or foresight could have averted. . . . On examination it was found that he died of a consumption. Mrs Coleridge was much fatigued during the child's illness, but her health was very good, and she very wisely kept up her spirits. . . .

I have thus, my deal Col., informed you of the whole truth. It was long contrary to my opinion to let you know of the child's death before your arrival in England. And I thought, and still think myself justified in that notion, by the OVER-anxiety you expressed in your former letters concerning the children. Doubtless the affection found to exist between parents and *infant* children is a wise law of nature, a mere instinct to preserve Man in his infant state. . . . But the moment you make this affection the creature of reason, you degrade reason. When the infant becomes a reasonable being, then let the affection be a thing of reason, not before. Brutes can only have an instinctive affection. Hence, when that ceases to be necessary, all affection ceases. This seems to me to be a great line of demarcation between Men and Beasts, between Reason and Instinct. If then the love of infants be a mere instinct, it is extraordinary that sensible men should be much disturbed at the counteraction of it, particularly when the end of that action, if I may so speak, becomes a nullity. . . . Hartley is brave and well, and like to give you grandchildren and great-grandchildren, *ad libitum*; and, I need not add, very likely to have a plenty of brothers and sisters. The truth is, my deal Col., it is idle to reason about a thing of this nature. . . . Only let your *mind* act, and not your *feelings*. Don't conjure up any scenes of distress which never happened. Mrs Coleridge felt as a mother . . . and, in an examplary manner, did all a mother could do. *But she never forgot herself.* She is now perfectly well, and does not make herself miserable by recalling the engaging, though, remember, mere instinctive attractions of an infant a few months old. Heaven and Earth! I have myself within the last month experienced disappointments more weighty than the death of ten infants. . . . Let us hear from you circumstantially, let us hear that you are happy. . . . We long to see you. But still I say, don't come till you have done your business. . . . Heaven bless you,

Thos. Poole.[19]

Sara's feelings on reading this letter may well be imagined. The dismissal of her beloved baby as a something merely to be regarded as little better than a particle of brute creation; the dismissal of Sara's own feelings towards the child as mere instinctive maternal response such as might be displayed by a rabbit or hedgehog, and this dismissal by an ignorant male who in his arrogance dared to claim that within the last month he had experienced "disappointments more weighty than the death of ten infants" . . . all this combined to produce in Sara an indignation amounting to utter contempt. And she was to sit by and let these things be said; and be said, moreover, in an attempt to shield

Samuel who, much as he had loved his baby, had been absent from home for months and had witnessed nothing of the infant's suffering and death! "Don't conjure up any scenes of distress that never happened." How did Poole dare to say that they had never happened? She could not let this pass. Men must be made to understand that infants, however young, were human beings; Samuel must be given to understand that a Mother stood for something far more than mere instinctive animal response. Samuel — and through Samuel, Thomas Poole — merited rebuke; rebuke she now dealt in the letter she penned to the S.T.C. whom Poole had hoped to featherbed from all that might make him miserable.

The letter was written on another of the vast sheets of paper and addressed to, "An den Herrn Coleridge/A la Poste restante/Gottingen/Germany". Beneath this address Sara was to write, many years later, "No secrets herein. I will not burn it for the sake of my sweet Berkeley".

[Easter Sunday 24th March 1799]

My dearest Love,

I hope you will not attribute my long silence to want of affection; if you have received Mr Poole's letter you will know the reason and acquit me. My darling infant left his wretched Mother on the tenth of February, and tho' the leisure that followed was intolerable to me, yet I could not employ myself in reading or writing, or in any way that prevented my thoughts from resting on him — this parting was the severest trial that I have ever yet undergone and I pray to God that I may never live to behold the death of another child for O my dear Samuel! it is a suffering beyond your conception! You will feel, and lament, the death of your child, but you will only recollect him a baby of fourteen weeks, but I am his Mother, and have carried him in my arms, and have fed him at my bosom, and have watched over him by day and by night for nine months; I have seen him twice at the brink of the grave but he has returned, and recovered and smiled upon me like an angel — and now I am lamenting that he is gone!

On the last day of the last year I shut up the house at Stowey, and in a chaise with Nanny and the children proceeded to Bristol; Berkeley was enveloped in flannel and kept at the breast the whole of the way: he travelled very well, and when we entered the City took great notice of the lamps and almost capered out of my arms. Mrs Lovell received us (she is in the same house with my mother) and when she carried him in to the light she was quite struck with the beauty and uncommon appearance of the child; the small pox had left so few marks and not to be discerned by candlelight. She could not believe that he had been ill so recently.

We had everything comfortable for our arrival and when we rose the next day, and he had taken no cold, I had great hopes that the change of air would soon cure his cough, but it returned in a week and I sent for Mr Morris: I believe he thought I was alarmed without reason from the appearance of the child; he asked what had been done, and he said he had been treated very properly, and he hoped when the weather changed that his breath and cough would mend — and he sent a little syrup, and called every other day, and when he perceived him worse he begged me to try a blister to the throat, for he thought the difficulty of breathing proceeded immediately from thence and not from the lungs; this produced no good effect, he continued to grow worse and Mr Morris perceiving he was in great danger begged me reconcile myself to his loss! This was a fortnight before his death — and from that time until he died continued we in the bed-chamber. Eliza and I were sitting up with him when about two o'clock I was so much alarmed as to call up Mrs Lovell and Nanny — I will never forget that Night!!!

Mr P. has related to you what followed, and now my dear Samuel I hope you will be perfectly satisfied that every thing was done for the dear babe that was likely to restore him, and endeavour to forget your own loss in contemplating mine. I cannot express how ardently I long for your return, or how much I shall be disappointed if I do not see you in May; I expect a letter from you daily, and am much surprised that you have not written from Gottingen; your last is dated Jan. the 5th and in it you say you will write again immediately — now this is Easter Sunday March the 24th. You will write once probably after you receive this, from Germany — and I wish you would be so good as write me a few lines from London that I may know the very day when I may see you; I shall go to Stowey in a fortnight. My sister Southey will accompany me and dear Hartley. Poor Nanny must remain with her mother; she is in a galloping consumption. She has had a cough ever since I lay-in with my dear lost child. I am happy that the fatigue of his illness rested entirely on me; she never sat up but one whole night — I was obliged to have people to assist at night on account of her cough, and I was obliged to sit up in bed with him the great part of every night to give the breast, for he could not lie down because of his difficulty of breathing; dear, patient Lamb! he was as little trouble as any child in his situation could possibly be. . . .

Our dear Hartley you will discover is grown a little. He has a most agreeable little tongue; he talks of his Father every day and I verily believe he will know you at your return, if you will try to come to us soon; if you do not hasten home I myself shall almost forget you! Ah no! indeed I shall not!

I am much pleased to see you wrote that you "languish to be at home". O God! I hope you never more will quit it! I sent your poems to your brother as you directed; in answer to my note, he returned me a most affectionate letter concluding it with an ardent wish to see me; I dare say you will take us down in the summer. . . .

God almighty bless you my dearest Love! Sara C — [20]

# CHAPTER ELEVEN

# *Decoy'd*

## I

Sara had anticipated that the news of Berkeley's death would bring S.T.C. home to her by the end of May. His letter in response to the dire news of the loss of his child was remarkably calm; almost detached in tone, as if he were writing in a dream and was fumbling to find the right things to say: "It is one of the discomforts of my absence, my dearest Love! that we feel the same calamities at different times — I would fain write words of consolation to you; yet I know that I shall only fan into new activity the pang which was growing dead and dull in your heart —Dear little Being! . . . although I know of his Death, yet . . . it seems to me as if I did not understand it . . . I confess that the more I think, the more I am discontented with the doctrines of Priestley. He builds the whole and sole hope of future existence on the words and miracles of Jesus — yet doubts or denies the future existence of Infants — only because according to his System of Materialism he has not discovered how they can be made unconscious." There was little comfort for a heartbroken young mother in any of this.

He concluded, "I trust, my Love! — I trust, my dear Sara! that this event which has forced us to think of the Death of what is most dear to us . . . will in many and various ways be good for us — To have shared — nay, I should say — to have divided with any human Being any one deep sensation of Joy or Sorrow, sinks deep the foundations of a lasting love."[1] Finally he assured her that if he followed his own impulses he would return home immediately, but he still had much work to do and therefore could not hope to be back with her for another two months.

Sara, in reply, did not hesitate to voice her disappointment that Samuel couldn't return to her immediately, though she conceded, "I am however fully satisfied with your reasons". This was in a letter of 15th May; she concluded, obviously from her heart:

> I hope you will soon be here — for oh! I am so tired of this cruel
> absence. My dear dear Samuel do not lose a moment of time in finishing
> your work — for I feel like a poor deserted thing — interesting to no
> one. You must not stay a minute by the way, but fly from Yarmouth and

be with me at quarter-day! Pray write a few lines from Yarmouth. . . .
My dear husband God almighty bless you and see you safe home to your
affectionate — Sara Coleridge.

May 15 — [2]

Most men, in response to that, would have strained every nerve and
muscle to be home by quarter day,* but instead Coleridge wrote back
saying that he was on the point of taking a walking tour in the Harz
mountains with some fellow students from Göttingen university. The
object of this tour, he explained, was to "see the mines and other
curiosities" and to climb the famous Brocken; perhaps even glimpse its
celebrated Spectre! Of course the material that he was collecting by this
extension of his stay in Germany would reap financial reward; if he had
returned earlier, he assured Sara, he and she would have found
themselves "embarrassed & in debt" whereas now there was "the moral
certainty" that they would be "more than cleared".

Following this walking tour S.T.C. returned to Göttingen; when at
length he left Göttingen on the alleged initial leg of his return to
England he organized his route, done entirely on foot, so that it became
a further circuitous pedestrian excursion. It was hard not to think that
he was procrastinating: this was scarcely the behaviour of a man as
homesick as he had repeatedly declared himself to be.

Without doubt this procrastination resulted from S.T.C.'s sense of
guilt at having abandoned Sara to such a long and grief-laden
separation; guilt intensified by the searing tone of reproach in her
Easter Sunday letter. This guilt manifested itself clearly in the letter he
wrote to Poole: "There are moments in which I have such a power of
Life within me, such a conceit of it, I mean — that I lay the blame of my
Child's Death to my absence — not intellectually; but I have a strange
sort of sensation, as if while I was present, none could die whom I
intensely loved."[3] Nursing these feelings of self-recrimination S.T.C.
could not steel himself to return to face Sara.

Southey, writing in later years of S.T.C.'s lifetime pattern of
absences and silences, a "wilful outlawry or excommunication of
himself", observed, "Never I believe did any other man for the sake of
sparing immediate pain to himself inflict so much upon all who were
connected with him, and lay up so heavy and unendurable burthen of
self condemnation".[4] While Dorothy Wordsworth, with her sympathetic insight into S.T.C.'s mind, was to sigh of another famous
occasion of Esteesian procrastination, "I know that his earnest desire to
return is the cause of his silence".[5] And this was true, inasmuch as the

*24th June.

stronger his feelings, the less Coleridge was able to face realities; as he put it, he always suffered from "the desire of running away and hiding myself from my personal feelings" when these were in any way stressful. For this reason, as he wrote in retrospect, "In *exact proportion* to the *importance* and *urgency* of any *Duty* was it . . . sure to be neglected. . . . In exact proportion, as I *loved* any person or persons more than others, & would have sacrificed my life to them, were *they* sure to be the most barbarously mistreated by silence, absence, or breach of promise".[6] From this knowledge of transgression arose self-condemnation; self-condemnation bred further sensations of guilt; the deeper the guilt the greater the self-condemnation; and so it went, an infinite regress of despair; a burden which became increasingly heavy and unendurable as it regressed.

## II

Towards the end of July Southey, Edith and Eliza, the youngest of the Fricker sisters, passed through Stowey in a chaise, on their way to Minehead where they were to holiday for a fortnight. Coleridge still had not arrived home. We may imagine Sara's feelings as she watched the happy holiday party bound for the sea, while she herself remained in her dreary little cottage, a grass widow.

However shortly afterwards S.T.C. was restored to her. Within days of being reunited the Coleridges were at odds with one another. The precise ins and outs of the matter we are not told; but we do know that she was in a sore and resentful frame of mind, as well as still suffering the tail-end effects of physical and nervous exhaustion, while he reacted to his feelings of guilt by being touchy, aggressive and sorry for himself in kaleidoscopic sequence.

Deep emotional issues between closely involved couples rarely surface nakedly, but appear clad in disguise; whereby the true reason of discord remains undiscussed and a substitute bone of contention is jointly gnawed and snarled over instead. Psychology tells us that this is subterfuge, by which violently disruptive explosion is by-passed. The Coleridges could not face overt discussion of what she, bitterly in her heart, thought of as betrayal by him while he, well aware that he had indeed betrayed her in her hour of need, became acutely miserable and therefore aggressive and quarrelsome. As their surrogate cause of dispute they chose the continuing coldness between Coleridge and Southey: in any case a matter of genuine concern to Sara.

She gave S.T.C. urgent accounts of the great kindness that she and

Hartley had received from Southey and Edith over the past months, of the affection which they had lavished upon Hartley and the debt of gratitude owed them by S.T.C. Sara, while in the company of Southey, had heard details of his side of the quarrel; he firmly believing himself to be the victim of S.T.C.'s malice. Sara must now have put all this to S.T.C. She concluded by requesting, if not demanding, that he should extend an olive branch to Southey in the form of a fraternal letter dispatched forthwith to Minehead. Among the arguments put forward by her must have been that it was decidedly awkward for herself and Edith to be married to men who would not speak to one another!

At last on 29th July, worn down by Sara's insistence, S.T.C. penned the demanded letter to Southey — a somewhat dehydrated olive branch: "I am perplexed what to write, or how to state the object of my writing." He explained that "domestic affliction" was hard upon him (in the shape of Sara's rebukes and animated upbraidings) and went on to make the plea that, in the event of himself and Southey meeting at any time, they should not withhold from each other "the outward Expressions of daily Kindliness"; if Southey could not soften his opinions regarding Coleridge, could he not make his feelings at least more tolerant: "A debit of humility which assuredly we all of us owe to our most feeble, imperfect and self-deceiving Nature."[7]

Now, Southey did not regard his own nature as either feeble or self-deceiving (if, indeed, imperfect) and his reply to this was an indignant outburst of recrimination tinctured with self-justification. This reply arrived at Stowey on 8th August, by which time Sara herself was at Minehead with the Southeys; she having received a communication that Edith was unwell and causing concern, that Southey was bent on making a solo walking tour to Lynmouth and the Valley of the Stones and that, as he didn't wish to leave Edith and Eliza alone in Minehead lodgings, it would be appreciated if they might visit Sara at Nether-Stowey. Sara had at once taken a chaise and hurried to Minehead to fetch Edith and Eliza back to Stowey.

The horrified S.T.C., realizing only too well that without peace with Southey there could be no peace with Sara, rushed round to Tom Poole to show him the letter and seek his advice. Poole, as usual, knew exactly what to do. He had seen some of Lloyd's malicious tittle-tattling letters and had a shrewd idea where the real trouble lay; an account of the true facts of Southey's misunderstanding of S.T.C. and *vice-versa* was penned by Poole and dispatched to Minehead without delay. In due course the ladies, all smiles, appeared in a chaise and announced that Southey was following on foot. Sure enough Southey was presently seen marching along Lime Street; S.T.C. went out to greet him on the threshold; the brothers-in-law embraced.[8]

As a result of this restoration of peace and trust the Southeys and Eliza spent a fortnight at Stowey; then the entire party, S.T.C., Sara, Hartley and his new nursemaid Fanny, Edith and Robert and Eliza, set forth for Ottery St Mary, to see Coleridge's family. The visit proved a great success; Sara, to her immense relief, made a good impression upon her husband's relatives; they could not have been more kind or attentive to her. Edith, Southey and Eliza were also asked to spend a few days at Ottery before going on to a nearby small watering place, Sidmouth.

On arrival at Sidmouth Southey could not find accommodation so his party sought rooms in Exeter. Here S.T.C. and his wife, child and nursemaid presently arrived; Robert and S.T.C. then took a five days' walking tour together, to Totnes and Dartmouth, arriving back at Exeter on 16th September. The Coleridges then returned to Ottery to spend another three weeks; however this stay was cut short by the discovery that Fanny had the Itch (scabies) and that Hartley too appeared to have caught it. Sara was overwhelmed by misery; compounded of disappointment that the visit must end, fear that the contagion might have spread to the Ottery Coleridges and their numerous children (not to mention Edith and Eliza in Exeter), and shame that her party had been instrumental in introducing such a low disease as the Itch into a household upon which she, Sara, had been so desirous of making a good impression! The Ottery Coleridges, to be sure, took the matter very well and remained kindness to the last; nonetheless Sara's chagrin was deep. The Samuel Coleridges packed themselves, Hartley and the shamefully itching Fanny into a chaise and returned to Stowey. The apothecary was sent for; Sara and S.T.C., neither of whom showed signs of infection, were instructed to wear mercurial girdles, as preventives; Hartley was anointed with brimstone. Fanny was packed off home first thing the following morning. Hartley found it all great fun, singing "I be a funny Fellow, And my name is Brimstonello".[9] For the now servantless, mercury-engirdled Sara the situation was anything but amusing as she embarked, singlehandedly, upon a mammoth operation of cleansing and fumigation, while S.T.C. retired with Spinoza into a quiet corner and did his best to remain "as undisturbed as a Toad in a Rock";[10] but Sara, it would seem, took umbrage at seeing him seated by the fire, deep in an "old Folio" or meditating upon philosophy and philosophers, and dosing himself with opium against a bout of rheumatism, while she struggled with her load of labour. S.T.C. grumbled in a letter to

Southey that Sara was lacking in sympathy with his habits and feelings as a man of Genius.[11]

Tempers began to rise again; domestic bliss was once more in eclipse; apparently very much so. It seems that Poole attempted to pour oil on the troubled waters and caused further annoyance to S.T.C. by so doing. Finally S.T.C. announced that he was going to Bristol to collect his travelling chests, which had not yet arrived home; if he couldn't find them at Bristol he would go to London in search of them. And with this he left the house.

Sara completed her wearisome chores in the cottage; this took a week. She had heard nothing from Samuel; presuming therefore that he must have gone to London, she and Hartley, now perfectly well (in addition to the Itch he had badly bruised his arm falling downstairs) took the opportunity to stay with friends at Old Cleve, near Watchet. From here, on 2nd November, Sara wrote to Mrs George Coleridge,

                                        Old Cleve Vicarage.
                                        November 2nd

My dear Madam

You will perceive by the date of this that all my troubles respecting the child are at an end; he is I thank God! in all respects perfectly well. We have been at this place above a week; that is, myself and Hartley for Samuel has been in Bristol nearly a fortnight; he left Stowey with an intention of proceeding to London in search of his travelling chests if he did not find them in Bristol, but fortunately they arrived at Stowey two days after his departure. I am going to Stowey to-morrow and hope to find him safe at Mr Poole's, for our cottage is shut up.

When we parted at Ottery, my dear Mrs C., you were so good as to express a wish to hear some particulars respecting the cause of our departure. I should have troubled you with them sooner but was not quite certain of its termination until just before I made this visit, and here I am never a moment without company; even now I write with five ladies in the room, all sisters of one family; but to the Subject! We took Fanny quite home with us; she was in great trouble all the first part of the journey. We arrived about four o'clock in the evening; we immediately sent for our apothecary. He advised girdles for Coleridge and myself, and brimstone for the child. I anointed him for a fortnight but the few people to whom we showed him, said, they did not think he had got the Itch as he did not scratch himself; however I persevered, and expected that when he was washed it would probably appear, but in this I was deceived.

Fanny left us on the morrow for her father's house: in a week after I wrote a note to enquire how she was; she answered, that her father did not chuse she should anoint, that he had after much persuasion permitted her to wear a girdle, that she had been to Bristol, offered at a place, was accepted, and begged I would send her a character: I sent her the best I could, but cautioned her respecting her complaint; since this I have heard nothing of her. My sister Eliza is perfectly safe and thus far, all is well. You, however, will readily believe that the business of anointing, the affairs of the house, etc, without a servant, was more than sufficient for my abilities; I was fatigued beyond description, notwithstanding Mrs Rich did all in her power to assist me, by lighting fires, cooking etc etc. Samuel too, at the same time, had the rheumatism by getting wet through and remaining unchanged; he went to Upcott in the midst of his pain, that I might have the house, sheets, blankets and cloaths washed and the latter buried, but the scent still remains. When Mr Coleridge assured us in his letter that Sally and your dear George were in no danger, and when Eliza wrote to the same effect, it lightened my trouble so considerably that I felt no regret but having been obliged to leave so soon my esteemed friends at Ottery. Hartley's arm is also quite well; we applied "Steery Aepodeldoc".*

I expect when I return to Stowey, if Coleridge is not there, to find a letter inviting me and the child to Bristol, for as I have no maid I cannot remain in the house alone. . . . [12]

Sara returned to Stowey, but no Coleridge was there. However she learned through Southey that he had darted off on a walking tour with Wordsworth in the Lake Country. Fresh developments unfolded at speed for Sara; the next thing she knew, she and Hartley were being summoned to London where Coleridge had been offered regular employment as political writer on the *Morning Post*. By 19th December husband, wife and child were reunited and in residence in lodgings at Number 21, Buckingham Street, just off the Strand, and conveniently near to the *Morning Post* offices.

The trip to Germany and the expenses of Berkeley's illness had saddled the Coleridges with significant debts and it was to defray these that S.T.C. had turned to journalism. In addition to being political writer for the *Morning Post* he also contributed miscellaneous features, articles and odd pieces of poetry. He worked hard and professionally; for the first time in his life he found himself earning a steady and good income, with the assurance of a lucrative and successful career ahead of him should he choose to pursue it. This general process of settling down introduced a settled mood into the Coleridge marriage; Sara was soon pregnant again; S.T.C. was telling Southey of his conjugal content-

*Stearin Opodeldoc*, a popular liniment of the day, composed of stearin, the chief ingredient of hard animal fat, and opodeldoc, a solution of soap in alcohol with camphor and menthol oils.

ment and happiness: domestic bliss had been recaptured. It is probable that to this period belongs S.T.C.'s poem, *The Happy Husband*:

> Oft, oft methinks, the while with Thee
> I breathe, as from the heart, thy Dear
> And dedicated name, I hear
> A promise and a mystery.
> A pledge of more than passing life,
> Yea, in that very name of Wife!
>
> A pulse of love, that ne'er can sleep!
> A feeling that upbraids the heart
> With happiness beyond desert,
> That gladness half requests to weep!
> Nor bless I not the keener sense
> And unalarming turbulence
>
> Of transient joys, that ask no sting
>   From jealous fears, or coy denying;
>   But born beneath Love's brooding wing,
> And into tenderness soon dying,
>   Wheel out their giddy moment, then
>   Resign the soul to love again; —
>
> A more precipitated vein
>   Of notes, that eddy in the flow
>   Of Smoothest song, they come, they go,
> And leave their sweeter understrain
>   It's own sweet self — a love of Thee
>   That seems, yet cannot greater be![13]

The Coleridges did a fair amount of entertaining of friends at Buckingham Street; informal, decidedly convivial occasions, to judge by surviving accounts: "I have been drunk two nights running at Coleridge's — how my Head burns!" Charles Lamb wrote to his friend Thomas Manning, early in February 1800.[14] Lamb, when tipsy, tended all too often to become an embarrassment and it is on record that on one occasion at Buckingham Street he insulted Godwin, who fortunately remained cool; though poor Sara felt anything but comfortable to have this happening at her supper table. It was possibly at her urging that Coleridge called on Lamb early the following morning to remonstrate with him over such undesirable behaviour; Coleridge found "Mr Gobwin" (as Hartley called him) breakfasting with Lamb, all forgiven and forgotten.[15]

Sara loved the Lambs and would have pardoned Lamb any transgression, but she would seem to have nursed reservations about "Mister Gobwin"; possibly he felt the same about her, for on another occasion, while paying a visit to Buckingham Street, Godwin received a sharp blow on the shin from Hartley wielding a ninepin. "Force is no substitute for reason" as the great man had himself observed elsewhere; Hartley was plainly growing up to be far too boisterous and Sara received a vehement lecture there and then on child upbringing, delivered by a "Gobwin in huge pain". Sara, it seems, was not over-contrite.[16]

Hartley, of course, was being reared on progressive, Rousseauist lines of free expression; with the result that he tended, as his parents were obliged to admit, to be "somewhat too rough & noisy". Poole described him as "a little chattering inquisitive, amusing rogue";[17] S.T.C. was fond of alluding to his first born (during this London period) as "rampant" and "in high force". It is significant that even S.T.C. was determined that the next house he lived in should have a study "out of the noise of Women & children".[18]

For the Coleridges were now house-hunting: Coleridge had no intention of remaining in London, engaged in journalism. Poole, though he hated the thought of losing S.T.C.'s company at Stowey, nonetheless urged him to continue working on the *Morning Post*; but this Coleridge was emphatic he would not do. He had, he said, no interest in making money; his one aim was to live a simple life, in the country.

The problem was, whereabouts in the country? The Wordsworths, on their return from Germany, had moved to Grasmere in Westmorland, and wished Coleridge to settle near them. Sara not unnaturally voiced a strong disinclination to leave Somerset, her birthplace and home, where she had all her roots, relatives, and friends.

Coleridge explained to Poole that Wordsworth badly needed as neighbour, "A person, or persons, who can feel & understand him, can reciprocate & react on him".[19] To this Poole responded that he, too, felt an equally deep need for the company of Coleridge, "I can truly say that your society is a principal ingredient in my happiness".[20]

Between Poole and the Wordsworths a species of tug-of-war was soon taking place, with Coleridge as the prize. The Wordsworths offered the scenery of the Lake Country as lure, "You speak of the pleasures of skating," Dorothy had written to Coleridge during the depths of his winter sojourn at Ratzeburg. "In the North of England, amongst the mountains whither we wish to decoy you, you might enjoy it with every possible advantage."[21] Meantime Poole had commenced searching for a house in the neighbourhood of Stowey, telling S.T.C., "You *may be certain* I shall keep an eye on every house to be had here . . . *I will not part from you*, if you will not part from me; be assured of that".[22]

We will let Sara take over the rest of the tale, in a letter to Mrs George Coleridge, postmarked "16. Sept. 1800. Keswick" and reading as follows:

Keswick Sepr. 10 — 1800

. . . By the date of this you will have perceived that we are transported far North; you will remember my speaking of Samuel's predilection for this country when I was with you. We resigned the house at Stowey last Christmas at the expiration of a term of 3 years; it was sold and re-built and tenanted by the proprietor. We passed the winter in London and when we returned to Stowey in May we could by no means suit ourselves in a house in or near Stowey; Allfoxden was involved in many difficulties and we were obliged to resign all thoughts of it. Samuel had seen a house at Keswick that was being built and was to be let this midsummer — he urged me to take it — but three hundred miles mean mighty and numerous objections! But the time was come that made it necessary to be settled somewhere — a home must be procured; this house was accordingly secured for us by means of Mr Wordsworth. My mother and family were much against our removing to such a distance; indeed it was the only objection on my part, for we are most delightfully situated, we have a large and very convenient house furnished with every article of comfort (but without elegance) and we are to pay a very moderate rent. The circumstances of removing the furniture so far would have prevented our coming hither if we had been obliged to it, but the gentleman who built this house offered to furnish it also as he had a furnished house (beside his own) in the town of Keswick which was left him by a relation, very recently, and he had it removed for our use which suited us exactly; so our goods were sold, except the linnen which came hither by water.

Since our arrival the neighbouring families have most of them visited us: a Colonel Peachy who lives in the Summer in a very beautiful house on an island in the Lake Derwent Water — it is just opposite to our house about a mile across; a Mr Spedding and his wife and her unmarried sisters, all young persons, seem to be an agreeable family — and they live here all the year. The Revd Mr Wilkinson; Mr Losh etc — all of whose visits Samuel has returned, but my present situation precludes me from accompanying him as I look every day for an addition to the family and do not chuse to exhibit my figure before strangers.

My dear Mrs Coleridge I often live over again the pleasant fortnight I passed amongst you — except indeed the last day; which for misery made up of disappointment, terror for future consequences and I think

a presentiment that it would be very, very long before we shall meet again
— that day I always endeavour not to recall!

I beseech you to spare a few minutes to write to me; I want to know
how you all are; if poor Mrs Phillips is quite well; if I have, or am likely to
have any new cousins; if George and Nelson can talk. Hartley remembers
all about Ottery; the children and the Boy with the Flute, as he has
forgotten the name; but I remember his face perfectly; he was a
handsome lad. I hope Mrs Coleridge (our mother) is in good health;
please to present our affectionate duty to her; to the Colonel and his lady;
to Mr Edward, and your Mr Coleridge; and to all and every one; all kind
wishes from both of us. . . .

In the hope of hearing from you immediately I remain

Dear Madam/yours affectionately/Sara Coleridge.
Mrs Coleridge/Keswick/Cumberland[23]

# CHAPTER TWELVE

## Farewell to Happiness

Greta Hall, the Coleridges' new home, stood perched on a low hill just outside the little town of Keswick, in Cumberland. In front of the house spread a field and an "enormous garden", the greater part of which was nursery garden. Round the foot of the hill on which the house stood wound the river Greta.[1] Facing the house was a magnificent view of the Newlands and distant Coledale fells; "An encamped army of tent-like mountains," Coleridge described them to Southey. On the right lay the lake of Bassenthwaite; "on our left Derwentwater and Lodore in full view, and the fantastic mountains of Borrowdale. Behind us is the massy Skiddaw. . . . A fairer scene you have not seen in all your wanderings."[2]

The views from within the house were as sublime as those from without. William Jackson, the landlord, had been a highly successful carrier in the region who had made enough money to retire and build this "gentleman's residence" with ravishing views; some less impressive accommodation at the rear of the house was intended for himself and his housekeeper, Mrs Wilson, while the fine front part of the building was designed to attract some wealthy and unwary foreigner (meaning a non-Cumbrian) with an enthusiasm for the picturesque who would not notice that the windows commanding the sublime vistas also faced the prevailing winds. The house itself had been erected at top speed and was a jerry-built affair (in 1803 the front part of the building threatened to fall down and had to be rebuilt).[3] The rear portion would seem to have been better constructed and the rooms, though much smaller and lacking vistas, were sheltered and could be kept warm. Here the canny Mr Jackson, interested in creature comforts rather than the sublime, kept himself snug.

The "front house" of Greta Hall had yet to reveal itself to the Coleridges as a "palace of the winds": to date Greta Hall's one obvious disadvantage was its distance from Grasmere; fourteen miles by turnpike road.

S.T.C., in transports of sublime delight, raced out day after day to explore the mountains. Sara, too, was happy. Though now eight months pregnant she remained fit and energetic; after her daily inescapable round of household chores (all the toil of unpacking boxes and settling into a new home) she strolled with S.T.C. and Hartley upon the rolling flanks of Skiddaw, enjoying splendid sunsets in the western skies, or sampled wooded walks along the banks of the Greta. As for Hartley, he was "all Health & extacy".[4]

A new son was born on 14th September. S.T.C. immediately began writing joyful letters, giving the tidings to friends: "She [Sara] was brought to bed on Sunday Night ½ past 10" and "is as well as any woman in her situation . . . ever was or can be — the child is a very large one", he told Godwin.[5] And, on 17th September, to Tobin: "My wife was safely and speedily delivered of a very fine boy on last Sunday Night — both he & she are as well as it is possible that Mother & new born Child can be. She dined & drank Tea up, in the parlour with me, this day — and this is only Wednesday Night! — There's for you."[6]

Thus we glimpse S.T.C. proudly contemplating his Sally Pally and the "very fine boy" she had produced with such admirable lack of fuss: the candlelight and firelight together illuminate the Greta Hall parlour on this night of Wednesday 17th September 1800; Sally Pally lying on the couch, the infant asleep, the father beaming; all is cosy, all is loving pride, all seems secure. And then, the candles gutter, the warm fire dies, darkness falls.

Coleridge had been ill at the time of the removal to the Lakes, having caught a bad cold during the journey north.[7] In London, busy and content, he had kept his health and had regulated his opium, keeping it under control, but his illness had resulted in heavy medicinal doses of laudanum to hold a threatened "rheumatic fever" at bay; while his blissful euphoria on taking up residence among the mountains had been heightened by opium taken (as he himself was to describe it) to assist to bring "forth Thoughts, hidden in him before . . . [and] to call forth the deepest feelings".[8]

In truth he should not have been out among the hills, but in his study writing, as he was under contract to do, for the *Morning Post* and for Longman and for Phillips, the booksellers, each of whom had paid him an advance on a promised manuscript. Not only had Coleridge a great deal of work to do; it was essential that it should be done speedily, for the removal north had been expensive and the new baby was a further expense. Now once more alarmingly short of money, he could not afford to stay away from his desk. Nonetheless, he either spent his time among the mountains, or at Grasmere assisting Wordsworth to prepare a new, two-volume edition of *Lyrical Ballads*. For this edition Coleridge extensively rewrote *The Ancient Mariner* and composed the second part of *Christabel*, it being intended that this poem should conclude the second volume.

It seems that he was jolted back into a sense of duty to his family by the fact that the new baby caught cold, rapidly developing a dangerous bronchitis. The illness was followed by convulsive fits. Sara's distress knew no bounds; it seemed that she was to lose this infant too. The neighbours, Mr Jackson and Mrs Wilson, convinced like everyone else that the baby was dying, begged that it should be given Christian baptism; accordingly it was baptized by the name of Derwent,* after the neighbouring lake. But Derwent did not die; he recovered and rapidly waxed into an exceptionally fat and healthy infant, "A very Stout Boy indeed"; "A fat pretty child, healthy and hungry".[9]

While Sara nursed Derwent into robust health and smiles S.T.C. attempted, by stints of day-long and night-long work, to catch up on his journalism for Daniel Stuart, Editor of the *Morning Post*. For the energy necessary to carry through this frenetic bout of work S.T.C. resorted to his faithful friend, opium. Opium, which never let him down, whichever role he called upon it to play: the miraculous drug that could be physician, philosopher, companion, or fund of inexhaustible vigour. "O just, subtle, and all-conquering opium! . . . Eloquent opium. . . . Thou has the keys of Paradise, O just, subtle, and mighty opium!"[10]

S.T.C. had no premonition that opium was about to reveal its other face; that the glorious glowing poetry of its courtship would be transformed, virtually overnight, into the frowning black-browed rock of reality. Like a traveller in the mountains poised, unknowingly, in the moment of tremble before the crash of an avalanche, he was poised on the brink of inevitable morphine disaster.

De Quincey, in tracing, in his *Confessions of an Opium Eater*, his own descent into the pains of opium, was to note that his bodily sufferings were provoked by distress of mind connected with a melancholy event. In the case of Coleridge collapse into opium's dark side coincided with a crisis in his poet's relationship with Wordsworth.

Though Wordsworth's initial reception of *Christabel* was one of delight, within forty-eight hours of this display of enthusiasm he was finding reasons why the poem should not be included in *Lyrical Ballads*. The revised *Ancient Mariner* had already been subjected to similar disparaging scrutiny by the Wordsworths. Coleridge sank into profound depression. "I abandon Poetry altogether," he wrote to Tobin. And to Godwin: "As an Author . . . I have neither Vanity nor ambition — I think meanly of all that I have done: and if ever I hope proudly of my future Self, this Hot Fit is uniformly followed & punished by Languor, & Despondency — or rather, by lazy & unhoping indifference."[11]

---

*Then pronounced *Darwent* (as Berkeley was Barkeley). Even today local Cumbrian pronunciation is *Darrant Wutter*.

Coleridge's letters and notebooks leave the reader in no doubt that Wordsworth's dismissal of him as a poet (and even if Wordsworth were not aware that he was so dismissing him then Coleridge certainly felt himself dismissed) contributed significantly to the triggering of the moment when, poised as he already was on the verge of destruction by opium, he had his feet (metaphorically speaking) knocked from under him. Feeling that he was now virtually finished as a productive poetic force, he still saw himself with a role to play in poetry: "I reserve for myself the honorable attempt to make others feel and understand their writings, as they deserve to be felt & understood."[12] This meant that he could continue as mentor to Wordsworth, and Wordsworth was not only happy but anxious to have Coleridge constantly at his side in that capacity. Clearly, Wordsworth had no conception of the trauma he had inflicted upon Coleridge, while Coleridge, who had a strong streak of masochism in his make-up, was increasingly prepared to dedicate himself to the establishment of Wordsworth's reputation at the cost of irreparably damaging his own. From this point his already notorious "idolatry" of Wordsworth assumed a frenetic aspect.

In this late autumn of 1800, S.T.C. succumbed to a succession of rheumatic chills and violent stomach upsets. Each time that he showed signs of the slightest improvement he immediately set out in the wintry wind and wet for Grasmere. Each time he went to Grasmere he succumbed to renewed rheumatic symptoms, not infrequently being obliged to return to Keswick in a chaise, far too ill to walk. Yet, within a few days, despite his wife's remonstrances, he would be staggering back over Dunmail Raise to Grasmere, in due course once more to return to Greta Hall in a condition of near collapse. Sara complained bitterly at this neglect of his health and professional interests on behalf of Wordsworth and *Lyrical Ballads* (her view of the situation is undoubtedly mirrored in Southey's subsequent observation, "Wordsworth and his sister who pride themselves upon having no selfishness, are of all human beings whom I have ever known the most intensely selfish. The one thing to which W. would sacrifice all others is his own reputation").[13]

The days drew in, the darkness of the northern winter solstice enveloped Greta Hall. The voice of De Quincey, speaking once more as opium eater, for all opium eaters, reaches us through the thickening gloom, "Farewell, a long farewell to happiness. . . . Farewell to smiles and laughter! farewell to peace of mind, to tranquil dreams, and to the blessed consolation of sleep! . . . Here opens upon me an Iliad of woes: for now I enter upon THE PAINS OF OPIUM".[14]

# CHAPTER THIRTEEN

# The Pains of Opium

## I

The landscape of intensifying opium misery has been drawn, in vivid detail by De Quincey,[1] whose account tallies remarkably closely with the details of Coleridge's experience: a sudden decline in bodily health; the outstanding physical affliction being appalling stomach irritations and bowel attacks, together with what De Quincey called "internal rheumatism" (attributed by him to his damp Lake Country cottage and the local climate) and what Coleridge named "the flying gout" (which he similarly blamed upon the damp climate). For these opium-induced physical miseries each man consumed more opium as an anodyne; inevitably, their respective conditions worsened.

These vastly increased doses of opium induced "intellectual torpor" (to quote De Quincey again): a state of affairs "most oppressive and tormenting, from the sense of incapacity and feebleness, from the direct embarrassments incident to the neglect and procrastination of each day's appropriate labours, and from . . . remorse".

Now came fresh and further manifestation of the drug's malignant effects: optical hallucinations; followed by fearful nightmares accompanied (said De Quincey) by "Deep seated anxiety and funereal melancholy" amounting to "suicidal despondency". In these terrible dreams he saw "scenes of abomination, circumstances of physical horror". He became "awestruck" at the approach of sleep and did all he could to stay awake, fearing "death through overwhelming nervous terrors" (this should be compared with S.T.C.'s "Terror & Cowardice . . . of sudden Death" in relation to opium nightmares; "The fear of dying suddenly in my Sleep").[2]

These pains and miseries of opium, catalogued by De Quincey, and counterparted by what we read from the pen of S.T.C., were accompanied, for both men, by bewildering changes in personal relationships. The happiest and closest of relationships assumed diametrically different guises, as if mirrored in reverse; those relatives and friends formerly nearest the heart now becoming those to be most scorned as despicable. Into this country of distortion and dreadful night stepped S.T.C. at the close of 1800 and in it he was to flounder for the next sixteen years, inevitably dragging Sara after him into the morass of misery and confusion.

## II

The start of 1801 was a gloomy one for the Coleridges; S.T.C. was straightway confined to his bed with rheumatic fever and a hydrocele. He was up to the eyes in debt: owing £20 to Wordsworth, £25 to various Keswick tradesmen and his landlord, £15 to Mrs Fricker (it will be recalled that he paid her an annual allowance), £25 to Phillips the bookseller, £30 to Longman, £17 to Poole and £13 to Charles Lamb. Moreover he had drawn in advance (and spent) at least £40 of next year's Wedgwood annuity.

S.T.C. continued without hope of defraying any of these debts; he was in bed, far too ill to work for much of the time, and when he recovered sufficiently he was too sunk in opium torpor and dejection to address himself to anything. The local doctor, John Edmondson, visited almost daily; knowing nothing of opium addiction he admitted himself perfectly perplexed. At some point in time of this spring of 1801, S.T.C. discovered the notorious "Kendal Black Drop", a particularly powerful tincture of opium, which he consumed in increasingly large doses, declaring that it did him sufficient good to justify its high price. (In 1825 Kendal Black Drop sold at eleven shillings for a phial of four ounces, an extortionate price, and would seem to have been much the same price from the commencement of its manufacture in the late eighteenth century.) In addition to the doctor's fees and the opiates there was also the cost of S.T.C.'s increasing consumption of brandy to be reckoned with; brandy being necessary to keep the laudanum on his stomach.

Sara became progressively distraught with anxiety over her husband's health, the desperate state of the family finances, the darkness of the future. The strain was beginning to tell upon her; robust as she was, the stress from S.T.C.'s illness, the draughts and damp of a house that they could not afford to keep warm, the frugality of diet, lowered her resistance and she succumbed to violent colds, an ulcerated throat and rheumatism.

As she had scant opportunity to leave the house she had so far made few friends among her neighbours; her closest acquaintances were the Misses Spedding (described by S.T.C. as "Chatty sensible women, republicans in opinion, and just like other Ladies of their rank, in practice").[3] Otherwise, Sara's chief society was found in Mrs Wilson; it was, said S.T.C., no small joy for Sara to have "a good affectionate motherly woman" divided from her merely by a wall.[4] But for the greater part of her time, between November 1800 and May 1801, Sara was confined to S.T.C.'s sick room; her sole "amusement", as she sat at his bedside, being found in reading copies of the *Morning Post*, regularly supplied by Stuart in the expectation that S.T.C. would be contributing to the paper. But he lay submerged in despondency; in fits of self-disgust and loathing; hopeless torpors that rendered him unfit for any kind of breadwinning.

The enormous and ever-increasing quantities of opium now consumed at Greta Hall were ostensibly required for medicinal purposes, but at some point during that winter Sara began to remonstrate with her husband, declaring that the opium, far from alleviating his sufferings, was clearly contributing to his languors and dejections, while the brandy was equally bad for him. The natural irritability of the sick rendered S.T.C. sufficiently "fretful and splenetic" without criticism from Sara as an additional exacerbation. The more urgently she remonstrated with him for his damaging self-indulgence, the more did he, in turn, reproach her for lacking wifely sympathy and understanding. The Wordsworths, he pointed out, never criticized him as she did; never gave him "blunt advice" on his habits. On the contrary, they commiserated with him in his sufferings, as loving friends should. Sara retorted, baldly, that in her view the Wordsworths, far from being his friends, were his worst enemies. He was sacrificing not only himself but his own family in the interests of Wordsworth. She pointed to the bundles of bills on S.T.C.'s desk; begged him to consider how they were to live, let alone bring up the children properly, with not a penny coming into the house with the exception of the Wedgwood annuity, which was insufficient for a household such as theirs.

Coleridge argued back that, as long as there was love and happiness, what did it matter if they were poor? He drew a romantic and touching portrait of domestic bliss on a round-the-year diet of potatoes; there was more to life than money. Sara, in reply, "ostentatiously avowed" sentiments which he "held most base":[5] it was not enough to live on potatoes, she wanted a better life than that for herself and her children. It was not right that he should inflict poverty and suffering upon them: cold, fireless rooms; wretched, insufficient meals; a chronic shortage of candles and coals and comfort; a pinched existence of eking out a pittance. Buried in debts, obliged to borrow from his friends and rely on the charity of his landlord: where was it all to end? Had S.T.C. no pride? Was he really prepared to see his family finish as paupers? Unless he gave up making himself ill with imprudent habits and behaviour he would live to see his wife and children sharing the fate of the beggars who came to the door of Greta Hall. Had he no wish to see his sons enjoy the advantages of upbringing and education and a station in life such as he himself had enjoyed?

S.T.C.'s contemptuous reply was that he had no pride as the world understood it. Nor did he have any desire to be thought of highly by his fellow men. As for his children, so long as they lived joyous, innocent lives, what could a lack of money matter? He had no wish to see his sons grow up to be fine gentlemen. "I love warm Rooms, comfortable fires, & food, books, natural scenery, music &c; but I do not care what *binding* the Books have, whether they are dusty or clean — & I *dislike* fine furniture, handsome cloathes, & all the ordinary symbols & appendages of artificial superiority — or what is called, *Gentility*."[6]

Sara's fears for the future were natural and rational. Her own experiences of girlhood, when an improvident and feckless father had plunged his family into bankruptcy, had taught her the harsh meaning of failure of a breadwinner; while the "romantic" aspects of a Rousseauist simple life in a humble country cottage had been tried and found tragically wanting in the "old hovel". She no longer believed in domestic bliss on a diet of potatoes and the strains of an Eolian harp. The "sanguine season of youth" was over; cold reality showed its wolf's teeth at the door.

In his heart S.T.C. knew that Sara was right in all that she said in the way of warning and reproach. He became riddled with guilt and remorse; with the inevitable result that he withdrew into himself, away from her. The instant he was able to rise from bed he hurried over the Raise to seek solace at Dove Cottage, while the angry Sara (distraught with anxiety as much as with anger) sent "ill tempered speeches" after him. Invariably he returned home with renewed sickness upon him, fetching a fresh spate of "ill tempered speeches" down upon his head. He buried himself among his pillows and swallowed more laudanum, more brandy, lashing out at Sara — and Hartley when the latter came near him — with a tongue made "wrong and bitter".

Hartley was depicted by his father in letters to friends as, "A fairy elf — all life, all motion — indefatigable in joy — a spirit of Joy dancing on an Aspen Leaf. From morning to night he whirls about and about, whisks, whirls, and eddies, like a blossom in a May breeze."[7] Yet the evidence is that the father was to some extent deluding himself over Hartley's alleged morn to night joyousness. The child, exposed to his father's irritable tongue-lashing, retired into his own world; either remaining out of view with Mr Jackson and Mrs Wilson, ("Wilsy") or, when the finer weather came, burying himself in the kitchen garden among thickets of burgeoning raspberry canes and jungles of jerusalem artichokes; daydreaming; inventing a fantasy world of his own: Ejuxria. Coleridge spoke of this seemingly contented reclusiveness as further proof of Hartley's joyous Rousseauist temperament and uniqueness; but there are subtle indications that, privately, he nursed guilty suspicions that he had done wrong to Hartley,

> A little child, a limber Elf
> Singing, dancing to itself;
> A faery Thing with red round Cheeks,
> That always *finds*, and never *seeks* —
> Doth make a Vision to the Sight,
> Which fills a Father's Eyes with Light!
> And Pleasures flow in so thick & fast
> Upon his Heart, that he at last
> Must needs express his Love's Excess
> In Words of Wrong and Bitterness. . . .

A copy of these self-revealing lines was sent to Southey with the equally revealing comment, "A very metaphysical account of Fathers calling their children rogues, rascals, & little varlets — &c — ".[8]

"Love's excess" could find no outlet except "in Words of Wrong and Bitterness"; an attitude common to those who for one reason or the other have lost their equilibrium; above all common to the victim of morphine, who expresses "the *alter ego* of erstwhile happiness" in terms of his drug-induced moral and intellectual perplexities, thereby bringing "anguish and remorse to the conscience".

The beloved elf, Hartley, had to be upbraided; Sara, the "beautiful Flower", the very sight of whom gave S.T.C. surges of delight and pride,[9] must be rebuked, belittled, insulted. Sara, unable to steal away like a child, instead reacted by bursting into distraught "screams of passion" and torrents of frenzied recrimination which (as S.T.C. recognized, in his better moments) revealed her bewilderment and perplexity and a strong element of fear which, in turn, triggered her to anger.[10] These outbursts were followed by prolonged silences between husband and wife; until darkness and S.T.C.'s frightful nightmare screams brought Sara hastening to wake him and assure him that he had been dreaming; trying to soothe and calm him; shawl over her nightgown; candle in hand.

S.T.C. now became privately convinced that he had not long to live. He anticipated that his brothers would protect his wife and children. Anxious not to prejudice the chances of Ottery assistance for his widow and orphaned sons he asked Thelwall, who was writing a volume of memoirs, to omit from this book all mention of his own activities in radical politics; indeed, any mention of his name. Thelwall complied with this request.[11]

Sickness, pain, wretchedness, gloom: yet it was not the sickness, nor the pain which caused Coleridge his intense sufferings. He wrote to Poole on 18th April, "I am rendered useless & wretched — not that my bodily pain afflicts me — God forbid! Were I a single man & independent, I should be ashamed to think myself wretched merely because I suffered Pain . . . I would rather be in Hell, deserving Heaven, than be in Heaven, deserving Hell. It is not my bodily Pain — but the gloom & distresses of those around me for whom I ought to be labouring & cannot."[12]

## III

Despite agonized bouts of guilt and remorse the addict entertains a basic conviction that "the diviner part of his nature is paramount. . . . The moral affections are in a state of cloudless serenity, and high over all the great light of majestic intellect."[13] Opium, or no opium, Coleridge (with justification) never entertained any doubts regarding the majesty of his intellect; but, as his morphine saturation increased, not only the cerebral Coleridge but the Coleridge of feeling, of the "moral affections" (and moral perceptions, too) was self-appraised as being of a superior stamp to lesser hearts and natures around him — always, of course, excepting the Wordsworths. Coleridge became increasingly contemptuous of commoner clay: during 1801 and 1802 we find Poole, Godwin, Cottle, Davy, all his old friends and cronies being measured against exacting Esteesian standards and found wanting in such qualities as disinterested affection, unworldliness, organic sensibility, depth of heart as weighed against a calculating head, and so on; with the inevitable corollary of rejection of the erstwhile friend as "unworthy".

Sara Coleridge was relegated to the ranks of the "contemptible". Contempt now became the prevailing note in S.T.C.'s voice whenever he referred to his wife (a contempt echoed in almost all that Dorothy now had to say about her and which has been repeated by innumerable pens down the ensuing one hundred and eighty years or so that have elapsed since S.T.C. abruptly began to tell everyone that his wife was proving the ruination of his "moral character"; "incapacitating" him for "any worthy" exertion of his faculties). This change in S.T.C.'s overtly expressed feelings for Sara took place with remarkable abruptness, between the autumn of 1800 and April of 1801. In early October 1800 he was still speaking of her with loving pride; by the following midsummer he had, he said, reached the "heart withering" conclusion that he could not be happy without his children and "could not but be miserable with the mother of them".[14]

We should remind ourselves, at this point, of Sara *fille*'s subsequent observations on the subject of her parents' incompatibility; how her mother's "honesty stood in the way" of her living harmoniously with her father "unless at the same time she had possessed that meekness and forbearance which softens everything and can be conciliating by utter silence on all unpeaceful topics and the constant recurrence to soothing cheering themes". Meekness and forbearance were not Mrs S.T.C.'s strong points; nor did she enjoy that "dexterity in managing the temper of others which is often a substitute for an even temper in the possessor".[15]

Sara showed no hesitation when she judged that it was her duty, as his wife and mother of his children, to confront her husband with the dangers of his increasing opium indulgence and the imprudence of his behaviour in general; furthermore, not only to caution him, but to do her best to oppose his pursuance of these damaging habits. This, however, was seen by S.T.C. as "Thwarting and Dispathy";[16] evidence of her lack of sympathy and affection.

Increasingly S.T.C. deluged the Wordsworths with recitations about Sara's tantrums; her total lack of affectionate understanding and wifely sympathy. Herein, he alleged, lay the true reason for his consumption of vast quantities of laudanum; opium was essential to lull that "constant dread in my mind respecting Mrs Coleridge's Temper"; discord between himself and Mrs Coleridge was, he affirmed, the root cause of all his trouble.

Accepting the truth of every word that S.T.C. uttered, it was natural that Dorothy should exclaim, "Is it not a hopeless case? So insensible and irritable that she [Mrs S.T.C.] never can come to good, and poor C!"[17] This to Mary and Sarah Hutchinson. The Dove Cottage circle, seeing his wife as the prime source of Coleridge's problems, began to mull over plans to separate the pair.

Sara herself, on the other hand, remained convinced that the Wordsworths with their, in her view, misplaced tolerant sympathy for S.T.C. were "the great means for his self-indulgence" and thereby his self-destruction. As she saw it they, who were allegedly his dearest friends, should have joined her in denunciation of his indulgences; instead they "humoured him in all his follies".[18] No small wonder, then, that Sara now greeted the Wordsworths with "freezing looks"[19] when they visited Greta Hall.

One of Coleridge's notebook entries exclaims: "Of the one mighty Defect of Female Education — every thing is taught but Reason & the Means of retaining Affection . . . how to quit a Husband, how to receive him on his Return, how never to recriminate — in short, the power of [promoting] pleasurable Thoughts & Feelings — & the *Mischief* of giving pain, or (as often happens, when a Husband comes Home from a Party of old Friends, Joyous & full of Heart) the love killing Effect of cold dry, uninterested looks & Manners."[20]

She continued to pursue what she saw as the correct course of criticism, rebuke and warning, despite her husband's riposte that "blunt advice" invariably did him more harm than good. Sara, ignoring this, persevered with her blunt outspokenness. Somebody had to tell him the truth! Nor was she entirely wasting her breath. S.T.C. refused to admit it, but in his heart he knew that Sara was right. His opium habit had to be broken or it would get the upper hand of him (the fact that this had already occurred was something he could not accept). He drew up a plan which he outlined to Poole in a letter of 17th May: "Thro' the whole Summer I will observe every rule of the most scrupulous Prudence & Forecast with religious strictness, using *regulated* Diet & *regulated* Exercise — at the close of the summer if I should be so far re-established, that I no longer feel my health affected by the changes of the Weather, I shall have nothing to do, but to pass the Winter in quiet industry, with unremitted caution as to Wet & cold. — If the contrary should be the case, I am determined to go to St Miguel's (one of the Azores . . . ) . . . Captn Wordsworth (W's Brother . . . ) . . . warmly recommends a Wintering there."[21]

It will be seen from this that S.T.C. had accepted advice from each side of the Raise. Despite his voiced violent repudiation of the counsel bluntly put to him by Sara the first part of the plan obviously derives from all that she had said to him; "every rule" of her "Prudence and Forecast" was embodied in his scheme. As for the Wordsworths, from them had come the suggestion of wintering in a warm climate, thereby sparing himself injurious damp Cumbrian months and, moreover, separating him, at least for a while, from his wife. Dorothy and William "with generous Friendship" had offered to settle in the Azores with him; Sara and the children to remain in England. If possible he would later "send over" for them (but Sara herself was given the firm impression, by her husband, that she and the children would accompany the party from the very start).[22]

Sara was not averse to the plan to live for a while in a warm climate but she pointed out the financial impossibility of going to the Azores at that moment in time and urged S.T.C. to do "nothing rashly" but first to give a trial to the aforesaid winter of "quiet industry" in his study at Greta Hall.[23]

Of course, the scheme for "scrupulous Prudence" foundered; instead the opium excesses and consequent strife at Greta Hall intensified: S.T.C. entered a further deepening phase of drug-distorted perspective and Sara became further perplexed and angry,

> And so we whirl round & round in perpetual
> & vertiginous agitation — agitation and vertigo.[24]

# CHAPTER FOURTEEN

## The Advent of Asra

Some time in the spring or summer of 1801 Sara Coleridge made the discovery that her husband was developing a tender friendship with Miss Sarah Hutchinson, twenty-six years of age and a sister of Mary Hutchinson (who, during the autumn of that same year was to become betrothed to William Wordsworth). S.T.C. had first met the Hutchinson sisters at Gallow Hill, Sockburn, Yorkshire, in the autumn of 1799. On this occasion he had been greatly charmed by the tall and gentle Mary and had playfully flirted with the jolly little Sarah who, at just over five feet in height and plump to go with it, was the sort of small, well-rounded female he always found attractive.

On his second visit to the north, in the spring of 1800, S.T.C. again called on the Hutchinsons.[1] They were a friendly, hospitable family of brothers and sisters, whose total lack of intellectual pretence combined with earthy humour and genuine good-heartedness appealed to the Devon countryman in S.T.C. At this time Mary and Sarah were housekeeping for their brothers Thomas and George who farmed at Gallow Hill (their eldest brother, John, farmed at Stockton; the other surviving brother, Henry, was a sailor). This time, when S.T.C. said goodbye, he departed with a little of Sarah Hutchinson's luxurious brown hair in his pocket, as a keepsake.[2]

During the winter-spring of 1800–1 she was staying at Dove Cottage as part of the Wordsworth circle to whom S.T.C. constantly bruited complaints about his wife. Miss Hutchinson's sympathetic listening encouraged him, a man "disappointed in marriage" as he put it, to attempt to make a compensation to himself by developing "a virtuous & tender & brotherly friendship" with "an amiable Woman"; viz. Miss Hutchinson.[3] In February 1801 Miss Hutchinson paid a visit to Greta Hall and it may have been at this time that Sara first became suspicious, and certainly a little jealous, of S.T.C.'s friendly manner towards the young woman. S.T.C. saw Sara's reaction as the culminating evidence of her total want of sympathetic understanding. "One mere Thought, one feeling of Suspicion or Jealousy or resentment can remove two human Beings farther from each other, than winds or seas can separate their bodies."[4] Sara and her husband now had all the oceans of the globe between them.

At some point during that progressively despair-ridden and opium-sodden spring of 1801 S.T.C.'s feelings of "brotherly friendship" for Miss Hutchinson were suddenly transformed into hopeless infatuation: "the abrupt creation of a moment".[5] This infatuation for another woman he did not attempt to conceal from his wife; had he not a perfect right to love whom and how he chose? Did the fact that he was a husband mean that he might only love one individual in the world, his wife? The stipulation was an impossible one. He had a right to love many persons other than Sara Coleridge. She retorted that wives, as well as husbands, had rights: of loyalty, support, consideration, priority.

Their disputes over this question of his rights as opposed to hers raged between them during the course of the next eighteen months and were encapsulated in a series of, as it were, "situation appreciation" memoranda which he wrote in the autumn of 1802: to quote two sections, relevant here:

1. . . . I can neither retain my Happiness nor my Faculties, unless I move, live, & love, in perfect Freedom, limited only by my own purity & self-respect, & by my incapability of loving any person, man or woman, unless I at the same time honour & esteem them. My Love is made up 9/10ths of fervent wishes for the permanent *Peace* of mind in those, whom I love, be it man or woman; & for their Progression in purity, goodness, & true Knowledge. Such being the nature of my Love, no human Being can have a right to be jealous. . . . That we can love but one person, is a miserable mistake, & the cause of abundant unhappiness. I can & do love many people, dearly — so dearly, that I really scarcely know, which I love the best. . . . Would any good & wise man, any warm & wide hearted man marry at all, if it were part of the Contract — Henceforth this Woman is your only friend, your sole beloved! all the rest of mankind, however amiable & akin to you, must be only your acquaintance! — ? It were well, if every woman wrote down before her marriage all, she thought she had a *right* to, from her Husband — & to examine each in this form — By what *Law* of God, of Man, or of general reason, do I claim *this* Right? I suspect, that this Process would make a ludicrous Quantity of Blots and Erasures in most of the first rude Draughts of these Rights of Wives — infinitely however to their own Advantage, & to the security of their true & genuine Rights. 2. — Permit me, my dear Sara! without offence to you, as Heaven knows! it is without any feeling of Pride in myself, to say — that in sex, acquirements, and in the quantity and quality of natural endowments whether of Feeling, or of Intellect, you are the Inferior. Therefore it would be preposterous to expect that I should see with your eyes, & dismiss my Friends from *my* heart, only because you have not chosen to give them any Share of *your* Heart; but it is not preposterous, in me, on the contrary I have a *right* to expect &

demand, that you should to a certain degree love, & act kindly to, those whom I deem worthy of my love.[6]

Despite the fact that he claimed to be her superior on every possible count, the paragraph with which he concludes reveals an unease closely akin to fear of the retaliatory gun power of his small but indomitable opponent, "If you read this Letter with half the Tenderness, with which it is written, it will do you & both of us, GOOD; & contribute it's share to the turning of a mere Cat-hole into a Dove's nest! You know, Sally Pally! I must have a Joke — or it would not be me! —"

Although Samuel had now so manifestly abandoned his former enthusiasm for Wollstonecraftist principles Sara clung staunchly to them. "For man and woman the truth must be the same". S.T.C. was claiming that what was preposterous in Sara was not preposterous in him; what kind of truth was that? Sara did not see it. She refused to regard herself as an inferior who was not entitled to decide with whom she should, or should not, share her heart. Nor, in her integral honesty, did she see why she should not speak out when she felt that she should; why she might not voice her objections. So she continued to behave in an independent-minded style, making it clear that she did not agree with Samuel's view of their respective rights.

He decided that he no longer loved her, on the grounds that she herself was totally incapable of loving; indeed, as he now confided to his notebook, Sara was unable to experience any feelings apart from anger and wounded pride:

"By an habitual absence of *reality* in her affection I have had an hundred instances that the being beloved, or not being beloved, is a thing indifferent: but the *notion* of not being beloved — that wounds her pride deeply." (The reader should compare this with S.T.C.'s similar reproach to Godwin: "It did appear to me, as if without any attachment to me you were simply gratified by the notion of my attachment to you." And also with Coleridge's complaints to Southey that Poole was too interested in money and lacking in generosity towards his friends, particularly himself, "No doubt he was very fond of my *conversation* & the instruction he derived from it/but. . . . " And then a long string of complaints against the man who had not so long since been, "My beloved . . . dearest, and most esteemed friend — Friend of my Soul! and Brother of my Choice!")[7]

Sara, S.T.C. decided, suffered from "Coldness . . . & paralysis in all *tangible* ideas & sensations . . . all that forms *real* self. . . . Nothing affects her with pain or pleasure as it is but only as other people will *say* it is." He could no longer make contact with, let alone love, this frozen image, "To love is to *know*, at least to imagine that you *know* (not always indeed *understand*); what is strange to you, you cannot love, (Mrs C. is all *strange*, & the *Terra incognita* always lies near to or under the frozen Poles)." Sara was "cold & calm as a deep Frost"; "uncommonly *cold* in her feelings of animal Love". (There is a strong possibility that Sara, to demonstrate her disapproval of her husband's enthusiasm for Miss Hutchinson, had had recourse to the strategy of Lysistrata.) He moaned that he was "heart starved by selfishness and frost-bitten by moral frigidity". And suddenly he saw it all, or thought that he did; the stark truth of the matter was that this "heart starving" inflicted upon him by "Mrs C" (a heart starving which he now traced back to the very first days of their marriage) had "cankered in the bud" not his happiness alone, but his health, his genius, his activity: "Hence too the general weakening and wasting of the Will that brought on an increasing cowardice of mental pain and distressing bodily symptoms. Hence . . .

> Lured by no fond Belief,
> No Hope that flatter'd Grief,
> But blank Despair my Plea,
> I borrowed short relief
> At frightful usury![8]"

Upon Sara was laid the blame for all his pains and woes. Opium itself he exonerated; indeed to opium he turned for relief from these evils; yet, "at frightful usury" — which immediately reveals that he recognized the role of havoc that opium was playing, even though he was overtly identifying Sara as the root cause of it. The element of guilty self-knowledge is painfully apparent. He found refuge from his guilt by making the ultimate gesture of self-deception, "I often say — in the words of Christ — Father forgive her! she knows not what she does!"[9] (Of course he let Sara know that he said this: she must be left in no doubt that *hers* was the guilt; that it was *she* who was the destructive agent.)

He consoled himself with opium, dreaming of an ideal union with a perfect other half. "Every generous mind . . . feels its Halfness and cannot *think* without a Symbol — neither can it *love* without something that is at once to be its Symbol, & its other half"; "the outward Interpreter" of the "incessant music" of his heart. It went without saying that Mrs C. (as he now invariably called her in his notebooks, as if she had indeed become a total stranger to him) could not possibly fulfil the role of "other half" as viewed within this context; it was possible to *join* sexually with her but he and she "could never *unify*". "There might be addition, but there could be no combination."[10]

He saw himself now as a man seeking for "a completeness of whose moral nature he shall be the completion". This, he decided, was "the innermost & holiest instinct". But where, who, was this sacred other half? And then he "discovered the Object, as by a flash of Lightning, or the Strike of a Horse's Shoe, or a Flint, in utter darkness": Sarah Hutchinson, with whom he had developed the feelings of brotherly friendship and "tenderest affection", gave him a signal, "*One look* of the eyes, one *vision* of the countenance, seen *only* by the *Being* on whom it worked, & by him only to be seen".[11]

Thus Asra was born (the *h* being dropped from Miss Hutchinson's first name, Sarah, followed by an inversion of the letters of the name Sara). A vague image, as "in a glass darkly", is projected for us of "the meek eyed maiden mild" with the "angel countenance"; a "compassionate Comforter . . . most innocent and full of love"; she whom he loved "as never woman was beloved! in body, in soul, in brain, in heart, in hope, in fear, in prospect, in retrospect! Not he alone in the vulgar meaning of *he*, but every living atom that composed him was wedded and faithful to you. Every single thought, every image, every perception was no sooner itself than it became *you* by some wish that you saw it and felt it or had — or by some recollection that it suggested — some way or other it always became a symbol of *you*. I played with them as with *your shadow*".[12]

"My love of Asra," he ruminated, at a later date, "is not so much in my soul as my soul in it. . . . To bid me not love you were to bid me annihilate myself, for to love you is all I know of my life as far as my life is an object of my consciousness or my free will. . . . You have been, and you alone have been, my conscience — in what form, with what voice, under what modification, can I imagine God to work upon me, in which *you* have not worked?".[13] "To be in love" with a woman "is to associate all our obscure feelings with a real form,"[14] he declared, thus giving love, in the sense of "being in love", a vast Piranesian dimension.

This vast dimension the decade of notebook entries certainly does bestow upon Asra; but where is the "real form", the real woman, with whom his obscure feelings were associated? The woman of whom Sara Coleridge was jealous? The truth of the matter was that Asra was a mirage; Asra, as a real woman, did not exist. She was a mirage of S.T.C.'s ideal Adam's rib woman (we must remind ourselves, it was his conviction that, "The perfection of every woman is to be characterless . . . Creatures who, though they may not always understand you . . . always feel you and feel with you"). In other words

Asra, the symbol of perfection, the ideal other half, was no more than a reflection of Esteesee; a species of Brocken spectre.

Opium destroyed Coleridge's sense of proportion and grossly affected his judgement. Opium-torpor weighed him down with dejection; cloyed him with disgust and loathing. "I was once a Volume of Gold Leaf, rising and riding on every breath of Fancy — but I have beaten myself back into weight & density, & now I remain squat and square on the earth," as he told Godwin.[15] Costive and sunk in lethargy, his responses of mind and heart acquired the sluggish viscosity of slurry; as he was to cry to his wife in heart-rending lament, "[I have never] known any woman for whom I had an equal personal fondness. . . . Till the very latest period, when my health & spirits rendered me dead to every thing, I had a PRIDE in you, . . . I never saw you at the top of our Hill, when I returned from a Walk, without a sort of pleasurable Feeling of Sight . . . some little akin to the delight in a beautiful Flower joined with the consciousness — 'And it is in *my* garden'."[16] To this garden he now lost the key. He subsided into a contorted underworld; a kind of subterranean hall of curved mirrors where grotesque distortions confronted him at every turn.

Reading the vituperation levelled by S.T.C. at Poole, Davy, Godwin, and above all at his wife, following his rejection of them, we do not recognize, in these bitter caricatures, anything that we have previously known; indeed the reverse: the generous democratic Poole is a mean capitalist; the spontaneous and dedicated Davy is worldly and conceited, thinking only of self-promotion; the warm and beddable Sara is physically, as well as emotionally, ice cold.

De Quincey, writing of Coleridge's "monomaniac antipathies", compared them with his "many strange likings — equally monomaniac". De Quincey's conclusion was that antipathies and likings (these "crazes of Coleridge") shared a root cause: they were "derangements worked by opium".[17]

And so what of Miss Sarah Hutchinson; she who, wittingly or unwittingly, allegedly triggered the signal that flashed Asra into S.T.C.'s exclusive view? In youth, plain and dumpy, her abundant hair her one beauty, she comes across as good, naïve and inexperienced, with an innocently sharp tongue and a fondness for poetry. We can well understand Mrs Coleridge's baffled comment that she could see "nothing extraordinary" about her. S.T.C. complained to his notebook that his wife was unable to appreciate "the mild and retired kind",[18] but in truth nothing that we learn about Sarah Hutchinson, either from her own pen or from those persons who knew her, indicates that here was a character either mild or retired. Her letters reveal that she gathered strength, so to speak, as she advanced in years; becoming the very epitome of a lively and aggressive old maid, always brimful with brisk counsel, prejudiced opinions (she was a rabid Tory) and a crusty (not infrequently acid) tongue. Hartley Coleridge described her as being "without a spark of malice in her heart" but added that she had, "from the perfect faultlessness of her own life, a good deal of intolerance in her head. . . . Not that she was so illiberal as to dislike people for differing from her own opinions (she certainly and naturally liked them better when they agreed) but hers was pre-eminently a one-side mind."[9] She became a tower of strength to the Wordsworth, Hutchinson and Southey families: whenever there was a crisis this opinionated, confident, energetic, cocky spinster lady soon turned up, handing out advice; suggesting that this love-lorn youth should look elsewhere, this nervous young lady should pull herself together, this nephew work harder, this invalid try sea-bathing.

What miraculous alchemy made it possible for such a one to be transformed into an Asra? We must remember that, when S.T.C.'s urgent need for an Asra arose, Sarah Hutchinson was virtually the only available female on the scene, with the exception of Dorothy (who already filled an important role in his life simply as herself, tutelary genius of the wild) and Mary Hutchinson, who was on the point of becoming betrothed to William. Moreover Sarah Hutchinson answered S.T.C.'s requirements perfectly inasmuch as her naïveté and inexperience enabled him to trap her in an intolerable situation which a more experienced and worldly woman would have avoided. She was young, and therefore flattered by his attentions; she was romantic-minded, as all young women are, and she was essentially chaste and therefore eager to acquiesce in expressions of some sublime, spiritual "love" which did not implicate her in sexual transgression. Moreover she was warm-hearted and kind and she pitied him; as Coleridge at last perceived only too clearly.[20] It is easy to understand how Sarah Hutchinson drifted into becoming Asra. But whether she consciously gave him that fatal signal seen only by himself is another matter: he was determined to see it whether she gave it or not.

Between 1801 and 1810, the years of her association with S.T.C., Sarah Hutchinson underwent a curious species of eclipse. Her health was almost continuously bad; she was beset with neuralgic pains, unspecified illness and debility. Everything points to her extreme unhappiness as the object of S.T.C.'s infatuation; indeed, in a letter dated at a much later period she writes in a manner which indicates that he "intruded upon her" and "persecuted her" with his attention; while he himself, in a notebook entry, complains that, "You never *sate* near me ten minutes in your life without showing a restlessness and a thought of going, etc — for at least five minutes out of the ten". In the final stages of the relationship Dorothy Wordsworth recorded that S.T.C. continually harassed and agitated Sarah Hutchinson's mind.[21]

S.T.C. recognized that he made her miserable. In a masochistic notebook entry he exclaimed, "Why we two made to be a Joy to each other, should for so many years constitute each other's melancholy — O! but the melancholy is Joy — ".[22]

However, in the early months of the affair, if such a relationship may be described as an "affair", Sarah Hutchinson apparently found it in her heart to write him letters "full of explicit Love & Feeling". When she flagged in these protestations of devotion he constructed "happy" opium day dreams out of his misery caused by her "neglect"; a favourite theme being that she came to his bedside where he lay deserted in some lonely inn, "There you have found me — there you are weeping over me! — Dear, dear Woman!"[23]

Or, significantly, he opium-dreamed ("My eyes make pictures, when they are shut")[24] of both Hutchinson sisters, Mary and Sarah, crooning over him and comforting him in some quiet, firelit room,

> The shadows dance upon the wall,
>   By the still dancing fire-flames made;
> And now they slumber, moveless all!
>   And now they melt to one deep shade!
> But not from me shall this mild darkness steal thee:
> I dream thee with mine eyes, and at my heart I feel thee![25]

These lines, entitled *A Day Dream* and dated 1802, invoke Asra; but as we read we find that we are seeing the same firelit room of that earlier *Day Dream: from an immigrant to his absent wife*, written by Coleridge in Germany in 1798 (above pp. 103–4),

> I saw the couch, I saw the quiet Room,
> The heaving Shadows and the fire-light gloom . . .

A notebook entry describes an Asra-inspired dream when she and he and Mary are together on a lazy bed (a couch, or *chaise longue*) in a quiet firelight glow, "Prest to my bosom and felt there . . . I felt her as *part* of my being — twas all spectral".[26] An echo, this, of "Across my chest there liv'd a weight so warm", from the 1798 poem. The second day dream poem is manifestly a form of variation upon the first: Asra upon the lazy bed is a transposition of Sara upon the Nether-Stowey couch — and, too, this firelit parlour of Nether-Stowey with Hartley playing and the infant Berkeley slumbering in his cradle beside the couch where Sara lies was, as we remember, echoed by the scene in the Greta Hall parlour following the birth of Derwent, when Sally Pally came downstairs to dine and drink Tea and rest on a couch by the fire following a triumphant recovery from childbirth: to the pride and delight of her husband: "There's for you!" Sara, mother and wife, upon a couch in a quiet, firelit room: the eternal epitome of domestic bliss.

But now, under the pains of opium, that sweet reality has vanished: Sara has become a frozen heart-starver; her *alter ego*, Asra, sympathetic and understanding, lies, "all spectral", upon the couch instead. Asra, the *alter-ego*, is essentially a symbol, and thus a product of the imagination: "That reconciling and mediatory power, which incorporating the reason in images of the sense, and organising . . . the flux of the senses by the permanence and self-circling energies of the reason, gives birth to a system of symbols, harmonious in themselves, and consubstantial with the truths of which they are conductors".[27] Asra: symbol of the ideal other half; "a Wife in the *truest* sense"; "a completeness of whose moral nature" he should be the completion: a couch, as he confides in a notebook entry, being a symbol of a Beloved; "our only means of quiet Heart-repose!"[28]

Of Asra, the symbol, he opium-dreamed by day. At night opium presented him with different dreams — not constructed or, as it were, remote-controlled by himself, but springing, unbidden, from recesses of his unconscious mind: deformed dwarfs crouched in corners, filling him with horror; hideous strangers threatened him with obscenities. The dormitory terrors of Christ's Hospital returned, bringing "confusion to the reason . . . anguish and remorse to the conscience":

> A lurid light, a trampling throng,
> Sense of intolerable wrong,
> And whom I scorned, those only strong! . . .
> Desire with loathing strangely mixed
> On wild or hateful objects fixed.
> Fantastic passions! maddening brawl!
> And shame and terror over all!
> Deeds to be hid which were not hid,
> Which all confused I could not know,
> Whether I suffered, or I did;
> For all seemed guilt, remorse or woe,
> My own or others' still the same
> Life-stifling fear, soul-stifling shame. . . .[29]

He yelled and screamed; bringing his wife, Sara Coleridge, to his bedside; wigless, her hair cropped like a nun's in dedication to a vocation; a constant reminder to him of what, in his heart, he knew to have been the first of the betrayals.

# CHAPTER FIFTEEN

# Constancy to an Ideal Object

## I

Unbeknown to Mrs Coleridge the Wordsworths now began urging S.T.C. to separate from her; on the rational grounds that if, as he claimed, she was ruining his life and driving him to an early grave the only sane decision was to live apart from her. Better that, than cease to live! Coleridge agreed with them that this was the only rational course open to him, but stipulated that he should first make one last trial "to bring Mrs C. to a change of temper, and something like communion with him in his enjoyments",[1] as Dorothy put it to the Hutchinson sisters.

Yet even Dorothy, prone as she was to accept every word that came from Coleridge, and ignorant as she was of the salient role which opium played in the Coleridge marital disaster, remained sufficiently fair-minded to be able to sympathize in some degree with Sara Coleridge, "She is much, very much to be pitied, for when one party is ill-matched the other necessarily must be so too". Dorothy recognized that "Mrs C." had "several great merits" which would have made her "a very good wife to many another man, but for Coleridge!! Her radical point is want of sensibility, and what can such a woman be to Coleridge?"[2]

Dorothy's sympathy encouraged S.T.C. to deluge her with laments about his marital misery; she in turn became increasingly "melancholy" on his behalf. What she seems not to have realized (doubtless because she did not wish to realize it) was that a man does not spend hours on end lamenting, unless he has sustained a grievous loss. However gratifying it might be to Coleridge's ego to have Dorothy weeping and Sarah and Mary Hutchinson crooning over him, and however much play Asra/Sarah Hutchinson might provide for masochistic opium-dreaming, the truth was that he still yearned profoundly for the recapture of domestic bliss with Sara Coleridge, (he wrote poignantly to Southey, reproaching him for writing her name as Sar*ah*, "Why, dear Southey, will you write it always, Sar*ah*? — Sar*a*, methinks, is associated with times that you & I cannot & do not wish ever to forget").[3]

Nonetheless the regenerated Sara for whom he longed should be of changed temper; of Hutchinson-like sympathy; of meekness and mildness; a compliant Sara, sharing his opinions; loving his friends.

But how to bring this about? S.T.C. drew up a plan of campaign which he outlined to Southey (now living and working in Westminster);[4] S.T.C. would winter alone in London, working for Stuart, and would practise "self-discipline" (a euphemism for giving up opium, or at least drastically cutting his consumption); he would attempt to draw his wife closer to him with a series of letters, in which he would explore all the sources of their unhappiness. After which he would return to Greta Hall for another trial of marital cohabitation and, if this failed, then they must live apart.

S.T.C. arrived in London on 15th November 1801 and resumed working for Stuart. Unfortunately some time that autumn S.T.C. had discovered that his wife had sent Sarah Hutchinson an "anonymous note" (the contents of which we may only guess). His yearnings for Sara were abruptly checked; he veered round to a determination to part from her and (to Southey's indignation) regaled London with accounts of her temper tantrums, polar coldness, and general impossibility as a wife.

However 1802 brought another change of heart. By early February S.T.C. was speaking of his determination to return to Keswick and, after that, removing with his family and the Wordsworths to the south of France. He wrote in friendly vein to Sara; assuring her of his improved health, which he attributed "to the chearfulness inspired by the thought of speedily returning to you in love & peace. . . . I drive away from me every thought but those of Hope & the tenderest yearnings after you — And it is my frequent prayer, & my almost perpetual aspiration, that we may meet to part no more — & live together as affectionate Husband & Wife ought to do."[5]

At the end of that month, he returned north, not going straight home to Keswick but spending eleven days at Gallow Hill *en route*; here he saw Sarah, as well as Mary Hutchinson. He then returned to Greta Hall and the arms of his wife: reaching Keswick on 15th March or thereabouts. By the end of March Samuel had got his wife with child again, as a result of their reconciliation; yet, during that same period of reconciliation with Sara Coleridge he had, "in a fretting hour", written Sarah Hutchinson "a complaining Scroll" lamenting the hopelessness of his passion for her and his misery; a letter which made her so nervously ill that she was obliged to take to her bed, as she informed him in a letter of reply, which in turn brought from him a further opium-sodden letter in the form of a lengthy poem; the first draft of the celebrated *Dejection Ode* (in part a reply to her; in part a counter to Wordsworth's *Ode to Immortality*, then undergoing composition). In this first, intimate draft of *Dejection*, Coleridge indulged himself in some particularly vehement complaints about life with the wife with whom, supposedly, he was at that very moment attempting conciliation,

> . . . my coarse domestic Life has known
> No Habits of heart-nursing Sympathy . . .
> No hopes of it's own Vintage, None, O! none. . . . [6]

A month later he was writing grumpily to Poole, "Mrs Coleridge is indisposed, & I have too much reason to suspect that she is breeding again/an event, which was to have been deprecated".[7] The pattern of daily domestic quarrelling was now fully resumed at Greta Hall. S.T.C. once more spent his time vanishing over the Raise to discuss with the Wordsworths his melancholy married life; the Wordsworths continued to urge separation for the Coleridges.

One of Wollstonecraft's firmest principles was that no motive on earth should make a man and woman live together a moment after mutual love and regard were gone. This thinking had influenced the Pantisocrats in their deliberations as to whether, in their ideal community in the New World, the marriage contract should be dissolved "if agreeable to one or both parties". It was an idea which found enthusiastic theoretical support among radicals (it should be remembered that divorce was then not commonly available). It is possible that Sara as well as Samuel had professed approval of separation by mutual agreement, in those heady days of Pantisocracy: she and Samuel had then been secure and happy in their love. Now it all looked rather different (as Nixon has observed of Mary Wollstonecraft's own predicament, in connection with her consort Gilbert Imlay, so similar to that of the Coleridges), "It had been easy to make such positive statements when she was confident of Imlay's devotion, but at the present moment [with Imlay's love wavering] there seemed to be need for further reflection on the subject".[8]

S.T.C. now saw separation as "a very aweful Step", but after violent mental struggle he made up his mind to take that step and summoned the nerve to broach the matter to his wife. Her reaction was so vehement that S.T.C., already in a seriously agitated state, was seized with violent stomach spasms and prostration.[9] He declared himself on the point of dying. Sara was "shocked & frightened beyond measure" by this and, forty-eight hours later, S.T.C. still being alarmingly weak and "pale as death", she flung herself upon him begging for forgiveness, together with "a solemn promise of amendment" of her behaviour. Together they sat down to a frank discussion of the problem, as in the good old days of Bristol and Stowey, and drew up a pact: she promised "to set about an alteration in her external manners & looks & language, & to fight against her inveterate habits of puny Thwarting & unintermitting Dyspathy — this immediately — and to do her best endeavours to cherish other *feelings*." S.T.C., on his part, promised to be more attentive to her feelings of pride and try to correct his habits of "impetuous and bitter censure".

S.T.C. reported all this to Southey (adding the inevitable rider that Sara's rejection of the idea of separation had had nothing whatever to do with affection for him, but had been due solely to her own wounded pride; her feelings throughout had been wholly selfish). Nonetheless they had made her *serious*; with the result that "for the first time since our marriage she *felt* and acted, as beseemed a Wife & a Mother to a Husband, & the Father of her children". By this, of course, he meant that she now gave up voicing her own opinions; stopped criticizing him; concurred with all that he thought, said and did; and, in general, tried her best to appear the epitome of meek and mild subservience, as he had stipulated.

Sara, we know, had now drawn the conclusion that Samuel required very special handling, like some puny infant. The state of his health was such that the least vexation did him great injury; "Nothing but tranquillity keeps him tolerable, care and anxiety destroy him". Henceforth *she* would have to be the man in the family; the strong one.

Samuel, blissfully unaware that *he* was the one who had been tried and found lamentably wanting, was pleasantly surprised by her compliant response. "She has kept her promise beyond any hope, I could have flattered myself with", he informed Tom Wedgwood, adding that Sara now felt "as a Wife ought to feel". To Southey he declared that he had the most confident hopes "that this happy Revolution in our domestic affairs will be permanent, & that this external Conformity will gradually generate a greater inward Likeness of thoughts, & attachments, than has hitherto existed between us".[10]

One of the first demands made by S.T.C. upon Sara's new wifely feeling was that the Wordsworths, following William's imminent marriage, should come to live at Greta Hall (Dove Cottage would be too small for them). Sara would seem to have acquiesced (it is hard to escape the cynical thought that she doubtless knew that Mary and Dorothy would no more wish to share a house with her than she with them). This proved to be the case.[11]

The Coleridges, during the months of June to October of 1802, knew more happiness together than they had known for a long time: "At home all is Peace & Love".[12] But even so S.T.C. quailed at the thought of wintering at Greta Hall; he was still maintaining that the damp northern climate was responsible for his agonizing seizures of "flying gout" and had accepted a proposal from Tom Wedgwood that the two should winter together in some warmer climate. In order that Sara should not be left on her own (she was due to give birth to the new baby at Christmas) it was arranged that the Southeys should come to stay during his absence; Southey having decided to give up his post in London and to live henceforth by writing. Mary Lovell was speaking of coming with the Southeys, who, by the time that they moved north, would have an infant of their own.*

The front half of Greta Hall was now being rebuilt: "As soon as the new house is finished, the whole front of the old one will be pulled down, if it does not fall before."[13] The work was supposed to be completed by October, but took much longer than had been anticipated and the Southeys were obliged to postpone their plan to join the Coleridges. Then, abruptly, Wedgwood wrote asking S.T.C. to travel with him to Italy. S.T.C. left without delay, at the urging of Sara herself, "To lose Time is merely to lose Spirits".[14] Wedgwood's letter arrived at Greta Hall on 3rd November; S.T.C. departed at half past four next morning by chaise to Penrith, there to catch the London coach.

Unfortunately he visited Sarah Hutchinson during his stop at Penrith and this brought some complaint in a letter from his wife which reached him at Bristol. Her "Feelings concerning Penrith" he was ready to pass over as "merely a little tiny Fretfulness — but there was one whole sentence of a very, very different cast". We do not know what this was (Sara's side of this correspondence is missing) but, judging by his reaction, it was probably highly critical of him: upon reading it (he told her) he immediately became disordered in "the Heart and Bowels".[15] Upon recovering he sent her a return letter heavy with indignant rebuke which in turn would seem to have upset Sara; at all events, she had a fainting fit, a thing normally utterly unknown to her. S.T.C., now in Wales with Thomas Wedgwood, upon receiving this piece of news had a "fluttering of the Heart" resulting in a "violent Diarrhoea" so that he was "obliged at last to take 20 drops of Laudanum. . . . You must see by this . . . the Importance of *Tranquility* to me", he informed her in a letter written at five-thirty the next morning; "The desire of writing you lay so heavy on my mind, that I awoke at 4 o/clock . . . [I] beg you, INSTANTLY to get a Nurse. If Mary's Aunt cannot come do try to get Mrs Railton. To be sure, there is a mawkish 'so-vary-good'-ness about her character, & her Face & Dress have far too much of the SMUG-DOLEFUL

*Margaret, born 31st August 1802.

in them, for *my* Taste; but she is certainly an excellent Nurse. — At all events, get somebody immediately — have a fire in your Bedroom. . . . If you are seriously ill, or unhappy at my absence, I will return at all Hazards: for I know, you would not *will* it, tho' you might *wish* it, except for a serious cause."[16]

He then proceeded to write her yet another lengthy analysis of the sources of their unhappinesses together. He was in Wales, at Crescelly,[17] when Sara's reply reached him — a reply so warm in response, so tenderly anxious to reciprocate his desires for peace and happiness that he was "overpowered" by "Joy & anxious Love". He wrote back at once, in a rush of feeling:

God love you & have you in his keeping, My blessed Sara! — & speedily restore me to you. — I have a faith, a heavenly Faith, that our future Days will be Days of Peace, & affectionate Happiness. — O that I were now with you! I feel it very, very hard to be from you at this trying Time — I dare not think a moment concerning you in this Relation, or I should be immediately ill. But I shall soon return — & bring you back a confident & affectionate Husband. Again, and again, my dearest dearest Sara! — my Wife & my Love, & indeed my very Hope/May God preserve you![18]

So happy was he made by Sara's letter, so joyous an omen for a future of domestic bliss did he see it, that he informed her that if their new child turned out to be a boy (which he had no serious doubts would be the case) it must be named Crescelly Coleridge.

Sara went ahead with engaging Mrs Railton and concealed from S.T.C. the forebodings now besetting her in respect of her coming confinement. However she allowed herself to confide in Mrs George Coleridge (to whom she wrote on 12th December in reply to a "long and kind letter" from Ottery). "You were mistaken in the number of my little ones," wrote Sara, "I have only two alive — but in the course of eight or ten days I expect and hope to have another; I would to Heaven those 8 or 10 days were past! for I am such a fool to get more and more a coward, and (at times) full of *fears and dread* (if you should chance to see Samuel before I am confined, do not tell him *this*). I know it is his intention if he can so manage matters to peep in at his native spot, unless he is suddenly hurried off by Mr T.W. to some distant place, though upon second thoughts it is not likely he can be with you before the time of my confinement. I always write cheerfully to him, because the state of his health is such that the least vexation affects his stomach and bowels and does him great injury; nothing but tranquillity keeps him tolerable, care and anxiety destroy him."[19]

Thomas Wedgwood and S.T.C. did not set off for Italy; instead S.T.C. took Thomas Wedgwood up to the Lakes, intending to be in Keswick for Christmas Day, by which time the new baby would be arrived, or arriving. Sara received instructions that Wedgwood's room must be thoroughly warmed and aired; likewise the bed and bedding. A young lass was hired to help with the extra work; fowls were ordered, and "a pound or so of the best salt potted Butter — which Mr Wedgwood likes". The guest was not intending to stay above a night or two.

Mr Jackson was to arrange for a message to meet S.T.C. at Kendal post office, letting him know the latest news about Mrs S.T.C.; news that her husband expected would tell him that he now had another son. Coleridge and Wedgwood arrived at Kendal in the early hours of Christmas Eve; no message had as yet reached Kendal. The travellers pushed on by chaise to Grasmere; there to be met with the news that Sara Coleridge, at half past six the previous morning, had been safely delivered "of a healthy — GIRL!" S.T.C. hurried home to Greta Hall, to find, "Both Mrs Coleridge & the Coleridgiella . . . as well as can be". After a few emotional moments he "left the little one sucking at a great rate" and went to his study to write a letter to Southey: "I had never thought of a Girl as a possible event . . . however I bore the sex with great Fortitude — & she shall be called Sara."[20]


## II

That the Coleridges each made such desperate and repeated attempts to save their marriage reveals how much that marriage meant to them. Their tragedy was that they were combating an enemy too powerfully insidious to be defeated by resolution; even by that strength of resolution which love gives people. It only slowly dawned upon the couple that the real enemy was morphine and not Sara's lack of organic sensibility, or S.T.C.'s adulation of the Wordsworths. The year of 1803 proved to be the year in which not their marriage, but opium, was revealed as the frowning Rock of Reality upon which they had shipwrecked; their marriage, in truth, was a species of shattered mizzen mast to which they clung as they tossed in the engulfing sea.

The year of 1803 from the first went badly for the Coleridges; he became ill with rheumatic fever, resulting from crossing the Kirkstone Pass on foot in a fearful tempest; Sara took longer than usual to recover from her confinement. Sarah Hutchinson, ravaged by nervous tooth-ache and general depression, came to stay at Greta Hall (the object being that Mrs Coleridge should get to know her better and therefore love her better) and completed the triangle of indisposition and dejection. Baby Sara developed the thrush, Hartley succumbed to scarlet fever and the croup. The weather was appallingly wild and wet. S.T.C.'s opium consumption was once again on the upsurge.

From this point onward there lurks, in all the surviving letters from S.T.C. to his wife, an unspelled-out but nonetheless fearful dread; an underlying sense of horror at what they at last both perceived to be happening; S.T.C.'s descent into the clutches of the infamous "opium habit". He was now unmistakably receiving dire signals that opium itself was the root cause of his "gout", his disturbed bowels, constipations, nightmares and "hysterical seizures"; but when he tried to relinquish the drug he was inevitably smitten with a "dreadful falling-abroad" of his "whole frame" which could only be remedied by more opium.[21] He was caught: but he could not get himself to admit this awful truth.

Sara, for her part, saw what was happening (though even she was unwilling to face, as yet, that he was actually trapped, and spoke of the danger as if it still loomed, rather than that it had occurred). She warned him that, unless he stopped taking opium *now*, he would be "unable to break" the habit. He voiced vehement denials that he was in danger, declaring to her repeatedly and loudly that he was capable of giving up wine, brandy, beer, rum, opium, tea; anything that she might mention, at any time he chose; "So very little does anything grow into a Habit with me".[22]

Nevertheless, he added, if she wished it he would resolve to take no more opium. But resolve proved worse than useless; each attempted relinquishment of the drug resulted in a "falling-abroad" and, for relief from the withdrawal symptoms, he reached desperately for the laudanum bottle. In his notebook he scrawled, despairingly, "And sapp'd Resolves, the rotten Banks of Fools against the swelling Tide of Habit".[23]

Both he and Sara now made silent gestures which revealed that each now acknowledged that he had fallen prey to that "Habit". He insured his life for £1,000 with the Equitable Assurance Society (at an initial premium of £31, the annual payments henceforth to be £27). He also made his will, bequeathing the interest on the Assurance policy to his wife and, after her death, the sum itself to Sara *fille*. Sara likewise attempted to make some provision against the terrifying uncertainty of the future; she quietly locked away in her desk the sum of ten pounds: an "iron ration" that was not to be used except in the final extreme of misfortune (in fact this ten pounds was never touched, but was found inviolate in her desk following her own death forty years later; neither Sara *fille* nor Derwent, upon discovering it, could get themselves to spend it; the money was given to charity).[24]

There is evidence that the awful extent of Coleridge's plight was, at this stage, known only to himself and Sara. She could display great discretion when necessary (S.T.C. told her, as one of his backhanded compliments, "In one thing, my dear Love! I do prefer you to any woman, I ever knew — I have the most unbounded Confidence in your Discretion").[25] This confidence was never betrayed by her; as far as she was concerned his "opium habit" remained a secret.

As a result of this secret between them, this sense of being beleaguered against a common enemy, the disillusioned, bed-rock camaraderie of long-established marriage (a little weary at times, a little frayed at the edges, but staunch at the core — a baffling relationship to those who have not experienced it for themselves) increasingly welded the Coleridges together, mysteriously but irrevocably: despite all his outbursts of vilification directed against her in his talk, his letters, his notebooks, the deep undercurrent of truly wedded attachment plugged doggedly along, surfacing spasmodically to reveal itself, then sinking out of sight again.

Sara knew that, on many counts, she was pitied by her family and friends. This she spiritedly resented, she would not have anyone pitying her; above all she would not listen to a word against her husband. She, as his wife, maintained the right to speak to him bluntly in private (yet with discretion, now that she understood the effect that blunt speech had upon him) but to hear him harshly judged by others was a thing she would not tolerate. It seems that at some point during that summer either Southey, or Edith, or perhaps both, voiced some sympathy with her in her predicament. She sent a stout rebuff, "My husband is a good man — his prejudices — and his prepossessions sometimes give me pain, but we all have a somewhat to encounter in this life — I should be a very, very happy Woman if it were not for a few things — and my husband's ill health stands at the head of these evils!"[26]

Plans were laid for him to sojourn abroad for a year or so; Sara now shared his conviction that his only hope of recovery lay in a change of climate and an opportunity to fight his opium habit undisturbed by domestic worries or her interference: an interference entirely well meant but only serving to agitate and irritate S.T.C. and thus worsen his condition. During his opium-sodden weeks before departure he never gave any hint in his conversation with her that this overseas trip might lead to definite separation from her; indeed the reverse, as the time approached for his departure from Greta Hall he showed every sign of sincere reluctance to leave her. The plans he had made for her financial security and general welfare during his absence were exemplary. She, for her part, promised to write him long and regular letters, plying him with detailed news about herself and the children.

Meantime Southey, Edith, and Mary Lovell had arrived at Keswick, but without little Margaret, the child having died, one year old, from "water on the brain from teething" (almost certainly tubercular meningitis). S.T.C. repeatedly expressed his relief at knowing that Sara would have their company during his absence. A scheme had been clinched that he should go to Malta, through the good offices of John Stoddart.[27]

Coleridge left Greta Hall for London on Christmas Eve, 1803; his farewells to his wife were deeply affectionate. He stayed at Dove Cottage over Christmas; his stay prolonged by illness. The former Mary Hutchinson, now married to William (the wedding had taken place the previous October), assisted Dorothy in devotedly tending him; nursing him "with more than Mother's Love",[28] as he reported to Greta Hall, adding that he lay for days "so weak, as scarcely to be able to smile with tenderness & thanks on Mrs Wordsworth & Dorothy".

The reply to this somewhat cloying news was "A BOTTLE OF INK"; lobbed, as it were, like a spluttering grenade from the other side of the Raise. S.T.C. had asked his wife to send him some of Southey's best ink (a particularly strong and indelible mixture) and with this request she now complied; but, no doubt inadvertently, she had put the ink in a cracked bottle and moreover had wrapped the bottle (presumably for safety's sake) in such a way as to make it a *large* parcel, not in the least indicative that it contained ink; nor was "INK" written, by way of warning, on the outside: with the result that when the parcel arrived and was unguardedly opened, the side of the damaged bottle fell out and the ink went all over Dorothy's carpet. The "tender smile" was wiped from S.T.C.'s face and a letter of reprimand and instructions on how to pack ink correctly were sent to Mrs S.T.C.[29]

Coleridge reached London on 23rd January 1804. He spent the next three months waiting for a ship and endeavouring to ensure that Sara would be left free from all outstanding debts ("Save that which we both owe to Southey for his Vice-fathership").[30] He did his best to conceal from his friends and acquaintances in Town that he was what he privately believed himself to be: opium-doomed. Thanks to his drug and drink he quarrelled with everyone (except Charles Lamb) and made embarrassing scenes wherever he went; all this was passed back, by various pens, to Southey at Greta Hall; Southey took pains to keep it from Sara. A letter to Coleridge, from Sarah Hutchinson, expressing her desire to end their unhappy friendship, further disintegrated him.

Because of war with France, Coleridge would have to travel to Malta by convoy; he had booked a passage on a merchant vessel, *Speedwell*, sailing at the close of March from Portsmouth. His final letters, opium-drenched and dejected, made painful reading. His farewell to Sara, written on 1st April, was a bedrugged, fumbling jumble of words, making almost no sense. But words, what were words? Feeling suddenly burst from him with moving poignancy, "What we have been to each other, our understandings will not permit our Hearts to forget!"[31]

He believed he would never return; that he would live out the brief remainder of his life on foreign soil. All hope of Domestic bliss in a home of his own was lost to him: *Speedwell* sped with the wind, placing an ever-widening distance between himself and his wife and children. Lost, all tangible reality, such as it was, of that mysteriously ambiguous ideal other half; who would elude him now to the end of his story. Sara — Asra, Asra — Sara, floated in the opium mists enclosing him like shifting banks of sea fog. He filled his notebooks with laments: for Sara the wife; for Asra the symbol. And always, behind the fog of opium, confusion and despair, there lurked the memory of a vision, "a dream remembered in a dream":[32] a cottage, in frost at midnight by moonlight; an orchard on spring evenings when the thrushes sang; summer mornings of lark rise; a happy young woman with a laughing baby, "a very seraph in clouts", in her arms. He had had it all; and he had lost it. And he swallowed more laudanum and brandy and travelled back through the misty paths of the past, losing himself and wondering, stretching out to reach spectres which dissolved, leaving him sitting in his solitude with his brandy, his laudanum and his notebook, "The Soul in its round & round flight forming narrower circles, till at every Gyre its wings beat against the *personal Self*".[33]

CONSTANCY TO AN IDEAL OBJECT

Since all that beat about in Nature's range,
Or veer or vanish; why should'st thou remain
The only constant in a world of change,
O yearning Thought! that liv'st but in the brain?
Call to the Hours, that in the distance play,
The faery people of the future day —
Fond Thought! not one of all that shining swarm
Will breathe on thee with life-enkindling breath,
Till when, like strangers shelt'ring from a storm,
Hope and Despair meet in the porch of Death!

Yet still thou haunt'st me; and though well I see,
She is not thou, and only thou art she,
Still, still as though some dear embodied Good,
Some living Love before my eyes there stood
With answering look a ready ear to lend,
I mourn to thee and say — "Ah! loveliest friend!
That this the meed of all my toils might be,
To have a home, an English home, and thee!"
Vain repetition! Home and Thou are one.
The peacefull'st cot, the moon shall shine upon,
Lulled by the thrush and wakened by the lark,
Without thee were but a becalmed bark,
Whose Helmsman on an ocean waste and wide
Sits mute and pale his mouldering helm beside.

And art thou nothing? Such thou art, as when
The woodman winding westward up the glen
At wintry dawn, where o'er the sheep-track's maze
The viewless snow-mist weaves a glist'ning haze,
Sees full before him, gliding without tread,
An image with a glory round its head;
The enamoured rustic worships its fair hues,
Nor knows he makes the shadow, he pursues![34]

# CHAPTER SIXTEEN

# Constancy to an Ideal Object —
# Variation on the Theme

My dear Mrs Coleridge . . .

I take it for granted you *know* all that concerns my poor Samuel; that
he is now performing his voyage to the island of Malta, and that he is gone
thither by the advice of many of his friends — medical, and others, to try
the efficacy of the climate. Dr Stoddart, who is lately gone to Malta with
his wife and sister, is an intimate acquaintance of ours, which is to me a
great source of comfort; for although Samuel has been abroad, and is as
well calculated as most men to visit foreign climes, yet he has such
frequent and severe attacks in his bowels that, unless he could have most
minute attention, it might end in very dreadful consequences. I shall be
full of fears until he is safe in the island; partly on account of the French
and partly on his health's account. . . . I expect with impatience a letter
from Gibraltar, & I think I had best not trouble you with this till it
arrives. . . . [1]

Thus Mrs Samuel Taylor Coleridge ("Mrs Sam" to the Ottery
Coleridges) writing to her sister-in-law, Mrs George Coleridge at
Ottery, the date being 20th May 1804. A little over three months later
we find Sara writing again (in a letter undated, but postmarked 1st
September 1804 — there would seem to have been correspondence
between these two dates, but it has not survived),

[Undated. Postmarked September 1 1804]

My dear Mrs Coleridge,

. . . I believe I told you in my last that we had all [received] letters from
Gibraltar; that he was in tolerable health and spirits and would write to
*all* his connections immediately on his arrival at the Island. I have long
concluded that you will be informed of the situation as early as myself —
and I ardently pray it may be soon, for I am now very impatient and
cannot help feeling the time long, but no news has arrived from Malta
since the probable time of his arrival and Southey tells me I must not
expect any news, or be at all anxious until the King has received his
dispatches, which same vessel, he expects, will bring tidings for us. You
will now see the reason I had not written, & I trust, pardon *me*.

I am just returned from a visit of five weeks with our friends the
Wordsworths at Grasmere; I took my three children and servant with
me, and left my sisters & the two Mr Southeys in possession of the house,
and it happened very fortunately just at that time; as they had a

succession of visitors which nearly filled all my part of the house, some of them students from Edinburgh, to visit Mr Henry Southey[2] who is staying here during the four months recess at Edinburgh; he is about one and twenty, and is studying physic.

During my stay at Grasmere Mrs W. was unexpectedly brought to bed of her second child[3] three weeks before we looked for it, but happily all turned out well, both for the mother and child. Before I went to Grasmere Dr Crompton came to Keswick, with his whole family, and they gave me a seat in one of the carriages, and I travelled with them the whole tour of the Lakes. Coleridge had spent a fortnight with them previous to his going abroad, and we were both visiting them at their house near Liverpool on our journey hither from Bristol, with our, then, only child Hartley: they gave me a very pressing invitation to come from Grasmere to their house, to spend some time, and Hartley if I thought proper might fit in the school with their younger children; but I declined taking my family, and intend going in the winter with Derwent only; for Hartley now goes to school, to a day school in Keswick, and it is best he should remain in it until he can have better instruction.

Believe me, dear Mrs C. I was much delighted with the accounts you favoured me with, respecting the families of the name of Coleridge; I am thankful to the Almighty for all the blessings we all enjoy! The first of blessings, health, myself & family partake with you; and although my husband's state of health must necessarily preclude prosperity, yet, if it please God to restore him, I have no doubt but we shall be enabled to live comfortably and bring up the dear children in credit. Respecting my present circumstances, you shall be informed: my husband, (I am told,) is to have a small appointment at Malta in which case I am to receive *the annuity* at home, 150£ a year, for the use of my mother, and my own expences. If he is not able to keep the place from ill health, or he is not appointed from any other cause, he still assures me he shall not receive any of it — he can do without it; but of course, I shall practise the strictest economy during his residence abroad and if any may be reserved, no doubt my endeavour ought not to be wanting. . . .

With respect to his length of stay abroad, I cannot tell until I get a letter, but I should suppose he would undoubtedly continue a year. In any case I shall not expect him until next summer — and I think it is possible not until the summer after! . . . I shall most likely be in London, and Bristol, in the spring of the next year, as my mother wishes much to see me, and the journey is too fatiguing for one in her miserable state of health to undertake, a journey into Cumberland. *The Post*!!!

I was most pleasantly interrupted by the Post, bringing the *long-expected letter*! and was too much agitated by its contents to finish this last night — he has written to no one but me at present. . . . He was very ill during the latter part of the voyage; so ill that the Captain hung out signals of distress to the Commodore, who as soon as possible sent the surgeon on board the *Speedwell*, to his assistance; it was a desperate bowel attack, — and it was many days before he recovered any strength — he had several fainting fits and a difficulty of breathing; but he was quite well when the vessel arrived at the Port of Volletta [sic]; and was received with an "explosion of affection" by Dr Stoddart and his family. . . . Samuel tells me that the heat, great as it is, does not at all annoy him; he meant to take a trip to Sicily and return in September. His letter is dated June 11, 1804.

And now my dear Mrs C. I congratulate you that my letter is nearly ended; and that after I have entreated you to write soon, and to present my most sincerely affectionate regards to each and all of our several connexions, I have only to add that I am most truly, yours ever — Sara Coleridge.

Wednesday night. Keswick.

Hartley begs his kind love to his dear cousins, and wishes they lived near him that they might be his playmates — he says he would take them up the great mountains & shew them how to slide down again, which he says is the finest sport in the world. His birthday is Sepr 19 — he will be 8 years old. Derwent will be 4 on Sepr 14. Sara — 2 years old Decr 23d — she cannot talk yet.[4]

At the time that the second of these letters was written Coleridge had been absent from England for four months and from Greta Hall for eight. There was no denying that these eight months had been restorative ones for Sara. Over the past three years she had been enclosed in bondage with a man in an advanced condition of morphine reliance; an experience always resembling hell on earth and in her case made particularly unbearable because she had been living in a remote situation cut off from the relatives and friends to whom she might otherwise have looked for support. But now all that had changed. Southey and Edith had reappeared upon the scene: Greta Hall no longer echoed to the groans, lamentations and nightmare screams of S.T.C., or the agitated shrieks and imprecations of domestic strife, but instead had become a cheerful, flourishing household (for though S.T.C. has left us a morose account of the daily outbursts of discord and ill-temper between the three sisters *née* Fricker,[5] the portrait drawn by all other pens of Greta Hall during the forty years of Southey's occupancy is, save for the very last period, predominantly a most happy one).

If further proof were required of the disruptive effects of morphine addiction not only upon the victim of the drug but upon all those in any way involved with that victim it is amply provided by the manner in which, once S.T.C. had departed from Keswick, the parties who had hitherto been at odds with each other suddenly found it possible to unite in apparently effortless friendship.[6] "I am just returned from a visit of five weeks to our friends at Grasmere" is a startling statement to hear from Mrs S.T.C.

With Coleridge's frenetic presence removed from the scene all things were viewed in a more reasoned manner.[7] Even Sarah Hutchinson fell into perspective: at the close of 1804 Mrs S.T.C. and Derwent went to stay with her at Park House, a farm near Penrith recently taken by Thomas Hutchinson. Later we find Miss Hutchinson staying at Greta Hall as a guest of the Southeys: indeed, in due course, she became a great favourite. The stock romantic concept of Coleridge and Sarah Hutchinson as unrequited lovers has the ground cut from under it by Greta Hall's acceptance of Miss Hutchinson. The Southeys would never have received a woman whom they in any way believed to have been implicated in an intrigue with Coleridge, nor would Sara have cultivated friendship with such a woman, even to please Samuel. But the better they knew her, the more the Greta Hall inmates liked the commonsensical, pithy, cheerful, in every respect decent Miss Hutchinson who, as in the case of everyone else, with S.T.C. gone from the scene had become quite a different person. Sarah/Asra, the harassed nervous sufferer, vanished now that there was no opium-impregnated poet to pester her with his dejected attentions.

As Sara Coleridge and Sarah Hutchinson would seem (from evidence in surviving correspondence) to have been capable of perfectly frank dialogue together concerning S.T.C., it is probable that Miss Hutchinson, now that she had become intimately friendly with Mrs S.T.C., clarified her position in relation to the absent poet. She did not disguise her "love" for him,[8] but it was of an elevated description, quite removed from vulgar interpretation. Miss Hutchinson's inherent and transparent innocence must have been clearly apparent to Mrs S.T.C.: from now onward we find nothing to suggest that she in any respect regarded Sarah Hutchinson as a rival; whatever the recurring ambivalences of feeling between Mrs S.T.C. and the Wordsworths, for Sarah Hutchinson we find no animosities, or even criticism, expressed either by Mrs S.T.C. or the Southeys. She is never, at any time, referred to or treated as a factor in the breakdown of the Coleridge marriage. This speaks for itself.

Sara herself preserved the hope that if S.T.C. recovered his health, freed himself from opium and thus returned home a restored man, he and she might recover the happiness they had known earlier in their marriage. She realized well enough that his inability to handle any kind of stress precluded his ever achieving the eminence and wealth which might have been his, had he not been so handicapped; nonetheless he might still enjoy a more modest success in life, bringing them simple comforts (at which she would by no manner of means turn up her nose) and enabling them to raise their children to do credit to themselves and the family name. This, then, was Sara's ideal, and to this ideal she clung.

Meanwhile she was happy as a member of the Southey family circle. With Robert and Edith at Greta Hall she did not (as she had remarked to Mrs George Coleridge) miss S.T.C. "in society"; by this she meant that, as a grass widow living alone, she would have been unable to receive or visit any but old friends (such as the Wordsworths or the Cromptons) or spinster or widowed ladies of her local acquaintance living similarly socially circumscribed lives as herself. Under the conventions of that era to be invited everywhere, as she was with the Southeys, or to entertain a non-stop summer cavalcade of Lakers, as the Southeys did with Sara as assisting hostess, would have been out of the question for a respectable matron whose husband was absent from home. But with her sister and brother-in-law (himself now becoming something of a literary lion) in residence with her, all was pleasantly different. Sara was accepted everywhere, by everyone; life was immeasurably gayer than it had ever been with poor Samuel as head of the household. Relieved of the tensions, anxieties and miseries of life with a morphine victim, Sara bloomed. All commented upon her healthy appearance; her plump and sparkling beauty was extensively admired (except by the Wordsworth ladies who, both being thin, in the way of the lean passed disapproving comments upon the better padded).

News from S.T.C. was received but rarely: he left Malta for Syracuse on 25th September 1805, lingering in Sicily until late October. He then went to Rome, travelling there via Naples where he was unable to stay, as he had planned, because of the advance of Napoleon's armies. In December Sara received a letter from S.T.C. in which he assured her that he would shortly be returning home via Vienna: news also reached Grasmere and Keswick from Stoddart, through the Lambs, that S.T.C. was returning home and, when last heard from, had been in Trieste. By the end of December both Greta Hall and Dove Cottage were in daily expectation of his arrival in England. His failure to appear prompted much concern lest he should have been taken by the French. "Heaven preserve him from Captivity in France!"[9]

But Coleridge was still in Rome (where he finally wintered). Despite his assurances that he had intended returning home without delay he remained in Rome until May 1806, when the spring campaigning and renewed advance of the French necessitated his departure from Italy. With a companion, Thomas Russell (a friend of the Ottery Coleridges) he made for Leghorn, via Florence and Pisa. From there he and Russell set sail for England on 22nd June, in an American ship, *Gosport*, and entered quarantine at Stangate Creek, Portsmouth on 11th August. S.T.C. finally set foot once more on his native land on 17th August, at Halstow, in Kent.

It was on 15th August that news first reached Sara, via Ottery, that his ship was lying off Portsmouth, in quarantine. Overcome with happiness she at once began writing letters to all her relatives and friends, giving them the joyful news. The past lay in the past; a new start was now to be made. "I have no doubt but we shall be enabled to live comfortably and bring up the dear children in credit."

# CHAPTER SEVENTEEN

## *"The Best Friends in the World"* (1)

I

While Sara, full of buoyant optimism, was writing her happy letters, S.T.C. moved in with the Lambs and began telling everyone that he could not face the prospect of returning to his wife. "He dare not go home, he recoils so much from the thought of domesticating with Mrs Coleridge, with whom, though on many counts he much respects her, he is so miserable that he dare not encounter it. What a deplorable thing!"[1]

The only person to whom S.T.C. did not make his dismal admission was Sara herself. He would not write a line to her, but instead begged Mary Lamb to write to Southey and Wordsworth asking them to exert pressure upon Sara to persuade her to agree to a separation, without his having to confront her himself. Mary Lamb, however, balked; refusing to do his dirty work for him. She wrote to Dorothy Wordsworth: "I think of the letter I received from Mrs Coleridge, telling me, as joyful news, that her husband is arrived, and I feel it very wrong in me even in the remotest degree to do anything to prevent her seeing her husband — she and her husband being the only people who ought to be concerned in the affair."[2]

In the past, when discussing with Coleridge the possibility of separation, the Wordsworths had rashly (though with undoubted sincerity) promised that he might live with them. Now they found themselves hoisted with their own petard. Coleridge expressed not only his intention of seeking refuge under their roof, but also of bringing Hartley and Derwent with him. He explained to the Wordsworths that he must have the boys in his care; if they remained with their mother they would act as "bird lime", fastening him to her inasmuch as whenever he wished to see them he would have to see her also. She, of course, was so far in utter ignorance of all this talk, but at last, upon Mary Lamb's adamant and persistent insistence, S.T.C. wrote to his wife. But he made no mention of separation; sending, instead, affectionate greetings and indicating that he was all anxiety to be back with her and the children and that his return was imminent.

He failed to materialize. Sara's initial joy at his arrival in England had by now changed to acute anxiety. At length Wordsworth took up the cudgels on her behalf and sent S.T.C. a sharpish note saying that he was prepared to meet him in London to discuss plans for the future, if he did not propose coming northward; but in any case, "[It] is absolutely necessary that you should decide upon something immediately to be done; or that Mrs Coleridge should be furnished with some reason for your not coming down as her present uncertainty and suspense is intolerable".[3]

Dorothy, for her part, was describing the problem to Lady Beaumont,

> We have long known how unfit Coleridge and his wife were for each other; but we had hoped that his ill-health, and the present need his children have of his care and fatherly instructions, and the reflections of his own mind during this long absence would have so wrought upon him that he might have returned home with comfort, ready to partake of the blessings of friendship . . . and to devote himself to his studies and his children. I now trust he has brought himself into this state of mind . . . [and] I hope things will not be so bad as he imagines when he finds himself once again with his Children under his own roof.[4]

Spurred by Wordsworth's letter to him, S.T.C. now informed Sara that he would be home on 29th September; he had delayed returning, he explained, because he was arranging a series of lectures to be given by him in Town that coming winter. But once more he failed to appear; he remained in London. Meanwhile the Wordsworths were removing themselves southward for the winter. They now had three children (a second son, Thomas, having been born on 15th June of that year) and though they could, as they put it, "make shift to summer in Dove Cottage"[5] they could no longer winter comfortably therein; four adults (Sarah Hutchinson was increasingly becoming a member of the household) and three little ones filled the cottage to overflowing (if S.T.C. joined them with his two boys the situation would be impossible). Sir George Beaumont, who was rebuilding Coleorton Hall, near Ashby-de-la-Zouch, Leicestershire, and who was consulting Wordsworth on the picturesque laying out of the grounds, had offered the Wordsworths the estate farmhouse as a winter residence and this they had accepted.

They were, at the close of October, on the point of departure for Coleorton when S.T.C. arrived unexpectedly in Penrith, *en route*, at last, for Keswick. A hasty meeting between himself and the Wordsworths, at Kendal, was arranged. The Wordsworths were shattered by both S.T.C.'s appearance and manner. He was "utterly changed": bloated, dazed; avoiding in his conversation anything remotely connec-

ted with personal affairs. At last however he volunteered the announcement that he must either part from his wife or die. The Wordsworths,
de spite their heartfelt hope that he might still learn to live happily with
Sara, were now overborne by pity and concern for him; they heard
themselves assuring him that, once he had seen Mrs S.T.C. and the
details of a separation had been "resolutely" arranged he, with Hartley
and Derwent, must come to Coleorton. The Wordsworths then hurried
away to catch the Leicestershire coach and S.T.C. hired a chaise to take
him to Keswick; where he, abruptly and brutally, would demand a
divorce.

The term "divorce" was, in that day and age, used in the figurative
sense of the "putting aside" or repudiation of a spouse; the legal
dissolution of marriage being virtually unobtainable in England except
for the highly influential few, and even then being of very rare
occurrence. Separation ("divorce") cast inevitable stigma upon the
wife; it invariably suggested to the world that she, for some reason or
other, had failed as a spouse, else why should her husband be "putting
her aside"? Furthermore, since a man would only go to the lengths of
putting his wife aside for some exceedingly serious reason, it was
equally invariably assumed by the world that the wife must be guilty of
some moral transgression (the common mind instantly flew to the
notion of adultery). Whether she deserved it or not, a "divorced"
woman's reputation always suffered.

The terms of the separation, too, invariably went against the wife.
Married women, unless some specific settlement had been made in their
favour, enjoyed no property rights; thus separation could mean real
penury for a woman whose husband refused, or neglected, to make
proper provision for her. Nor had she any powers when it came to her
children; they could be removed from her care without her retaining
any right of access to them. In short, in a totally male-oriented society,
separation could spell complete disaster for the wife, depriving her of
home, money, children, reputation. Nor did she have any redress
against the injustice of her predicament.

Sara and her children received S.T.C. home with joyousness and
touching excitement. Sara knew that he had been talking about
separation while with the Lambs in London, but his affectionate letters
to her had allayed her natural alarm upon hearing these rumours from
Town. Now he informed her, without any prior discussion, that he was
removing Hartley and Derwent to live henceforth with the Wordsworths: her marital status was, for all intents and purposes, to be taken
from her; her good name irretrievably eroded. She had no certainty
that, once Samuel had walked out of her life, he would continue to

provide for her in any way. In short, her entire future was at stake. And for what reason? He could only repeat, over and over again, that he could no longer live with her because of their "unfitness" for one another; due pre-eminently to her "temper & general tone of feeling".[6]

Sara put up an immense fight in the face of what she, not surprisingly, saw as a rank affront and gross injustice (this response he described as "outrageous";[7] she should have accepted the situation meekly). She made impassioned references to their former happiness together; to their children. She appealed to his better nature; did he fully understand what the envisaged separation would mean for her? Did he really wish all the world to see her as an abandoned wife, whose sons had been removed from her care? To leave her, taking the boys with him, was cruel not only to her as a mother but must suggest to the world at large that she was of unprincipled character, no longer to be entrusted with her own children! How could she hope to keep her reputation as a respectable woman? Even if he had no pride (as he boasted he had not) surely he would respect *her* feelings of pride? Had he forgotten her sufferings in Stowey and Bristol; all that painful mortification she had suffered from uncharitable tongues! This had then angered him; would he in the future no longer care whether she was insulted? What had she done to deserve this treatment at his hands?

He remained unmoved (he had dosed himself recklessly with opium in an attempt to anaesthetize himself against her appeals).[8] His (in her view) callous and unjust behaviour moved Sara to remind him of his obligations; to compare his wretched conduct with that of Southey, "the best of men". In the account of all this which S.T.C. sent the Wordsworths he said that Mrs S.T.C., in her arguments against parting, had made every attack upon human weakness (his better nature, in other words) that could be made, but "fortunately there was an indelicacy and artifice which tho' they did not perceptibly lessen my anguish, yet . . . made me see always, and without the possibility of a doubt, that mere selfish desire to have a *rank* in life and not be believed to be that which she really was" (a divorced woman) "without the slightest wish that what was should be otherwise, was at the bottom of all. Her temper, and selfishness, her manifest dislike of me (as far as her nature is capable of a *positive* feeling) and her self-encouraged admiration of Southey as a vindictive feeling in which she delights herself as satirizing me etc etc".[9] And so he mumbled on.

However, as husband and wife disputed their way through the impasse, old sensations of affection and mutual esteem surfaced. By 24th November a parting had been agreed upon and terms drawn up: civilized terms, with them remaining "good friends". "It is his wish that she should be in such a state of mind as [for him] to be able to visit her in a friendly way," Dorothy reported to Mrs Clarkson.[10] For Sara's part, all her surviving comments indicate that she finally agreed to "a friendly separation, with visits" because she became frightened by Samuel's vehement insistence that if he lived with her continuously it would be the death of him.

S.T.C., anxious to show the Wordsworths that he had followed their advice and had been "resolute" in his handling of the matter, assured them that, in spite of the envisaged visits, "We have determined to part absolutely and finally; Hartley and Derwent to be with me but to visit their Mother [during holiday times] as they would do if at a publick school".[11] Little Sara would remain with her mother, apart from occasional visits to her father. Mrs S.T.C. was to be provided with an adequate and regular allowance.

It is not improbable that Southey had a part to play in advising Sara to agree to a separation which, with its careful stipulations, gave her continuing access to her sons, protection of her good name, and financial security. If S.T.C. continued to visit her "in a friendly way", as he professed to hope to be the case, nothing would, in fact, be greatly altered in her life; her marriage, for several years past, had been little more than visits (not always particularly friendly ones, moreover) from S.T.C. between his protracted absences from home.

Towards the end of November S.T.C. departed for Coleorton, taking Hartley with him. The six-year-old Derwent remained with his mother and sister.

## II

The Coleridge who returned to England in 1806 was in an immeasurably worse state of morphine confusion than the man who had left in 1804. He had quit home vowing to himself that he would conquer opium or die in the attempt: far from beating opium he had sunk even more hopelessly into its clutches. How close he had come to suicide while in Malta and Italy the notebooks reveal: he had been held back only by the knowledge that if he took his life there would be no chance of his children benefiting from his life insurance; the Wedgwood annuity would be lost; his family would be left utterly destitute. So he had struggled on.

Now, in the autumn of 1806, he was in a state of advanced organic psychosis, his body's entire chemistry radically altered by the drug; completely oriented to morphine and thus disoriented to all else (a condition then unrecognized by medicine). He himself was, intermittently, able to discern that he was in the clutches of delusion, but these glimpses came like rare appearances of clear sky between veil upon veil of cloud. For him, for the greater part of the time, delusion *was* his reality. Much later, when he was able to look back upon himself as he had been during this terrible passage through oceans of opium, he perceived that his deluded condition had indeed been (as De Quincey described it) a "looking thro' the magic glass of an opium-poisoned imagination": in short, something resembling a hideous bewitchment: possession by the daemon of opium "Old Black" himself.

The Wordsworths still failed to recognize the full extent of S.T.C.'s destruction by opium, though they accepted that he brought most of his troubles upon himself through "mismanagement". Their response to the situation was classic; like thousands of other good people who have supposed that a drug victim may be saved by firm, yet sympathetic handling, they now determined to save Coleridge. Hitherto they had never had him fully to themselves; Mrs S.T.C., they knew, had attemped to be firm with him but she had *lacked sympathy*. Under the Wordsworth roof firm handling would be partnered by *sensibility*; the prevailing mood of the household would be entirely, happily, sympathetic; Coleridge would be truly tranquil, which he had never had the chance to be, before: he would no longer need opium.

The Wordsworths had no conception of the real nature of the problem. Thus Dorothy, writing to Lady Beaumont to tell her that S.T.C. would be joining the Wordsworths at Coleorton, remarked confidently, "If he is not inclined to manage himself, we can manage him".[12] It was the voice of blissful ignorance.

The much harder-headed Robert Southey, on the other hand, upon having his brother-in-law back at Greta Hall had quickly reached the conclusion that S.T.C. was no longer worth trying to manage. "His habits are so murderous of all domestic comfort that I am only surprised Mrs C. is not rejoiced at being rid of him," Southey wrote confidentially to Rickman,

[He] besots himself with opium, or with spirits, till his eyes look like a Turk's who is half reduced to idiotcy by the practise — he calls up the servants at all hours of the night to prepare food for him — he does in short all things at all times except the proper time — does nothing which he ought to do, and every thing which he ought not. His present scheme is to live with Wordsworth — it is from his idolatry of that family that this has begun — they have always humoured him in all his follies, listened to his complaints of his wife, and when he has complained of his itch, helped him to scratch, instead of covering him with brimstone ointment, and shutting him up by himself. . . . I myself, as I have told Coleridge, think it highly fit that the separation should take place, but by no means so that it should ever have been necessary.[13]

To this Rickman replied, "If Wordsworth is to blame (as seems likely) he will suffer adequate punishment I think in the society of a Man, as lost as C."[14] A prophetic observation.

Thus it was that, while the Wordsworths were convinced that they (at considerable inconvenience to themselves) were about to rescue S.T.C. from a tragic condition into which he had fallen chiefly because of an unsuitable wife's lack of sympathetic understanding, on the other side of the Raise opinion held, with equal conviction, that it was the Wordsworths who were responsible for the failure of the Coleridge marriage.

The warmly fraternal relationship between Sara and Southey and her frankly avowed admiration for him had somehow persuaded S.T.C. that she would henceforth remain in the Southey household. The Wordsworths were now anxiously casting their minds over the necessity of finding a larger place than Dove Cottage: S.T.C. suggested Greta Hall, assuring the Wordsworths that Southey intended quitting Keswick in the near future and that where the Southeys went Mrs S.T.C. would go too; Greta Hall would therefore fall vacant. Dorothy and Mary were not happy with the idea (they had "a hundred objections" to Greta Hall as a house and "a hundred more to taking Mrs C.'s place there", said Dorothy); at last they consented to the idea but only out of consideration of S.T.C.'s feelings, the convenience of his books being at Greta Hall, and his wish not to part Hartley and Wilsy[15] (no fatherly qualms were voiced over the separating of Hartley from his mother).

On 7th February S.T.C. wrote to Sara (the letter has not survived) enquiring, through her, after Southey's plans and making it clear that, if and when Southey vacated his part of the house, S.T.C. hoped to establish himself therein with the Wordsworths.

Although there had been considerable talk of the Southeys leaving Greta Hall there had been no suggestion that Sara might accompany them; all her plans were built around her remaining at Greta Hall, returning there after a visit to Ottery. But if, Southey having left, S.T.C. and the Wordsworths were to move into the vacant "front house" Sara would be obliged to quit, though she had nowhere else to go. In effect, S.T.C.'s scheme would result in Sara being turned out of her own home: an intolerable situation. Almost frantic with alarm and indignation she ran to show S.T.C.'s letter to Southey.

He responded with a vehement "That be hanged for a tale!" With his assistance Sara immediately penned a categorical letter of reply; "Southey has no thought of leaving Keswick, it is out of the question," going on to add that, after her visit to Ottery, she would return to Greta Hall and remain there "as long as the Southeys do". In this abrupt, wholly unpremeditated fashion, Southey made his decision to settle in Keswick for good. He wrote to Danvers,

If I had not remained here C. has so little regard to common decency of appearances that he would have brought the Wordsworths here, and his wife must have removed: that is if Jackson (who tho' C. does not know it abominates that family for their systematic selfishness) would have permitted it, which he says flatly to me he would not. . . . For her [the separation] is a very happy thing, for not only his habits are destructive of all comfort, but — what I should once never have thought possible, his temper has become so too: and as the thing is done with systematic civility, and they are to continue the best friends in the world, I think it the wisest thing they can do, things being as they are, tho' that they are as they are, I consider, as I have told him, are his own fault.[16]

# CHAPTER EIGHTEEN

# "The Best Friends in the World" (2)

## I

The Wordsworths were now discovering precisely what it meant to live with a man in the nadir of morphine reliance. They could not "manage" Coleridge any more successfully than his wife had been able to manage him. He was impossible. Dorothy attempted to convince herself that Coleridge did not take such strong stimulants as formerly, but she confided to Lady Beaumont, "I feel he will never be able to leave them off entirely". He ailed "at some time in every day" and was in fact far more of a trial to the Wordsworths than they were prepared, at that time, to admit.

Wordsworth's reading aloud, over the New Year at Coleorton, of his now completed *Poem on the Growth of an Individual Mind* (later to be known as *The Prelude*), a work dedicated to S.T.C., had the effect of first stimulating him with excitement and joy, then flooding him with dejection at his own failure as a poet and jealousy of Wordsworth's achievement. There was further, even more painful, ground for jealousy. Sarah Hutchinson was making it increasingly clear that she found S.T.C.'s infatuated attentions unwelcome: indeed, the notebook's despairing entries indicate that she found them positively repugnant. She tried, tactfully but unmistakably, to discourage and avoid S.T.C. Upon the other hand, as an integrated and beloved member of the Wordsworth household she entertained a deep and undisguised, albeit wholly sisterly, love for William; while he was similarly strongly attached to her. Sarah's preference for William's company drove S.T.C. to a frenzy of jealousy and self-pity. He kept his despairing broodings to himself; but Wordsworth noted the change in his manner: the coldness and manifest withdrawal of love. Wordsworth, in his turn, was deeply hurt.

Dorothy Wordsworth, writing several months later about this winter spent with Coleridge, was to confess, "We had long experience at Coleorton, that we could not make him happy".[1]

Coleridge's dream of adoptive domestic bliss with the Wordsworths having evaporated, an alternative scheme now began to occupy his thoughts. In pursuance of their intention to remain "the best friends in the world" S.T.C. and Sara had agreed to pay a visit to Ottery before parting "absolutely and finally" (occasional friendly meetings excluded). A visit had been requested by the George Coleridges, during S.T.C.'s absence in Malta; Sara had promised them that, when he returned home, he, the children and herself, should travel to Ottery to see Mrs Coleridge senior (now very old and frail) and Samuel's brothers, sisters-in-law, nephews and nieces. As Sara saw it, despite the separation, this visit must still take place; partly because it had been promised and partly because such a visit accompanied by a little tactful explaining that Samuel would henceforth mainly be working and therefore residing in London while she remained at Greta Hall, and that the boys were to go away to school at Ottery, but, of course, would return to her during the holidays, was a perfect solution to what must otherwise be a most damaging and painful situation for her. Ottery would never accept her as a divorced woman, but she did not intend that the word "divorce" should be mentioned. She was proud and happy at belonging to the Coleridge family and wished desperately to continue to remain an acknowledged member; also it was most important for the children that they should not be associated with an openly broken marriage. For their sakes, if for no other reason, discretion was imperative. She impressed this upon Samuel; he appeared to be in agreement.

Meanwhile Thomas Russell, who had been S.T.C.'s companion during the journey back to England, and had formed a strong regard for him, had drawn for Ottery a moving picture of S.T.C. in his misfortunes: nine-tenths of his papers and manuscripts lost (owing to the rapid advance of the French upon Naples), no more than a few guineas in his pocket, and, greatest affliction of all, in a "miserably hypochondriacal state".[2] George Coleridge (who, despite occasional uncomfortable doubts about Samuel's sanity, always entertained a warm affection for his youngest brother, as well as high regard for him as a classical scholar) consequently wrote to Samuel saying that their brother Edward was resigning as assistant master at the King's School, Ottery; George was hoping that Samuel would take his place.[3]

Now that S.T.C. had lost his obsessive desire to live with the Wordsworths, Ottery seemed to him the best alternative refuge: it afforded the prospect of free boarding and schooling for Hartley and Derwent and a home and occupation for himself; Sara would remain at Greta Hall with Southey. There was only one obstacle to be surmounted with regard to Ottery; if S.T.C. and Sara did not take up residence there together as man and wife explanation would certainly be demanded by George, who, as a priest as well as a schoolmaster, might be relied upon to object to the separation of Samuel and Sara and find it out of the question, on moral grounds, to have as assistant master in his school a man who was "divorced" from his wife.

Thus S.T.C. now cautiously wrote to George Coleridge, attempting to make clear that the responsibility for the breakdown of the marriage rested entirely with Sara; he was, as he told George, without "self reproach" in the matter:

> . . . with many excellent qualities, of strict modesty, attention to her children, and economy, Mrs Coleridge has a temper & general tone of feeling which after a long [and] . . . patient Trial I have found wholly incompatible with even an endurable Life, & such as to preclude all chance of my ever developing the talents, which my Maker has entrusted to me. . . . The few friends, who have been Witnesses of my domestic Life, have long advised separation, as the necessary condition of every thing desirable for me — nor does Mrs Coleridge herself state or pretend to any objection on the score of attachment to me; — that it will not look *respectable* for her, is the sum into which all her objections resolve themselves. At length, however, it is settled . . . but Mrs Coleridge wishes — & very naturally — to accompany me into Devonshire that our separation may appear free from all shadow of suspicion of any other cause than that of unfitness & unconquerable difference of Temper. . . . However, we part as Friends — the boys of course will be with me. What more need be said, I shall have an opportunity of saying when we are together. — If you wish to write to me, before my arrival, my address will be — Mr Wade's, Aggs' Printing-office, St Augustin's Back, Bristol.[4]

Sara Coleridge knew nothing of these developments and had no idea that S.T.C. had informed Ottery of the impending separation. In March of that year 1807 she, with Derwent and little Sara, set out on the first leg of her journey to Bristol; where S.T.C., with Hartley, was due to collect her in April. They would then all go to stay with Poole in Nether-Stowey, and from there would go to Ottery.

On 4th April S.T.C., Hartley and the Wordsworths left Coleorton and set out for London, where they would holiday for a while and from where S.T.C. and Hartley would presently take the coach for Bristol. During the course of the journey S.T.C., enmeshed darkly in his jealousy of Wordsworth, persuaded himself that Sarah Hutchinson, at an hotel where the party stayed, had been to bed with Wordsworth.[5] It was pure hallucination on his part: "the magic glass of an opium-poisoned imagination" had been at work again, distorting his view of Wordsworth just as the same magic glass had distorted the way in which he saw his wife, saw Poole. The more the morphine addict loves a person and the closer the relationship, the more terrible are the distortions in relation to that person. On the other hand, the part which Sarah/Asra played in his hallucinatory experience (basically a masochistic exercise on the part of Coleridge's diseased imagination) was essentially a gratifying one, since it allowed him to tear himself apart with agonized laments and address wildly reproachful soliloquies to Asra in the privacy of his notebook.

Yet, while all this fearful turmoil was seething within him (like fire hidden in the heart of a volcano) on the surface all remained friendly: he permitted himself to give no hint of his awful suspicions. His old special warmth for Wordsworth no longer evinced itself, but nonetheless the friendship was in no way ruptured, despite S.T.C.'s dreadful inner broodings. The party pursued London pleasures and distractions, including seeing a play at Covent Garden (*Town and Country* with Kemble in the lead), with plenty of "sliding scenes" or illusions; Hartley was particularly delighted by a moon which Sarah Hutchinson disparagingly compared to a copper warming-pan. The play was followed by a pantomime, *Mother Goose*, with the celebrated clown, Grimaldi, "in all his glory".

On another occasion (two occasions, to be precise) the party saw the Drury Lane melodrama, *The Wood Demon*, by "Monk" Lewis, with Bannister in the lead as the blood-curdling villain. Hartley was privately furious at Sarah Hutchinson's refusal to admire the show: she was unable to conceal her "disgust at adult noise and nonsense"; she was especially disgusted at the way in which "the galleries and pit laughed immoderately" at the comic scenes. Indeed Hartley never forgave her for this; years later getting his own back on her in a piece he wrote about this play in a collection of essays entitled *The Wisdom of our Ancestors*.[6]

If Hartley had ever been the joyous dancing elf that his elders loved to enthuse over, that joyous elf had now disappeared. The months spent at Coleorton could not have been happy for the child. He had long known that the relationship between his parents was a troubled one and at Coleorton he undoubtedly decided that his father's attachment to Sarah Hutchinson was the source of the trouble. For this he bore her intense resentment (his dislike of her is manifest in his letters; as Griggs remarks, Sarah Hutchinson hardly ever receives praise from Hartley). He also (as he confessed in adulthood) resented the exclusive element in the close union of the Wordsworth family (the knowledge that they would never really admit his mother to their "inner circle"). Finally, "the ladies . . . were somewhat too apt to 'season their fire-side with personal talk'".[7] Some of this personal talk touched on his parents and was overheard by the child.

Meanwhile Sara had arrived at Bristol and Derwent and little Sara had been introduced, at College Street, to their aunts Martha and Eliza and "an old lady, very invalidish" who was their "mother's mother".[8] S.T.C. was expected, with Hartley, in Bristol by the end of April; he was a month late in arriving and he no sooner appeared than he was taken ill, which further delayed the departure to Stowey. However at last he rallied and on 5th June — or possibly 6th — (to quote Sara), "We all 5 proceeded to Stowey to Mr Poole's most hospitable abode, remaining most pleasantly with him for 2 months, and did not go to Ottery St Mary *at all*".[9]

## II

Why they never went to Ottery, a visit there having been the sole reason for the prolonged and expensive family trek, was a matter which Sara never completely fathomed.

The five of them arrived, as stated, at Stowey, to receive the warmest possible welcome from the ever-generous Poole (who, of course, had been the first of the loved ones to fall victim to the distortions of the "magic glass"). Yet Poole, in spite of long neglectful silences from Coleridge, interspersed by a few highly critical letters, and a distinctly unhappy visit from him during Poole's sojourn in London in the early months of 1804, was now overjoyed to have Coleridge and his family under his roof in Stowey, seeing it as a revival of the happy past.

Despite the warmth of the welcome Coleridge was dejected, uncommunicative and unwell; though he accompanied Sara and the children on social rounds and on these occasions recaptured some of his old bonhomie. Sara, it went without saying, quite apart from her joy at being back in Poole's "beloved abode" was in raptures at meeting so many old friends; "We made visits to Asholt (Mr Brice's), to Enmire (the Cruikshanks) and to Bridgwater at the Chubb's".[10] But never a word from S.T.C. that it was time to proceed to Ottery.

Sara sensed that something had gone wrong, but feared to ask questions lest she upset her husband. The children, less inhibited, enquired artlessly and with increasing impatience, "When were they going to visit 'Father's Mamma'?". Somehow it leaked out that there had been a letter from Uncle George Coleridge; there was illness at Ottery, explained S.T.C., the visit could not take place. Sara pressed him for details; he changed the story of vague illness to the more specific one that the Ottery children had all had measles and the families had gone to Sidmouth to recuperate.[11] Sara, her suspicions increasingly roused, asked to be allowed to see the letter; S.T.C. became truculent and refused her request. Finally she gave up asking (of course, as she told Mrs Lovell many years later, she could always have seen the letter simply by taking it herself from S.T.C.'s portable desk; but she had her pride and self-respect and so "didn't chuse to" adopt this subterfuge).

The true facts behind this mystery were as follows: George Coleridge's letter, in reply to S.T.C.'s of 2nd April, had been written on 6th April and sent, as requested, to Bristol, where it had lain until S.T.C.'s delayed arrival there at the end of May. S.T.C., guessing only too well what George would have to say about the severence of marriage vows and fearing a firm rebuff from one who had always been for him a father figure rather than a brother, delayed opening the letter until after 27th June; then, further procrastination being impossible, the letter was opened.

George made it clear that the Samuel Coleridges would not be received. Obviously (though he did not actually say so in words) George Coleridge, who over the years had come to know Samuel disconcertingly well, suspected that once Mrs Sam and the children had been fetched to Ottery, Sam would make one of his celebrated bolts leaving Ottery to support the abandoned ones. This dark intimation of Samuel's possible true intentions filled George with agitation; he spilled out every reason he could think of that would prevent Samuel from coming: everyone was ill; "We have now ten patients in bed . . . and our poor aged mother is with difficulty carried up and down stairs and cannot of course be at this period of her frail existence incommoded. . . . Mrs James Coleridge who has an hereditary nervousness and despondency and who at present is in little less than a state of wretchedness, would be out of her senses at the very approach of a family in addition to her own". Furthermore George had made arrangements to give up the school, so that there was no chance that Hartley and Derwent might be there as boarders under his care. "As you are going to Bristol and determine to separate from your Wife (a step which in my own opinion no argument in your situation can justify), make your arrangements there among her Friends. To come to Ottery for such a purpose would be to create a fresh expence for yourself and to load my feelings with what they could not bear without endangering my life — I pray you therefore do not so." He gave brotherly advice, "Your situation is in no way desperate if your mind does not make it so. . . . For God's sake strive to put on some fortitude and do nothing rashly. . . . Your male children might be properly sent out and a settlement would probably be made by Mrs Coleridge's friends for the maintainance of herself and Daughter, when you might live apart for some time till you had better considered the nature of what you were doing."[12]

It was certainly not a letter to show Sara.

S.T.C. was deeply incensed by George's reaction and comments, even though they were far from unexpected. As usual he at once exonerated himself of all blame and commenced wild recriminations against George and the entire tribe of Ottery Coleridges, complaining that he had been insulted by them; however by mid-September he had decided that, by their behaviour towards him, they had at least "released his conscience wholly from all connection with a family to whom he was indebted only for misery".[13]

Although he did not realize it, S.T.C. was indebted to George for having prevented (or, more correctly, in the light of what was to transpire, for having delayed) a rupture with Josiah Wedgwood. News of Thomas Wedgwood's death in 1805 had been withheld from S.T.C. by Sara, with well-meant motives. Josiah, not realizing this, had been surprised at not having heard from Coleridge in connection with the event, but had excused him, on the grounds of his genius, "as privileged to dispense with the ordinary rules that govern the conduct of common men".[14]

When Coleridge was announced as being back in England, Wedgwood applied to him for material for a "Life" of Thomas Wedgwood which Mackintosh was writing. No reply whatever came from Coleridge, despite all urgent appeals. By January Wedgwood had lost all his benign feelings towards genius and was deeply hurt and annoyed. However it so happened that his eldest son was a pupil at George Coleridge's school and the boy was now taken ill with scarlet fever; his parents hastened to his bedside. George Coleridge, during the course of the weeks of anxiety which kept the Wedgwoods much at Ottery (receiving "hospitality and cordial kindness" from the George Coleridges) was able, when the subject of S.T.C. and his apparently inexcusable behaviour came under discussion, to mollify Wedgwood by offering tactful excuses on S.T.C.'s behalf and describing "his miserably hypochondriacal state" which prevented him from keeping up any kind of a regular correspondence. Josiah, who had known only too well the effects of Thomas Wedgwood's "hypochondria", was flooded with pity for S.T.C.

But when another two months had passed without a line from S.T.C., Wedgwood, not surprisingly, lost all patience. He sent Poole an ominous, "Have you heard or seen anything of Coleridge? . . . I wish to write to him, though I shall do it unwillingly, for, feeling as I do, I cannot write to him as a friend, and I would rather have no communication with him than as a mere stranger. Or, if you know where Mrs Coleridge is, I would write to her, as it is a matter of business."[15] This suggests that Wedgwood was approaching the point where the Coleridge annuity might be coming under unfavourable scrutiny. This letter, fortunately, arrived at Stowey shortly after the Coleridges had arrived there and, shown the letter and urged by Poole, S.T.C. at last wrote to Wedgwood: the profuse apologies, excuses and explanations once more moved the patron to sympathy, and ominous sounds from Etruria (temporarily) ceased. Poole, to seal the good work, also wrote on S.T.C.'s behalf.

This visit to Stowey cemented the old alliance of Poole and Sara Coleridge. During her stay at Poole's she and he discussed S.T.C.'s problems, which also meant her problems. The subsequent exchange of letters between Poole and Sara over the next twenty-seven years (her letters have survived, his were doubtless burned in the great letter holocaust) reveal that there were few secrets between the two friends, who, drawn together from the outset by their shared love and anxiety for Coleridge, continued to share the melancholy embers of that love and an undiminishing anxiety for him who had once been Samuel, "my adored, divine husband"; Col, "a meteor from the clouds".

# CHAPTER NINETEEN

## *"The Best Friends in the World" (3)*

Sara and her children returned to Bristol on 30th July; S.T.C. lingered at Stowey with Poole for a little longer. He then joined his wife in Bristol; his plan was to go to London, to organize his new lecture season, while Mrs S.T.C. would return to Keswick, escorted by a young "Mr de Quincey, who was a frequent visitor to C. in College St".[1] Accordingly Sara, the children and De Quincey departed for the North at the close of October, while S.T.C. removed himself not to London, but the home of some Bristol acquaintances, a John Morgan, his wife and her sister: kind, generous people who succumbed to S.T.C.'s fatal charm as though he had indeed cast a spell over them.

He had first met Morgan, through Southey, in 1795; Morgan had subsequently married a Miss Mary Brent, whose sister, Charlotte, made her home with them. Coleridge rapidly persuaded himself that, in these two young women, he had rediscovered the Hutchinson sisters, Mary and Sarah: the clock had been miraculously put back by a decade; here once again, regenerated through the magic looking glass of opium, were those "dear, dear Sisters, prized all price above!" Before long S.T.C. was carrying in his vest pocket locks of hair from the heads of Mary and Charlotte, who were comforting him, as had Mary and Sarah Hutchinson, with "more than sisters' love". There was even a couch, or sofa, scene; as we learn from a letter he wrote to Mary Morgan, recalling the evening "when dear Morgan was asleep in the Parlour, and you and beloved Caroletta asleep at opposite Corners of the Sopha in the Drawing Room, of which I occupied the center in a state of blessed self-consciousness, as a drowsy Guardian of your Slumbers". From this sofa scene there resulted, of course, a poem, *To Two Sisters*; a fresh variation upon the *Day Dream* theme, commencing,

> To know, to esteem, to love, — and then to part —
> Makes up Life's tale to many a feeling heart;
> Alas for some abiding-place of Love
> O'er which my spirit, like the mother dove,
> Might brood with warming wings! . . .[2]

The poet went on to lament his "soul and body" wasting "daily with the poison of sad thought" arising from "one guiltless fault" (his mistaken marriage). The poem, signed SIESTI, appeared in *The Courier*, 10th December 1807. Early in the New Year of 1808 he went one step further in his attempt to recapture the past; he tried to create an Asra situation with Charlotte Brent, sending her, it would seem, a letter of wild lament, such as he had inflicted upon Sarah Hutchinson, torturing and wooing her simultaneously. But the Morgans were not Wordsworths; there was a lack of organic sensibility in St James' Square, Bristol, which resulted in these advances being looked upon with manifest disapproval. S.T.C. wrote again hastily, entreating "dear Miss Brent to think of what I wrote as the mere *light-headedness* of a diseased Body, and a heart sore stricken". Nonetheless he couldn't restrain himself from one more despairing howl of anguish, "I love her most dearly! O had I health and youth, and were what I once was — but I played the fool, and cut the throat of my Happiness, of my genius, of my utility, in compliment to the merest phantom of overstrained Honor! — O Southey! Southey! an unthinking man were you — and are — & will be"[3] (Southey, it must be remembered, was on cordial terms of friendship with John Morgan and maintained a correspondence with him; in abusing Southey to the Morgans Coleridge was upon uncertain ground).

The appearance of *To Two Sisters* caused deep indignation and resentment at Greta Hall; for Mrs S.T.C. it was the final Esteesian straw. When Mary and Dorothy Wordsworth made yet one more attempt to persuade Mrs S.T.C. of the importance of a categorical public announcement about the separation rather than to allow things to drift on as they were now, with Coleridge at one end of the country and herself at the other (giving the world strong cause to suspect that he had brutally deserted his wife rather than having had a civilized "separation"), Mrs S.T.C. replied, "Well, he may stay away if he likes; I care nothing about it if he will not talk of it". And with this she put an end to discussion. The Dove Cottage ladies were appalled by her apparent flippancy. "If she had not so little feeling I should pity her very much," Dorothy reiterated in the ever-receptive ear of Catharine Clarkson. However, that said, "I feel and know that wounded pride and the world's remarks are all that give her pain".[4] The truth was that Sara Coleridge had been flayed to a standstill.

News presently reached the north that Coleridge's lectures, which had begun at the Royal Institution, on 15th January 1808, were proving to be something less than an outstanding success, due to postponements and non-appearances occasioned by his "ill health". A spate of confused and alarming letters from him suddenly burst in all directions. To his wife went an overwrought missive, describing his most recent frightening bout of illness, his inflamed bowels, his dark suspicions of the stone and the imminence of his death, together with assurances that, with his end now so near at hand, he forgave her for all the sorrows and torments which she had brought upon him and begged to be forgiven for any pain that he might "wilfully" have caused her. Sara, wearied beyond endurance by his complaints, his threats of imminent death, his bosom-beating; with being forgiven for transgressions she hadn't committed; with his general hypochondria and self-induced miseries; responded with a calculated breeziness which almost choked him with indignation and self-pity, poured out in a wild effusion to the Morgans,

> I wrote her 3 letters, the last of them, almost a farewell to her & to my Children — written with great effort during Pain and desperate weakness, in which I assured her of my forgiveness & begged her's in return for whatever pain I had wilfully caused her — in short, I will venture to say, that that Letter would draw Tears down the face of your Servant — this day I received the answer. From the beginning to end it is in a strain of *dancing, frisking high spirits* . . . quite the letter of a gay woman writing to some female acquaintance in an hour of mirth — and she notices my illness, the particulars of which and the strong & fearful suspicions entertained of the Stone, in these words — neither more nor less — "*Lord! how often you are ill! YOU must be MORE careful about Colds!*" . . . Not a word respecting my tender & tearful advice to her about the Children — not a single acknowledgement for having nearly doubled the sum for the year, which she herself had stated & settled . . . no! not one simple expression that she was sorry I was obliged to work and lecture while I was so ill. . . . O shocking! it is too clear, that she is glad that her Children are about to be fatherless![5]

This letter was followed by a further tirade directed against his wife, concluding with a demented outburst of ranting, "Did this Woman bring me a Fortune? or give me rank? or procure me introductions & interest? or am I now maintained in Idleness by her money? — O that I had the Heart to do what Justice & Wisdom would dictate — & bring her to her Senses!" And he rambled on,

> Henceforward, I will trouble you no more with this hateful Subject. But only think just enough of it, not to remain too much surprized that my Spirit was so weighed down by her unfeelingness, her seeming pleasure at the anticipation of my being speedily got quit of — me, who in the worst of times had ever felt & expressed as much Joy in her Health, as my Wife, and mother of my Children, as if I had been married to you, or Charlotte, or Mrs Wordsworth or Sarah Hutchinson — I say, wonder not that I was overset — that I seemed to look round a Wilderness, to hear in the

distance the yell & roar of fierce animals, & to see no one that would give me even the Help of Comfort — !⁶

Finally S.T.C. concluded that, as a result of fever induced by Mrs S.T.C.'s cruelty, he would be obliged to postpone his next lecture.

He was now thinking of going to Bristol to stay with the Morgans while placing himself under the medical care of Dr Beddoes; "Wither else can I go?" he asked the Morgans pathetically. "To Keswick? The *sight* of that Woman would destroy me. To Grasmere? — They are still in their Cottage . . . & they have not room scarcely for a Cat . . . And shall I stay here? Alas! it is sad, it is very sad."⁷ As things turned out he remained in London during the entire spring and summer, lecturing, and assisting Wordsworth over negotiations with Longman for *The White Doe*. Meantime, in the Lakes, the Wordsworths removed from Dove Cottage to Allan Bank; a roomy villa that had been built by a Mr Crump, a wealthy Liverpool attorney, on rising ground overlooking Grasmere village and lake.

This removal meant that the Wordsworths would be able to accommodate Coleridge without difficulty if and when he came to them; the question now was, did they still wish him to come? Growing realization of how burdensome domestication with Coleridge could be filled them with serious apprehension. Nevertheless they didn't wish him to feel that they had deserted him, thereby giving him "an excuse for considering himself utterly homeless" and "a handle for despair". "We would fain give him assistance if anything can be done," Dorothy concluded, in her inevitable blow-by-blow bulletin to Mrs Clarkson.⁸

Again and again Dorothy returned to the theme of the Coleridge separation and how unfortunate it was that S.T.C. had as yet "failed to make public" his determination never to live again with Mrs C.: "I lament the weakness which has prevented him from putting it out of her power to torment him any more". Unless and until he announced the separation officially and acted upon it for good and all he would always "have something to make him uneasy and disturbed, something hanging over his head". However, S.T.C. having shown such a sorry reluctance to make a public announcement of separation from his wife (and the wife having made clear her repugnance of having the matter bruited abroad because of the disgrace it would bring upon her and the effect that it would have upon the children), Dorothy took it upon herself to rectify the situation as far as it lay within her power to do so; she spread the word to all her friends who might still be in ignorance of the news, "Mr Coleridge and his wife are separated, and I hope they will both be the happier for it. They are upon friendly terms, and occasionally see each other."⁹ Dorothy was determined that there should be no loopholes by which Mrs S.T.C. might retain a tormenting hold upon Coleridge. Now or never, he must be saved.

The tone of her letters during the period covering the Coleridges' separation reveals how deeply, one might say obsessively, she had become emotionally involved in the matter. Her feelings for Coleridge and his welfare were intense; she longed to see this now tragic failure of a man restored to the brilliant and joyous poet whom she had loved in the days of Alfoxden. Through his collapse Dorothy had suffered acutely. Additional further trauma was inflicted upon her by the removal from Dove Cottage (long after leaving it she could scarcely bear to hear the beloved cottage mentioned). All this agitation built up into a state of acute anxiety during which she permitted herself to think and say things which were not in keeping with her normally kind and generous nature. Coleridge himself noticed the change in her, "A decaying of genial Hope & former light-heartedness"; "Compare Dorothy with Dorothy of ten years ago"¹⁰ (oblivious to the fact that distress caused by him and his behaviour might have been a contributing factor).

De Quincey, who first met Dorothy in the autumn of 1807, has also left us a glimpse of an obviously disturbed woman (she was then thirty-six years of age); her movements of "a glancing quickness", her speech suffering from an impediment, or stammer, arising from "the agitation of her extreme organic sensibility", her eyes not simply wild (the "wild eyes" with their "shooting lights" immortalized in *Tintern Abbey*) but "startling and hurried in their motion"; some "subtle fire" burning within her, giving "her whole demeanor and . . . conversation" an impression "of self-conflict that was almost distressing to witness".¹¹ The palpable agitation noted in Dorothy by both De Quincey and Coleridge in 1807–8 suggests that Dorothy was at that time in a state of extreme nervous agitation amounting to threatened breakdown.

Sarah Hutchinson also had her problems now that Coleridge was expected to rejoin the Wordsworths. Whether the ladies of that household realized it or not, Miss Hutchinson's own good name and reputation were being placed at hazard through her association with the "separated" S.T.C. Thanks in no small part to Mrs Clarkson and her friend Crabb Robinson (both indefatigable gossips), in London there was now "buzz" about the part that Miss Hutchinson's alleged romantic involvement (the kind of subject dear to the hearts of all persons of organic sensibility) might, or might not, have played in the failure of the Coleridge marriage (indeed, we find S.T.C. having to defend Miss Hutchinson in a letter to Stuart, who had been "somehow or other led to misunderstand" her character).[12] Dorothy's artless correspondence with Mrs Clarkson was a contributory factor, doubtless, to this.

Coleridge at last appeared at Allan Bank on Thursday 1st September. He could not have chosen a more inconvenient time: Mary Wordsworth was expecting to give birth, within the coming week, to her fourth child. Accordingly S.T.C. and William were bundled from Allan Bank to keep them out of the way; they walked over to Keswick and spent the next few days at Greta Hall.

Thanks to opium S.T.C. rarely could recall what he had said to, or about people, in his worst fits of anger; "wholly forgotten, as is commonly the unfortunate case with things said or written in a passion . . . forgotten by the Aggressor & for ever remembered by the Receiver". Fortunately for him Sara was of an exceptionally loyal and magnanimous disposition. She revealed, throughout her life, "a union of . . . steady, deep affection for those she was connected with by blood or friendship . . . Hasty she was at the moments of provocation, but never was anyone more just to all mankind, as far as her knowledge and insight extended, less swayed by peevish resentment in her deliberate judgements" (thus wrote her daughter Sara, paraphrasing a tribute paid to Mrs S.T.C.'s character, following her death, by one of her old friends). And never more abundantly were these virtues revealed by Mrs S.T.C. than in this autumn of 1808 when she received S.T.C. back at Greta Hall with "a kind behaviour" that made "a deep impression" on his mind; as he told her in a subsequent letter of thanks.[13]

During the visit husband and wife amicably discussed plans to send the boys to the Reverend John Dawes' school in Ambleside. Then, news reaching Greta Hall that Mary Wordsworth had safely been delivered of a daughter (Catharine), Wordsworth and S.T.C. returned to Grasmere taking little Sara Coleridge with them.

Adults rarely give sufficient credit to the perceptive powers of small children. Despite their heightened sensibilities S.T.C. and Dorothy were no exception to this rule; apparently neither of them appreciated the subtle insight which the diminutive Sara *fille* brought to bear upon Allan Bank and its occupants when she was carried off by her father to stay there at the age of six, in September 1808.

Sara, a shy and over-protected child, was alarmed and depressed at being borne away by the father who was not so much "beloved" by her as "an object of admiring wonder" (she had had little chance to learn to love him; he had been absent from home for the greater part of her short life). Her mother, on the other hand, was a "guardian" who was "ever most near and dear". From the security of mother and Greta Hall little Sara was now removed and taken over the Raise to Grasmere. Thirty years later and more Sara could still recall this momentous leaving home for the first time without her mother; "That journey to Grasmere gleams before me as the shadow of a shade. My father's wish it was to have me for a month with him at Grasmere, where he was domesticated with the Wordsworths. He insisted upon it that I became rosier and hardier during my absence from mama" (he had insisted upon the same thing with both Hartley and Derwent; the latter in particular having allegedly become "more manly and less timid", his skin clearer and his bowels healthier, when staying at Grasmere). "Mama" continued Sara,

> did not much like to part with me . . . I think my father's motive, at bottom must have been a wish to fasten my affections upon him. I slept with him, and he would tell me fairy stories when he came to bed at twelve and one o'clock. I remember his telling me a wild tale, too, in his study, and my trying to repeat it to the maids afterwards.
>
> I have no doubt there was much enjoyment in my young life at that time, but some of my recollections are tinged with pain. I think my dear father was anxious that I should learn to love him and the Wordsworths and their children, and not cling so exclusively to my mother, and all around me at home. He was therefore much annoyed when, on my mother's coming to Allan Bank, I flew to her, and wished not to be separated from her anymore. I remember his showing displeasure to me, and accusing me of want of affection. I could not understand why. The young Wordsworths came in and caressed him. I sate benumbed. . . . The sense that you have done very wrong, or at least given great offence, you know not how or why — that you are dunned for some payment of love or feeling which you know not how to produce or to demonstrate on a sudden, chills the heart, and fills it with perplexity and bitterness. My father reproached me, and contrasted my coldness with the childish caresses of the little Wordsworths. I slunk away, and hid myself.

Sara had blotted her copy book immediately upon arrival at Allan Bank when she had been led up to Dora Wordsworth: the two little girls had not met for several months, a long lapse in acquaintance for little children. Dora, four years of age, was (to quote Sara *fille*), "At this time very picturesque in her appearance, with her long, thick, yellow locks, which were never cut, but curled with papers, a thing which seems much out of keeping with the poetic simplicity of the household. I remember being asked, by my father and Miss Wordsworth, the poet's sister, if I did not think her very pretty. 'No', said I, bluntly; for which I met a rebuff which made me feel as if I was a culprit."

Dora, as a child, had "wild eyes, impetuous movements, and [this] long, floating yellow hair" (her father called it "angelic"). Like her namesake, Miss Dorothy Wordsworth senior, the child was unrestrained and impulsive to the point of being wayward. Little Sara recalled Miss Wordsworth as "gladsome" and of "most poetic eye and temper"; she "took a great part with the children" and was given to saying "alternately sharp and kind things" (a trait shared by Miss Hutchinson). "Miss Wordsworth . . . told us once a pretty story of a primrose, I think, which she spied by the way-side when she went to see me soon after my birth, though that was at Christmas, and how this same primrose was still blooming when she went back to Grasmere.

"My father used to talk to me with much admiration and affection of Sarah Hutchinson. . . . She had fine, long, light brown hair, I think her only beauty, except a fair skin, for her features were plain and contracted, her figure dumpy, and devoid of grace and dignity. She was a plump woman, of little more than five feet. I remember my father talking to me admiringly of her long light locks, and saying how mildly she bore it when the baby pulled them hard in play."[14]

Thus Allan Bank, in an unvarnished nutshell.

Once Hartley and Derwent had entered Mr Dawes' school at Ambleside, as weekly boarders, they settled into a routine of spending term time week-ends at Allan Bank and their vacations at home at Greta Hall. Significantly neither of them, in adult life, was to have much to say in the way of memories of life at Allan Bank: the Wordsworths showed every kindness, but it was a troubled time for the Coleridge children, knowing that their parents were estranged and now virtually living apart; while, again, disturbing adult conversations were overheard which only added to the general sense of disorientation. Nor was the addition of the Coleridge boys to the Allan Bank household entirely a boon for the Wordsworths; Hartley and Derwent, as Dorothy not infrequently commented, made a great deal of noise and caused a lot of extra work. The brothers had now arrived at that stage of fraternal development where they spent much of their time together quarrelling; entirely without malice, but with a good deal of rowdy vehemence, thereby making a nuisance of themselves to all adults in their vicinity.

Coleridge remained at Grasmere until well into the spring of 1809; he then began visiting Keswick and Penrith in connection with printing and publication of *The Friend* (a weekly subscription journal which was proving more difficult to launch than he had anticipated). He became increasingly discouraged; he was anxious and morose and "was not managing himself well" (a Wordsworth euphemism for his opium). The Wordsworths attempted to rally him to prevent his "indulgence", but this merely produced a worsened mood in him: resentful, guilty, miserable, he did what he had so often done in the old days, when his wife, at Greta Hall, had reprimanded him and complained of his behaviour, he removed himself to the other side of the Raise; only, now, it was a removal in reverse; not from Keswick to Grasmere, but Grasmere to Keswick.

The rain fell all summer; Coleridge travelled back and forth between Keswick and Grasmere, "We never know when Coleridge may come, nor if he comes when he may go," commented Southey in weary resignation.

In September Mr Jackson died at Greta Hall, after a "cruel Illness". Southey took a lease on that part of the house (Mrs Wilson was promised that she should live out the remainder of her days there, as one of the Southey family). On 4th November two other deaths occurred: Mrs Fricker and Mrs Coleridge Senior ("our Mothers") died: by strange coincidence on the same day. Sara hated losing links with the past; "old familiar faces", "dear scenes of yore" were, throughout her life, warming themes to her heart. Now, within the space of two months, three links had vanished for ever.

On 18th November she escorted little Sara to Grasmere; Coleridge, now settled at Allan Bank for the winter, had expressed the wish to have his daughter with him for a while. Straws in the wind were silently observed by Mrs S.T.C. during the brief stay which she herself spent at Allan Bank: it became her private conviction that S.T.C. was rapidly exhausting the patience of the Wordsworths, and that they likewise were exhausting him with their "management", or attempted "management" of him; she foresaw that he would presently be returning to her for good, as a roaming barque at last heads for the home harbour.

On arriving back at Greta Hall herself she voiced this expectation of S.T.C. to Southey; he however was adamant that nothing would induce him to have Coleridge perpetually resident and disturbing *his* domestic harmony. Therefore Sara took over the part of the house which formerly had been Jackson's (at that time more distinctly a separate residence than subsequently, when changes were made to convert the two "houses" into one): this meant, as Southey observed with grim satisfaction, that Coleridge might come and go as he pleased and make as much domestic upheaval as he chose: "A thing which cannot be with my establishment, ought not, and shall not."[15]

In mid-February Sara received a letter from her husband: "My dear Sara . . . as soon as ever I can look a fortnight in the face . . . I will unrust my toes, and perform a walk to Greta Hall."[16] A month later he was writing again, addressing her as "My dear Love" (an endearment he had not used in years) and going on to say that he desired to be with her and little Sara for a while. He put in no appearance, however, until early in May, when another letter arrived, addressed as before to "My dear Love" and voicing his intention of being with her very shortly. Within days he was at Greta Hall, in amazingly good humour and a "kind disposition". He remained at Greta Hall, in residence with his wife, for the next five months; "His spirits better than I have known them for years,"[17] as the undisguisedly astonished Sara told Poole. She had expected his ultimate return, but not the accompanying good humour.

The story behind his return to his wife was never detailed to her by him; he merely told her that he had thought it expedient both for himself and the Wordsworths that he should remove from Allan Bank to Greta Hall for a while: Mary was expecting another child (William, born on 12th May) while little Catharine in April had had some kind of a convulsive seizure.[18] But his departure from Allan Bank had been prompted by deeper reasons: a point had been reached where Coleridge's presence at Allan Bank could no longer be tolerated and he himself could no longer tolerate having become intolerable.

Sarah Hutchinson, at Allan Bank, had decided (in a forthright and sensible manner) to place her friendship with S.T.C. upon "an unequivocal" footing which, while revealing "an interest in the Man more than in a common acquaintance" left no room for the tortures of love.[19] Pursuing this intention, she had dedicated herself unsparingly to his literary interests, in the role of amanuensis and goad. She had kept his nose to the grindstone, "teizing him and driving him on". All in all, over a period of ten months, twenty-seven numbers of *The Friend* had appeared, the last upon 15th March 1810. Without Miss Hutchinson this certainly could not have been achieved.

A steady falling off in the subscribers to *The Friend* had justified Southey's forecast that the journal was "so utterly unsuitable to the public taste as to preclude all rational hopes of its success".[20] This realization had flung Coleridge into increasing dejection and plunged him into taking vast quantities of opium. Sarah Hutchinson had struggled to prevent him from drowning himself in laudanum; had coaxed, cajoled, scolded, upbraided; in short she had played the part which earlier had been Sara Coleridge's, and with the same results: as Dorothy described it to Catharine Clarkson, "His love for her is no more than a fanciful dream. . . . He likes to have her about him as his own, as one devoted to him, but when she stood in the way of other gratifications, it was all over".[21]

In mid-March Miss Hutchinson had slipped quietly away to Wales and her brother Tom, now farming in Radnorshire. Coleridge had shut himself up for hours on end alone in his room at Allan Bank, swallowing laudanum and filling his notebook with wild lamentations. Every now and again he would tell Dorothy that he had been working on *The Friend*, but, sighed Dorothy (the scales having at last fallen from her eyes), "I know that he has not written a single line".

Her disillusionment was complete, and tragic. She poured her heart out to Catharine Clarkson, "We have no hope of him. . . . His whole time and thoughts . . . are employed in deceiving himself, and seeking to deceive others. . . . This Habit pervades all his words and actions, and you feel perpetual new hollowness, and emptiness". She concluded: "It has been misery, God knows, to me to see the truths which I now see."[22]

# CHAPTER TWENTY

# *The Best of Friends — "On his Side Quite"*

## I

For Greta Hall the summer of 1810 saw the usual flow of visitors as Keswick enjoyed its annual influx of Lakers. Coleridge, when opium permitted, emerged from his lair and made himself universally charming; he was described as "a great addition" to Keswick society, his conversation was "uniformly admired". In between social activities (and solitary bouts of imbibing laudanum) he taught the two Saras, mother and daughter, Italian. But, despite his excellent spirits and reasonably good state of health he did not work, though he repeatedly assured his wife that he was "employed in composition". She wrote sadly to Poole,

> The last N° of the "Friend" lies on his Desk, the sight of which fills my heart with grief, and my Eyes with tears; but am obliged to conceal my trouble as much as possible, as the slightest expression of regret never fails to excite resentment — Poor Man! — I have not the least doubt but he is the most unhappy of the two; and the reason is too obvious to need any explanation. —[1]

Coleridge had now done no work since March; *The Friend* had brought in virtually no income so far and, if left discontinued, would bring none in the future. "Heaven knows, I am so bewildered about our affairs that I know not what to wish or what to *do*," Sara confessed to Poole.

She had long since learned the uselessness of reprimanding and upbraiding; or attempting, with coaxing or cajoling, to persuade him to cut down on his consumption of his drug. She cast a coolly clinical eye on his periodic outbursts of violent irritability, "Have you taken too much or too little opium?" she asked, in the weary accents of experience. To his notebook S.T.C. lamented, "Too much? or too little? Alas! alas! needs must it always be the one or the other: for of a poison there is no 'Enough'. — "[2]

Family concern at his condition, together with his own ever-nagging sense of guilt, at length prompted him to speak of going to a highly recommended "retreat" in Edinburgh where cases similar to his had been allegedly successfully treated. Sara and Southey were, however, strenuously against this scheme; they no longer entertained the slightest hope of a cure for his "opium habit" and believed that, instead of going away among strangers, he should remain with those who knew and loved him. With patience and encouragement some kind of improvement might at length be effected at Greta Hall; but in a "retreat" in Edinburgh where he knew nobody, dejection would soon engulf him, and dejection always spelled disaster for him.

At this juncture Basil Montagu came over from Grasmere with his wife; they had been staying with the Wordsworths and were full of a scheme to take Coleridge back to London with them and to keep him under their care in tranquillity, while he learned "industrious habits" from Montagu, an ambitious barrister who was (to quote Dorothy), "The most industrious creature in the world".[3]

The present Mrs Montagu was the third (Montagu having been twice a widower). Before her marriage to Montagu she had been Mrs Skipper: a lively and handsome widow who, it was rumoured, had rather "managed" Montagu into marrying her. She had presided as hostess over his widower's dinner table and had kept an eye on his children and his neglected housekeeping and, one way and another, had made herself indispensable, thereby prompting him to decide upon taking her as his wife. The Montagus were ardent Romantics: he was a lifelong Rousseauist and had been a keen disciple of Godwin, particularly espousing the Godwin ideal of "total sincerity" (since Montagu was a successful as well as an ambitious K.C., one must suppose that he curbed his Godwinism when in action at the Bar); Mrs Montagu was all heightened organic sensibility and gushing with enthusiasm for poetry and poets. Having missed Coleridge at Allan Bank the Montagus insisted upon going over to Greta Hall to see him (Montagu having known the Coleridges since Nether-Stowey days). Wordsworth had imparted to the Montagus the tale of the failure of *The Friend*, due to the author's incurable "indolence" (Wordsworth had stopped short of confiding to Montagu that "indolence" was a euphemism for "opium"; Montagu was, in any case, not wholly unaware of Coleridge's "opium habit" though having no conception of its real extent). The result of all this had been that Montagu had become determined to mount a rescue operation; he convinced himself that he would be able, by persuasion and example "to have so much influence over [Coleridge] as to lead him into the way of following up his schemes with industry".

Wordsworth, knowing (through bitter experience) that the experiment could only end in "mutual dissatisfaction" took it upon himself to persuade Montagu that the idea of having Coleridge in his house would never work. Montagu merely repeated that: "He would do all that could be done for Coleridge and would have him at his house" (his London home at 55 Frith Street, Soho). Wordsworth then spoke out and frankly revealed to Montagu the nature and extent of Coleridge's habits. Montagu replied that nevertheless he was still determined to have Coleridge with him in London; conceding, however, that it would perhaps be better if Coleridge had lodgings close by to Frith Street, rather than being actually domesticated with the Montagus.[4]

(It is difficult to see how Wordsworth could have acted other than he did when confronted with Montagu's determination to take Coleridge under his roof in a — misguided and foredoomed — rescue operation: common friendship dictated that Montagu had to be alerted to the harsh realities of the situation. Moreover we know that Wordsworth, on innumerable occasions, had spoken frankly and forcibly to Coleridge on the subject of his opium and drinking habits: it was not true that, as Coleridge was to allege subsequently, Wordsworth had never voiced criticism to his face.)

It would seem that, once away from Allan Bank, the Montagus dismissed Wordsworth's warnings. At Greta Hall they enthusiastically unfolded their scheme: tranquillity; every inducement to industry; "a quiet bedroom" in Frith Street. Mrs Montagu declared how much she and Montagu hoped to "have their little dwelling hallowed by the presence of such a friend" as Coleridge.[5] Certainly Greta Hall was given every impression that Coleridge would be a guest at Frith Street under the Montagu roof. Furthermore Mrs Montagu voiced her intention of placing Coleridge in the care of her friend Anthony Carlisle, a physician of distinguished reputation.

S.T.C. nursed reservations: he had never been close to Montagu; moreover Mrs Montagu was the kind of woman he particularly disliked. However Sara, impressed by Mrs Montagu's "earnest professions of watching and nursing" S.T.C., became strongly in favour of the scheme; accordingly S.T.C. accepted the Montagu invitation.[6]

Sara wrote that on 16th October she, the Montagus and S.T.C. left Keswick; Sara accompanied the party as far as Ambleside where S.T.C. took leave of Hartley and Derwent and of the Wordsworths "whom he had not seen for some months before".[7] S.T.C. then set off with the Montagus to London.

Following which no more was heard from Coleridge, directly, for several months, either by Greta Hall or Grasmere. A letter arrived for Wordsworth from Montagu describing how, on arrival in London, he had explained his inability to accommodate Coleridge at 55 Frith Street; and repeated Wordsworth's confidential disclosures. Coleridge, said Montagu, had thereupon removed himself, deeply wounded and insulted, to Hudson's Hotel. Wordsworth, upon receiving this information, made no attempt to contact Coleridge, but confined himself to telling Montagu that he had "done unwisely".[8] There also came news that Mary Lamb had had a most distressing interview with Coleridge who (to quote his own later account) had arrived faint and trembling, wild and pale with an agitation which he was unable to conceal, unable to speak in answer to her entreaties to tell her what was the matter. He had burst into "an agony of weeping", at last bringing out, "convulsively", the words "Wordsworth — Wordsworth has given me up. He has no hope of me — I have been an absolute Nuisance in his family."[9]

Meantime Greta Hall learned that Coleridge was staying with the Morgans, who were now living in London, at Portland Place, Hammersmith; he was ill, dejected and in a bad way with opium. It seems that his shattering experience with Montagu was not disclosed to Greta Hall. He had already told all to the Morgans and in all likelihood they automatically assumed that Greta Hall knew the facts.

A letter from Southey to Grosvenor Bedford on 22nd December provides a fitting epilogue to Coleridge's tragic year of 1810:

> Coleridge is a guest of John Morgan's at Hammersmith . . . Coleridge . . . went to London professedly to put himself under medical advice for — bad habits, and as we knew very well would be the case, he is going on in those habits. When he is tired of his London and Hammersmith friends he will come back again as if he had done nothing amiss or absurd, and we whose resentment has long since given place to regret and compassion, shall receive him as kindly as we took leave of him, but more chearfully, or rather with less inward sorrow, for if he will destroy himself with self-indulgence, it is better he should do it here than among strangers. O Grosvenor what a mind is here overthrown![10]

## II

The new year of 1811 failed to bring the Lake Country any word from Coleridge. Insistent letters from his wife and Southey, addressed to him at the Morgans, begging him to write, evoked no response: there could be but little doubt that they lay in his desk, unopened. At last however, in May, S.T.C. wrote to his wife asking for "the immediate Transition, per coach" of all MSS poems of his at Greta Hall as he had received an advance from Longman for a volume of original poems.[11] In his letter to Sara he gave an incoherent account of the

Wordsworth-Montagu incident; asking her not to acquaint the Words-worths with the contents of his letter. But Sara's immediate reaction of furious indignation with Wordsworth for having betrayed S.T.C.'s "failings" to Montagu prompted her to inform Allan Bank of S.T.C.'s self-described "frenzy of the heart" amounting to "a derangement of the brain" brought on by Wordsworth's "cruel conduct".

S.T.C.'s actual letter to Sara was burned in the famous holocaust; Sara's letter to Dorothy has not survived; but Dorothy's (inevitable) letter to Mrs Clarkson, dated 12th May, gives a full account of all that was in the two missing letters. Dorothy's "soul burned with indignation that William should thus (by implication) be charged with having caused disarrangement in his Friend's mind". She was, she explained, passing on these "irksome" details to Mrs Clarkson because she didn't wish some "mutilated tale" to reach her; "though I am sure you would not be inclined to blame my Brother whatever you might hear from other quarters". Coleridge "is apt to make anyone who listens to him the confidant of his gloomy fancies or wild dreams of injuries — his best friends are not exempted from his accusations upon these occasions — let me caution you therefore against believing any thing to the prejudice of W.W."[12] It was a pity that there had been nobody at hand to caution Dorothy similarly, when Coleridge had poured into her ear "wild dreams of injuries" to the prejudice of Sara.

The quarrel between the two men quickly developed into the literary *cause célèbre* of the day. Neither Wordsworth nor Coleridge would communicate direct with the other. Mutual friends, principally Charles Lamb and Crabb Robinson, in turn attempted to act as intermediary parties but each attempt at reconciliation failed.

Greta Hall rallied, without hesitation, to the side of Coleridge, making no attempt to conceal a severe condemnation both of Words-worth and of "that miscreant Montagu", who, declared Southey, had "acted with a degree of folly which would be absolutely incredible in any other person. . . . W. is no otherwise blameable than as having said anything to such a man which he would have felt any dislike to seeing in the *Morning Post*". Concluded Southey, "I do not wonder at C.'s resentment".[13]

Edith and Sara "twice debated the matter with Wordsworth and his sister". Sara, "Never in her whole life saw her Sister so vehement, or so compleatly overcome her natural timidity as when she answered Wordsworth's excuses — She would not suffer him to wander from the true point — Never mind sir! — Coleridge does not heed *what* was said — whatever is true, his friends all know, & he himself never made a secret of — but that *you*, that *you*, should say all this — & to Montagu

— & having never at any one time during a 15 years' friendship given him even a *hint* of the state of your opinions concerning him — it is *you*, Sir! *you* — not the things said, true or false!"[4] Thus Edith, the "meek lily of the vale" suddenly revealing something of her more fiery sister Sara's gun power.

The attitude of the Wordsworths was that William had said to Montagu things which, in fact, *had* already been spoken on several occasions to Coleridge at Grasmere and that, in any case, they were not things to which Coleridge might justly take very great exception; Wordsworth had been correct to warn Montagu of Coleridge's habits; Coleridge was inflating the episode out of all proportion.

Sarah Hutchinson, during a visit to Greta Hall, reported to Wordsworth, "Mrs C. and I have many a battle [on the subject of the breach] — but we do not quarrel — she wonders how I could ever love any one of whom I think so ill; and thinks he [S.T.C.] ought to know what I *do* think of him — why, I say, every thing that I say to you *have I said to himself* — and all that I believe of him now I believed formerly (except that he should ever have behaved as he has done to [Words-worth]). . . . *She* is angry and thinks I speak resentfully. . . . She is sure that we think far worse of him than ever she did and is now on his *side quite*".[15]

The Wordsworths, who at no time had shown any sympathy with, or understanding of, the Coleridge marriage, never grasping the funda-mental depth of attachment which lay beneath the turbulent surface ("What we have been to each other, our understandings will not permit our Hearts to forget!") were baffled by the loyalty to her spouse which Sara now displayed. Equally, it would seem, they were baffled by Coleridge's behaviour throughout this crisis of ruptured friendship. Indignation and pride (and the moral support of Greta Hall together with the hospitality and kindness of the Morgans) kept him afloat; his pride evinced by his determined display of high spirits when in company, and the habit he had now adopted of having "his hair dressed and powdered by a hairdresser every day". Wordsworth, however, saw these things not as manifestations of Coleridge's determination to keep his flag flying, but derided the "reported High Spirits & . . . wearing Powder" as "proof positive" that his alleged "pain of mind from the affair . . . was all pretence".[16]

In mid-February of the new year, 1812, S.T.C. travelled up to Keswick, for a stay of six weeks. During this period Sara received numerous letters and messages from Dorothy Wordsworth begging her to urge S.T.C. not to leave Cumberland without seeing them; but "he would not go to *them* and *they* did not come to him".[17] S.T.C. found this aspect of his visit deeply distressing; especially when he learned from Greta Hall that Wordsworth was treating the whole Montagu business "as a trifle" and only "wondered at Coleridge's resenting it". As for any possibility that he might pay a visit to the Wordsworths, S.T.C.'s response to this was to explode, "I, who 'for years past had been an ABSOLUTE NUISANCE in the family!' — "[18]

At Grasmere the belief was that Coleridge would never have come north at all but for the fact that he had been "in the hope of a reconciliation" with them.[19] However they were possibly wrong on this point: though Coleridge was undoubtedly hoping for a gesture of apology and reconciliation from Grasmere, he also had another, quite different matter on his mind.

Rupture with the Wordsworths had swung him fully back into his old orbit centred upon Sara Coleridge and Thomas Poole: to Poole he was now to write, "Love so deep & domesticated with the whole Being, as mine was to you can never cease to be",[20] while to Sara, much to her astonishment, he made the proposal that she and the children should, within a year or so, settle with him in London. Optimistically he assured her that he was now anticipating regular lecture engagements which would bring him an annual income of at least £800 a year; furthermore *The Friend* was to be resumed and published quarterly, which would ensure another source of income. If Mrs Coleridge didn't come to London, or until she came, he proposed allowing her £200 a year in addition to what she already received; further money would be put aside for the education of Hartley and Derwent.

Once upon a time Sara would have leapt to agree with his proposals; impulsively anxious to please him, eager to believe in his "fair promises". But the years had taught her a melancholy wisdom; now she treated his propositions with admirable diplomacy, handling him with smooth skill tinctured by compassion. She described the episode to Poole, thus,

When C, was here in Feb$^{ry}$ he was cheerful & good natured & full of fair promises — he talked of our settling finally in London, that is, when he had gone on for a year or so giving me, and all his friends satisfaction as to the possibility of making a livelihood by his writings so as to enable us to live in great credit there — I listened, I own, with incredulous ears, while he was building these "airy castles" and calmly told him that I thought it was much better that I and the children should remain in the country until the Boys had finished their School-education and then, if he found himself in circumstances that would admit of it, & would engage not to leave us all alone in that wide city, I would cheerfully take leave of dear Keswick, and follow his amended fortunes: he agreed to this, & in the meantime, a regular correspondence was to be kept up between himself, and me, and the children; and never more was he to keep a letter of mine, or the Boys', or Southey's unopened — [21]

Coleridge returned to London and the Morgans, now living at 71 Berners Street. Initially he settled down to the promised regular correspondence with his wife, writing in a most cheerful and cheering strain about his "Health & Spirits, & . . . smiling Prospects", which, together with his new "Disposition to activity" had struck everyone: "The Morgans say, they had never before seen me *myself*. I feel myself an altered man, and dare promise you that you shall never have to complain of, or to apprehend, my not opening & reading your Letters". His forthcoming new series of lectures was receiving promise of enthusiastic support; *The Friend*, now published as a volume by Gale and Curtis, was confidently expected to have good sales. "Everything, my dear; goes on as prosperously as you yourself would wish". Coleridge was falling over himself in the attempt to please, and impress, his wife. The dream of recaptured domestic bliss once more lured him; constancy to the ideal object, the meed of all his toils. [22]

## III

Coleridge's failure to visit Grasmere during his sojourn in the north finally convinced the Wordsworths of what they had suspected, that Coleridge was "glad of a pretext" to break with them. (Coleridge, for his part, was now convinced that Wordsworth had spoken to Montagu as a means to putting an end to their long friendship.) Following his return to Town with the breach with Wordsworth unhealed there was an increase of "buzz" at London dinner parties and in drawing-rooms: Wordsworth, much incensed upon learning of this gossip, went down to London himself at the end of April, determined to deal decisively with the whole business and clear it up, once and for all. A month later news arrived in the Lakes that Wordsworth and Coleridge had become "reconciled": Wordsworth had given Coleridge an assurance that Montagu's statements during the Frith Street interview had contained, "Absolutely NOTHING of the spirit of the truth"; Coleridge had responded with expression of his faith in Wordsworth's assurance.

The Wordsworths, who seemed incapable of realizing how deeply Coleridge had been wounded, now anticipated that the friendship with him would be resumed on the same happy footing as in the old days. Sara, with her clearer perception, held a different view. To Poole she confided, succinctly,

I think, I may venture to say, there will never more be that between them which was in days of yore — but it has taught C. one useful lesson; that even his dearest & most indulgent friends, even those very persons who have been the great means of his self-indulgence, when he comes to live wholly with them, are as clear-sighted to his failings, & much less delicate in speaking of them, than his Wife, who being the Mother of his children, even if she had not the slightest regard for himself, would naturally feel a reluctance to the exposing of his faults.[23]

# PART THREE

*Snouterumpater*

(MAY 1812–JUNE 1834)

# A Case of Desertion

Following Coleridge's departure from Keswick (he having extracted the promise that his wife and children would join him in Town at some unspecified date) and his ensuing few letters in highly optimistic vein with their assurances of prosperity to come, no more was heard from him. This did not unduly surprise his wife; she by now knew him through and through, warp and woof. "His promises, poor fellow, are like Castles, — airy nothings! — "[1] she sighed resignedly to Poole.

Nonetheless she began to experience a certain dismay as the summer wore on into autumn and autumn towards winter and yet still no word came from her husband. It seemed almost beyond belief that, having been so (apparently) well-disposed to his family's interests earlier in the year, he should now put his dependents so entirely out of his mind: particularly disconcerting was his neglect of Hartley, always closest to S.T.C. and, now that his schooldays were rapidly drawing to an end and the question of his future looming near at hand, especially in need of his father's attention.

Hartley, just turned sixteen, was voicing a preference for the church as his future profession; however, "Many persons have thought that his talents would be more useful in the Law — as he has the 'Gift of the Gab' — in no small degree," Sara told Poole. But, whichever profession Hartley finally decided upon, he would need to go to university, and university cost money. Therefore when Sara learned, in the early autumn of 1812 (through Charles Lamb) that S.T.C. had offered his tragedy *Osorio* (renamed *Remorse*) to "one of the Theatres" the news understandably filled her with anxious excitement: "Heaven grant that it succeed, for never were his exertions so absolutely, so imperiously necessary to his family as now."[2]

Some six weeks later the dire news reached Sara (through Wordsworth) that Josiah Wedgwood had withdrawn his half of S.T.C.'s annuity (the other half could not be withdrawn as Thomas Wedgwood had bequeathed it in his will). This meant that there would be in future, as their sole reliable annual income, a mere sixty-seven pounds ten shillings (after tax had been deducted).

Sara wrote in despair to her husband: it is clear that he read her letter (mostly, these days, letters to him went unread) for he commented to Stuart, "Poor woman! she is sadly out of heart".[3] But, this said, S.T.C.

could not bring himself to write to her and it was through Martha Fricker (now in London and embarking upon a millinery and dressmaking business "with a Lady in Tichfield Street") that Sara learned that her husband's course of lectures at the Surrey Institution for the winter season 1812–1813 was going well and that she should be receiving money from that source.[4]

At the close of 1812 came the news that *Remorse* had gone into rehearsal at Drury Lane, where it was produced on 23rd January as a New Year sensation, being received with immense applause. It played for twenty consecutive nights (an excellent run in those days), and made some four hundred pounds, of which Coleridge promptly sent his wife a hundred, with promise of another hundred to come within the month.[5] Sara's relief knew no bounds. The bleak future suddenly looked rosy. Better still, S.T.C. was reported to be brimming with ideas for further musical dramas and comedies: "There is more reason to expect something from him now than there has ever been."[6] He stood, it seemed, on the threshold of a new and brilliant career. "Mrs Coleridge is much elated as you can guess."[7]

But after that first hundred pounds Sara saw no more of the money from *Remorse*. John Morgan, through a series of misfortunes, went bankrupt and Coleridge felt himself in honour bound to give Mary Morgan and Charlotte Brent any financial assistance of which he was capable. News of the Morgan disaster reached Greta Hall through Southey's Bristol contacts; from S.T.C. himself nothing was heard, he had lapsed back into impenetrable silence.

August of 1813 saw Southey travelling to London on business matters; during this visit he was appointed Poet Laureate. He met S.T.C., who declared his intention of returning to Keswick and his family as soon as he had completed negotiation for another piece to be presented at Covent Garden. He shortly afterwards vanished to Bristol on business on behalf of the Morgans; nonetheless it was understood that he would soon return to Keswick.[8]

Hartley, during his years at Mr Dawes's school, after "lights out" in the dormitory each night had entertained his companions with an extraordinary serial story of which the chief characters were "a subtle, intellectual villain, Scauzan, and his father, a man of gigantic stature, outlawed and persecuted through the machinations of his son". Derwent, one of the spellbound nightly listeners to this tale, was to recall many years later how: "The struggles between parental affection and resentment against the injuries of his son were . . . powerfully depicted. . . . The interest excited was occasionally so great as to become painful."[9]

Clearly, guilt heavily shadowed this labyrinthine landscape of Hartley's subconscious mind; but whose guilt? The father, "a man of gigantic stature, outlawed and persecuted", loomed through the mists; guilt was reflected in resentment; but whose resentment?

Hartley, as a little child, had enjoyed an exceptionally close and special relationship with his father, who, from the first, had virtually worshipped the infant: had written poems beside his cradle; had presently carried him out on moonlit walks in Alfoxden glades filled with nightingales; later had raced him down the slopes of Skiddaw and dipped him in rocky pools of the river Greta. Then, abruptly, this doting, divine father had been transformed; alternately withdrawn, ignoring Hartley utterly, or, stirred from lethargy, ranting at the child in "Words of Wrong and Bitterness". The bewildered five-year-old boy, unable to understand what had happened, aware only that somehow he had displeased his father, had made him angry, responded as his sister would respond when her turn came to experience inexplicable paternal rejection and rebuke, "I slunk away and hid myself". Hartley had hidden himself, had retreated into the Greta Hall vegetable garden, there to spin fantasies of Ejuxria; another country, far away: free from distressful feelings of bewilderment, guilt and resentment.

However guilt and resentment, once implanted in the heart, remain there, to reappear perhaps years later in the guise of dreams and fairy tales, strange patterns of thought and behaviour, skeins of memory tangled into knots, mysterious tokens from the maze of burrows in the mind's subterraneous territory, surfacing spontaneously as fragmented archaic weapons do from the soil of old battlefields. So, Hartley's nightly saga of guilt-fraught strife between gigantic, outlawed father and small, but wily son: a tale which poured out from him, holding his schoolboy listeners captive.

Yet Hartley, in real life (as opposed to subconscious fantasy life) firmly anticipated that his father would return home from exile, to advance plans for a university education for his son, leading to some professional career. This was what fathers did, in their walk of life; this was what his father would do. At Ambleside, with Mr Dawes, Hartley waited confidently for the letter from his mother telling him that his father was back at Greta Hall, ready to see him, perhaps to tutor him in preparation for Oxford, or Cambridge.

But Coleridge, in Bristol and engaged to give a series of lectures, sent no word of any kind to Greta Hall.[10] The truth was that he was now in the utter nadir of opium crisis: totally incapacitated. The crisis had overtaken him at Bath in transit for Bristol. A doctor, summoned to the inn where Coleridge lay, had managed to pull him together sufficiently for him to be able to travel to Bristol, where Wade had taken him under his roof. And in Bristol he remained: too ill to give his course of lectures; his one desperate wish, he declared, being for two hundred pounds, "Half to send to Mrs Coleridge & half to place myself in a private madhouse" — in such an institution, under constant surveillance and medical treatment, there might be hope of his release from opium, "Now there is none!"[11]

Cottle, in this tragic spring of 1814, decided to raise a subscription for Coleridge that he might enter the desired private madhouse. Southey, however, sent Cottle brisk advice to drop all idea of the subscription. "This, Cottle, is an insanity which none but the Soul's physician can cure."[12] Let Coleridge make an effort and he would prove as capable of exertion as Southey himself. Cottle therefore dropped the idea of the subscription.

Southey did not show Sara Cottle's letters; there was no point in distressing her further by baring to her all the painful details of S.T.C.'s descent into the gutter of self-degradation.[13] "Any other woman would have broken her heart ere this, and happily as she has been constituted for her situation, her spirits and health are beginning to sink under it,"[14] Southey informed Cottle, adding that if an "humiliating solicitation" proved necessary for Coleridge (supposing that he utterly refused "to do that, which he can and ought to do") it should take the form of a subscription for his children, left dependent "upon chance and charity".[15]

Southey's angry indignation was understandable. His day and age had no real understanding of what morphine reliance does to its victims, literally rendering them powerless in terms of self-control and exertion; his tolerant attitude towards Coleridge of some three and a half years previously ("We whose resentment has long since given place to regret and compassion" — above, p. 200), had now hardened once more into resentment; an intensified resentment, because of the intensification of the suffering inflicted upon Sara by her husband's neglect.

Southey quietly shouldered the burden of paying the rent and taxes for Sara's part of the house and the support of herself and her daughter; the halved annuity wouldn't stretch beyond covering the expenses of the two boys. Sara henceforth was painfully aware that the house which she had called home for the past fourteen years was no longer, any part of it, hers by right, but remained "home" for herself and her children solely through the kindness of her brother-in-law; it was "Southey's house". "I have bitter feelings attached to the word HOME",[16] she told Poole (her children remained blissfully unaware of the true implication of their Uncle Southey's generous assumption of rents and taxes on their behalf; to them Greta Hall, always *their* house and home, was still theirs). To Poole Sara continued to unburden herself, "Ah my dear Sir, — Mr Wedgewood, I daresay, little guesses the *increase of anxieties* his withdrawing his half of the annuity has caused me — but it was not to be expected that he could be interested about those whom he had never seen — I think if [he] *had* ever seen these children, he would not have had the heart to have withdrawn it — at least until one of them was in a way of providing for himself — but I blame *nobody* — and these *murmurs* of an oppressed heart, are only for the ears of an indulgent friend — this much more — and I have done — if it were not for the protection that Southey's house affords me — I know not how we should all have gone on at this present writing — I remain however in *much trouble* yet thankful for the *blessings* remaining to me — (I need not name them) and in hope of better prospects or C's return even. . . ."[17]

But Coleridge did not return; indeed no sound came from him whatever.

Much anxiety was now being voiced both at Keswick and Grasmere concerning Hartley's future. "Coleridge . . . *ought* to come to see after Hartley!" was the repeated exclamation heard from Greta Hall and Rydal Mount (the house into which the Wordsworths had moved in May of that year following the deaths of Catharine and Thomas).[18] But what Coleridge ought to do and what he actually did were always two markedly different things and gradually it became clear to his relatives and friends that, insofar as Hartley's further education was concerned, Coleridge had come to the conclusion that it was *they* who ought to do something about the matter.

When, by April 1814, Coleridge (still in Bristol) showed absolutely no sign of doing anything about his elder son's future, it was decided (after consultation between Wordsworth and Southey) that Poole should go to him and attempt to stir him to some kind of activity: it was, said Wordsworth, incumbent upon Coleridge's friends "to do their best to prevent the father's weaknesses being ruinous to the Son". Added Wordsworth, "I do not expect that C will be able to do anything himself, but his consent will be indispensable before any of his Friends can openly stir in exertions for H".[19]

When Poole visited Coleridge in Bristol, Coleridge (still enmeshed in his opium crisis) virtually dismissed the matter: he refused to discuss, let alone consent to, any plans on Hartley's behalf. Poole reported this disheartening news to the Wordsworths; they, meanwhile, had learned that Coleridge had been telling casual acquaintances that his elder son was going to university. "So you see he expects the thing to take place," wrote Wordsworth to Poole, "though he wished to put it off when you conversed with him".[20]

The Ottery Coleridges, approached by Southey on Hartley's behalf, procured for him the office of Postmaster (the equivalent of a scholarship worth fifty pounds a year and lasting four years) at Merton College, Oxford. Ottery also promised Hartley a further £40 per annum. Lady Beaumont promised an annual £30, Poole £10, Cottle £5. This was expected to provide an income adequate to support Hartley with "frugality". Southey and Wordsworth promised further money should it be "absolutely" required and Basil Montagu also came forward with offers of help. Sara wrote to S.T.C. to acquaint him with the news of this generosity extended to Hartley from all sides, but there came no reply.

George Coleridge, in the course of his correspondence with Southey, had referred to Hartley in touching terms as a "fatherless child". Sara had found this deeply affecting. But the entire episode of S.T.C.'s total silence upon the issue of Hartley's future, the apparent complete indifference of this man for his wife and children, shook her profoundly. She confided to Poole, "You will be shocked to hear that I never hear from C. I dare not dwell upon the painful consequences of his desertion."[21]

For, by 1813, she was obliged to see herself, starkly, for what she was: a wife who had been deserted by her husband.

Yet even now there were rays of sunshine to pierce the gloom: from every side shone the smiles of friends rallying to the assistance of her "poor children". In a letter of thanks to Poole for his help with Hartley she touchingly voiced her indebtedness to him, going on to speak of "the great kindness and solicitude we have experienced from Wordsworth & his family . . . and to Southey I am in every manner everlastingly bound: I pray to heaven to reward you all for your goodness!"[22]

Hartley, too, properly expressed his thanks where thanks were due; but his heart was bruised beyond recovery by the knowledge that his father had failed him and that others had had to come forward to perform the duties which should, by right and in parental pride, have been Coleridge's. Worse still, criticism of their father was heard on all sides and the young Coleridges flinched every time his name was spoken: Sara, well aware of this, sighed to Poole, "The poor children are miserable if their father is mentioned for fear they should hear anything like blame attached to it. . . . I believe I mentioned to you before their great sensibility on this unhappy subject."[23]

But perhaps their uncle George Coleridge was right: they were not so much children who had been deserted by their father as children who were truly orphaned. The "meteor from the clouds", the "adored divine" Coleridge was now all but drowned in laudanum. In Bristol he, a trembling, stunned-visaged, blear-eyed wreck was clinging in a final spasm of despair to the last splintered spar of himself, while the appalled onlookers (most of whom who had known him in his miraculous youth) speculated that it could only be a matter of weeks before S.T.C., the wretched struggler drowning in an ocean of morphine, became a washed up cadaver lolling in the shallows of a final outgone tide.

# Snouterumpater in Full Confabulumpatus

## I

Hartley was due to commence at Merton at Eastertide, 1815. He departed for the south and his new life accompanied by William and Mary Wordsworth; the party was joined by Charles Lamb and with these loyal supporters Hartley went to Oxford, where he matriculated successfully and, by 16th May, felt himself "tolerably established as a Collegian" as he wrote to Lamb.[1]

Letters from Hartley to his mother described his settling in at Merton and his good progress there. His cousin, William Coleridge,[2] made Hartley "acquainted with all things needful" and gave him "every possible assistance"; in short Sara, to her immense relief, "received pleasing accounts" in every respect.[3] An offer for further assistance now came from an utterly unexpected quarter; S.T.C. wanted to tutor Hartley in Greek during the Long Vacation.

S.T.C., that existential mariner, had not perished in the ocean of laudanum, but, by a superhuman effort had struck out for the distant shores of salvation. During his nine months stay in Bristol, struggling with opium, he had uttered all the usual exclamations and sworn all the usual vows of the drug victim, "Woe be to me, if this last Warning is not taken! . . . May God grant me power to struggle to become *not another* but a *better man*".[4] He vowed to devote the remainder of his life to, firstly, saving his immortal soul (which necessarily involved liberating himself from the curse of opium and the inevitable moral degradation which it brought in its train) and, secondly, to salvaging and re-establishing his literary and personal reputation which opium had reduced to tatters.

He had rightly concluded that all voluntary efforts to give up his drug, however devotedly assisted by loyal and loving friends or family, must be doomed to failure. He continued to insist that to emancipate himself from his most pitiable slavery (as he himself phrased it) he needed to be placed "in a private madhouse" where he could procure no laudanum but what a physician thought proper, and where a medical attendant could be constantly with him.[5] But such treatment would cost money; S.T.C. was penniless. So he determined to earn the necessary money with professional writing. This would demand discipline. But he was now totally committed:

"I have a great, a gigantic effort to make & I will go through with it or die".[6]

He had left Bristol and had returned to live with the Morgans; first at Box, near Bath, and then at Calne in Wiltshire. Here he had now commenced a stint of writing which would have been commendable in any author but which, in the case of Coleridge, was nothing short of miraculous. Yet, as he was well aware from past calamitous experience, work must be steady and regularized in order to avoid the kind of pressure which led inevitably, in his case, to increased opium and consequent disaster. "All I can do," he had concluded, "is to be quite regular [in a daily work routine] and never to exceed the smallest dose of Poison that will suffice to keep me tranquil and capable of literary labour".[7]

He evolved a daily routine: "I breakfast every morning before nine — work till one — & walk or read till 3 — thence till Tea time chat or read some lownge-book — or correct what I have written — from 6 to 8, work again — from 8 to bed time play whist, or the little mock-billiard, called Bagatelle, & then sup & go to bed".[8] With the support and encouragement of the Morgans he managed to keep to this routine.

Sara now received encouraging news of S.T.C., which she passed on to Poole, "Mr Morgan . . . says he is not entirely without hope that C. will do something now for his family, as he is now in good health & spirits, & talks of beginning in good earnest a German translation which will be profitable and which Mr M. kindly promises to take all the fag of, & only require the business of correction from C. which will leave him at liberty to get his Poems ready for the press."[9] Even better, S.T.C. now expressed the desire to tutor Hartley; John Morgan accordingly invited him to stay. Both Hartley and his mother were overjoyed by this; she wrote to her son, "It is exceedingly kind of Mr M. to ask you to his house for the long vacation and I own it is a great satisfaction to me that you should see and be with your father, and that he should examine you in Greek and Latin and give you . . . instruction."[10]

Hartley's stay at Calne (from mid-June until 20th October) was a happy time for him; he not only received the promised tutoring but enjoyed long discursive conversations with his father.[11] Hartley developed a warm affection for the Morgans, "Good, comfortable, unintellectual people, in whose company I always thought S.T.C. more than usually pleasant", he was subsequently to confide to his own notebook.[12] To his mother Hartley sent "frequent letters" describing his father in a much improved state of health and working steadily at his "literary life" (*Biographia Literaria*). Sara passed on this good news to Poole and on 20th September was able to tell him: "Coleridge, it appears, has sent 2 vols: to the press; a republication of the former poems, with others, & a literary life of the Author, which has grown out of the preface; & is, if we may believe his son, an interesting part of the work; it is printing at Bristol but is to be, I suppose, published in London."[3]

## II

Hartley came home to Keswick at Christmas to add to the general happiness of the Aunt Hill (as Greta Hall was nicknamed, on account of the number of Aunts who lived there). He was received with rapture by his sister Sara, now about to celebrate her thirteenth birthday, and a swarm of little Southeys: Edith May, aged ten years; Herbert, aged eight years; Bertha, not quite five years; Katharine (Kate) aged three and a half years and Isabel, eighteen months of age (who was held up by Edith May for Hartley to kiss). Now in his nineteenth year Hartley was of an extraordinary appearance; remarkably small in stature, with a heavy black beard and equally heavy black eyebrows. Children universally adored him and he delighted in them.

The new year of 1816 started in the most unexpected style: a letter from S.T.C. to his wife, "The first for almost three years!" she kept exclaiming, almost unable to believe it. In it he told her that he was shortly going to London with a new play for Covent Garden: *A Christmas Tale*. He was, he added, in good health and good spirits.

Sara spread the agreeable news. Derwent became sanguine that there might, after all, be money to send him to Cambridge.

But, following this letter, no more was heard from S.T.C. or of *A Christmas Tale*. Sara resigned herself to the realization that it would probably be another three years before she heard from him again. Resolutely she, as Christmas and New Year holidays ended and term time began again, marched into the Greta Hall schoolroom and took her place behind teacher's desk. Samuel Taylor Coleridge or no Samuel Taylor Coleridge, life had to go on.

The Greta Hall children were lucky in being surrounded by adults who were capable of running an excellent, so to speak "home grown", schoolroom: Mrs Lovell taught English and Latin; Mrs S.T.C. French, Italian, writing, arithmetic and needlework; Southey taught Spanish and Greek; Miss Barker, a neighbour, gave instruction in drawing and music. "We keep regular School from $\frac{1}{2}$ past nine until 4 with the exception of an hour for walking and an half hour for dressing," Sara informed Poole.[14]

This Greta Hall schoolroom would see the daughters educated beyond the capacity of any outside educational establishment for young females; a son of course, would pass out of the schoolroom and on to a boys' school at the age of nine or ten. Herbert, a precocious child, was already learning Latin and his father had great hopes of him.

But early in March of that year 1816 Herbert became ill with an undiagnosed illness which began with a cough and fever and steadily worsened; he died in April, in his tenth year. Southey went to his study and wrote to his physician brother Henry: "All is over, and no equal affliction can ever again befall me — for here was the very heart and life of my happiness and hopes."[5] Sara, acquainting Poole with the tragic news, wrote, "Never was child more lamented by a father than this is, and will be to the latest hour of his life. . . . My poor Sister is not to be consoled at present — the Almighty will, I trust, enable them to bear their affliction, & time will, no doubt, do something for them! but they are deeply smitten."[16]

As an antidote to the sorrow which engulfed him Southey hurled himself at his work with increased intensity. "Southey has . . . done great things, even in the bitterest days of his most bitter sorrow . . . he is a most extraordinary being — good & great & deserves to be happy", declared Sara to Poole.[17] Happiness, however, rarely comes because it is deserved. Southey, perhaps, would never be truly happy again; but, just as he stoically forced himself to work during his hours of grief, so did he similarly force himself to wear a cheerful face and keep up a flow of high spirits, so that within months of Herbert's death Sara was remarking of her brother-in-law that, "Strangers think him the happiest man alive".[18]

She herself knew what it was to maintain a show of light, frisking high spirits while privately deeply miserable and consumed with anxiety; she had been doing this for years, *"Toujours gai!"* It was her form of personal gallantry, nor did it go unnoticed or unappreciated by Southey, who even before Herbert's death, had always been under a certain tension, introduced into his life by his zealous and unremitting devotion to work and duty; while, at the same time, Edith's chronic depression tinctured his daily domestic life with a certain twilit quality which was only prevented from being dampening to himself and his children by his determination to keep Greta Hall resonant with fun and puns, chatter, bustle and laughter.

Edith was "Mrs Southey", the Laureate's "dignified and gracious" wife (her fine figure, now become Junoesque by motherhood, and her apathy, gave her an air of stately languor which was considerably admired by visiting Lakers):[19] but it was "Mrs C." (as Sara came to be known to an ever-widening circle of friends and distinguished acquaintances) who played what in effect was leading lady, opposite Southey, in the charade of merriment which set the seal on Greta Hall's reputation as the social centre of Keswick's high season: and Keswick's high season then stood at the apex of Laker festivity and enjoyment.

It was an age which loved "innocent" jollity and laughter. The non-stop flow of bishops, politicians, academicians, poets, judges, dons, merchant bankers and Harley Street consultants who, with their wives, visited Greta Hall during those summer seasons, revelled in what might be termed the Southey-Sara double comedy act. Middle age had brought Sara a rotund "embonpoint" (as it was kindly described) which she found increasingly tiresome: she sighed to Sarah Hutchinson that no matter "what you put on, you can never look one bit nice" (Miss Hutchinson congratulated herself "on never having been a beauty" and thus being spared the pangs of losing her looks);[20] Mary Wordsworth commented to daughter Dora, on one occasion of a dinner party, that "poor dear Mrs C. looked like *a stuffed Turkey*"[21] (the Wordsworth ladies grew increasingly lean with the passing years and lost their teeth; Mrs C. wrote to Poole about Dorothy's "nut-cracker nose and chin").[22] But despite these "ravages of the hand of time" Sara's popularity with the Lakers was apparently enhanced by her rotundity and "full-moon phiz" (as she herself described it):[23] she *looked* her part of irrepressible laughter provoker and *comedienne*.

She had a natural and unselfconscious propensity for "funny things" and ridiculous disasters. Many of her scrapes occurred during the course of picturesque excursions in the company of visitors seeking sublime experiences gratifying to their organic sensibilities. Southey tells us of taking a party of enthusing ladies (including Miss Betham, the portrait painter) up Skiddaw and "on the way down Mrs C. got into a bog some way above her knees, and I saved her life! . . . Afterwards I washed her petticoat in one of the gills, and carried it home on my stick."[24] On another occasion she disrupted a literary picnic by seating herself on an ant-infested bank; while her sons never forgot how she once blew her nose in a handkerchief only to discover, too late, that it was a nightcap.[25]

Because of her incorrigible propensity for ridiculous accidents and incidents Southey nicknamed her "Bumble-cum-Tumble" after the nursery-rhyme character:

> The only society I have left now,
> Is Bumble-cum-Tumble and Doggy-bow-wow[26]

he observed, when the season ended, the last of the visitors had gone, and the last of the boats put away for the winter.

Many of the "funny things" were connected with the elaborate practical jokes and hoaxes that Southey loved to set up, with Mrs C. frequently the butt. We are told that she "played, not unwillingly, her good-humoured part in these pantomimic scenes, which [Southey] enjoyed with boyish delight". One such practical joke (or charade) involving an antique mail coach horn (chosen because Mrs C. professed a horror of noise) was described by Southey to Grosvenor Bedford, who, as one of Mrs C.'s warmest friends and admirers, liked to be kept informed of her hilarious diversions. To quote from Southey's letter (of particular interest to Bedford on this occasion because it was his own brother who had provided the horn):

> I [must] . . . describe . . . how Mrs Coleridge looked when the fatal horn [was] exhibited to her astonished eyes. . . . It had been packed . . . carefully with my umbrella in brown paper, so that no person could possibly discover what the mysterious package contained. . . . Mrs C. stood by . . . while the unpacking was deliberately performed. . . . The first emotion was an expression of contemptuous disappointment at sight of the umbrella, which I was careful should be first discovered. But when the horn appeared, the fatal horn, then, oh then — Grosvenor, it was an expression of dolorous dismay which Richter or Wilkie could hardly represent unless they had witnessed it, — it was at once so piteous and so comical. Up went the brows, down went the chin, and yet the face appeared to widen as much as it was elongated, by an indefinable drawing of the lips which seemed to flatten all the features. I know not whether sorrow or resentment predominated in the eyes; sorrow as . . . she pitied herself; or anger when she thought of me, and of your brother from whom I received the precious gift; and whose benevolence I loudly lauded. She wished him at Mo-ko (where that is I know not),* and me she wished to a worse place, if any worse there be. . . . Here I blew a blast . . . [and] out she ran.[27]

It was to Grosvenor Bedford that Southey (as we have already discovered) sent accounts of Mrs C.'s *lingo grande*; acclaimed as possibly the funniest of all her funny things. Southey, with his interest in etymology in general and nonsense-rhyming in particular clearly suspected that there was more to the *lingo grande* than met the eye, or ear, "There is a mystery in an unknown tongue; and they who speak it," he wrote musingly. "There may be an unknown inspiration as well as an

---

*To wish a person to Mo-ko was then (and for the rest of the century) a popular phrase, deriving from Napoleon's ill-fated Moscow campaign of 1812.

unknown tongue. If so what . . . revelations may lie unrevealed."[28]
But, as he informed Grosvenor, try as he might he could not get to the
bottom of Mrs C.'s *lingo grande*;

> . . . If the children — the childeroapusses I should say — are
> bangrampating about the house, they are said to be rudderish and
> roughcumtatherick. . . . [A] mouth is sometimes called a jabber-
> umpeter, sometimes a towsalowset. When the word comfortabuttle is
> used, I suppose it may be designed to mean that there is comfort in a
> bottle. But by what imaginable process of language and association
> snouterumpater can be, as she declares it to be, a short way of calling
> mother, I am altogether unable to comprehend.
>
> On one occasion, however, I was fortunate enough to see this
> extraordinary language in the mint, if I may so express myself, and in the
> very act of its coinage. Speaking of a labourer, she said, "the thumper, the
> what-d'ye-callder — the undoer, — I can't hit upon it, — the cutter-up."
> These were the very words, received and noted as they came from the die;
> and they meant a man who was chopping wood. . . . [29]

Had Southey lived in an era more psychologically aware he might
have understood better what the *lingo grande* was fundamentally
revealing. Sara had deep-seated needs for inventing a private language
— needs never analysed but only felt: release from the tensions of
constant suppressed anxiety; the necessity to have something of her
very own that could not be taken from her as everything else was taken;
the need for privacy in a world which gossiped freely about her as the
deserted wife of Samuel Taylor Coleridge. Fundamentally her language was a cypher affording her a species of cover (it is significant that
one of the *aliases* which she bestowed upon herself was "Mrs Codian").
Equally fundamentally it was her safety-valve, permitting her, as it
were, to let off steam. She was of an ironical turn of mind: a dangerous
thing to be at the best of times. By using a private language she was able
to give vent in safety to her irony; to pass comments on men and
manners; to express herself without inhibition. By using a method of
verbal shorthand she could reach to the heart of things in a flash: for
instance, to describe a man chopping wood as a "thumper", an "undoer"
and a "cutter-up" is to express, in a mere four words, a myriad of
associated ideas and comments ranging from the sexual to the social.

By such means and methods of jokes and hoaxes, puns and facetious
pranks, funny things and *lingo grande*, did Sara Coleridge and Southey
attempt to relieve the tensions which their respective burdens in life laid
upon them: an opium-ridden husband, a chronically depressed wife.
Southey was the sort of man who would sooner have died than bruit his

domestic problems to the world, but there is a revealing passage in a letter he wrote to Wynn in June 1815 (before the disruptive tragedy of Herbert's death, it should be noted) which may be read as a subconscious comment upon his domestic impasse. The subject he was touching upon was the question (at that time receiving considerable public debate) of the legality of marriage to a deceased wife's sister. "Has it never occurred to you my dear Wynn that this law [prohibiting such marriages] is an abominable relic of ecclesiastical tyranny? Of all second marriages, I have no hesitation in saying that these are the most natural, the most suitable, and likely to be the most frequent, if the law did not prevent them."[30] This speaks volumes.

## *"Without Hope or Heart"*

I

In the spring of 1816 Coleridge, pursuing his plan of deliverance from opium and self-redemption, had placed himself under the roof of Mr James Gillman, an apothecary and surgeon of Highgate, who had undertaken to "cure him of opium".[1] A year later Coleridge was still at Highgate; his opium had been successfully brought under control. There was now talk of his returning to Greta Hall and correspondence between himself and Mrs C. was exchanged on the subject; he saying that he would return if she wanted him back and she replying that she would agree to whatever he wished.[2]

Southey, however, finally put his foot down when he learned from Morgan (it ultimately proved to have been a groundless allegation) that Coleridge owed Gillman a large sum for board and lodging and, being unable to discharge the debt, was proposing to abscond to Keswick. Morgan added that Gillman would assuredly have Coleridge pursued by bailiffs. The thought of S.T.C. being arrested by bailiffs on Greta Hall doorstep filled Southey with horror and he informed Mrs C., in no uncertain terms, that if she and S.T.C. wished to live together it must be in an abode of their own. This, of course, was tantamount to saying that there was no possibility of their ever again resuming domesticity together; the chances of S.T.C. acquiring the means to provide a family home was a notion beyond the wildest dreams. Mrs C. put on a philosophical front, maintaining that she really considered it for the best that she and Coleridge should remain apart: though she was privately filled with anguish at the thought that her "poor children" could have no home that was truly theirs.

In point of fact there was little, if any, risk of Southey finding himself encumbered with Coleridge at Greta Hall. Morgan was totally wrong about Mr and Mrs Gillman, who were two of the kindest and most generous people ever born. Once they discovered the true state of Coleridge's finances they refused all payment for board, lodging or medical treatment, excepting if and when he found himself able to give them money without inconvenience to himself and his own family.

Nevertheless, relieved as Coleridge now was of any necessity to pay the Gillmans board and lodging, he had no money worth mentioning coming in from his pen. True, he had been writing hard enough: 1816 had seen the publication of *Christabel* and *The Statesman's Manual* (the first of his "Lay Sermons") while 1817 saw the appearance of the second Lay Sermon, "Blessed are ye that sow beside all waters!", *Biographia Literaria*, and *Sibylline Leaves*. 1818 was noteworthy for the highly successful course of lectures which he gave in the new year; from the lectures he made some money, but with his publications he met with nothing but financial disappointment, due to scurrilous treatment from his publishers.

Poole wrote cheerfully about these literary productions; falling back into his old habit of encouraging and rallying S.T.C. ("Proceed, my dear Friend, in the manner you are going on . . . you cannot estimate the happiness it will give me"),[3] and confiding to Mrs C. that at last it seemed that S.T.C. would come into his own and bring to fruition the promise of his youth. But Mrs C., taught by experience never to be over-sanguine where her husband was concerned, could only reply that: "What you say about S.T.C. is likely enough to happen; Alas, I dare not look forward." However well S.T.C. might prove to be capable of reviving his former self, one thing was certain to her; their "domestic bliss" could never be recaptured. There was, as she pointed out to Poole, no chance of seeing S.T.C. at Greta Hall (in fact we know that Poole himself had been vehemently against the idea of his return there, "I think no circumstance should induce you to leave your *present residence*," he had written to him at Highgate on 31st July 1817, "You are happy in your friends near you. Mr Gillman is an invaluable treasure").[4] And, when Hartley's visit to Stowey later in that same summer would seem to have veered Poole round to feeling that, for the sake of his children, S.T.C. might possibly endeavour to unite himself once more with his family in a proper home of their own, Mrs C.'s reponse was, "It seems to me impossible we ever should live together under a roof of our own, for we have not the means". With complete honesty she went on to add, "Our separation has, on the whole, been for the best, you will easily see why". But, "I grieve on the children's account, poor things".[5]

With his vision no longer opium-distorted Coleridge turned increasingly towards his own family and longed to have his children around him, but unless he could offer them a home of their own (which he could not) then he must content himself with seeing them on visits. Such visits depended, of course, upon the kindness and convenience of the Gillmans. Hartley came frequently during vacations, and Derwent, too, was able to visit; it was not difficult to accommodate the boys, who were able to share their father's room, but a visit from the young Sara (whom Coleridge longed to see) was fraught with complication, due to bedroom shortage. "Poor C.," exclaimed Charles Lamb. "I wish he had a home to receive his daughter in. But he is a stranger or a visitor in this world."[6]

Meanwhile Hartley was working hard for his degree and after that his fellowship. Outwardly he seemed cheerful and reasonably confident, but to Derwent he confided that he felt "obscure forebodings of evil to come".[7]

These forebodings were concealed from his parents. And indeed such presentiments seemed at this period to be irrational, ridiculous. Hartley was on the crest of a wave of success: in early December 1818 his parents learned that he had been awarded a second class *in literis humanioribus* and, although S.T.C. "was a little galled that the student did not reach the *first class*" (Mrs C. to Poole), when it was considered that he had never attended any school but Mr Dawes's at Ambleside and had not been able to afford any private tutor to assist him with his cramming on the final lap, "no blame could possibly fall on the lad, if he could not reach the rank which his cousins had reached before him, wanting their advantages; and Southey, Wordsworth and Sir George B. and many others said, he gained as much credit in his circumstances, being second, as some of those, who had hundreds bestowed on their education did in being first".[8] Thus his proud mother, who was raised to such a pitch of irrepressible high spirits by her good news that Southey teasingly threatened her that he would "import an *aunt*-eater from Brazil".[9]

The new year of 1819 opened with an even greater flourish: when Poole received his customary news bulletin he found himself reading the ecstatic communication, "Hartley Coleridge has had the singular good-fortune to be elected Fellow of Oriel-College, Oxford!"

Following the magnificent news about Hartley there soon came good tidings concerning Derwent: Coleridge's old friend and admirer, John Hookham Frere,[10] had offered to "put aside" three hundred pounds towards Derwent's university expenses and the ever-generous Lady Beaumont[11] had also offered assistance. Mrs C.'s joy knew no bounds. The new generation of Ottery Coleridges was proving to be exceptionally brilliant; particularly the sons of S.T.C.'s brother, Colonel James Coleridge: of these John Taylor Coleridge and Henry Nelson Coleridge[12] were shining stars in the scholastic firmament, while other brothers and cousins reaped distinctions which only seemed less impressive when compared with the achievements of John and Henry. The name "Coleridge" was becoming a byword for outstanding success at both Oxford and Cambridge and now Hartley had joined this family *élite* and Mrs C. had no doubt that in due course Derwent would do the same.

Hartley's success had overjoyed his father, whose pride and satisfaction, like Mrs C.'s, was boundless. But for S.T.C. the satisfaction was, if possible, even keener; he saw in his son's success at Oxford a compensation for his own failure: "Whatever I am, my Hartley is Fellow of Oriel!"

II

Hartley began his Oriel Fellowship in the Michaelmas term of 1819. At Christmas he was invited to Ottery, to the further gratification of his parents; S.T.C. took particular comfort from the sight of "the chasm of the first generation closing and healing up in the second".[13] In May, to augment family satisfaction, Derwent was entered at St John's College, Cambridge.

Strictly speaking Hartley was not yet a full Fellow; at Oriel a Fellow had to serve a probationary year before his election was confirmed. Nevertheless, the authorities were invariably so exacting in their selection of probationary Fellows that it was unheard of for confirmation to be denied.

Oriel was encouraged by its provost, Dr Edward Copleston,[14] to set an example to the other colleges by its pursuit of knowledge, its devotion to its pupils, and by the conduct of its Fellows even in the smallest details of their everyday life. The Fellows of Oriel were a byword at Cambridge for "passing round the teapot in preference to the port". Their Common Room was renowned for its critical style of conversation, insisting on clear definition of forms and logical sequence in argument. Senior Fellows were given to cutting short the discourse of the Junior Fellows (particularly the probationers) and demanding that they should prove a point more conclusively or define more accurately. This was not Hartley's style at all. At Merton he had made a name for himself by "his extraordinary powers as a converser (or rather a declaimer)", resulting in innumerable invitations to wine parties, where he was expected to talk. He was happy to do so, he loved nothing better: "Leaning his head on one shoulder, turning up his dark bright eyes, and swinging backwards and forwards in his chair, he would hold forth by the hour" in a manner which his admirers claimed might only be surpassed by S.T.C. himself.[15]

Moreover, and most importantly, the Oriel common room was, at this time, what might be termed the labour ward of the Oxford Movement. Here, within a few months, Newman would arrive as a probationary Fellow; here Tractarian thinking already had its

mainspring stirring to life in Keble;[16] here, in short, the kernel of
nineteenth-century morals and mores was undergoing definition. The
nineteenth century, particularly in England, overturned the ethics,
ideals and style of the eighteenth; the overall landscape was totally
changed. Hartley did not belong to the nineteenth century; he could
not, did not fit. In the Oriel common room he was in the new era and he
felt, and was perceived to be, a fish out of water.

Hartley, of course, knew that he was on probation and that this meant
that he was expected to eschew the society of undergraduate friends at
Merton and instead cultivate that of the Fellows and probationers of
Oriel; he knew he must act with dignity befitting his new station in the
university; that he was expected to attend morning chapel regularly;
that he must conform with the habits, principles and prejudices of those
whose company he had joined (indeed professed himself to be proud
and honoured to have joined). Unfortunately Hartley, by nature and
upbringing, was the exact antithesis of a conformist. He disdained the
ancient wisdom, "When in Rome do as the Romans". Dr Copleston
himself, during this probationary year, found it necessary on occasions
to "advise and expostulate" with Hartley concerning his conduct. But
Hartley, despite such warnings, continued to fail to attend morning
chapel, to "keep irregular hours" and to return home late of nights after
prolonged convivial sessions with his old friends. The popular version
of what happened next was that the crisis came when Dr Copleston
happened to be in the porter's lodge one evening when there was a
knock on the door, the porter opened it, and Hartley fell "prostrate
through it".[17]

By now the Dean, Richard Whateley,[18] had decided that he must act.
He informed Dr Copleston that "he had heard very disagreeable
accounts lately of the conduct of Mr Coleridge, Probationer Fellow". It
was agreed that all the resident Fellows should assemble on 30th May
(1820) to confer upon the subject. In the meanwhile various enquiries
were quietly made about Hartley's conduct and "it was learnt that the
suspicions of the College were but too well founded"; Hartley Coleridge
was "often guilty of intemperance" attested the college servants and
"came home in a state in which it was not safe to trust him with a
candle".[19]

The resident Fellows convened on 30th May and after a careful
review of Hartley's conduct arrived at the unanimous opinion that he
was not fit to be admitted an Actual Fellow — and that had they "known
a tenth part of what his Probationary year had brought to light, he never
would have been elected at all". The accusations formally presented
against Hartley were "sottishness, a love of low company, and general

inattention to college rules".[20] The Dean informed Hartley of the charges, and of the decision of the Fellows, with the suggestion that he should resign his Fellowship before October, when a formal general meeting was to be held; in this way Hartley would be spared the disgrace of being openly rejected.

At this interview with the Dean Hartley made a "very humble and contrite acknowledgment of the justice" of the decision (thereby tacitly admitting the substance of the accusations made against him). He went on to supplicate to have his probation extended for another year, giving him opportunity to reform (another tacit confession) but was informed that this was out of the question; such a measure would be inconsistent with the very idea of probation, which was not intended to form and discipline a Junior Fellow, but to reveal his real character.[21]

Hartley, during this crisis, confided in no one outside the university; his family knew nothing of what was happening. At length John Taylor Coleridge, informed by Keble, passed on the news to Southey and at last the tragic news was broken to S.T.C. by Dr Gillman (on 30th June). Derwent was at Highgate at the time and was to recall that, "I have never seen any human being before or since, so deeply afflicted".[22]

Derwent was now dispatched to fetch Hartley back to Highgate. On arriving at Oxford Derwent discovered that Hartley had fled, leaving no clue to his whereabouts, though it was thought that he might be on his way to Keswick. Derwent at once sent this information to S.T.C., whose immediate reaction was one of intense chagrin (heavily laced with his chronic, and now intensified, sense of guilt): chagrin that Hartley had at no time in this crisis turned to his father but instead was now hastening back to his mother and Robert Southey, thereby confirming S.T.C.'s ever-lurking self-reproach that he had failed as a father. His hasty reply to Derwent (written on 3rd July) is agonizingly revealing, ·

> I were, methinks, to be pardoned if even on my own account I felt it an aggravation of my sore affliction, that your Brother without writing or any other mode of communication should have bent his course to the North as tho' I were not his Father. . . . Had it been his object to make it known and felt, that he considered me . . . as a Defaulter in the Duties, which I owed his Youth, he could not have chosen a more intelligible . . . way of realizing it.[23]

Derwent now learned that Dr Whately had advised Hartley to go to Canada "on grounds that damaged goods do best for the Colonies".[24] This news flung S.T.C. into a state of complete panic; he visualized

Hartley "wandering on some wild scheme, in no dissimilar mood or chaos of thoughts and feelings to that which possessed his unhappy father at an earlier age . . . he may even be scheming to take passage from Liverpool to America".[25]

But Hartley had not gone either to Canada or Keswick. He emerged from his hiding place (we are not told where he had been) and presented himself at Highgate. Having initially admitted to his peers the justice of their charges, Hartley changed his tune completely when reunited with his father; veering round to vehement denial of any drinking habit and claiming that, in essence, the Fellows had been harsh and unjust, that the irregularities of his behaviour had been grossly exaggerated and that lying testimonies had been made by the college servants.[26] In sum, concluded Hartley, unknown enemies had been at work.

Coleridge accepted Hartley's version of what had happened and rapidly convinced himself that Hartley's personal "oddities" had aroused prejudice and antagonism against him at Oriel: Southey, too, was of this opinion. Indeed at this stage Hartley's denials and excuses were fully accepted by his immediate family and a loyal handful of old friends (Ottery, informed upon the catastrophe by John Keble, framed a distinctly less sympathetic, more objective view).

Precisely who it was that broke to Mrs C. the tragic news about her firstborn is not certain; in all likelihood the task fell to Southey. Every effort was made, from all sides, to shield her from learning the full abrasive details of the Oriel charges; above all the opprobrious word "sottishness" (indeed S.T.C. could not get himself to face that word).[27] Hartley himself plied her with letters putting forward the version of his "disgrace" which he had already given his father; Mrs C. accepted that Hartley had been sinned against, rather than that he had sinned and comforted herself with the assurances which he gave her that his future was not as clouded as some now tried to paint it. Thus we find her writing to Mrs George Coleridge: "With regard to his future prospects, which have been so cruelly darkened by the harsh, I think I may add, unprecedented measure at Oriel, he thinks he shall be able to show himself not wholly unworthy of applying for Ordination some time hence . . . I must venture to assure you that he professes himself *greatly injured* inasmuch as his faults were multiplied and magnified to the College by some unknown enemies."[28]

Meanwhile, S.T.C. devoted his time and energies to preparing a rebuttal of Oriel's charges against Hartley. It is highly significant that Hartley had to caution his father not to attempt to defend him upon "untenable points" and was obliged to put forward a "plain statement of facts" which revealed to S.T.C. the hard truth that there was more substance in Oriel's accusations than Hartley had at first suggested.[29] But S.T.C. had all the makings of a brilliant lawyer and the increasing and formidable complexity of the case he was handling would seem to have stimulated rather than to have dejected him. He revealed fascinating subtleties of argument in defence of this youth who was so palpably at least half guilty: when S.T.C. finally obtained, on October 15, an interview with Dr Copleston at Oxford the encounter became, as so many lawyers' arguments become, a suave and highly sophisticated matter of semantics rather than of anything else; the two gentlemen probing and defining the precise meaning of the word "sottishness" in the best Oriel style: S.T.C. submitting that sottishness meant "addiction to solitary drinking" as opposed to "intemperance". Dr Copleston clearly appreciated the interview and sympathized with S.T.C.'s dignified plea that the Fellows should consider the injurious effects which their charges might have upon Hartley's future character and career, charges calculated to injure him permanently, to an "awful extent and degree";[30] nonetheless, this said, Oriel neither would, nor could, rescind its decision about Hartley.[31]

Tragic as Hartley's disgrace was for the poor youth himself it was equally tragic for the father. The miraculous ground that S.T.C. had regained over the past four years was substantially eroded. Mrs C., while immeasurably distressed by Hartley's calamity, had righteous indignation to buoy her up; being kept in ignorance of the subtleties and complexities of the matter she was able to remain wholly convinced that Hartley's "oddities" had been the sole real cause of the disaster. But at Highgate, once the attempt to re-establish Hartley was seen conclusively to have failed (accompanied by a, so to speak, muffled realization that there had been at least a portion of truth in the Oriel charges) S.T.C. virtually collapsed, becoming distraught, dejected and seeking consolation in opium.[32]

For the two years following his ignominious departure from Oxford Hartley remained in London (mostly in residence in Bedford Square with the Basil Montagus) attempting, unsuccessfully, to earn a living by writing. He was obliged to turn to his family and friends for support. He succumbed to frequent moods of despondency and self-condemnation. Derwent was to write of this period of his brother's life that Hartley "lost his power of will" (he believed himself a toy of Fate).[33] His alcoholism was becoming confirmed; from time to time he would vanish from the Montagus and sequester himself for weeks on end at pot houses, or with friends who were prepared to tolerate him while he was engulfed in his drinking.

By the close of 1821 it was becoming increasingly difficult for

Highgate to ignore the tragic truth of Hartley's drinking habit and in the spring of 1822 there occurred some traumatic crisis (we have not the details) which revealed to S.T.C. the stark fact that Oriel had been right about Hartley and that Hartley's version of his disgrace had consisted of "sophisms".[34] S.T.C. decided that Hartley must be packed off back to the Lake Country and after some cogitation he decided to approach Mr Dawes to see if he might engage Hartley as an assistant teacher at his school. In taking this step S.T.C.'s overt reason was that the Lake Country would not proffer Hartley the temptation such as he experienced in the metropolis; but there can be little doubt, from the evidence afforded in letters, that S.T.C. now found Hartley too grievous to contemplate and was following an urge to put him out of sight and thereby out of mind ("The Rock of Reality"). The Gillmans, too, were anxious to see Hartley removed to a distance; his presence as a frequent visitor at Highgate was having a serious effect upon his father.

Mr Dawes proved willing to take Hartley on his teaching staff, but Hartley dreaded the idea of being a teacher (it must be borne in mind that he was physically smaller than many boys of fifteen and sixteen). Above all he dreaded being a teacher at the school where the news of his election as a probationary Fellow of Oriel had, upon announcement, raised the loudest cheer ever heard in Ambleside.[35] He was being asked to return, an abject failure, to his former scene of triumph. It was a harsh request to be made of him, and an especially harsh request to come from his father. Hartley protested; he begged to be allowed to make another trial of his literary talents in London.[36] But S.T.C. remained adamant; Hartley was not being given any choice; to Mr Dawes he must go: it was a "pronouncement of final sentence" of the father against his son.[37] Mr Gillman wrote to Southey saying that Hartley would be coming up to Greta Hall forthwith, there to await taking up his appointment with Mr Dawes. Southey objected violently.

Poor Mrs C. understood his objections only too well. The Greta Hall household contained three innocent adolescent girls, two children, a mistress of the household who was in a chronic state of depression, and a Poet Laureate and man of letters to whom peace and quiet was a professional necessity. It was beyond contemplation to introduce into such a household an intemperate Hartley and all the consequences that would inevitably be incurred thereby. Furthermore it would mean that Hartley would be flung upon Southey's charity: an extra burden which Southey could not be asked, or expected, to bear. And, final, bitter truth; Greta Hall was not Mrs C.'s house, it was Southey's and therefore the decision of whether to receive Hartley or not rested exclusively with Southey. Mrs C. had no choice but to bow before the inexorable. Southey put the matter in a nutshell with the brisk message which he now dispatched to Wordsworth: "If you have not heard that they have already packed him [Hartley] off for Westmorland, I think you had better write to Mr Gillman and tell him our thorough disapprobation of the scheme; and remind him, which he seems to have forgotten, that Mrs C. has no establishment in which H. can be received."[38]

Hartley was being cast adrift: homeless. His drinking could no longer be hidden; the future held little, if any, tolerable prospect for him. His mother, heartbroken, wrote that she herself felt like "one without plan or purpose; without hope or heart".[39]

# The House of Bondage

I

Hartley joined Mr Dawes in December 1822. He saw the Wordsworths, who invited him to spend part of his Christmas holiday at Rydal Mount, but he did not go to Greta Hall. In any case his mother and sister were themselves now in the south, to have a Christmas reunion with S.T.C.

Young Sara was overwhelmed at the thought of meeting her father. It was ten years since they had last met; for her he was a shadowy, Jove-like figure, to be revered rather than loved. As she was subsequently to write, her relationship with him was one of virtual lifelong separation: "I never lived with him for more than a few weeks at time."[1] Southey had been far more of a true father to Sara than had her own; it might be said that her attitude now was that of an adopted girl who, though dearly loving her step-father, could not subdue her deep-seated desire to know her sire. For S.T.C. it was a moment of discovery of a lost child whom he had last seen as a little capering tomboy and who had now become a brilliant and breathtaking young woman: author of a recently published scholarly work and about to be acclaimed by London as one of the exceptional beauties of the day.

The learned work was a translation from crabbed Latin into English of Martin Dobrizhoffer's account of the Abipones, an equestrian people of Paraguay (a book unearthed and used by Southey while writing his recent history of Brazil); Murray published the translation in three volumes, anonymously, early in 1822 and paid Sara £125 for it. She had worked at the translation as a form of enjoyable relaxation. Always the star of the Greta Hall schoolroom, at an early age she had revealed remarkable intellectual capacities; it was she, rather than either of her brothers, who was the direct heir to her father's cerebral prowess. The adults at Greta Hall had given her encouragement to study; her uncle's large library had been at her disposal. Wordsworth, too, had shown interest in her. Mrs C. had refused to listen to the other mamas who had warned of the dangers of overwork for Sara with her books; even more resolutely had Mrs C. ignored the many persons of both sexes (including Poole) who had pointed out the undesirability of scholarship in a female (it took an exceptional woman, in the first decades of the nineteenth century, to encourage her daughter to acquire learning as Mrs C. encouraged Sara).

Not only was Sara outstandingly brilliant intellectually; she had blossomed into a beauty. When William Collins, the painter, had come to stay at Keswick with the Beaumonts during the summer of 1818 he had been so enchanted by her that he had painted her portrait, in the character of a Highland girl. This portrait had been exhibited in London, where it had caused something of a Romantic sensation. Subsequently it had been presented to Coleridge who had been overwhelmed to learn that this lovely young girl was his daughter and that (as Hartley assured him) the likeness was a true one.

Most mothers would have dreamed of a brilliant match for such a daughter, but Mrs C. privately nursed the hope that Sara would remain single, engaged as a governess to some congenial and reputable family; enabled thereby to pursue her intellectual interests and saved from the anxiety and hardship, let alone the heartbreak, which Mrs C. had come to associate with the state of holy matrimony.

The appearance of the delicious "Highland Girl" in London, in the flesh, created little short of a furore. The metropolis hailed her as "Exquisite Sara . . . Flower of the Lakes" and "Sylph of Ullswater". At the theatre people stood on their seats to catch a glimpse of her and in the drawing-rooms into which Lady Beaumont introduced her all heads were turned in Sara's direction. According to one admirer, Henry Taylor, her beauty at this time was something "which could not but remain in one's memory for life": delicate, regular features, an exquisite complexion, masses of auburn hair, and large eyes of a deep "celestial blue" shining "with the serene lustre of her father's".[2] In build she was small, slight and elegant (to her immense satisfaction she was exactly an inch taller than her mother).

The occasion of S.T.C.'s reunion with this bewitching daughter whom he had only known through her portrait was moving in the extreme; she was, he declared, everything that any father's heart might desire. Equally moving was the touching affection with which he greeted his wife; affection which she, equally touchingly, returned.[3]

A number of visitors came to Highgate to meet Sara and her mother. Lamb, invited to dine, was enchanted by the girl: "I wish I had just such a — daughter!" S.T.C. in his usual manner regaled the dinner party with a lengthy monologue upon a variety of subjects and Lamb was secretly highly amused by the way in which Sara from time to time interspersed, "Uncle Southey doesn't think so".[4]

After Christmas Sara's cousins, John Taylor Coleridge and Henry Nelson Coleridge, sons of S.T.C.'s brother Colonel James Coleridge, called to pay their respects to their Aunt Sam and Sara. John, thirty-two years of age and recently married, was establishing himself as a leading lawyer on the Western circuit while Henry, at twenty-four, with an exceptionally brilliant career at King's College, Cambridge, behind him, was embarking on a promising future as Chancery barrister. Each of them wrote regularly for the magazines and papers and John was on the point of becoming editor of the celebrated *Quarterly Review*. Nonetheless the pair approached the meeting with their cousin Sara in a somewhat nervous mood: the knowledge that she was the translator of Dobrizhoffer had an inhibiting effect upon their customary masculine confidence. Even the ebullient Henry, handsome, charming, full of audacious wit and (at least in his own opinion) immensely sophisticated, cultivating a veneer of what Southey referred to as "Eton bronze",[5] even Henry was intimidated by the notion of a "sylph of Ullswater" who could tackle Dobrizhoffer's archaic Latin. Nonetheless John, summoning his nerve, "swore he would kiss her". However he quailed at the moment of trial; weakened not by her air of intellect but by her breathtaking beauty. Henry (equally bowled over) made do "with the most affectionate, prolonged diminuendo and crescendo squeeze with both hands".[6]

Barely three months later Henry and Sara were deeply in love and secretly and solemnly engaged to each other. "She has promised never to marry anyone but me," Henry confided to his diary. "I can never meet any woman so exquisitely sweet again, and who loves me more devoutly."[7]

Henry and Sara fell in love during the visit that mother and daughter made to Ottery after having left Highgate. They were received most hospitably by the Ottery Coleridges: Colonel James Coleridge wrote of Sara (he had as yet no inkling that Henry was falling in love with her), "Sara is indeed a sweet creature, and she has attached herself to me, and indeed to us all". Of Mrs C. he added: "We get on well with Mrs Sam and let her run on about all the literary World. And I begged her not to think ill of me because I only read the Bible, search the Encyclopaedia, etc, etc. I shall not quiz her for the love I feel of her Daughter."[8] This said, the colonel generously proposed contributing £20 annually towards Mrs Sam's support.

Henry confided the news of his engagement to nobody but his sister Fanny.[9] She, realizing that the engagement would be an unpopular one with the family, advised him to tell no one else for the time being. Henry had yet to advance firmly in his profession; undoubtedly he had a future at the Bar, but was in no position as yet to think of taking on the responsibilities of marriage. Neither he nor Sara possessed a penny of their own (apart from the £125 for Dobrizhoffer). The engagement was bound to be a long one; it should be kept a secret for as long as possible.

Sara, however, confided in her mother, who far from regarding Henry as a catch expressed alarm and horror at the news. Mrs C.'s own experience of impetuous marriage to a penniless youth had taught her to look with extreme apprehension, if not downright censure, upon any marital alliance in which financial security was not absolutely assured. A young barrister with years of hard work ahead in order to establish himself, a Coleridge (Mrs C.'s idea of a distinct risk in what she called the "marriage lottery") and a first cousin into the bargain was not what Mrs C. could envisage with equanimity as a husband for her cherished daughter — if that daughter need be so unfortunate as to be married in the first place. This said, it was obvious that Sara was as determined to marry Henry as he was to marry her. The thought of waiting several years for one another (they bravely spoke of a period as long as seven) in no way deterred them; it was left to Mrs C. to comment, "I daresay they will *now* in the prime and pride of youth agree to live on hope; but, how will it be when youth and charms are fled?"[10]

The visit to Ottery was followed up by visits to Nether-Stowey and Bristol. At Stowey Mrs C. "hinted" to Poole of Sara's "unfortunate attachment".[11] Poole counselled (how history continued to repeat itself!) that S.T.C. must be kept in ignorance of this development. Perhaps the engagement might, after all, come to nothing.

Hartley and Derwent between them were giving their "poor Father" (as Mrs C. now invariably referred to S.T.C.) sufficient to worry about without Sara's romance being introduced as further cause for agitation. During the Highgate visit the parents had several anxious discussions concerning their sons. Hartley, at present, seemed happy with Mr Dawes; but how long that arrangement might last would depend entirely upon how long Mr Dawes continued with his school (he was approaching retiring age). In the months immediately following the Oriel *débâcle* Hartley had spoken of taking Holy Orders; but clearly nothing would now come of that. As for Derwent, now at the close of his second year at St John's College, Cambridge, his progress at first had been excellent, but gradually there had been a falling-off in scholastic performance. Highgate and Greta Hall received roundabout news that he was overspending, finding his friends among the wealthier under-graduates, playing an active (and therefore expensive) social role and developing into a dandy and a beau (his father brusquely accused him of being a "coxcomb"). Rather than concentrating on working for his degree Derwent wrote poetry and articles for magazines[12] and, worst of all in the eyes of his family, abandoned his former orthodox Christian faith and began proclaiming himself an atheist. (S.T.C. would seem to have forgotten that he had caused his own family precisely this same anguish when he had faltered in his own faith some thirty years earlier; Mrs C. now gently reminded him of this and he endeavoured to find comfort in the thought that Derwent was passing through a young man's inevitable stage of "catterpillarage".)[13] Mrs C. had already been crisply told by Derwent that she mustn't interfere but should "let things take their course".[14]

Mrs C. and Sara, on their tour of visits after leaving Highgate, fleetingly saw Derwent at Cambridge; Mrs C., perfectly aware by this time that any further parental cautioning would be unavailing, did her best to keep the visit a troublefree one. Derwent bade his mother and sister goodbye with earnest and unsolicited vows to work hard for his degree and avoid running into debt through extravagance.

Mrs C. and Sara returned to Greta Hall in midsummer 1823; they had been absent for six months. The first news that they learned, on arriving back in the Lakes, was that Mr Dawes had decided to retire from teaching and Hartley was proposing to start a small school of his own in Ambleside. Mrs C. wryly commented to Poole, "With God's blessing he must maintain himself by his School & occasional literature — but how he will contrive to do it . . . I am at a loss to divine!"[15]

The second unpleasant discovery that Mrs C. and Sara made was that the atmosphere at Greta Hall had subtly changed during their absence. Mrs Southey's state of depression had increased and with it her "complaining ways" and irrational resentments. By various small subterfuges she now succeeded in making it clear to her returned sister and niece that their presence at Greta Hall was burdensome to the domestic purse. This naturally triggered in Mrs C. a mounting concern and sense of discomfort. She and Sara had no home to go to other than Greta Hall: in earlier days she had convinced herself that both Hartley and Derwent would be taking Holy Orders and, as clergymen, would be able to offer her happy years in tranquil parsonages: "How often have I drawn a picture in my imagination of seeing you and your brother comfortably settled in some pleasant village as respectable clergymen, enjoying the emoluments of fellowships which I always flatter'd myself you would gain, and being if not always, yet very often with you!"[16] This to Derwent. But now he had become a declared atheist, while Hartley obviously would never take the cloth either. Dreams of pleasant parsonages were no more. As for Henry, even if Sara's marriage did ultimately take place and Mrs C. was offered sanctuary beneath the roof of a lawyer instead of that of a cleric, this could not be for several years. Meantime, what if Edith Southey, in her morosely resentful and irrational state of mind, refused to have her sister and niece any longer at Greta Hall?

George Fricker had died and had left his sisters small legacies of something in the nature of £115 apiece. Mary Lovell had used this sum to purchase herself an annuity and Mrs C. determined to do the same; she would use the annuity to "contribute more towards the household expenditure" on behalf of Sara and herself.

Her sons endeavoured to convince their mother that the obligation between herself and Greta Hall was a mutual one.[17] Young Sara, for several years now, had been teaching in the Greta Hall schoolroom; she and her mother, over a long period, had saved the Southeys the expense of employing a governess. But Mrs C. refused to see this. "It is impossible for us ever to repay the obligations of such a home as we have had for so many years."[18]

In the autumn of that year of 1823 came the thunderbolt news that Derwent, having successfully gained his B.A., would be quitting Cambridge without trying for his fellowship and without prospects of a job and, worse still, with a substantial sum outstanding in debts. The news brought appalled reactions from all quarters. S.T.C., anguished that once again one of his sons had left university in disgrace, subsided into a fresh trough of ill-health and opium, leaving Mrs C. to face the problem of the debts (which gradually revealed themselves to be just under £200).

For the next two years she devoted her time to the repayment of the debts[19] (without hesitation offering her legacy towards this end); to writing letters of admonition and advice to Derwent (who had obtained the post of third master at Plymouth grammar school, but was still showing an inclination to live beyond his means) and to casting anxious glances in the direction of Ambleside where Hartley, his own school having failed, had opened another in partnership with a friend. Mrs C., with Sara, continued to teach full time in the Greta Hall schoolroom; the pupils being Bertha, Kate and Isabel (ranging from thirteen to ten years in age) with little Cuthbert (the latest and final addition to the Southey family, born in 1819) waiting to join them when he reached his fifth birthday.

In late July 1825, Mrs C. received a brief and hasty note from Derwent saying that he had left Plymouth school to become assistant master in classics at a private teaching establishment at Buckfastleigh (near Ashburton, Devon). The head of this establishment was the Reverend Mr Lowndes and Mrs C. instantly saw Derwent's association with a man of the cloth as a sign that her son's period of agnosticism was over and that he was heading in the direction of retrieved orthodoxy.

Other news from Derwent aroused less comfortable suspicions. He had, to his mother's alarm, invested in a horse; explaining that he had done so because he needed to travel about the country, visiting. Maternal intuition alerted Mrs C.; she sensed that there was more to the horse than Derwent cared to divulge. What call was there for so much visiting — *who* was he visiting? She showered him with questions and anxious comments in her strongest sermonizing vein. The inevitable result was that Derwent told his mother as little as possible, or fobbed her off with what she called "half truths". It was not until some six months later that she learned that he was returning, indeed had returned, to Cambridge to read theology and take Holy Orders, and that he had plans for an early marriage with a Miss Mary Pridham, a young lady of nineteen or thereabouts.

His sister wrote to Derwent, "Your hint about 'marrying as soon as may be' has plunged mama into one of those bogs of doubt and discomfort".[20] This was followed by a dire communication from Mrs C. herself: "I hope no child of mine will marry without a good certainty of supporting a family. I have known so many difficulties myself that I have reason to warn my children."[21] S.T.C. similarly sent Derwent a vigorous caution to "think and think again" before binding himself in marriage.[22]

Further admonitions and warnings were sent in ensuing letters but as the betrothal was now a confirmed fact Mrs C. became philosophical: "I do not now wish to give you pain and I will endeavour to hope that all may be well in the end. We must make the best of it."[23]

Meanwhile Hartley's second attempt at running a school had failed; he was now endeavouring to support himself by writing and what little remained of Wilsy's legacy. He drifted into a semi-vagrant way of life, making The Red Lion at Grasmere a kind of headquarters from which he set out on "wanderings" through the upland vales during which all track was lost of him. His mother was as well aware as anyone that these wanderings were really prolonged drinking sorties. From time to time he put in an appearance at Rydal Mount; tolerant as the Wordsworths were where Hartley was concerned ("They have more charity for the errors of those they love than is often found", observed Mrs C.)[24], his conversation caused offence: "He vexed dear Miss Wordsworth [Dorothy] by talking about suicide in a lax way — said he could not find it prohibited in scripture. . . . He talks too, in a wild way about destiny, signifying that a man's actions are not in his own power: absurd! He can govern himself well enough if he chooses to set about it, but self-indulgence and indolence is his ruin."[25]

It was no wonder that Mrs C. exclaimed to Derwent, whom she now saw as her chief hope for security: "I shall pass an anxious winter on *all* your accounts — your situation will, I trust, now *soon* afford me some fair place for the sole of my foot; I have not been on safe ground for a

Sarah Hutchinson, *circa* 1815. Silhouette portrait by artist unknown
(*Courtesy Dove Cottage Trustees*)

*Left:* Daguerreotype portrait of Hartley Coleridge, *circa* 1845 *(By permission of Mrs A.H.B. Coleridge)*

*Right:* Derwent Coleridge in 1819 or 1820, by E. Nash, sketched at Greta Hall *(Humanities Research Center, The University of Texas at Austin, Austin, Texas)*

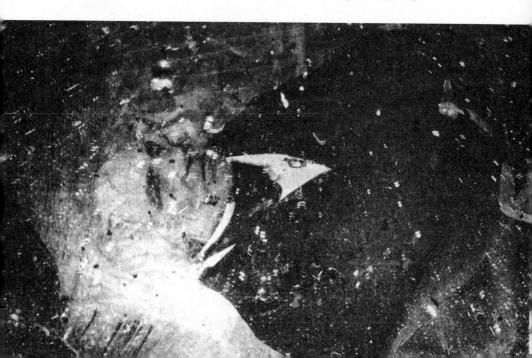

Engraving of the grounds of Greta Hall, with ladies of the Laureate's household, and a view of Crosthwaite church and Bassenthwaite Water beyond, *circa 1820*, drawn and engraved by W. Westall (see Notes to Illustrations 3)

Sara Coleridge *fille* (left) with her cousin Edith May Southey, painted at Greta Hall in 1820 by E. Nash (*National Portrait Gallery, London*)

very, very long time — I trusted long to frail reeds which broke, one by one, from my grasp, and never helped me to good land!"[26]

Meantime Greta Hall had become increasingly melancholy; in July (1826) Isabel Southey had died. It was too much for Mrs Southey who, even before Isabel's death, had been revealing alarming signs of impending breakdown: loss of appetite and weight, self-neglect, and an indefinable oppression of mind and spirit.[27] She now informed her husband that she thought that she was going mad. Southey did his best to put heart into her, assuring her that there was nothing amiss with her that a good diet, a cheerful attitude and counting her blessings would not cure; but deep within himself he knew that Edith had diagnosed her condition correctly. The way ahead promised to be dark indeed. Southey could not prevent his own mood from settling into a depressive mould. The year of 1827 dawned dismally.

A bright note was introduced, suddenly, for Mrs C. and Sara; Derwent had received Holy Orders, was to become curate in the Cornish parish of Helston and planned to open a boarding school. He wanted his mother and sister to be with him, his mother in the capacity of housekeeper. Here was the long-awaited chance to escape from Greta Hall! Mrs C. leapt at Derwent's proposal.

Mrs Southey and Mrs Lovell learned what was afoot; the Aunt Hill seethed with agitation. It was made clear to Mrs C. that the departure of herself and Sara would be considered an immense inconvenience; the Southeys had counted on Sara's tuition for Cuthbert "for some few years to come".[28] Hints were thrown out by Mrs Southey that if they *did* go, and failed to return within six months, they need not come back at all.

Much as Mrs C. and Sara now yearned to be away from Greta Hall and with their dearest Dervy, on further consideration they saw that the arrangement with Derwent might very well terminate when he married in a year or two's time; unable to return, in that case, to Greta Hall, they would find themsleves completely homeless: that dread now everlastingly haunting them and from which they seemed doomed to be unable to escape. Sara was still anticipating that several years must pass before she married Henry; there was no hope of a roof appearing over their heads from that direction! Yet, sighed Mrs C. to Derwent, "Heaven knows how much my heart yearns to look upon you once more!"[29]

Derwent continued to write urging her to join him; at Greta Hall the Southeys made it obvious that they felt that their interests were not being sufficiently considered. Mrs C. worried herself into a state of what was manifestly one of nervous exhaustion, "I have a strange sort of nervous shaking. . . . It seems like an ague; but aunt Lovell says it is entirely nervous." She was reduced to such a state of confusion that she didn't know what to do or where to go; in the end Southey convinced her that she should stay at Greta Hall by saying firmly, "You had better write and give it up, at once". Accordingly Mrs C. wrote to Derwent to say that she and Sara would be remaining in Keswick until Sara married.[30]

Derwent's marriage to Mary Pridham on 6th December of that same year persuaded his mother and sister that they had been right to stay at Keswick; nonetheless Mrs Southey's swings of mood, from silent dejection to feverish outbursts of resentment and suspicion, made Greta Hall's atmosphere increasingly uncongenial for them; their dread of being turned out became a nightmare (if we may believe Hartley) while, realizing the dependence of Mrs C. and Sara upon Southey generosity, the young girl cousins lamentably began assuming superior airs. Greta Hall, declared Hartley, had become a "house of bondage" for his mother and sister.[31]

## II

Early in 1829 came the long-awaited announcement that Henry had at last advanced ( sooner than had been anticipated) to a point in his career where he was able to offer Sara a modest home and security. Plans for the wedding were set in train; it would take place at Crosthwaite church on 3rd September and the honeymoon would be spent touring the Lake Country. Henry and Sara would then set up home together in apartments in London and Mrs C. would go to live with Derwent, his wife and newly arrived son, Derwent Moultrie Coleridge, in Cornwall.

Since there was not the remotest possibility that S.T.C. might be present at the wedding Southey undertook the full role of bride's father, making all the arrangements and paying all the expenses. Hartley wrote introspectively to his sister; Derwent was now married, said Hartley, Sara was about to marry, but he had been decreed by providence "single to live, and unlamented to die". To his mother he wrote, "I remain alone, bare and barren and blasted, ill omen'd and unsightly as Wordsworth's melancholy thorn on the bleak hill-top. So hath it been ordain'd."[32]

The month of August slipped into September. The bridegroom arrived in Keswick, full of high spirits. He brought a carriage with him; his brother-in-law, John Patteson's, kindly spared to the bridal pair for their honeymoon tour. The weather had been wet, but the day of the wedding was "fair, *all through*, for a wonder" (to quote Mrs C.). The officiating clergyman was the recently ordained John Wordsworth; there were eight bridesmaids, comprising the four young misses Senhouse, Dora Wordsworth, and the three Southey girls. The church was a smother of roses; the bridesmaids wore pale green dresses and carried roses and wore roses in their hair; the bride was gowned in rich brocaded white silk trimmed with satin and tulle; she too carried roses. She impressed everyone with her "gentle firmness". She was given away by her uncle Southey. Shortly before the wedding day Hartley had written to say, "I will be present at the celebration — if I walk all night, and all night again. In Justice, I ought to give her away, but. . . ."[33] He had left the sentence unfinished; it was a blessing that he had not been relied upon to give Sara away for he failed entirely to put in an appearance, despite his promise.

Aunt Martha Fricker had journeyed north for the occasion and was present in the church, but Aunty Southey, Aunt Lovell and Mrs C. did not attend the ceremony but remained indoors at Greta Hall; who knows what thoughts were theirs as they waited for the four carriages ("All private, over which was a saving of expense to us") to come bowling back up the drive, with the bride and bridegroom riding together in the leading carriage. "A very elegant breakfast was ready prepared (in part, on the evening before), under the superintendence of Edith [May] and her sisters; in Mr Southey's Study, which went off well, and at one o'clock the separations began — the pair, for Patterdale the rest for Derwent-Water bay, the present residence of Mr Senhouse, where a dinner, Ball, and supper was given and they separated at 4 the next morning" (Mrs C. giving Poole an account of the Great Day). "Do not suppose", she added, "that I went to this merry meeting; I remained at home with my poor sister Lovell, and, even, began some of my packing, such as books, which was better than sitting quite still, and thinking of the miseries of quitting a beloved residence of 29 years duration."

For, now that the time had really come to quit Greta Hall for ever, Mrs C.'s feelings were far from being totally joyful: to be withdrawn from Southey, from the Wordsworths to whom she was "yearly *more* and *more* attached; from this delicious country" where her beloved Derwent and Sara had been "*born* and *bred* and where all the interesting period" of Hartley's childhood had been passed; where she had known so many "excellent people now in the grave" — she exclaimed, "I cannot think of it without pain!"[34]

Southey, brooding upon the loss of his sister-in-law and his niece, miserably reflected that a marriage, next to a funeral, was "the most melancholy of domestic events", completely removing as it did "a beloved member of a family" (in this case two members). To Grosvenor Bedford he wrote, of Mrs C.'s departure: "We part, after six-and-twenty years' residence under the same roof. All change is mournful, and, if I thought of myself only, I should wish to be in a world where there will be none."[35]

The honeymooners, after their tour, returned briefly to Greta Hall and then departed for London. Mrs C. left a few days later, to stay for a short while at Rydal Mount, in order to see the Wordsworths and say goodbye to Hartley. She would then travel south in the carriage of one of the wedding guests, a Miss Trevenen, who was a neighbour of Derwent's, in Helston, and godmother to his child.

The main preoccupation of herself, Dorothy and Mary Wordsworth, during Mrs C.'s visit to Rydal Mount, was the drawing up of plans for the future care of Hartley. Mrs C. would provide regular sums of money for his board and lodging (using her legacy from Sir George Beaumont for this purpose),[36] together with parcels of clothing; the Wordsworths would undertake the responsibility of administering the money, ensuring that Hartley received the clothes, and generally doing their best to keep an eye on him, insofar as one of his vagrant disposition might have an eye kept on him.

Hartley, the subject of all this dedicated concern,[37] was daily expected at Rydal Mount. There was every probability that this might be his last meeting with his mother; she, now sixty, had no expectations of returning to the north once she had removed herself to the south and it was the firm conviction of all connected with Hartley that he must never leave the Lake Country, which afforded him a kind of security that he could not hope for elsewhere.

Mrs C. never doubted for one moment that Hartley would put in an appearance to say what perhaps might be a final goodbye to her; but he failed to present himself. It was learned that he had gone "wandering" once more. It was now becoming clear that Hartley's wanderings were something more than drinking sprees; they were attempts to hide away, to conceal himself. He was, as Derwent tells us, eternally haunted by "self reproach". Moreover there can be no doubt that Sara's marriage had had a traumatic effect upon Hartley, magnifying for him his sense of isolation from his own home and family.

His mother plied him with morale-raising letters; how could he ever expect to be happy, she asked, when he frittered his life and talents away in "desperate indolence", mixing with "low people" and indulging in low habits? She begged him, for the thousandth time, to exchange the society of The Red Lion for that of Rydal Mount. The training of the Oriel common room surfaced in the letter of reply which Hartley at length sent her: "We dispute about happiness, and yet we are not settled about the meaning of the term. . . . Were I a disembodied spirit . . . I doubt not that I should be active, benevolent, and happy. But all that is human is bounded; our life is all a fruitless effort to break the chain which only death can dissolve. . . . The wider my sympathies extend, the more . . . conscious I become of the state of circumscription in which I exist . . . [to be happy] I require a larger area, or in other terms, a greater degree of liberty than is compatible with the condition of humanity, which I nevertheless could not be content to enjoy for my particular self, unless those beings were participators which sympathy had made to me a multiplied self."[38] He concluded: "Never will I exclude from my heart that human creature which that heart welcomes, let its reception cost me what it will."[39]

The voice of the father heard in the son! The right to love where and whom he chose; the necessity for "participators" which "sympathy . . . made . . . a multiplied self"; above all the idea that the human condition was a species of bondage, "Were I a disembodied spirit . . . I doubt not that I should be . . . happy". We are reminded of S.T.C.'s definition of Joy: "That [which] cannot be entered into while I am embodied."[40]

Mrs C. had come to accept that "one so *very* extraordinary" as S.T.C. should "speak a lofty strain" and tread in "elevated realms of thought" (as she expressed it) far beyond her comprehension; she knew herself to be an earthling in comparison with her husband (and very thankful she was too that she had been cast in a more practical, everyday mould). She had long ceased to expect her husband to behave like a normal man; to dream his life away oblivious of the existence of the world around him, convinced that true happiness and love would only be known to him after he had shuffled off his mortal coil, was, perhaps, perfectly natural within the context of a Samuel Taylor Coleridge. She had even managed to persuade herself, over the past few years since the reconciliatory visit to Highgate, that in some strange way peculiar to himself S.T.C. *had* loved her throughout, *had* nourished a deep affection for her; that he had always, again in his own strange way, cherished in his heart the children whom he had too evidently left to "chance and charity".

But to make these concessions to the extraordinariness of S.T.C. was one thing; a son was quite another. A son was an extension of oneself; had, at first, been physically part of oneself; remained, even when a grown man, in some degree still attached by a mysterious, invisible umbilical cord of sympathy. Mrs C. had always been intense in her feelings of maternal love and devotion; she had been, and remained, the essence of selfless dedication to her children. Instinctively she assumed that they would reciprocate this dedication; that her love for them would flow back from them to her. She never imagined, for one moment, that Hartley, her first-born, despite all his lapses in his general behaviour, despite his painful omission to attend Sara's wedding, would not join her during her farewell visit to Rydal Mount.

His failure to return from his "wanderings" to see her and say goodbye to her inflicted a wound in her heart which was second only to that other wound dealt her thirty years earlier when S.T.C. had failed, despite her repeated pleas, to return to her from Germany following the death of Berkeley. Dismayed and broken now as she had been dismayed and broken then, she climbed into Miss Trevenen's carriage, having tearfully embraced her good old friends of Rydal Mount; Miss Trevenen's coachman whipped the horses into action, the carriage wheels revolved, the carriage rolled away between the Rydalian laurels of the driveway and, turning down the hill towards the turnpike road, bore Mrs C. southward. She never had an opportunity to return to the Lakes and as Hartley, for the rest of his days, never travelled further south than Leeds, mother and son never met again.[41]

## *Domestic Bliss — Reprise*

Half of Mrs C.'s dreams of having both sons installed in pleasant country parishes had come true: she at last saw her beloved Dervy officiating in church; heard him preach (he was making something of a name for himself in the pulpit). She was delighted beyond measure by her grandchild, "Little Derwent", and she quickly established a close and loving relationship with her daughter-in-law, "good and pretty Mary". There was also the "gratifying experience" of meeting the "highly thought of" Pridham family who paid Mrs C. "great, & kind attentions".[1] All in all, therefore, Helston was a satisfying dwelling place for Mrs C., but she was kept in a great state of concern while there, on account of Hartley, who was still on his "wanderings".

Mary Wordsworth wrote to say that "from time to time" Rydal Mount heard of him; "calling at this house or that — where he was supplied with a meal — and housing at night in Barns etc". The Wordsworths "commissioned everyone likely to see him with a message requesting him to come to R. Mt", but to no avail. It was not until March (1830) that Mary Wordsworth was able to tell Mrs C. that she knew for a fact that the message had definitely been delivered to Hartley in person. Despite this, he failed to appear at Rydal Mount, but continued to wander.[2] The tragic news had so far been kept from S.T.C., but now it was felt necessary that he should be informed. He was flung into "an agony of grief"; dropping on his knees in a paroxysm of tears and prayer, followed by nights of insomnia and weeping.

At last, in August, having been on the wander for virtually a year, Hartley was once more in correspondence with his mother and lodging with a Mrs Fleming, in Grasmere. He made no attempt to get in touch with his father; nor did his father attempt to write to him.

By this time Mrs C. was on her way down to London. In the spring of 1830 the news had arrived at Helston that Sara was pregnant. In the summer she and Henry rented, furnished, a newly built "small villa" in Downshire Place, at the top of Downshire Hill, Hampstead.[3] The house, with a squeeze, could accommodate Mrs C. and Sara was naturally anxious to have her mother with her during her confinement. Mrs C., in June, began her preparations to travel to London, taking in a visit to Tom Poole at Stowey *en route*. She and Poole gossiped for hours on end and discussed S.T.C.'s most recent work, "a small volume on Church & State &c" that contained, in the notes, an affectionate pen portrait of Poole; Mrs C. was "much pleased and affected by it" and Poole's eyes filled with tears whenever it was referred to.[4]

By mid-September Mrs C. was installed at her new address, 1 Downshire Place, and on 8th October she was able to send Poole the hoped for "happy announcement that,

> Yesterday forenoon, about 11 o'clock Sara was safely brought to bed of a boy who, with his mother, is going on well. He is about the middle size, a little more than 8 pounds in weight. All parties seem satisfied with his appearance, but his father thinks he [is] too much like himself to be pretty; he *wished* for a girl, but is too happy at the well-doing of his wife to care, very much, about the sex of the Child. . . . Poor father at Highgate, has been very nervous about her, he will be now relieved; for Mr Gillman [who delivered the child] will have carried him the good tidings.[5]

The baby was named Herbert,[6] after the ever-lamented cousin, Herbert Southey. Herbert (Herbie) Coleridge was a strong healthy infant with his mother's "azure blue" eyes and red gold hair; his complexion and colouring were so fine that he was soon known to a circle of doting ladies as "The Rose of Hampstead".[7] Sara was blissfully happy with him.[8]

Mrs C. had gone to Hampstead with no clear idea of how long she would stay there, apart from a vague statement that she would remain with Sara for "as long as she was needed".[9] How long that would be, "Time will shew", "We shall see" (these two philosophical observations became great favourites with her during the later years of her life). Mrs C., one way and another, was able to make herself immensely useful at Downshire Place; indeed she became invaluable, and her own happiness was fortified a hundredfold "in feeling herself so supremely useful".[10] Her feet had found good land at last!

The marriage of Henry and Sara and their setting up home with Mrs C. as one of their household, moreover their siting of this home of theirs at Hampstead, only a few miles distant from S.T.C. at Highgate, was to have a profound influence upon all parties concerned, effecting what Hartley was to call "the great reconcilement" within the Coleridge family and giving "peace and comfort and universal charity" to S.T.C.'s final days. Henry, particularly, was to be thanked for the role he played in this reconciliation; as Hartley fully acknowledged in a sonnet which he addressed to Henry in 1837,[11]

Kinsman, Yea — more than kinsman, brother, friend —
O more than Kinsman, more than Friend or Brother
My Sister's Spouse, Son to my widowed mother,
How shall I praise thee right and not offend?
For thou wert sent a sore heart-ill to mend:
Twin-stars were ye — Thou and thy wedded Love
Benign of aspect, as those Imps of Jove
In antique Faith commissioned to portend
To sad sea-wanderers peace. Or like the Tree
By Moses cast into the bitter pool
Which made the tear-salt water fresh and cool —
Or even as the Spring, that sets the boon Earth free
Free to be good, exempt from winter's rule
Such hast thou been to our poor family —[12]

"Our poor family", the Samuel Taylor Coleridges, certainly had been in a disrupted and discordant state at the time of Sara's marriage to Henry; more so than Mrs C. and Sara themselves had realized, for certain things had not been disclosed to them. Mrs C. in her letters had constantly enquired of her sons if they had recently written to their father; she suspected that they had not done so; she was anxious to know the reason for their lack of filial behaviour. Derwent, between his first coming down from Cambridge and his marriage to Mary Pridham had shown himself remarkably disinclined to keep up a correspondence with S.T.C., while Hartley, though repeatedly promising to do so, never wrote to his father after 1824.

Strange depths of constraint, resentment, jealousy, self-reproach, guilt, and dumbly fettered love lurk below the surface of all family group relationships. The Samuel Taylor Coleridges suffered especially from what might be called the accumulation of emotional deposit, which clogged and often hid from view what S.T.C. described as the "pulsating spring" of perfect love.[13] Over the years S.T.C. had accumulated his own (almost unbearable) burden of guilt, resulting from his sense of having failed his wife and children, of having neglected them, of betraying their natural trust in him. This guilt had in turn led to further failure, further neglect, which in turn had stimulated further guilt, and so on. The children, particularly the two sons, on their part had (very naturally) accumulated feelings of resentment against the father who had left them to "chance and charity". These feelings had been kept amazingly well under control out of filial respect zealously implanted in them by their mother; but at last, in 1822, the two young men had voiced to their father this resentment and had made perfectly clear to him their chagrin at always being under obligation for kindnesses and assistance of one kind and another received from persons outside the family. The brothers indicated that their father's failure to provide them with a proper home of their own and to pay for their education had had painful and inhibiting consequences for each of them.[14]

Having dared at last to accuse their sire of failing them as protector and provider, each son had experienced a reaction of shock at his own temerity. It was as if they had shattered a taboo; each was appalled at what he had done. Resultantly each had distanced himself from his father. Riddled with guilt (for in his heart he knew that the reproaches of his sons were just)[15] and paralysed by grief, S.T.C. for his part had shuffled out of his personal relationship with Hartley, banishing him to the far north and throwing the youth upon his own inadequate and tragically eroded self-resources of energy and determination. The result was total disaster. As for Derwent, he hadn't waited to be banished, but had stumped off to carve out his own future in a distinctly ruthless style.

Hartley had mentioned to S.T.C. his conviction that he was a toy in the hands of Fate; S.T.C., whose own sensations of having been rendered powerless, deprived of all self-volition by opium and Heaven knew by what else (even De Quincey at times had felt that it was something more than opium which had fettered Coleridge) had, upon hearing this from Hartley, exploded into that kind of indignation which is upbraiding itself rather than the avowed cause of the moral resentment: "Our own wandering Thoughts may be suffered to become Tyrants over the mind, of which they are the Offspring . . . & that these may end in a loss or rather forfeiture of Free-agency, I doubt not. . . . But for self-condemnation H. would never have tampered with Fatalism; and but for Fatalism he would never have had such cause to condemn himself."[16] Which of the two, father or son, most tortured himself with self-condemnation it would be hard to say.

Since his creation of *The Ancient Mariner* S.T.C. had associated himself, at a profoundly deep level, with the mariner of that epic poem. He had developed the habit of referring to himself as a seaman: a voyager travelling endlessly across the oceans of life, circumnavigating the globe of human experience; meeting with strange and darkly tragic adventures; involved in desperate battles for survival. He had been bowled along by the storm blast; carried to the frozen poles; had burst into silent seas where no man had been before; had destroyed the albatross, that pinioned flight of man soaring to unite with the archangel possible within himself ("O man, thou half-dead Angel", victim of "inward desolations").[17] He had been weighed down by intolerable guilt; had been rejected by old and young; had been rescued, shriven and, he trusted, forgiven: but, even so, he could not escape from the woeful agony which forced him to recount, relive, his past. Like some old sea dog, some retired *conquistador*, he ached with "those . . . wounds too deep & broad for the vis medicatrix of mortal Life to fill up wholly with new flesh, those that tho' healed, yet left an unsightly scar which too often, spite our best wishes . . . opened anew at other derangements & Indispositions of the mortal Health. . . . Even as the Scars of the Sailor, the reliques & remembrancers of Sword or Gun Shot Wounds . . . ache & throb at the coming of Rain or Easterly Winds, and open again & bleed anew."[18] Thus S.T.C. to his notebook, speaking of himself.

Hartley's fate as vagrant and wanderer, and the knowledge of the part which he, S.T.C., himself had played in casting Hartley adrift, constituted the "easterly wind" which, above all others, split the ancient mariner's old wounds wide open anew.

Into this family landscape with its chiaroscuro of tortured guilt and fatalistic shades, reminiscent of some Greek tragedy, now stepped Henry Nelson Coleridge: benign and blithe "imp of Jove". The home circumstances of his own childhood and youth had been remarkably happy and secure. If we are searching for instances of S.T.C.'s pathologically distorted powers of judgement we need only turn to those passages in his letters where he writes, contemptuously and not infrequently downright insultingly, of his brothers. Everything that we learn of them elsewhere presents them in a very different light.

Distinct genetic streams flowed through the Coleridges of S.T.C.'s generation: a practical, commonsensical countryman's approach to life, the essence of an "old cavalier toryism" as Hartley described it,[19] side by side with remarkable gifts of intellect and love of scholarship. The Ottery Coleridges were in every respect a brilliant family, a succession of generations making their mark upon their day by their outstanding achievements in the professions, but the most brilliant generation was that which succeeded that of S.T.C. and his brothers; the saliently endowed group of siblings being that sired by James Coleridge, "the Colonel", and, we are told, of that remarkable group Henry was "the most brilliant and captivating".[20]

Indeed Henry, with his love of fun, puns and anecdotes, his brilliance of mind, his irresistible charm and his sociability must have seemed to S.T.C. more like a son than a son-in-law; he was fond of referring to the young man as, "My dear Nephew and by a higher tie Son",[21] but the very fact that Henry was son-in-law and not son meant that the relationship between the pair was of a happier and freer intimacy than S.T.C. was now able to achieve with his own true sons; no trauma of the past lay between S.T.C. and Henry, no guilt, no resentments.

Nor had Henry any inhibitions when it came to calling upon his uncle Sam and discoursing with him; certainly he worshipped S.T.C. with an enthusiasm which to his brothers sometimes seemed to verge on the excessive, but Henry's hero worship of the sage of Highgate, the "marvellous spirit", was free of that painful element of filial reverence for "an erring, suffering saint"[22] that burdened Hartley and Derwent and Sara when they approached that father who, for so many years of their lives, had been a species of unseen, awesome godhead; a brooding weight upon them since, proud as their mother had taught them to be of him, they always trembled at what they might overhear being said of him. Henry's happy relationship with his own father, his sense of security when in his own home at Ottery, meant that he visited The Grove, Highgate, with equal ease of mind and spirit. So he now assumed the role of blithe, albeit respectful, liaison between Hampstead and Highgate, carrying messages of love from Sara and Mrs C. to Highgate, and returning to Downshire Hill laden with messages and blessings for the inmates thereof. Gradually Mrs C. and Sara grew accustomed to the feeling that "poor Father" was only a few miles distant, instead of three hundred, and Coleridge in his turn became aware that he had a real family of his own across the Heath. A point was reached where occasional visits were exchanged. It was eight years since Mrs C. and S.T.C. had last met. She now found him "very decrepit" physically (the Gillmans informed her that Coleridge had suffered a kind of "seizure" during early May of that year 1830, possibly connected with the shock he had received upon learning of Hartley's wanderings) but his mind and countenance were as vigorous and youthful as ever.

Henry's marriage to Sara had brought about an atmosphere of *rapprochement* between Ottery and Highgate; the Colonel, when in London, had once or twice called at Highgate and had been kindly received, while the Rev. George Coleridge, whose death occurred in 1828, before dying had expressed a strong wish to see S.T.C. again and, this being impossible, had dictated him a loving letter.

Derwent appeared in London in January 1831; he stayed at Highgate with his father, but came frequently to Downshire Place. Baby Herbert, too, was a visitor to Highgate; being taken over there, from time to time, to see his grandfather. Mrs C. described one visit, when Herbie was a year old: "Herbert was in raptures the whole time he stayed, raving at the pictures [in S.T.C.'s attic bedroom-study] . . .

S.T.C. laughed heartily at his funniness and hoped to see him again soon."[23]

Thus, thirty years after opium had forced him to abandon all "true" hope of domestic happiness, we find S.T.C. quietly but successfully reintegrating himself within his own family circle. Certainly he was encouraged in this by his son-in-law Henry, but nonetheless there was visible a stirring of genuine desire to be one of his family in an everyday sense, seemingly regardless of whether, or not, intellectual justification might be found for such participation. Perhaps this was merely a sign that he was growing old; that in his final years he was instinctively homing; subconsciously acknowledging the rudimentary pull of "the holiness of the heart's affections" as expressed in that simplest and most universal of all urges, to return home at the end of the day:

> Homeward I wind my way . . . recalled
> From bodings that have well nigh wearied me. . . .
> And now, belovéd Stowey! I behold
> Thy church-tower, and, methinks, the four huge elms
> Clustering, which mark the mansion of my friend;
> And close behind them, hidden from my view,
> Is my own lowly cottage, where my babe
> And my babe's mother dwell in peace! With light
> And quickened footsteps thitherward I tend,
> Remembering thee, O green and silent dell!
> And grateful, that by Nature's quietness
> And solitary musings, all my heart
> Is softened, and made worthy to indulge
> Love, and the thoughts that yearn for human kind.[24]

Alas, the babe of these lines, Hartley, alone remained isolated from the fresh tide of family feeling. His mother continued to send him regular remittances of money, parcels of clothes, and newsy letters, and, through the Wordsworths, she knew that these were safely delivered to him, but from him came no acknowledgement or reply of any kind.

At length, towards the close of that autumn of 1831, Mrs C. dispatched Hartley a strong letter reproaching him for his continuing neglect of his parents and accusing him of having outlived his affection for them. She cited his failure in coming to Rydal Mount to say goodbye to her at the time of her final departure from the Lakes, and his years of total silence towards his father (now, with the onset of winter, ailing again). Hartley, appalled by her accusations, was at last stung into a reply:

My dear Mother

I deserve it, and yet to hint the possibility that a son could outlive his affection for his mother, and such a mother, is sufficient reproach for a fault great as mine. You cannot, do not seriously suspect this, for if you did, no profession, scarce any performance of mine, could exorcise the evil spirit from your soul, for dead affections have no earthly resurrection — it is vain to puff at the cold ashes of extinguish'd love, to galvanize the corpse of tenderness to a mimicry of posthumous life. But no, my mother, I never ceased to love you, tho' times have been, when that love was more remorse and agony, proclaiming aloud the duties which it gave no strength to perform. You have not experienced as your main sorrow, what it is to fear the voice, to shrink from the eye of offended love, or you would know that any thing rather than indifference occasion'd my absence when you were paying your last visit to Rydal Mount. . . . With regard to my long silence, I have nothing to say, but that I have been always intending to write daily. . . . I must, I will write to my Father, and that forthwith.[25]

But no letter came to S.T.C. from Hartley. He remained silent; nor did his father write to him. Each was gripped in the paralysis which stems from remorse in the wake of "offended love". Hartley could not forgive himself for the disgrace that he had brought upon himself and his family; S.T.C. could not forget how he had "pronounced a final sentence against" his son; washing his hands of him and banishing him to the distant north. To pronounce final sentence against a friend was "almost irreligion" — but against a *son*! "O then what solace can we find? While we love him, how can there be solace? . . . There are sighs which cease to heave the Breast only when the Breast is no more to be heaved."[26]

This grievous sorrow of the Hartley tragedy weighed eternally upon S.T.C.'s heart, and upon Mrs C.'s too; casting a shadow across the otherwise increasingly sunny family landscape. In June 1832 Sara gave birth to a second child, named Edith. Henry and Sara were both anxious that S.T.C. should attend the christening and he had privately made up his mind to get there at all costs; having, as he expressed it, the wish "to stand beside Mrs Coleridge at this second birth of our common Off-spring — in proof that the lack of Oil or Anti-friction Powder in our Conjugal Carriage-wheels did not extend to our parental relations". This to his friend J. H. Green, to whom S.T.C. added, in a burst of confidence, "In fact, bating living in the same house with her there are few women, that I have a greater respect & *ratherish* liking for, than Mrs C. — ".[27]

Despite the note of irony S.T.C.'s behaviour towards his wife, during the christening and at the party afterwards, revealed a genuine tenderness; he spoke to her of "early days"; of Stowey and Tom Poole.[28] Not many weeks later he was again revealing tenderness and concern; Sara *fille* had succumbed to a severe attack of what her doctor called "nervous debility" when in conversation with her, but which he diagnosed as a "puerperal Depression" when discussing the illness with Mrs C. A month by the sea was recommended; accordingly arrangements were made for Sara to go to Brighton with her mother in attendance. S.T.C. declared himself anxious to go with them: it was planned that Henry would take them to Brighton, but after that mother and daughter would be on their own; "Father" felt that he should be there with them. However Mrs Gillman refused to agree to this scheme without the consent of her husband, who was in Paris; S.T.C. was reluctantly obliged to relinquish the idea. Mrs C. (who confessedly would have been relieved to have had a companion to stay on in Brighton with her and Sara after Henry's return to London) comforted herself with the thought that all was probably for the best, as she might well have found herself with two "sufferers" on her hands instead of one.[29] Nonetheless S.T.C.'s gesture touched her greatly.

Sara gradually recovered her health and in the spring of 1833 there was rejoicing in the family when Hartley's first volume of *Poems* appeared, dedicated to S.T.C.,

> Father, and Bard revered! to whom I owe,
> Whate'er it be, my little art of numbers . . .

S.T.C. was "much affected", and felt pride too when the work was well received and favourably noticed in the *Quarterly Review*.[30] But still no actual word came to him from Hartley: however, S.T.C.'s spirits had been raised. Indeed 1833 proved a happy year for him; his own three-volume *Poetical Works* was almost completed, while an unexpected spell of good health, following a course of bath treatment, enabled him to pay more visits and see more visitors than usual. In late June he visited Cambridge (Derwent, too, was there at the time). "S.T.C. is ten years younger in spirit: the tepid-salt-water-shower bath has done wonders!" Mrs C. reported jubilantly to Poole. At Cambridge, "Samuel was most highly gratified with his reception, and pleased to see his College & old haunts once more".[31] On his return to Highgate he went over to Hampstead to see his family; he was (noted daughter Sara): "In excellent spirits. Admired the darlints."[32]

Mrs C. makes affectionate mention of S.T.C. frequently in her letters to Poole during this period. Husband and wife were now seeing a fair amount of each other in the course of domestic visiting. Poole sent messages and news to S.T.C. through Mrs C.; she told Poole, "He receives all your kind messages with a peculiar look of satisfaction, and begins to talk of 'auld lang syne'".[33] In July 1833 we find her exclaiming to Poole: "S.T.C. will be delighted when I read to him that part of your letter, in which he is so affectionately mentioned: what a pity that such friends cannot see more of each other!"[34]

Thus, in the final eighteen months of his life we discover Samuel reunited with Sally Pally in that comfortably persistent friendship which underlies long-established marriages; she reading to him letters from dear Tom Poole, thereby inspiring S.T.C. to reminiscence; reviving in memory those now distant days spent in Poole's "comfortable brown house with the tanyard at the back, and the long garden" with its jasmine and lime-tree bowers, and the little path connecting this happy spot with "the old hovel", which, surveyed over a distance of forty years, itself assumed a blissful dreamlike aspect, bathed in transcendental glow.

If this seems a sentimental note to strike at the finish of the story of a marriage so notoriously bumpy in its progress as that of the Coleridges, then this is because they themselves were feeling sentimental, as grandparents have a right to feel. When we read of William and Mary Wordsworth "Darby and Joaning it" (as W.W. liked to say) we should remind ourselves (astonishing as it may seem) that Samuel and Sara Coleridge "Darby and Joan'd it" too, over Poole's letters, read together in the parlour at Downshire Place.

## Envoi

S.T.C. died on 25th July 1834. During this final illness it was his wish that neither his wife nor daughter should visit him; he wanted them to be spared distress. On the evening of 19th July a note from Highgate was delivered at Downshire Hill; as Henry was at church it was opened by Sara; it bore the news that S.T.C. had become "alarmingly worse". Sara jotted despairingly in her diary, "On Sunday Henry saw him twice — and again yesterday — We hear of him twice a day. His pain is great." Henry's last visit recorded here (it took place on the 22nd) was probably the occasion on which he said goodbye to S.T.C. who had announced that he desired henceforth to have nobody visit him except his doctor; the dying man wished to be disturbed as little as possible in order that he might meditate upon his Redeemer. Henry however was resolved to see him for a last time and S.T.C. was "just able" to send his blessing to his wife and daughter; "He articulated with difficulty . . . Henry kissed him & withdrew — never to see him alive again".[1] Three days later S.T.C. was dead. "A great spirit has passed, a very great one — and what have we not lost!" exclaimed Henry, breaking the news.

The funeral took place on Saturday 2nd August, Mrs C. and Sara did not go to it. The family had also decided that it would be "useless" to ask either Derwent or Hartley to make a long journey to be present. Edward Coleridge came from Eton to represent the Coleridge family, together with Henry. Mr Gillman was ill in bed; his son James came as the representative of the household in which S.T.C. had passed his final two decades. A number of friends and disciples of S.T.C. were also present. The funeral was "handsome": the hearse was drawn by four horses, and there was an "abundance of plumes — two mourning carriages etc". The remains were placed in a vault in Highgate churchyard.[2]

Now came the letters of respect and condolence. There were sheaves of them; among them a long one from Poole specifically for Mrs C. (unfortunately it was subsequently burned). Sara replied to it on behalf of her mother, who was "very far from well at present". "Your remarks on [my father's] character and genius have been delightful to us," wrote Sara, "they are among those valuable tributes from valued persons which have mingled sweetness with our cup of sorrow. We mourn not only one near and dear taken from our sight, but the extinction of a light such as can never beam on our earthly path again."[3]

From Hartley came a chaos of remorse, despair, "I lived in hopes of seeing our dear departed Parent. But for my . . . soul-withering procrastination, I might have seen him, might have comforted him." He exclaimed, tragically: "I can only hope that no painful thought of me adulterated the final outgushing of his spirit, that if he breathed a prayer for me, it was a prayer of comfortable love, foreseeing, in its intensity, its own effect."[4]

This to Derwent. In his letter to his mother Hartley was even more tragic in tone: "I grieve that I was not called away in my youth, that my beloved Parents did not close my eyes, that my death should have been the only sorrow I had ever caused them, that when they talked of me, they might weep tears of tender joy, thinking of what I might have been, and no painful thought of what I had been . . . ah, Mother, how little worthy was I of such a father."[5]

In his study at Greta Hall Southey, on 27th July, had opened his morning's mail to find amongst it a communication from Downshire Place informing him that Coleridge was dead. Great waves of recollection swept over him. Before addressing himself to penning a long letter of sympathy to the bereaved family he scribbled a short note to Grosvenor Bedford, "This day's post brings me word of Coleridge's death. It is just forty years since he and I first met, and from that meeting the course of my life received its bias. Even my present place of abode was determined in consequence of my coming to this very house to visit him after my return from Lisbon." Here Southey stopped, as if the tide of memory made it impossible for him to continue. He concluded the note, "God bless you. R.S."[6] Coleridge, as usual, had defeated him.

Wordsworth wrote to Henry and Sara on behalf of all the family at Rydal Mount; concluding with the wish that they might be remembered "tenderly" to Mrs C.[7]

Mrs C. survived her husband by eleven years; Southey she outlived by two. The final decade of her life was no more trouble-free than the rest had been. Sara suffered a succession of miscarriages and stillbirths, with intervening relapses into her nervous illness and in 1843 came the heavy blow of Henry's death from spinal paralysis. Tom Poole had died in September 1837, suddenly, from a sharp pleurisy: a sad milestone in Mrs C.'s life story. The following November had brought another blow: the death, under circumstances of insanity, of her sister, Edith Southey.

Sarah Hutchinson ("My dear, good old friend") had died in 1835; Dorothy Wordsworth had become a hopeless and tragic invalid. Southey, in 1839 (following his second marriage, to Caroline Bowles) had subsided into total memory loss and senility. To add to all these sorrows there had been the abrasive journalistic assault upon Coleridge's good name and reputation, with exposures of his opium and plagiarisms, and details of his private life, far from kind to Mrs C. Then had followed the traumatic holocaust: the burning of the great collection of letters with their "secrets", which, entailing reading them all, as it had, opened up old wounds anew for Mrs C.

It was no wonder that her own health had faltered under this constant stress: in 1836 she told the Derwents, "I am become, in looks and feelings, 10 years older".[8] But buoyancy had always been one of her saving characteristics and in spite of her infirmities she was, as she said in sincerely heartfelt gratitude, blessed with a loving family and friends, and though many of these had been removed by death, many remained to bring her comfort in her closing years with Sara at Chester Place, Regent's Park. The Derwents came to work and live at Chelsea, and their nearness brought great joy to "poor, old infirm Mother", as she now rather liked to refer to herself. Hartley kept up a fairly good correspondence with her and she kept him overprovided in articles of dress; he was now advancing in middle age and prematurely white-headed, but she insisted in thinking of him as a youthful and eternally wayward son.

Despite her inclination to see herself as "decrepit" her family noticed little real change in her essential self. "Her age and infirmities . . . had not made any sensible alteration in her mind or heart," Sara was to recall in her *Memoirs*, "[she] entered as fully into life, as if she had [remained for ever] fifty".[9] Mrs C. helped Edie with her arithmetic and sewing and cutting out paper animals; listened to Herbie's tales of his exploits at Eton and resigned herself, on wet days during holiday times, to the incessant sound of his hammering ("the carpentry craze") or his practising on the trumpet. On sunny days, equipped with parasol, she crossed the gravelled carriageway encircling Regent's Park and sat on a seat under the trees, quietly amusing herself with watching the occasional passers by, the odd pug dog or poodle, and listening to the bleating of distant sheep; that sound which always carried her back to "dear dear Keswick and the dear land of the Lakes". And, when bad or wintry weather prevented this, she sat on the sofa at the drawing-room windows, watching the world from there, or "scrawled" loving little notes to relatives and friends.

She died on the morning of 24th September 1845, in the act of getting up to start another day. Sara was away from home; Mrs C. had not been very well, breathless and with a pain in her chest, but she had made light of it; "Now, dearest Child, make yourself easy about me . . .

and pray do not think of coming home a minute sooner than you first intended . . . I am always better in the evening so I think it best to write now; and finish by the evening Post tomorrow,"[10] she wrote to Sara on the evening of Tuesday 23rd September. On that morrow, when the family's old nurse came into her room to help her to dress, Mrs C., as she rose from her bed, collapsed and died in mid-breath, mid-movement: an abrupt, almost accidental step into eternity.

# NOTES AND REFERENCES

## Key to References

| | |
|---|---|
| BL | *Biographia Literaria* |
| BM | British Museum |
| BMJ | *British Medical Journal* |
| CCL | Coleridge, S. T., *Collected Letters* (ed. Griggs) |
| C.F. | *Coleridge Fille*, Griggs |
| CNB | Coleridge, S. T., *Notebooks* (ed. Coburn) |
| CSL | *The Life and Correspondence of Robert Southey* (ed. C. C. Southey) |
| D.C. | Dove Cottage Library |
| Dev. House | *The Story of a Devonshire House*, Lord Coleridge, K.C. |
| D.Q. | De Quincey |
| EWL | Wordsworth Letters, *The Early Years* (ed. Selincourt) |
| HCL | Coleridge, Hartley, *Letters* (ed. Griggs) |
| HCPWM | Coleridge, Hartley, *Poetical Works, and Memoir of his Life by His Brother* |
| HCRL | Robinson, Henry Crabb, *Correspondence* (ed. Morley) |
| K.K. | *Kubla Khan* |
| LL | Lamb, Charles and Mary, *Letters* (L) ed. Lucas; (M) ed. Marrs |
| LWL | Wordsworth Letters, *The Later Years* (H) ed. Hill |
| Min. | *Minnow Among Tritons: Mrs S. T. Coleridge's Letters to Thomas Poole, 1799–1834* (ed. Potter) |
| MS HRC UTA | Humanities Research Center, The University of Texas at Austin |
| MS R | MS Rugby |
| MWL | Wordsworth Letters, *The Middle Years* (ed. Selincourt, rev. Mary Moorman and Alan G. Hill) |
| MWSL | Wordsworth, Mary, *Letters* (sel. and ed. Burton) |
| NSLC | *New Letters of Robert Southey* (ed. Curry) |
| P.W. | Coleridge, S. T., *Poetical Works* (Coleridge, E. H., 1912, unless indicated otherwise) |
| Rem. | *Reminiscences*, Cottle |
| S | Sandford, Mrs Henry, *Thomas Poole and his Friends* |
| SCCB | *Correspondence of Robert Southey with Caroline Bowles* (ed. Dowden) |
| SCML | Coleridge, Sara, *Memoir and Letters* (ed. her daughter — Edith Coleridge) |
| SHL | Hutchinson, Sara, *Collected Letters*, (ed. Coburn) |
| SMSS | Poole MS BL Add. 35,343 |
| SLW | *A Selection from the Letters of Robert Southey* (ed. Warter) |
| T.T. | Coleridge, S. T., *Table Talk* |

PREFACE

1 Henry Taylor (1800–86), distinguished civil servant and man of letters. Entered Colonial Office in 1824 and became a shaping influence upon the British Empire. He was Southey's closest link with the younger generation of writers and poets, including the "Cambridge Apostles" (among them Tennyson) who were associated with James Spedding (1808–81) the Bacon scholar of Mirehouse, Bassenthwaite, Cumberland. Taylor did not, in the end, write the Southey *Life and Letters*, relinquishing the work to Southey's son Cuthbert.

2 CCL L 597

CHAPTER ONE: *An Angry Young Man*

1 SLW iii 270–3
2 CCL L 676
3 HCPWM i xcviii
4 HCPWM: 1
5 MS HRC UTA, "Mrs Codian": all quoted passages concerning the Fricker and Southey families come from "Mrs Codian's Remembrancies" unless otherwise stated. Stephen Fricker (1738–86), a remarkably handsome young man, was reckoned a "good scholar" and there had been talk that he might take Holy Orders, but upon his father's death he had gone to Bristol to look for a commercial situation.
6 Mrs S.T.C. in "Mrs Codian" says it was of "some hundreds"; S.T.C. says £10,000 (CCL iii 238). Judging by the amount of money Stephen Fricker would seem to have had at his disposal one wonders if the latter figure may not have been the more likely.
7 CCL L 738; MS HRC UTA, "Mrs Codian"
8 CSL i. It is from this garment, based on a romanticized version of the costumes of American Indians, that we have derived our pyjamas.
9 Ibid.
10 Ibid.
11 Ibid.
12 SCCB 52
13 NSLC i 36
14 NSLC i 36, 37
15 Charles Watkin Williams Wynn (1775–

1850) was, with Grosvenor Bedford, Southey's life-long friend. Wynn was the second son of Sir Watkin Williams Wynn, a Welsh baronet. Through his mother Wynn was a nephew of Lord Grenville and a kinsman of the Duke of Buckingham. Wynn was called to the Bar in 1798. In 1797 he had become M.P. for Old Sarum; later he was M.P. for Montgomeryshire. He sat in the Cabinet 1822–1828; during Grey's administration he was Secretary of War, 1830–1831. George Burnett (1776–1811), a young man of brilliant intellectual promise, son of a farmer at Huntspill, Somerset. Grosvenor Charles Bedford (1773–1839); from c. 1804 onwards a good friend and admirer of Mrs S.T.C.; held posts at the Exchequer; Chief Clerk in the Auditor's Office 1822–34. A bachelor, he lived with his aged parents, two younger brothers and a cousin in Brixton.
16 NSLC i 36
17 NSLC i 36, 37
18 CCL L 676
19 "No niggard 'and" (the "h" deliberately dropped) became a Coleridge family saying, passed from one generation to the next (note by A. H. B. Coleridge).
20 *Min. Pref.* xxxiii
21 NSLC i 55
22 NSLC i 83, 84
23 NSLC i 54, 55
24 NSLC i 56

CHAPTER TWO: *Sarah Enchanted by a Meteor . . .*

1 Robert Allen (1772–1805); B.A. 1796, M.A. 1803, M.B. and M.D. 1803. In 1797 appointed assistant surgeon to the Second Royals, then serving in Portugal. Died of apoplexy at Sudbury, where he was on the medical staff.
2 LL (M) i 127–7
3 EWL 70; Wordsworth, *Extempore Effusions*
4 *Frost at Midnight*
5 *Sonnet: To Pantisocracy*
6 NSLC i 56
7 S i 97–98
8 CCL L 73
9 SCML i 11

10 David Hartley (1705–57), author of *Observations on Man, His Frame, His Duty, and his Expectations* (1749); a loosely Spinozistic philosophy combining associational psychology, Necessitarianism and Christianity.

11 Letter to R.S. CCL L 86; *Conciones ad Populum* and lectures 1 and 3 on *Revealed Religion: Works* i 45–46, 105–7, 163.

12 CCL L 168

13 *Min*. L 22

14 Joseph Priestley (1733–1804); author of an abridged (1775) version of Hartley's *Observations*, the Priestley version being entitled *Hartley's Theory of the Human Mind*. Also author of, among other works, an *Essay on the First Principles of Government* (1768) and *An History of the Corruptions of Christianity* (1782).

15 William Godwin (1756–1836), republican and author, member of the Revolutionists' Society, associated with Stanhope, Horne Tooke and Holcroft. From 1785 onwards wrote "Sketches of English History" for the *Annual Register*. His most famous work, a treatise on political science entitled *The Inquiry concerning Political Justice, and its Influence on General Virtue and Happiness* (1793) was followed in 1794 by a novel, *Caleb Williams, or Things as they are*. In that year he came bravely forward in support of fellow republicans arraigned for high treason. His other works include *The History of the Commonwealth*. He also attempted drama; in 1800 his *Tragedy of Antonio* was a disaster at Drury Lane. Tried business as a bookseller and among other works published Charles and Mary Lamb's *Tales from Shakespeare*. In 1833 Grey's government appointed him Yeoman Usher of the Exchequer, with grace and favour apartments in Palace Yard, where he died at the age of eighty.

16 McFarland, *Coleridge and the Pantheistic Tradition*, 171

17 *Polit. Justice*, i 316

18 *P.W.* (1840) i 71, 179

19 CCL L 667

20 T.T. 27.9.1830.

21 CNB 1601 21.361

22 NSLC i 72, 61–66

23 NSLC i 72

24 CNB 2398 21.564

25 NSLC i 61

26 NSLC i 56

27 S i 96–7

28 S i 122

29 NSLC i 70

30 CCL L 73

CHAPTER THREE: *Ebullience and Duty*

1 NSLC i 68

2 S i 103–4

3 S i 92–5

4 S i 40–3

5 S i 103–4. (We may form some idea of what was actually said by reading a letter from R.S. to Horace Bedford on 22.8.1794: "Poor Robespierre! . . . I believe him to have been sacrificed to the despair of fools and cowards. Coleridge . . . is now inclined to think with me that the [?actions] of a man so situated must not be judged by common laws, that Robespierre was the benefactor of mankind and that we should lament his death as the greatest misfortune Europe could have sustained". (NSLC i 73).

6 S i 98

7 S i 39

8 NSLC i 72

9 S i 97

10 NSLC i 71

11 CCL L 54

12 *Proceedings of the Delaware County Institute of Science*, xi 1–60 (1947)

13 NSLC i 70, 72

14 CCL L 58, 59, 60; for R.S.'s later account of S.T.C.'s behaviour and the Bristol and Bath perplexities arising therefrom, see NSLC ii 446–8.

15 CCL L 522

16 CCL L 77

17 CCL L 65

18 Ibid.

CHAPTER FOUR: *The Glowing Gorgeous Poetry . . .*

1 CCL L 680

2 D.Q. *Works* iii 57

3 CNB 4430 21½. 51. Derived by S.T.C. from Jean Paul, *Geist*.

4 CCL L 1169. Another glum notebook entry reads, "A man who marries for love is like a frog who leaps into a well. He has plenty of water but then he cannot get out." (*Anima Poetæ* 160).

5 *Min.* L 14

6 *Anima Poetæ* 158

7 CCL L 81

8 *Bondage of Opium* 65

9 CCL L 93

10 Cottle *Rem.*

11 George Dyer (1755–1841) educated at Christ's Hospital and Cambridge; journalist and active Reformist, friend of William Frend the Unitarian and seditionist. Further (delightful) acquaintance with him should be made through the pages of Charles Lamb.

12 NSLC i 93

13 NSLC i 511

14 Ibid.; R.S., at all events, alleged this authorship in the letter cited, to Charles Danvers, 15.6.1809.

15 Published as *Conciones ad Populum or Addresses to the People*; 16th Nov. 1795. See *Lectures 1795 on Politics and Religion*, ed. Lewis Patton and Peter Mann, *Works*, vol. I.

The Jacobins originally derived from the Breton deputation in the Third Estate of the Estates General of France in its early days (1789); the Breton deputation having earned a reputation for intransigence. From this deputation was formed the radical Breton Club, which in turn provided the nucleus of the Jacobin Club; its members being noted for their extreme radical views and academic oratory, and in due course for sans-culotte methods of violence.

In the popular English view anyone who urged reform, let alone revolution, even bloodless revolution (as S.T.C. did — see below) was a Jacobin. S.T.C.'s own view of the matter was that though he aided the Jacobins by some of his utterances he was never a Jacobin himself and this must be seen as a fundamentally correct, though very nice distinction.

There is no doubt (he confessed it himself) that when he was on the platform, speaking, S.T.C.'s ebullience led him into impromptu utterances which were of markedly more Jacobin tone than what we read in the published lectures; nevertheless his overall tone must be judged as remarkably balanced and moderate for so young a man speaking upon such inflammatory political topics at such a time: what he has to say is already all of a piece with what he will say in maturity. He sees revolution, reform, being absorbed into a great overall whole: an embracive System based upon theism and traditional social and moral values. At Bristol in 1795 he was already convinced of the necessity of "bottoming on fixed principles", as he called it; and convinced of the importance of establishing an educated leadership in both Church and State (atheism was abhorrent to him), and his major purpose in politics was already the salvation of the people through an education embracing the whole range of humanity's interests — which included the spiritual as well as the material: see editorial introduction, *Works*, I. This was radical thinking; but not Jacobin thinking.

16 CCL L 683

17 CNB 4430 21½.51

18 CCL L 1169; CNB 4430 21½.51

19 CCL L 1169

20 Mary Wollstonecraft (1759–1797); journalist and author, who first became famous in 1790 with her *Vindication of the Rights of Men*, a reply to Burke's *Reflections on the Revolution in France*. She quickly followed *Rights of Men* with her most celebrated production, *A Vindication of the Rights of Woman* (1792). Took her place among leading republicans of the day; moved from London to revolutionary Paris, where she planned to write a second volume of *Rights of Woman*, extending her theme that the education and emancipation of women would lead to a general reformation of society; this second volume remained unwritten: she was herself overtaken by the dilemmas of being a woman; falling in love, bearing a child, being betrayed by her lover, attempting suicide; finally finding tranquillity and happiness in marriage to William Godwin, to die

some five months later (in September 1797) following giving birth to his child (see also note Chap. 11, 16).

21 All quoted passages in this section unless stated otherwise are from *Rights of Woman*.

22 NSLC i 166; Lowes 161; CCL L 316

23 S i 128

24 NSLC i 72

25 D.Q. *Works* iii 195

26 CCL L 449

27 CCL L 93

28 *Times Lit. Sup.* 18.10.1928, p. 759

29 CCL L 80

30 NSLC i 96

31 *Rem.* 27–35; CCL L 87, 88, 93


CHAPTER FIVE: *The Fair Electric Flame*

1 CCL L 93

2 CCL L 87, 88, 93

3 S i 128

4 CCL L 91

5 *P.W.* (1840) i 193

6 MS R


CHAPTER SIX: *Domestic Bliss*

1 *Rem.*

2 CCL L 91; Cottle MSS

3 *P.W.* (1840), 193

4 It was at this time that S.T.C. and Wordsworth first met, in Bristol.

5 This lecture was advertised in the *Bristol Gazette* of the same day. It appeared as a pamphlet in early December of that year, entitled *The Plot Discovered. Conciones ad Populum* had been published shortly before, on 3rd Dec.

6 The chief objects of *The Watchman* were "to co-operate (1) with the WHIG CLUB in procuring a repeal of Lord Grenville's and Mr Pitt's bills, now passed into laws, and (2) with the PATRIOTIC SOCIETIES, for obtaining a Right of Suffrage general and frequent." *Watchman; Works* ii.

7 S i 133–4

8 SMSS

9 CCL L 91; S i 121

10 SMSS

11 S i 16

12 *Rem.*

13 NSLC i 102–6

14 CCL L 93

15 CCL L 105

16 CCL L 112

17 Ibid.

18 CCL L 119

19 CCL L 1723

20 CCL L 108

21 CCL L 66

22 CNB 4430 21$\frac{1}{2}$.51


CHAPTER SEVEN: *The Rock of Reality*

1 CCL L 174, 179, 208, 210, 234; the "autobiographical" letters.

2 See *The Pains of Sleep* (*P.W.*) for vivid suggestion of this: also his anxiety about Hartley and young Robert Lovell (CCL L 676) and S.T.C.'s much later concern for Henry Gillman's "moral danger" at Eton (CCL L 1489, 1490, 1491, 1493). See also B.L. 47555 for an account by Edward Coleridge of late 18th-century public school dormitory life. S.T.C. is naturally reticent on the subject of his own experiences within this context, but provides ample indirect evidence of his victimization.

3 CCL L 16

4 CCL L 156

5 CCL L 536; CNB 1601 21.361; CNB 1718 16.105; among many instances of loving maternal figures (real, or opium-dreamed) at his bedside, and of the bed as a symbol of infantile security.

6 CCL L 68

7 B.L. (1817) x, 86

8 CCL L 124

9 Mrs Elizabeth Evans was the daughter of a rich Quaker, Jedediah Strutt, and the widow of William Evans of Darley, Derbyshire.

10 MS HRC UTA "Mrs Codian"

11 CCL L 176

12 SMSS

13 CCL L 142

14 CCL L 74

15 *Min.* xiv (Potter in his introduction).

16 CCL L 317

17 *P.W.* (1796) *Ode to the Departing Year*, viii

18 Ibid ix

19 MS HRC UTA; letter from Mrs S.T.C. to Mrs Lovell, 1843.

20 CCL L 160

21 CCL L 163

22 CNB 283 G. 280
23 CCL L 163
24 CCL L 146, 151
25 CCL L 150, 151
26 *Rem*; SMSS
27 CCL L 162, 163
28 Ibid.
29 Count von Rumford (Sir Benjamin Thompson) 1753–1814, Fellow of the Royal Society and founder of the Royal Institution, who among many other activities investigated the improvement of smoky chimneys and fireplaces.
30 *Rem.*

CHAPTER EIGHT: *Domestic Bliss Continued*
1 CCL L 262
2 He proposed keeping pigs, fowls and to raise vegetables and "Corn . . . enough for my family" (CCL L 176)
3 *Min*. L 17
4 CCL L 341
5 CCL L 176
6 SMSS; CLL L 204
7 CCL L 173
8 CCL L 176; B.L. (1847); 355; Lamb *Works* iv 73–74
9 S i 199
10 SMSS
11 CCL L 195, 204; S i
12 LL (L) i 118
13 John Thelwall (1764–1834) was a member of Thomas Hardy's Corresponding Society. In 1704 he was sent to the Tower for sedition, with Hardy (1752–1832) and John Horne Tooke (1736–1812) and in October of that same year true bills were found against them and they were transferred to Newgate. Thelwall was acquitted in December; Horne Tooke and Hardy were similarly tried and acquitted.
14 CCL L 200
15 *Rem*. 150
16 John and Thomas Wedgwood spent five days at Alfoxden in September of that year and while there met S.T.C. (Tom Wedgwood was temporarily residing with his brother John at Cote House, near Bristol, in order to be near Dr Thomas Beddoes (1780–1808); an active democrat and Bristol physician of repute who, under Tom Wedgwood's patronage, in 1798 opened the celebrated "pulmonary institution" at Hot Wells, Clifton). The Wedgwoods were an ancient family of potters: Josiah Wedgwood Senior (1730–95), the youngest child of Thomas, of Burslem, Staffordshire, having been an exceptionally skilful potter, specializing in ornamental wares, manufacturing them at his pottery Etruria (named after his famous Etruscan ware), at Hanley. His eldest son, John, became a banker; Josiah junior succeeded as head of the family potteries, while Thomas, a chronic invalid, was a brilliant dilettante (he invented "heliotypes", the forerunners of photographs, was a distinguished metaphysician and theorized on advanced systems of education). John and Josiah married sisters, the Misses Allen, sisters of Robert Allen, the mutual friend of Southey and S.T.C. and early Pantisocrat. A third Miss Allen was married to James Mackintosh, whose first wife was sister of Daniel Stuart (1766–1846) who became owner-editor of *The Morning Post* in 1795, speedily raising the paper into eminence. He was subsequently equally successful with the *Courier*. S.T.C. was to work, brilliantly, for Stuart as a political journalist.
17 CCL L 217
18 The Reverend John Prior Estlin (1747–1817), Unitarian minister, St Michael's Hill, Bristol; author of an important pamphlet, *The Nature and Causes of Atheism*, printed by N. Biggs for J. Cottle, Bristol 1797.
19 CCL L 199
20 *First Acquaintance with Poets*
21 MS HCR UTA "Mrs Codian"

CHAPTER NINE: *Farewell, Sweet Youth*
1 D.Q. *Works* iii 196
2 CCL L 317
3 *Gras. Journ*. May 14 1800; CCL L 1788
4 D.Q. *Works* ii 62; iii 198; CCL L 195
5 *Coleridge Fille* 104–5
6 *Rec. of Henry Nelson Coleridge, By His Daughter* (Torquay, 1910), 9–10
7 D.Q. *Works* iii 198–9
8 Ibid, ii 64–5
9 S i 133–4
10 S i 174, 285

11 *Min*. L 7; see also S ii
12 CNB 2543 17.101
13 CCL L 248
14 CCL L 536; 248
15 CCL L 238
16 Thomas Percy's *Reliques of Ancient English Poetry* (1765), an anthology of traditional ballads. Matthew Gregory Lewis, a highly successful author of "picturesque" fiction and drama; his most famous spine chiller was *The Monk* (1797), universally and enthusiastically described as "perfectly horrid".
17 CCL L 183
18 *The Eolian Harp*: lines first introduced in *Sybilline Leaves*, 1817.
19 S i 283. For a detailed account of Lloyd's troublemaking and the quarrels see Courtney, *Young Charles Lamb*.
20 CCL L 478
21 CCL L 245
22 CCL L 246
23 SCML i 2–3
24 CCL L 256

CHAPTER TEN: *Calamity*
1 CCL L 255
2 CCL L 254
3 Ibid. Richard Lovell Edgeworth (1744–1817) author of *Practical Education* (1798); newly published, therefore, at this time and causing considerable interest, not to say sensation, in progressive circles. *Practical Education* was written in collaboration with Edgeworth's daughter, Maria. The views expressed in the book were based on Rousseau's theories, enlarged upon by Thomas Day (1748–89), disciple of Rousseau and author of *Sandford and Merton*, a moral story for children, written at Edgeworth's suggestion, demonstrating the power of reason and the practical wisdom of doing right. Day became a close friend of Edgeworth and worked with Maria Edgeworth on nursery stories embodying Rousseau doctrine. The Edgeworths were recognized as innovators in educational writing inasmuch as they brought scientific method to their work; with the assistance of the second Mrs Edgeworth (Honora Sneyd) they kept accurate records of children's conversations with their elders and methods of reasoning in children: these records were embodied in *Practical Education*. The Edgeworths placed particular importance upon the necessity of permitting young children to follow their own trains of reasoning, and upon spontaneity of behaviour. Subsequently S.T.C. was to remark to Mrs S.T.C. that, "J. Wedgwood informed me that the Edgeworths were most miserable when Children, & yet the Father, *in his book*, is ever vapouring about their Happiness! — ! — However there are very good things in the work — & some nonsense!" (CCL L 254). Posterity judged the good to outweigh the nonsense: the Edgeworths played an important part in the development of modern methods of education.
4 Part of this journal ultimately reached the public as *Satyrane's Letters; The Friend* 1809 and *Biog. Lit.* 1817.
5 The Wedgwoods shared Poole's distrust of S.T.C.'s "Wordsworth idolatry".
6 CCL L 254
7 CCL L 259
8 CCL L 262. The management, or construction, of dreams arising from opium narcosis is best described as a kind of subconscious remote control; nonetheless it is a control definitely exercised. The addict dreams the kind of dream he wants and avoids unpleasant or frightening sequences. S.T.C., in his notebooks, has described this process of day dreaming or half-asleep fantasy building performed while still sufficiently conscious to be able to *construct*; "*poising* the Thought while Fancy and Sleep *stream on*". (CNB 1421 4.108). Such day dreams, or fantasies, are founded on real events and situations, or memories from the past; in the latter instance, for example, the past will return so vividly and with such force that it is literally lived again, with an immensity of detail that has been lying wholly buried in oblivion during the everyday waking state, but which is now recaptured, as if by a miracle. Real life situations which dwindled to nothing, or ended abortively, may be revived, extended and a score of

delicious variations upon the original theme invented and explored: this alchemy wrought by "the marvellous velocity of Thought & Image in certain full Trances". (Ibid.)

9 MS DC G1/15/1

10 S i 277–81. Vaccination had been first introduced in 1796, a mere two years earlier. Edward Jenner, a country physician, had discovered in his practice at Berkeley in Gloucestershire how to prevent smallpox by deliberately inoculating people with cowpox. However Jenner had no clear idea as to what he was really doing, inasmuch as bacteria had not yet been discovered and the mechanism of infective disease was not understood at that time. It should be added that, at this early stage of its history, vaccination was always an uncomfortable and disconcerting experience for infants, though immeasurably less dangerous than the risk of catching actual smallpox.

11 CCL L 257

12 MS HRC UTA. *Postmark indecipherable. Written from Nether-Stowey. Addressed to*: Mr Coleridge/Pastor Unrake/Ratzburg/(7 Ger: miles from Hamburgh) Germany. *Dated*: 13th December 1798. *On back of fold is written, at a much later date, by Mrs S.T.C.*: Beginning of dear Berkeley's fatal complaint.

Some discursive postscript material has been omitted from the end of this letter. It deals with a living for Mr Roskilly, the curate of Stowey; that Martha Fricker has moved into new lodgings in Bristol; that Hartley sends a message, "Papa tome home"; that Sara has begun reading Edgeworth's books.

13 MS HRC UTA

14 CCL L 263

15 CCL L 270

16 S i 284–87

17 *Min.* L 1. The Mrs King here mentioned was Poole's sister.

18 *Min.* L 2

19 S i 290–4. Mrs Henry Sandford, Thomas Poole's biographer, comments indignantly, of this letter, that Poole wrote "as if, in his mind, a baby scarcely ranked as a human being" (S. i 288), and,

in a footnote to the letter (i 293) "Poor Mrs Coleridge! It may be questioned whether Tom Poole knew what he was talking about. . . . For years afterwards *she* [Mrs S.T.C.] alludes to him [Berkeley] again and again as a loved and living memory. . . . She remembers his birthday, realises what his age would have been, and once almost breaks down with emotion when a Stowey acquaintance visits her, of whom she recollects that, when they last met, she sat long by Berkeley's cradle."

20 MS HRC UTA. Some discursive postscripts omitted: that Cottle resented not having received any letters from S.T.C., though promised; the kindness shown her by Edith and R.S.; Charles Lloyd had written a tragedy; Lamb was writing one; Mary Lamb was again "under affliction" (suffering from one of her periodical attacks of insanity); Southey had published more poems and his "Madoc" was nearly finished; Chatterton's works were about to be published in two vols. for the benefit of his family. The *Lyrical Ballads* were not much esteemed in the Southey household, apart from "the Nightingale" and "the River Y" [Wye = "Tintern Abbey"]. She was alarmed by the amount of S.T.C.'s expenses; hers too had, unavoidably, been much higher than originally anticipated. Her brother George (who had gone to sea as a young merchant seaman) had been shipwrecked off the coast of Spain and had endured great hardship. Eliza Fricker had a lover, an American sea captain; old Mrs Fricker did not believe him to be serious (this in the event proved correct). Commented Sara: "His being a sailor would be sufficient objection to me; but I am very sore on the subject of absent husbands just at this time."

CHAPTER ELEVEN: *Decoy'd*

1 CCL L 275

2 MS HRC UTA

3 CCL L 277

4 NSLC ii 3–4

5 EWL L 235

6 CCL L 927

7 CCL L 286
8 MS HRC UTA. Mrs S.T.C. to Mrs Lovell, 1843.
9 CCL L 292
10 CCL L 294
11 CCL L 298
12 MS Sir Charles Cave
13 *P.W.* (1840) i 178. However S.T.C. himself dated this poem to 1802 — there is uncertainty attached to the date.
14 LL (M) i 183
15 Ibid. 586–7
16 CCL L 305. Following the death of his wife, Mary Wollstonecraft, Godwin was left with two tiny girls to bring up: Fanny Imlay, Wollstonecraft's daughter by Gilbert Imlay (an American speculator and adventurer) and the infant Mary whose birth had brought tragedy to the Polygon. Godwin was fundamentally fond of children; he gave little Fanny the name of Godwin and brought her up as his own daughter. Nonetheless he would seem to have subscribed to the adage that "little children should be seen and not heard": the Coleridges found the "cadaverous silence of Godwin's Children . . . quite catacomb-ish."
17 Poole to S.T.C., 8.5.1799, MS HRC UTA; CCL L 333
18 CCL L 318
19 CCL L 277
20 S i 286
21 EWL L 105
22 S i 286
23 MS HRC UTA. Letter endorsed by Geo. Coleridge, "Letter from Mrs Samuel Coleridge".

CHAPTER TWELVE: *Farewell to Happiness*
1 CCL L 344
2 CCL L 392
3 EWL L 110; 137
4 CCL L 344; also 343
5 CCL L 350
6 CCL L 351
7 S.T.C. was taken seriously ill at Liverpool, while staying with the Cromptons, formerly of Derby, whom S.T.C. had first met during his *Watchman* subscription-raising tour of 1797. The Cromptons had subsequently removed to Liverpool, where they had "a noble seat", Eton, or Eaton. They remained lifelong friends of Mrs Coleridge and her children.
8 CNB 3320 21½.14
9 CCL L 353; 354; 362; 366
10 D.Q. *Works* iii, *Confessions of an Opium Eater*
11 CCL L 351; 432
12 CCL L 400
13 NSLC i 449
14 D.Q. *Works* iii, *Confessions*

CHAPTER THIRTEEN: *The Pains of Opium*
1 *Works* iii: *Confessions of an Opium Eater*. All quotations from De Quincey in this chapter from *Confessions* unless stated otherwise.
2 CCL L 717
3 CCL L 351
4 CCL L 362
5 CCL L 464
6 CCL L 467
7 CCL L 376
8 CCL L 398
9 CCL L 683
10 CCL L 464; Biog. Lit.
11 CCL L 395
12 CCL L 394
13 D.Q. *Confessions of an Opium Eater*
14 CCL L 464; 432
15 C.F. 104–5
16 CCL L 449
17 EWL L 172
18 N.Y. Pub. Lib.
19 CCL L 464
20 CNB 3316 21½.10
21 CCL L 598
22 CCL L 400
23 CCL L 397; 437
24 CNB 909 21.109

CHAPTER FOURTEEN: *The Advent of Asra*
1 They were the children (originally ten in number) of John Hutchinson (1736–85), a tobacco merchant of Penrith, Cumberland, and Mary, née Monkhouse (d. 1783). The ten children comprised: John (bapt'd 1768, d. 1831); Henry (1769– 1839); Mary (1770–1859); Margaret (Peggy) (1772–96); Thomas (1773– 1849); Sarah (1775–1835); Elizabeth (1776–1832); George (1778– 1864); Joanna (1780–1841); William

(1783–85). Mary, George, Peggy and Joanna, following the death of their father, lived in Penrith with their maternal aunt Elizabeth Monkhouse and their great aunt Gamage; Mary, during this period, became the friend of Dorothy Wordsworth. Sarah Hutchinson was mainly living in Kendal; in 1788 she and Mary went to live at Sockburn, where Peggy (formerly a close Penrith companion of Dorothy Wordsworth), ill with tuberculosis, joined them and died in 1796.

2 CNB 718 5½.1
3 CNB 1065 21.190
4 CCL L 881
5 CCL L 814
6 CCL L 470
7 CNB 979 21.131; CCL L 151, 568
8 CNB 979 21.131; CCL L 1169; CNB 1816 16.200; CCL L 719
9 CCL L 470
10 CNB 745.19; CCL L 1169
11 CNB 2053 15.14
12 BL Add.MSS 47521; 74519
13 CNB 2053
14 CNB 2516 17.81
15 CCL L 390
16 CCL L 683
17 "Coleridge and Opium Eating" De Quincey
18 CNB 1394 8.122
19 HCL L 53
20 Raysor; SHL; CNB 3231; *Bondage of Opium* 347–9
21 Raysor; MWL L 149
22 CNB 1394 8.122
23 CNB 1601 21.361
24 *P.W.* (1840) ii 74
25 Ibid., 75
26 CNB 985 21.137
27 *Statesman's Manual*, 320
28 CNB 3298 25.24
29 *P.W.* (1840) i 270–271, *The Pains of Sleep*.

CHAPTER FIFTEEN: *Constancy to an Ideal Object*
1 MWL L 47
2 EWL L 121
3 CCL L 449
4 R.S. and Edith had spent April 1800–April 1801 in Portugal. On his return to England R.S. had received the appointment of private secretary to Isaac Corry, Chancellor of the Exchequer for Ireland. The Southeys took lodgings in Bridge Street, Westminster.
5 CCL L 435
6 *Dejection: An Ode* (original draft, addressed to Sarah Hutchinson).
7 CCL L 439
8 Nixon, 130
9 Though S.T.C. blamed his wife's "outburst" for this attack, in all probability these were withdrawal symptoms: S.T.C. at this time still did not recognize these for what they were.
10 CCL L 449, 464
11 EWL L 172
12 CCL L 454
13 CCL L 458
14 CCL L 465
15 CCL L 466, 467
16 CCL L 470. Mary Stamper, their servant girl. It seems that her aunt was Keswick's favourite midwife. Mrs Railton (recommended by Mrs Clarkson) was a more expensive and exclusive nurse from Penrith.
17 The home of the Allen family, South Wales.
18 CCL L 471
19 MS HRC UTA
20 CCL L 478
21 CCL L 919
22 CCL L 597
23 CNB 2990 11.59
24 Note by A.H.B.C. to the present author.
25 CCL L 417
26 MS N.Y. Pub. Lib.
27 Sir John Stoddart (1773–1856), Crown and Admiralty Advocate for Malta, 1803–7. His sister, Sara, married William Hazlitt.
28 CCL L 536
29 Ibid.
30 CCL L 555
31 CCL L 591
32 *P.W.* (1840) i 180
33 CNB 2531 17.89
34 *P.W.* 455–6. First pub. 1828. J. D. Campbell conjectured that it was written in Malta: everything points to a first draft written in Malta with further work done on the poem later.

CHAPTER SIXTEEN: *Constancy . . . Variation*
1 *Postmarked*: May 23 1804 Keswick. *Addressed*: To Mrs Geo. Coleridge/St Mary Ottery/Devon. *Dated*: May 20th 1804. MS in possession of Mrs Priscilla Coleridge Needham.
2 Henry Herbert Southey (1783–1865), Robert Southey's brother, third of the four brothers. He qualified in medicine at Edinburgh and after practising in Durham moved to London in 1812, where, in Harley Street, he became a fashionable and highly successful physician.
3 Dorothy (Dora) Wordsworth, b. 16th August 1804.
4 *Postmarked*: 1st Sept. 1804. *Addressed*: To Mrs G. Coleridge/St Mary Ottery/Devon. MS in possession of Mrs Priscilla Coleridge Needham.
5 CCL L 525
6 EWLS L 191
7 MWL L 47
8 D.C. MS G1/1/44
9 EWL L 236, 237

CHAPTER SEVENTEEN: *Best Friends in the World* (1)
1 MWL L 43
2 MWL ii 19–22
3 MWL L 44
4 MWL L 47
5 MWL L 45
6 CCL L 642
7 MWL L 58
8 CNB 2934 11.32
9 CCL L 635
10 MWL L 67
11 MWL L 55
12 MWL L 58
13 NSLC i 448–9
14 NSLC i 400n
15 MWL L 67
16 NSLC i 451

CHAPTER EIGHTEEN: *Best Friends in the World* (2)
1 MWL L 92
2 S ii 179
3 CCL L 653
4 CCL L 642
5 BL Add. MSS 74519

6 HCPWM ixxxix; ixl; App. B. ccxix–ccxxii
7 HCL p. 188 and n
8 SCML i *Mem.*
9 MS HRC UTA. Mrs Coleridge to Aunt Lovell *c.* June 1843.
10 Ibid.
11 SCML i 8; CCL L 705. To the Wordsworths S.T.C. wrote that, as he had neglected to inform his brothers that he was bringing his family to Ottery, they had all gone to a watering place for a summer holiday.
12 MS Sir Charles Cave
13 CCL L 656
14 S ii 176
15 S ii 180

CHAPTER NINETEEN: *Best Friends* (3)
1 *Min.* L 5
2 *P.W.* (1840) 410–412
3 CCL L 680
4 MWL L 90
5 CCL L 676
6 CCL L 677
7 CCL L 680
8 MWL L 14, 33, 73, 81, 92
9 MWL L 134
10 CCL L 708; CNB 3355 L.68
11 D.Q. *Works* iii
12 CCL L 682
13 CCL L 788; SCML ii 25; CCL L 713
14 SCML i 17–20
15 CSL iii 242
16 CCL L 802
17 *Min.* L 6
18 MWL L 188 describes how this seizure, resulting in partial paralysis of the right side, had been attributed by the Wordsworths to the child's consumption of a surfeit of raw carrot. Mr Scrambler, the attendant surgeon and apothecary, had concurred with this explanation but later was to confide that he had privately diagnosed a leaked cerebral aneurysm and had anticipated a further, and fatal, cerebral haemorrhage — as proved the case in June 1812.
19 SHL 28.2.1818
20 CSL iii 259
21 MWL L 188
22 MWL L 225

CHAPTER TWENTY: *Best of Friends — "On His Side Quite"*

1 *Min.* L 6
2 CNB 3874 18.97
3 MWL L 223. Basil Montagu, b. 1770, natural son of John Montagu, 4th earl of Sandwich. Basil Montagu had known Wordsworth since undergraduate days at Cambridge.
4 Ibid.
5 D.C. MS 61/1/44
6 CCL L 809, 867
7 Mrs S.T.C. is interesting on this point. We know that, during the latter half of that October, the Wordsworth children were staying at Hackett, in the Colwyth fells between Little Langdale and Elterwater, and this may explain why the farewell meeting with the Wordsworths took place at Ambleside rather than at Grasmere. Elsewhere the date for the departure of Coleridge and the Montagus is given as 18th October; Mrs S.T.C. makes no mention of any stop-over stay at Allan Bank or, even any calling in, at Allan Bank en route for Ambleside. There is every indication that the farewell meeting with the Wordsworths was brief: which would seem to indicate that Wordsworth's conversation with Montagu, warning the latter about S.T.C.'s opium habit, must have taken place on an earlier occasion and that Montagu had gone to Keswick determined to ignore the warning; subsequently Montagu was to say that what he had observed of S.T.C.'s habits while on the road with him had made him change his mind about accommodating S.T.C. under his own roof.

Mrs S.T.C. was, it seems, *en route* (on that morning of 16th or 18th October) for a stay with the Lloyds at Old Brathay.
8 MWL L 223
9 CCL L 867
10 NSLC i 584
11 CCL L 823
12 MWL L 223
13 Campbell *Life*, 180n
14 CCL L 859
15 D.C. Wordsworth MS G1/1/4
16 MWL L 223
17 *Min.* L 7
18 CCL L 856
19 CCL L 858 n1
20 CCL L 882
21 *Min.* L 6
22 CCL L 852, 861, 864
23 *Min.* L 7

CHAPTER TWENTY-ONE: *A Case of Desertion*

1 *Min.* L 7
2 Ibid.
3 CCL L 883
4 *Min.* L 7
5 CCL L 886
6 NSLC ii 49–50
7 MWL L 287
8 NLSC ii 65
9 HCPWM i lix
10 *Min.* L 9
11 CCL L 919
12 *Rem.* CCL L 921n2
13 NSLC ii 94, 97
14 NSLC ii 94
15 NSLC ii 96, 98
16 *Min.* L 9
17 *Min.* L 8
18 MWL L 234; 273. Catharine Wordsworth had finally succumbed to her cerebral aneurysm on 4th June 1812; Thomas had died of pneumonia, a complication of measles, on 1st December of that same year.
19 MWL L 287
20 MWL L 320
21 *Min.* L 9
22 Ibid.
23 Ibid.

CHAPTER TWENTY-TWO: *Snouterumpater*

1 HCL L 3
2 William Hart Coleridge (1789–1849), the "little Will" who made himself ill eating ripe plums in the orchard at Ottery, as S.T.C. tells us in a Long Vacation letter of 1793 (CCL L 30); only child of Luke Herman Coleridge (1765–90), surgeon and apothecary, and Sarah, née Hart (1760–1830), third daughter of Richard Hart, a "respectable druggist in the city of Exeter". William Hart Coleridge was a pupil at King's School, Ottery, 1795–1808: then at Christ Church, Oxford. 1811 First in both classics and mathematics. 1812 ordained

deacon and in 1814 ordained priest and accepted perpetual curacy of Cowley, near Oxford. Subsequently returned to Oxford (1815) and took his Master's degree. 1816 became curate of St Andrew's, Holborn. 1819 became joint secretary of the Society for Promoting Christian Knowledge. 1824 offered appointment as bishop of Barbados and the Leeward Islands. Accepted appointment; set sail for Barbados, accompanied by his cousin Henry Nelson Coleridge (1798–1843). They returned to England the following year; W.H.C. to hold discussions with governmental ministers. He married Sarah Elizabeth Rennell, daughter of the dean of Winchester, and returned with her to Barbados in 1826. Resigned his See for reasons of health in 1841. Returned to England; became first warden of the newly founded St Augustine's Missionary College at Canterbury. Held this office until his sudden death in 1849. One hundred and fifty years later his name is still esteemed in his old See.

3 *Min.* L 11
4 CCL L 909
5 CCL L 919
6 CCL L 984
7 CCL L 987
8 CCL L 951
9 *Min.* L 10
10 MS HRC UTA
11 HCL L 4
12 HCPWM i lxxii
13 *Min.* L 11
14 NSLC ii 137–9
15 Ibid.
16 *Min.* L 12
17 *Min.* L 13
18 *Min.* L 14
19 SCML i
20 SHL
21 MWSL L 104
22 *Min.* L 18
23 Ibid.
24 NSLC ii 159
25 HCPWM i; HCL L 21
26 NSLC ii 159
27 CL v 167–169
28 *The Doctor* (1848) 378–88
29 SLW iii 270–3

30 CSL v 114–115

CHAPTER TWENTY-THREE: *"Without Hope or Heart"*

1 *Min.* L 12
2 The actual correspondence between them has not survived, but can be reconstructed from NSLC, *Min.* and MSS HRC UTA.
3 S ii 256
4 S ii 257
5 *Min.* L 18
6 LL (L) ii 374
7 HCPWM i lxxiii–lxxviii
8 *Min.* L 19
9 CSL iii 108
10 John Hookham Frere (1769–1846), the translator of Aristophanes, was a devoted friend and disciple of S.T.C. and a useful acquaintance to R.S. (whom he had first met in Portugal in 1801, Frere having then been an envoy to that country). Personal meeting with both S.T.C. and R.S. had at first been embarrassing for Frere as he had earlier parodied both poets in the *Anti-Jacobin*.
11 Sir George Beaumont (1753–1827), patron of Hearne, Girtin, Constable, Wordsworth and Coleridge, among many other distinguished names in painting and literature. Founder of the National Gallery. A distinguished painter himself; pupil of Cozens, Wilson and Malchair. Painted in Lakes as early as 1777 and 1778 with Hearne and Farington. Became a regular "Laker"; he and Lady Beaumont were tenants for many years of "Jackson's House", Greta Hall.
12 John Taylor Coleridge (1790–1876), second son of Colonel James Coleridge, brother of S.T.C. Educated at the King's School, Ottery St Mary and Eton. 1809 won a scholarship to Corpus Christi college, Oxford; gained a first in classics in 1812. That same year elected a Fellow of Exeter college and went on to cover himself with academic honours. 1813 commenced law studies at Southampton Buildings, his companion being John Patteson (who subsequently became J.T.C.'s brother-in-law and a brother High Court judge). In 1816 J.T.C became a member of the Middle

Temple. 1818 married Mary Buchanan, daughter of the Rev. Dr Gilbert Buchanan of the Buchanans of Lenny, and rector of Woodmansterne, Surrey. J.T.C. now gave up Special Pleading and joined the Western Circuit. 1824–25, editor of *Quarterly Review*. J.T.C.'s first child, b. 1819, survived only a few months; his second, John Duke Coleridge (1820–94) became Lord Chief Justice.

Henry Nelson Coleridge (1798–1843), fifth son of Colonel James Coleridge. Educated King's School, Ottery; Eton, and King's college, Cambridge. Became fellow of King's (1821); winner of the Browne Medal for the Greek and Latin Odes, and for the Greek Ode. Afterwards practised as a Chancery barrister. 1829 married Sara Coleridge *fille*. Author of *Six Months in the West Indies* (1826); an *Introduction to the Greek Classics* (1834); *Table Talk of Samuel Taylor Coleridge* (1835). Commenced second ed. of S.T.C.'s *Works*, which was completed by H.N.C.'s widow in 1847. Of his several children, only two, Herbert (1830–61) and Edith (1832–1911) survived earliest infancy.

13 S ii 256–57
14 Edward Copleston (1776–1849) became provost of Oriel in 1814 and bishop of Llandaff in 1827.
15 HCPWM i lxix–lxx
16 John Keble (1792–1866), a close friend of J.T.C., was an outstanding academic, poet and High Anglican holding the Oxford chair in poetry 1831–1841: his 2 vol. book of poems, *The Christian Year*, appeared anonymously in 1827. Keble was, with Newman, the primary impetus of the Tractarian movement.
17 HCL App. A
18 Richard Whately (1787–1863) dean of Oriel, was a notable logician and theological writer, who in 1829 became professor of political economy at Oxford and in 1831 archbishop of Dublin.
19 HCPWM i lxix–lxx
20 HCL App. B
21 Ibid.
22 HCPWM i lxix–lxx
23 CCL L 1242

24 HCL L 11
25 CCL L 1242
26 HCL L 15
27 CCL L 1241
28 MS HRC UTA. *Postmarked*: Keswick. *Addressed*: To Mrs G. Coleridge/St Mary-Ottery/Devon. *Dated*: 2nd April 1821
29 HCL L 11
30 CCL L 1249A
31 HCL J App. A
32 CCL: letters following Hartley's disgrace draw a tragic self portrait of S.T.C.
33 HCPWM i xcv; CCL L 1317
34 HCL L 22
35 *Min.* L 17
36 HCL L 22
37 CCL L 1312; CNB 4039 18.176
38 NSLC ii 234–35
39 MS HRC UTA. Letter to Mrs George Coleridge.

CHAPTER TWENTY-FOUR: *The House of Bondage*

1 SCML i 2
2 SCML i 28
3 *Min.* L 23; MS HRC UTA
4 LL (L) ii 370
5 NSLC ii 280
6 *Dev. House*, quoting H.N.C.'s diary
7 Ibid.; C.F. 51
8 *Dev. House*, 282
9 Frances Duke Coleridge, two years Henry's senior.
10 MS HRC UTA, to Derwent Coleridge 6th October 1826
11 *Min.* L 26
12 Chiefly K.Q.M. to which Derwent contributed under the name of *Davenand Cecil*. His literary circle included Thomas Babington Macaulay, the poet John Moultrie, W. M. Praed, and H.N.C.
13 CCL L 1286
14 MS HRC UTA
15 *Min.* L 25
16 MS HRC UTA
17 HCL L 32
18 MS HRC UTA
19 *Min.* L 26
20 MS Mrs A. H. B. Coleridge
21 MS HRC UTA, to Derwent, dated 30th January 1826
22 CCL L 1515

23 MS HRC UTA. *Postmarked*: 4th April 1826. Undated
24 MS HRC UTA, to Derwent, dated 6th October 1826
25 Ibid.
26 Ibid.
27 NSLC ii 305
28 MS HRC UTA, to Derwent. Dated 1st–4th February 1827
29 Ibid.
30 MS HRC UTA. Undated. No postmark. Probably 6th or 13th February 1827, from internal evidence.
31 HCL L 32
32 HCL L 30
33 Ibid.
34 *Min*. L 34
35 CSL vi 74–75
36 Beaumont had left her a legacy of £100 upon his death in 1827.
37 Lady Beaumont had died 14 July 1829, leaving S.T.C. £50 which he sent to Mrs C. "to lay out, as she thinks needful, for Dear Hartley. Would to God! it had been twice ten times the sum" (S.T.C. to Derwent, CCL L 1673).
38 HCL L 31
39 Ibid.
40 CNB 13.278
41 Griggs says she returned in 1831 for a visit but evidence in her letters establishes otherwise.

CHAPTER TWENTY-FIVE: *Domestic Bliss — Reprise*
1 HCL L 38; *Min*. L 36
2 MWL i 451–52
3 Downshire Place no longer survives.
4 *Min*. L 36, 37; S ii 320, 288
5 *Min*. L 38
6 Herbert Coleridge (1830–1861) won the Newcastle and Balliol scholarships while at Eton and took a double first at Oxford in 1852. He was a distinguished member of the Philological Society, being learned in Sanskrit, and the northern languages including Icelandic. In 1859 he published his *Glossarial Index to the Printed English Literature of the Thirteenth Century* as a foundation for the *New English Dictionary* (subsequently published by the Clarendon Press as the *Oxford English Dictionary*). He married Ellen Penshouse Phillips in 1853; they had no children. He died at 10 Chester Place, his old home, of pulmonary tuberculosis, at the age of thirty-one.
7 *Rec. H.N.C.*
8 C.F.
9 SCML ii 366n
10 C.F. 65, 72; *Rec. H.N.C.* 10
11 *Poems*, 135
12 HCL L 61. The first draft of the sonnet, used in this text.
13 CNB 980 21.132
14 CCL L 1312
15 Ibid.
16 CCL L 1317
17 CNB 273 G. 270
18 CNB 3309 23.13
19 HCL L 53
20 *Dev. House* 138
21 CCL L 1673
22 HCL L 36
23 MS HRC UTA
24 *Fears in Solitude*
25 HCL L 36. Mrs C.'s letter has not survived.
26 CNB 4039 18.176
27 CCL L 1752
28 *Min*. 39
29 *Min*. 40
30 HCPWM i
31 *Min*. 41
32 MS HRC UTA. *Sara's Journal*
33 *Min*. L 40
34 *Min*. L 41

ENVOI
1 MS HRC UTA Sara to Hartley 5.8. 1834
2 Ibid.
3 S ii 297
4 HCL L 46
5 HCL L 47
6 NSLC ii 415
7 LWL (H) ii L 832
8 MS HRC UTA *Addressed* to: Miss Emily Trevenen. *Postmarked*: 23rd November 1836. Undated.
9 SCML i 344–45
10 MS HRC UTA

# NOTES TO THE ILLUSTRATIONS

1. (*Frontispiece*) Mary Matilda Betham (1776–1852), miniature portrait painter, poet, and author of a *Biographical Dictionary of the Celebrated Women of every Age and Country* (1804). Together with her brother Charles she spent the summer and early autumn of 1809 at Greta Hall, during which period she did miniatures of the entire Southey family, and of Mrs Coleridge, S.T.C., their little daughter Sara, and Mary Lovell.

2. (*Following page 80*) Watercolour, artist unknown, but evidently amateur. The subject is shown as a young woman; her costume belongs to *circa* the first decade of the nineteenth century. Believed to be a keepsake portrait of Dorothy Wordsworth given by her niece Dora to Maria Jane Jewsbury, who at the age of twenty four, in May 1825, presented Wordsworth with her poems, dedicated to him. She was invited to stay at Rydal Mount where she formed an enthusiastic admiration for Dorothy Wordsworth and struck up cordial – and lasting – friendships with Dora Wordsworth and Sara Coleridge *fille*. In 1832 Miss Jewsbury married a Reverend Mr Fletcher, a missionary, and in September of that year left with him for India (where she died of cholera soon after her arrival). Before leaving England she decided to leave her portrait of Dorothy with Dora, to whom she wrote to that effect on 2 August 1832. However Dora did not want the portrait (it seems she did not much like it) and when Maria Jane and her husband arrived in London, prior to joining ship at Gravesend, they visited Sara *fille* and Henry Coleridge in Hampstead and soon afterwards the portrait was handed to Henry (letter to Dora from Maria Jane, 17 September 1832) and in this way, with Dora's full knowledge and acquiescence, the portrait came into, and remained in, the possession of Sara *fille* and the Coleridge family. (Dove Cottage MSS: A/Jewsbury/38, 39).

3. (*Following page 240*) William Westall (1781–1850). First visited the Lakes in 1811 and became an enthusiastic member of Laker society, and very friendly with the Southey family. His set of aquatints of *Views of the Lake and Vale of Keswick* appeared in 1820: in this view of Crosthwaite Church the ladies in the grounds of Greta Hall are said to represent members of the Southey household; the figure in the large bonnet, presenting her back view, is Mrs Southey; her companion in conversation with her is unidentifiable; the girl seated under the tree with a book represents Sara *fille*.

# SELECTED BIBLIOGRAPHY

ALLSOP, T., ed., *Letters, Conversations, and Recollections of S. T. Coleridge*, New York, 1836.

ARMITT, M. L., *Rydal*, Kendal, 1916.

BARTH, J., ROBERT, S. J., *The Symbolic Imagination: Coleridge and the Romantic Tradition*, Princeton Essays in Literature, Princeton N. J., 1977.

BOUCH, C. M. L. and JONES, G. P., *The Lake Counties (1500–1830), A Social and Economic History*, Manchester, 1961.

CAMPBELL, J. D., *Samuel Taylor Coleridge: A Narrative of the Events of his Life*, London, 1894.

COLERIDGE, EDITH, *Some Recollections of Henry Nelson Coleridge and his Family*, Torquay, 1910.

COLERIDGE, HARTLEY, *Letters of Hartley Coleridge*, ed. G. E. Griggs and E. L. Griggs, London, 1936.

*Poetical Works, and a Memoir of his Life by his Brother*, London, 1851.

COLERIDGE, H. N., *Six Months in the West Indies in 1825*, London, 1826.

COLERIDGE, J. T., *Memoir of John Keble*, 2 vols., London 1869.

COLERIDGE, LORD, *The Story of a Devonshire House*, London, 1905.

COLERIDGE, S. T., *Aids to Reflection*, ed. H. N. Coleridge, 2 vols., London, 1843.

*Biographia Literaria . . . and Two Lay Sermons*, London, 1817.

*Collected Letters*, ed. E. L. Griggs, 6 vols., Oxford 1956–1972.

*Coll. Works*: 1. *Lectures 1795: On Politics and Religion*, ed. Lewis Patton and Peter Mann (1970) Princeton N. J., 1967.

*Coll. Works*: 3. *Essays on his Times*, ed. David Erdman, 3 vols. (1978)

*Notebooks of Samuel Taylor Coleridge*, ed. Kathleen Coburn, 3 double vols., London, 1957–1973.

*The Complete Poetical Works of Samuel Taylor Coleridge*, ed. E. H. Coleridge, Oxford, 1912.

*The Table Talk and Omniana of Samuel Taylor Coleridge*, London, 1835.

COLERIDGE, SARA (Mrs S.T.C.), *Minnow Among Tritons: Letters of Mrs Sara Coleridge to Thomas Poole*, ed. S. Potter, London, 1934.

COLERIDGE, SARA, *Memoir and Letters*, ed. Edith Coleridge, 2 vols., London, 1873.

COLLIER, J. P., *An Old Man's Diary, Forty Years Ago*, London, 1872.

COTTLE, J., *Early Recollections; Chiefly Relating to the Late Samuel Taylor Coleridge during his Long Residence in Bristol*, London, 1837.

*Reminiscences of Samuel Taylor Coleridge and Robert Southey*, London, 1847.

COURTNEY, W. F., *Young Charles Lamb 1775–1802*, New York and London, 1982.

*Cumberland and Westmorland Antiquarian and Archaeological Society's Transactions*, Old Series (CW) and New Series (CW2), Kendal.

DE QUINCEY, T., *The Collected Writings of Thomas De Quincey*, ed. Masson, Edinburgh, 1889–90.

DE VERE, AUBREY, *Recollections*, London, 1897.

FOSKETT, D., *John Harden of Brathay Hall 1772–1847*, Kendal, 1974.

GODWIN, WILLIAM, *An Enquiry Concerning Political Justice, and Its Influence on General Virtue and Happiness*, London, 1793.

*Memoirs of the Author of the Rights of Woman*, London 1798.

GRIGGS, E. L., *Coleridge Fille*, Oxford, 1940.

HALLER, W., *The Early Life of Robert Southey*, New York, 1917.

HARDING, A. J., *Coleridge and the Idea of Love: Aspects of Relationship in Coleridge's Thought and Writing*, Cambridge, 1974.

HAYDON, BENJAMIN R., *The Autobiography and Memoirs of Benjamin Robert Haydon*, ed. Tom Taylor, 2 vols., London, 1926.

HAZLITT, WILLIAM, *The Complete Works of William Hazlitt*, ed. P. P. Howe, after the ed. of A. R. Waller and Arnold Glover, London and Toronto, 1930–34.

HUGHES, EDWARD, *North Country Life in the Eighteenth Century*, ii., 2 vols., London, 1965.

HUTCHINSON, SARA, *Collected Letters*, ed. K. Coburn, Oxford, 1954.

HUTCHINSON, W., *History of the County of Cumberland and some Places Adjacent*, 2 vols., Carlisle, 1794.

IMLAY, GILBERT, *A Topographical Description of the Western Territory of North America*, London, 1791.

JERDAN, W., *The Autobiography of William Jerdan*, 4 vols., London, 1852–3.

KEATS, JOHN, *Letters of John Keats, 1814–1821*, ed. Hyder E. Rollins, 2 vols., Cambridge, 1958.

KNIGHT, FRIDA, *University Rebel: The Life of William Frend*, London, 1971.

LAMB, CHARLES and MARY, *The Letters of Charles Lamb, to Which are Added Those of his Sister Mary Lamb*, ed. E. V. Lucas, 3 vols., London, 1935.
*The Letters of Charles and Mary Anne Lamb*, ed. E. W. Marrs (to Oct. 1817), Ithaca, 1975–.

LATIMER, JOHN, ed., *Annals of Bristol in the Nineteenth Century; Bristol Mercury*, Bristol, 1887.

LOCKHART, J. G., *Memoirs of the Life of Sir Walter Scott, Bart.*, 7 vols., London, 1837–8.

LYNN LINTON, E., *The Lake Country*, illus. W. J. Linton, London, 1864.

LYSONS, D. and S., *Magna Britannia, vol. iv Cumberland*, London, 1816.

McFARLAND, THOMAS, *Coleridge and the Pantheist Tradition*, Oxford, 1969.

METYARD, ELIZA, *A Group of Englishmen (1795–1815)*, London, 1871.

MOORMAN, MARY, *William Wordsworth, a Biography*, 2 vols., Oxford, 1957–65.

MOZLEY, T., *Reminiscences chiefly of Oriel College, and the Oxford Movement*, 2 vols., London, 1882.

NICHOLSON R. A., *The Mystics of Islam*, London, 1914.

NIXON, EDNA, *Mary Wollstonecraft: Her Life and Times*, London, 1971.

PARSONS, W. and WHITE, W., *History, Directory and Gazeteer of the Counties of Cumberland and Westmorland with that part of the Lake District in Lancashire, etc.*, Leeds, 1829.

PAUL, C. K., *William Godwin: His Friends and Contemporaries*, 2 vols., London, 1876.

PRIESTLEY, JOSEPH, *Hartley's Theory of the Human Mind, on the Principle of the Association of Ideas; with Essays Relating to the Subject of It*, London, 1775.

*Proceedings of the Delaware County Institute of Science*, xi, 1–60, 1947.

RAWNSLEY, REV. H. D., *Literary Associations of the English Lakes*, 2 vols., Galashiels, 1894.

RAYSOR, T. M., ed., *Samuel Taylor Coleridge; Shakespearean Criticism*, second ed., London and New York, 1960.

REED, MARK L., *Wordsworth: the Chronology of the Early Years, 1770–1799; The Middle Years, 1800–1815*, Boston, 1967, 1975.

ROBINSON, HENRY CRABB, *The Correspondence of Henry Crabb Robinson with the Wordsworth Circle*, ed. E. J. Morley, 2 vols., Oxford, 1927.

SANDFORD, MRS HENRY, *Thomas Poole and his Friends*, 2 vols., London, 1888.

SAUNDERS, ANN, *Regent's Park: A Study of the Development of the Area from 1086 to the Present Day*, London, 1969.

*Scott, Sir Walter. Familiar Letters Of . . .* ed. D. Douglas, 2 vols., London, 1894.

SIMMONS, JACK, *Southey*, London, 1945.

SLATER's, late Pigot & Co's *Royal National Commercial Directory of Northern Counties* . . . vol. 2; Isaac Slater, Manchester & London, 1855.

SOUTHEY, ROBERT, *Common-Place Book*, ed. J. W. Warter, London, 1876. Four Series.
*Correspondence of Robert Southey with Caroline Bowles*, ed. E. Dowden, London 1881.
*Life and Correspondence of the late Robert Southey*, ed. C. C. Southey, 6 vols., 1849-50, New York, 1851.
*New Letters of Robert Southey*, ed. Kenneth Curry, 2 vols., New York and London, 1965.
*Selections from the Letters of Robert Southey*, ed. J. W. Warter, 4 vols., London, 1856.
*The Doctor*, ed. J. W. Warter, London, 1848.

STEPHENS, FRAN. C., *The Hartley Coleridge Letters, A Calendar and Index*, Austin, Texas, 1978.

STERNE, LAURENCE, *The Life and Opinions of Tristram Shandy, Gentleman*, London, 1948.

SWIFT, A. M., *Derwent Coleridge, Scholar, Pastor, Educator*, New York, 1883.

TAYLOR, H., *The Autobiography of Henry Taylor*, 2 vols., London, 1885.

TREVELYAN, SIR GEORGE OTTO, *The Life and Letters of Lord Macaulay*, 2 vols., London, 1876.

VIZETELLY, HENRY, *Glancing back through Seventy Years*, 2 vols., London, 1893.

WATSON, LUCY E., née Gillman, *Coleridge at Highgate*, London, 1925.

WEST, T., *A Guide to the Lakes*, 1799 ed., London.

WHALLEY, GEORGE, *Coleridge and Sara Hutchinson and the Asra Poems*, London, 1955.

WOLLSTONECRAFT, MARY, *A Vindication of the Rights of Woman*, London, 1792.

WOODCOCK, GEORGE, *William Godwin*, London, 1946.

WORDSWORTH, DOROTHY, *Journals of Dorothy Wordsworth*, ed. M. Moorman, Oxford, 1971.

WORDSWORTH, MARY, *Letters of Mary Wordsworth*, sel. and ed. Mary E. Burton, Oxford, 1958.

WORDSWORTH, WILLIAM and DOROTHY, *Letters of William and Dorothy Wordsworth*, ed. de Selincourt, *The Early Years 1787–1805*, rev. Chester Shaver; 2, *The Middle Years 1806–1811*, rev. M. Moorman, Oxford 1937–1970.
*The Letters of William and Dorothy Wordsworth, The Later Years*, revised, arr. and ed. by Alan G. Hill from the first edition ed. de Selincourt. Part I 1821–1828; Part II 1829–1834, Oxford, 1979.

# INDEX

Adscombe, 82–84, 94
Alfoxden, 89, 127, 211
Allan Bank, 189, 191–196; child's eye view of, 191–193
Allen family (*see also* Crescelly), 266
Allen, Robert, 35, 36, 40, 266
Ambleside (*see also under* Dawes), 199, 272

Bannister, John (in *The Wood Demon*), 181
Bath (*see also under* Coleridge, Sara, *and* Southey, Robert), 24, 28–31, 41, 42, 44; "milliners of", 61, 62; Bath-Bristol Repertory Company, 30
Beaumont, Sir George, 171, 244, 273; legacy for Mrs S.T.C., 275; as tenant of "Jackson's House", Greta Hall, 273
Beaumont, Lady, 175, 178; help for Hartley, 214; for Derwent, 226; legacy for S.T.C., 275
Beddoes, Dr Thomas, 189, 266
Bedford, Grosvenor Charles, 21, 29, 32, 33, 63, 262
Bedford, Horace, 29, 263
Berkeley, George, Bishop of Cloyne, 97, 98
Betham, Mary Matilda, 220 (*see also* List of Illustrations)
Birmingham, 79
Bowles, Caroline, 258
Brent, Charlotte, 186, 210; attempted Asra situation with, 187
Brighton, 255
Bristol, 27, 44–46, 56, 57, 61, 62, 70, 73–75; as scene of early life for Sara, Southey and S.T.C., 23–85 *passim*; as radical city, 24; Sara's childhood and girlhood in, 23–26, 31, 41, 47; Coleridge courtship in, 41, 53–57, 61–68 *passim*; Coleridge marriage at St Mary Redcliff, 69; early married life of Coleridges in, 70–85 *passim*; death of Berkeley in, 111–113; S.T.C.'s and Sara's 1807 visit there, 180, 186; meeting De Quincey there, 186; opium crisis at, 211–215; Mrs S.T.C.'s and Sara *fille*'s 1823 visit, 237; Mrs S.T.C.'s residences in, b. 1770 Thomas St or Stokes Croft, 23; Westbury, *c.* 1776–1780, 23;

Redcliff Hill, 1786–Oct. 1795, 25–69 *passim*; Nov. 1795–March 1796, 70–74 *passim*; Oxford St, Kingsdown, March–Dec. 1796, 74–85 *passim*
Brunton, Elizabeth, 48; Ann, 48
Burnett, George, 29, 35, 37, 40, 44, 56, 65, 73, 74, 262
Byron, George Gordon, Lord, 61

Calne, 217
"Cambridge Apostles", 262
Cambridge University, 47, 48, 49, 66, 226–240 *passim*; S.T.C.'s last visit (1833), 255; Colleges: King's, 274; St John's, 227, 237
Chatterton, Thomas, 268
Chepstow, 63–65
Chester, John, 98, 102
Christ's Hospital, 34, 37, 54, 76, 77
Clarkson, Catharine (Mrs Thomas Clarkson, née Buck, wife of the abolitionist), 174, 187, 189, 190, 191, 195, 196, 201, 270
Clevedon, 66–70
Coleorton, 171, 174, 175, 178, 181
Coleridge family, 122, 124, 128, 256; the "great family reconcilement", 252
Coleridge, Ann (Mrs Coleridge Snr: "Our mother"), née Bowden, 76, 128, 179, 183; death of, 194
Coleridge, Berkeley, birth of, 97, 98; a remarkable child, 98, 106, 107, 116; his illness and death, 102–118; 124, 131; surviving in Mrs S.T.C.'s memory, 268
Coleridge, Derwent, 22; birth of, 130, 131; 1807 visit to Bristol, 182; at Mr Dawes's school, 191, 193; at Allan Bank, 193; in hopes of Cambridge, 218; visits Highgate, 225; scholastic success, 226, 227; enters St John's, Cambridge, 227; involved in Hartley crisis, 229; Derwent's "catterpillarage", 237–239; schoolmaster at Plymouth, 239; at Buckfastleigh, 239; return to orthodoxy, 239; engaged to Mary Pridham, 240; takes Holy Orders, 240, 241; at Helston, 241–247 *passim*;

marriage, 242; birth of son, 242; rupture with S.T.C., 249, 250; reconciled, 252; success in pulpit, 247; at Cambridge with S.T.C. in 1833, 255; at St Mark's Teachers' Training College, Chelsea, 259; as poet, 274

Coleridge, Mrs Derwent, née Mary Pridham, 242, 247

Coleridge, Derwent Moultrie, their son, 242, 247

Coleridge, Edith (daughter of Henry and Sara *fille*), 254, 259

Coleridge, Edward (brother of S.T.C.), 179

Coleridge, Edward (Fellow of Eton, nephew of S.T.C.), 256, 265

Coleridge, Frances Duke (Fanny), 236, 274

Coleridge, George, Master of King's School Ottery and Chaplain Priest, Ottery St Mary, 42; rescues S.T.C., 43, 48, 49; hoping to have S.T.C. at Ottery, 179, 180; determined not to have S.T.C. at Ottery, 183, 184; help for Hartley, 213, 214; death of, 252

Coleridge, Mrs George, née Jane Hart, Sara's letters to, 123, 124, 127, 128, 157, 164–166, 230

Coleridge, George May, their son, 128

Coleridge, Hartley, 15–17, 22; birth of, 79, 80; infancy, 88–90, 98, 211; learning by Edgeworth methods, 101, 267, 268; illness at Stowey, 104, 109; 111–113, 117; and the Itch, 122–124; and "Mr Gobwin", 126; arrival in Lakes, 129, 130; effect of father's opium habit upon him, 136, 137, 211; boyhood, 165, 166, 210, 211, 242, 182, 192; to Coleorton with S.T.C., 174, 181; trauma from his parents' separation, 176, 181, 193; dislike of Sarah Hutchinson, 148, 181; pupil at Mr Dawes's school, 191, 193, 199, 210, 211, 219, 226; paternal neglect of his future, 209, 211, 212–214; assistance from friends, 213, 214, 216; traumatic relationship with S.T.C., 136, 137, 210, 211, 214; to Merton College, Oxford, 214, 215; coached by S.T.C. in 1815 Long Vac., 217; strange appearance, 218; adored by children, 218; scholastic prowess, 226; visits Ottery, 227; becomes probationary Fellow, Oriel, 227; the Oriel catastrophe, 227–231; his alcoholism confirmed, 231; banished by S.T.C., 232;

homeless, 233; assistant to Mr Dawes, 232, 234, 237, 238; Hartley's Ambleside school, 238, 240; a vagrant, 240–247 *passim*, 251; his "blasted" existence, 242, 243, 246; tragically isolated, 249–251, 253–255; his grief at S.T.C.'s death, 258; his mother's "eternally youthful and wayward son", 259; his fatalism, 226, 250;
Essays: *The Wisdom of our Ancestors*, 181;
Poems: *Poems* (1833), a collection, 255; *Sonnet to H.N.C.*, 248, 249

Coleridge, Henry, Nelson, 16, 128; a shining scholar, 226, 274; engaged to Sara *fille*, 236–238, 241; to Barbados, 273; wedding, 242–244; as family "reconciler", 248–252; his charm and brilliancy, 251; as son to S.T.C., 251, 252; as family man, 247, 254, 255; S.T.C. death-bed farewells and grief, 257; editor of S.T.C.'s *Works*, 274; death of Henry, 258

Coleridge, Mrs Henry, née Sara Coleridge – see under Coleridge, Sara *fille*

Coleridge, Herbert, their son, 248, 252, 259; his brilliant career and premature death, 275

Coleridge, James (Colonel), 226, 236; on "Mrs Sam", 236; 251, 252

Coleridge, Mrs James, nèe Frances Duke Taylor, 183

Coleridge, John (father of S.T.C.), Master of King's School and vicar of Ottery St Mary, 42; S.T.C. his "Benjamin", 76

Coleridge, John Taylor, 226, 235, 236, 273, 274

Coleridge, Mrs John Taylor, née Mary Buchanan, 274

Coleridge, Luke Herman, 272

Coleridge, Mrs Luke, née Sarah Hart, 272; William Hart, their son, *see under separate entry*

Coleridge, Samuel Taylor, 15–18 *passim*, 34–36, 41; as S.T.C., 17; as Ancient Mariner, 250, 251; early history and neurotic personality of, 42, 43, 76–78, 82–84, 88, 94–97, 119, 120, 150, 186; as Pantisocrat, 35–36 *passim*, 61–65; reputation as Jacobin, 44, 46, 56, 57, 69, 70, 84, 87, 264; political lectures, 56, 57, 70; as genius and poet (*see also* Poems of), 34, 35, 94–97; as Unitarian, 97; as upholder of woman's rights, 58, 61, 80, 82, 91, 92; as reactionary on same, 57, 58, 143, 144, 155; his dislike of "bluestockingism", 57,

58, 92, 139–140; on love and marriage, 37–40, 77, 78, 80, 81, 143, 144; malignment of his wife, 15–18 *passim*, 139, 140, 144, 145, 147, 153, 155, 173, 180, 188, 189; and of his friends, 138, 144, 147, 180; first meeting with Southey, 33, 35; the "scheme" to wed Sara, 37–40; first meeting with Sara, 41; proposes, 42; attempts to jilt her, 47–52; reconciliation with, 51–53, 81, 82; whirlwind courtship, 53–69; plans to elope, 56; quarrels with Southey, 65, 67, 73, 97, 121, 122; marriage and honeymoon, 69–71; realities and hardships of early married life, 73–85; Poole to the rescue, 71–79 *passim*; friendship with Poole – see under Poole; friendship with S.T.C.; domestic bliss, 69–75, 80–98 *passim*; one man Pantisocrat, 81–87; Nether Stowey, 72, 86–111; 1807 visit, 182–186; Germany and the Berkeley tragedy, 101–120; reconciliation with Sara, 120–125; 153–160; escape to the Lakes, 124; London and journalism, 124–126; removal to Greta Hall, 126–131; opium and destruction of marital happiness, 130, 134–151; trauma with Hartley, 136–138; advent of Asra, 142–151; constancy to the ideal of domestic bliss, 152–163; Malta and Italy, 164–166, 168, 169; return to England: the "divorce" that never was, 170–205; at Coleorton, 174, 178, 181; at Allan Bank, 191–195; quarrel with Wordsworth: return to Greta Hall and Sara, 195–205; Wedgwood annuity (*see under* Wedgwood); struggles to resume marriage, 152–160; desertion and neglect, 219–223 *passim*; struggle to save his soul and reputation, 216, 217; Highgate (*see under own entry*); coaching Hartley, 217; *Biographia Literaria*, 217, 218; visits from sons, 225, 226; the Hartley catastrophe, 229–232; visit of wife and daughter, 225, 226, 234–238; estrangement from Hartley, 232, 249–254; from Derwent, 239, 249, 250, 252; "poor father", 237, 238, 240, 242, 245, 252, 254, 255; as grandfather, 252, 254, 255; final reconciliation, 248–256; death of, 257; funeral, 257;
Opium: early addiction, 54, 55, 65; under marital stress, 75; the Adscombe crisis, 81, 83, 84, 94; the writing on the wall, 83, 84; influence of Wordsworths, 95, 96;

opium in Germany, 102, 103; "The Pains of Opium", 130–163 *passim*; misplaced sympathy of Wordsworths, 135, 139; struggle against drug, 140, 153, 156, 158–160; realization of "opium habit", 158–160; organic psychosis, 171–181, 187–189; a trial to Wordsworths on account of, 178, 189, 193, 195, 196; improvement at Highgate, 225; thrown back by the Oriel disaster, 231, 250; and by Derwent, 239; by Hartley's vagrancy, 247, 251; De Quincey on S.T.C.'s "opium fetters", 250; final improvement, 253, 255;
Poems: *Ancient Mariner, The*, 96, 130, 131, 251; *Christabel*, 97, 130, 131, 137, 225; *Christmas Tale, A*, (poetic drama), 218; *Constancy to an Ideal Object*, 162, 163; *Day Dream: From an immigrant to his Absent Wife*, 103, 104; *Day Dream, A*, 149; *Dejection: an Ode*, 153, 154; *Destiny of Nations, The*, 88; *Eolian Harp, The*, 67, 97; *Fall of Robespierre, The* (co-author with Southey), 47; *Fears in Solitude*, 253; *Frost at Midnight*, 35; *Happy Husband, The*, 125; *Kubla Khan*, 34, 96; *Lyrical Ballads* (*see also under own heading, and* Wordsworth), 91, 96, 130, 132, "not much esteemed" by Southey, 268; *Nightingale, The*, 268; *Ode to the Departing Year*, 81, 88; *Ode to Sara: written at Shurton Bars*, 67, 68; *Osorio* (*Remorse* – poetic drama), 87, 88, 90, 97, 209, 210; *Pains of Sleep, The*, 150; *Poetical Works*, 255; *Reflections on Having left a place of Retirement*, 66; *Remorse* (*see Osorio*); *Sibylline Leaves* (coll.), 225; *Sonnet: To Pantisocracy*, 35; *To Two Sisters*, 186, 187
Day Dream sequences: constancy to his ideal of domestic bliss, 103, 104, 149, 150, 186;
Prose Works: *Biographia Literaria*, 217, 218, 225; *Friend, The*, 193, 195, 196, 197, 203, 204; *Lay Sermons: The Statesman's Manual*, 225, 248; *Watchman, The*, 70, 73–75, 78
Coleridge, Sara (Mrs Samuel Taylor Coleridge, née Fricker), 15–18, 23–26, 37–40, 45–47; an unknown character, 18; misrepresented and maligned, 15–18; 93, 94, 138, 139, 144, 145; personality, 25, 31, 32, 92, 191; temper, 25, 26, 57, 136, 137,

139; environment and upbringing, 23, 24, 29, 30; her intellect, 91; her education, 24, 91; her unconventionality, 62; as democrat and forward-looking young woman, 24, 45, 46, 62; as upholder of woman's rights and sexual equality, 24, 29, 61–64, 143, 144, 155; as believer in women's education, 24, 218, 219, 234; as household "oeconomist" 75, 82; as chatelaine and hostess at Greta Hall, 168, 219, 220; as Bumble-cum-Tumble and joker, 219–222; her Lingo Grande, 21, 22, 221, 222; relationship with Robert Southey, 16, 17, 22, 23, 26, 29–32, 65, 67, 81, 82, 113, 120, 121, 164–166, 168, 173, 177, 212, 213, 219–223, 242–244; friendship with Poole, 16, 71, 72, 87, 88, 94–97, 185, 237, 247, 248, 256, 257; grief at death of, 258; relationship with Wordsworths: from foes to friends, 17, 91–97, 135, 139, 140, 164, 167, 220, 243–246, 258 (*see also* Wordsworth, Dorothy *and* William); birth of, 23; *Mrs Codian's Remembrancies*, 16, 17, 23–98 *passim*; childhood and girlhood, 16, 23–33; in Bristol, 16, 23–85 *passim*; in Bath, 24–26, 29–31, 41, 42; influence of Miss Tyler and Bath, 29–32, 93; as designated Pantisocratic bride, 37–41; first meeting with S.T.C., 41; proposed to by him, 42; jilted by him, 47–52; ecstatically courted by him, 51–69; emancipated behaviour of Sara, 61–66; her damaged reputation thereby, 61, 62, 65, 66, 68, 69, 87; marriage and honeymoon, 69–71; Sally Pally, 80; domestic bliss, 69–98 *passim*; pregnancy and hard lessons of Necessitarianism, 73–75; birth of Hartley, 79, 80; laudanum: the writing on the wall, 81, 83, 84; projected experiment of self sufficiency and simple life, 81–87; Nether Stowey, domestic bliss in "wretched hovel", 86–90; arrival of Wordsworths, 89, 91–97; Sara lacks organic sensibility, 91–94; birth of Berkeley, 97, 98; pride and delight in, 98, 106, 107; death of Berkeley: Sara's tragedy and betrayal, 104–120; domestic strife, 120–124; London, 124–126; househunting, 126, 127; Greta Hall and birth of Derwent, 127–131; the Pains of Opium: catastrophe, 130–141; freezing looks for the Wordsworths, 139; Sarah Hutchinson as rival,

142–144, 147,153, 156; as friend, 167, 202, 258; a strong marital relationship at the core, 143, 144, 153–162, 173, 174, 191, 194–204, 224, 225, 235, 237, 238, 245; battle with S.T.C.'s "opium habit", 135–141, 158–160 (*see also* opium, its role in her marriage); S.T.C. to Malta, 160–169; Sara's tour of the Lakes, 165; a "friendly" separation, 170–195; 1807 visit to Stowey but never reached Ottery, 182–184; S.T.C.'s return to Sara, 194; the Wordsworth-S.T.C. quarrel, "on his side quite", 197–205; "battles" with Sarah Hutchinson, 202; as deserted wife, 210–218; officially homeless, 212, 213, 224, 225; financial hardship, 134–136, 209, 212, 213; as Snouterumpater and matriarch, 216–223, 226, 235, 236, 239–248; middle-aged spread, 220; broken-hearted by Hartley, 230–233, 244–246, 253, 254; visit to Highgate, 235; alarmed by Sara's engagement, 237; aversion to marriage for her children, 235, 237, 240; troubled by Derwent, 237–242; departure from Lakes, 243–246; domiciled in Derwent ménage, 242, 247; solacement in Sara *fille*, 247, 248, 255, 259; reunited with S.T.C., 195–204, 235, 248–256; "auld lang syne", 256; death of S.T.C., 257, 258; death of Poole, 258; old age of Sara, 258, 259; her death, 259, 260;
The role of opium in her marriage: courtship period, 54, 55; as impediment to her marriage, 55, 56, 65; as alarming factor, 83, 84, 94–97; engulfed by S.T.C.'s catastrophe, 132–141; "Asra", 142–151; joint battle against opium, 158–160; her concern, 197–199
Coleridge, Sara *fille*, 15, 16, 22, 92; birth of, 158; childhood, 182, 191–194; at Allan Bank, 191–194; girlhood, development into beauty and scholar, 234–236; as the *Highland Girl*, 235; at Highgate, 235, 236; engagement to Henry Coleridge, 236–238; the House of Bondage, 238–242; her wedding, 242–244; marriage and motherhood at Hampstead, 247–258; widowhood and Regent's Park, 259; on her parents' incompatibility, 92, 139; on her mother's magnanimity, 191; lack of close attachment to her father, 191, 192, 234, 242, 252; on his death, 257
Coleridge, William Hart (Bishop of

Barbados), 216, 272, 273
Collins, William, *The Highland Girl*, 235
Cooper, Thomas, 46
Copleston, Edward, 227, 228, 231, 274
Cottle, Joseph, 55, 62–64, 69, 73, 85, 86, 89, 90, 138; a subscription for S.T.C., 212; help for Hartley, 214; 266, 268; *Reminiscences*, 57, 89, 90
Covent Garden Theatre, 181, 210

Danvers, Charles, 177, 264
Darwin, Erasmus, 88
Davy, Humphrey, 138, 147
Dawes, Rev. John and his Ambleside school, 191, 193, 199, 210, 211, 219, 226, 234, 237, 238
Day, Thomas, 267
De Quincey, Thomas, 15, 16; on the Coleridge courtship, 52; on "milliners of Bath", 61, 62; on opium consumption, 83; on Wordsworths and Mrs S.T.C., 91–93; on S.T.C.'s "monomaniac" antipathies and likings, 147; on Dorothy Wordsworth, 91–93, 190; on S.T.C.'s opium, 250; *Confessions of an Opium Eater*, 131–133
Derwent Water, 127, 129, 131
Dove Cottage, 15, 136, 139; at Christmas 1803, 161; Mrs S.T.C.'s 1803 and 1804 visits, 164, 167; overcrowded, 171, 189; removal from, to Allan Bank, 189; Dorothy's trauma at leaving, 190
Drury Lane Theatre, 87, 181, 210
Dyer, George, 56, 78

Edgeworth, Maria, 267
Edgeworth, Richard Lovell, *Practical Education*, 102, 267, 268
Edmondson, John (Keswick apothecary-surgeon), 134
Estlin, Rev. John Prior, 90, 266
Eton College, 257, 259, 265, 273, 274, 275; "Eton Bronze", 236
Evans, Elizabeth (Mrs Evans of Darley, née Strutt), 78, 79, 87, 265
Evans, Mary, 37, 49, 77

Fordyce, James, *Sermons to Young Women*, 59
Frend, William, 264
Frere, John Hookham, 226, 273
Fricker family, 23–26, 81; opposition to Sara's marriage, 53–56; Fricker sisters,

general, 23–26, 29–32, 37; emancipation of, 45, 46, 61–64, 66; estrangement of, 64, 66; in Stowey, 120–122
Fricker, Edith (*see also* Southey, Mrs Edith), 23, 30, 32, 37, 39, 46, 49, 61–64; marriage, 72, 73
Fricker, Eliza, 23, 120–124; 182, 268
Fricker, George, 23, 83, 84, 239, 268
Fricker, Martha, 23, 37, 182, 210, 243
Fricker, Martha (Mrs Stephen, née Rowles), 23–25, 49, 64, 69, 73, 75, 83, 84, 134, 182; death of, 194
Fricker, Mary (*see* Lovell, Mary)
Fricker, Sara (*see* Coleridge, Sara, Mrs S.T.C.)
Fricker, Stephen, 23–25

Gallow Hill, 142, 153
Germany, 78, 90, 97–119 *passim*; Brocken Spectre, 119
Gillman, Mrs Ann, 224, 255
Gillman, Henry, 265
Gillman, Dr James, 224, 225, 229, 232, 233, 257
Gillman, James Jnr, 257
Godwin, William, 38, 61, 125, 126, 130, 131, 138, 144, 147; *Political Justice*, 39
Grasmere, 15, 126, 130, 132, 164, 167, 168; distance from Keswick, 129; Red Lion Inn, as H.Q. for Hartley, 240, 244
Green, J.H., 254
Grenville, William Wyndham (Lord Grenville), 33; and the "Gagging Acts", 70
Greta Hall, 15, 21, 127–244 *passim*; as jerry-built "picturesque lure", 129; to be shared with Wordsworths, 155; with the Southeys, 156, 161; rebuilding of, 156; arrival of Southeys, 161; social life under Southey's influence, 168; Southey's decision to settle there, 176; attempt by S.T.C. to turn his wife out and install Wordsworths instead, 176, 177; S.T.C.'s 1808 visit, 191; in connection with *The Friend*, 193, 195, 196; S.T.C.'s return to Mrs S.T.C. in 1809, 194–197; and his 1812 visit, 202–204; as "Aunt Hill", 218; family life, 218–223; the schoolroom, 218–219; as hub of Lakes society, 220; no longer "home" for Coleridges, 212, 213, 232, 233; as "House of Bondage", 238–242; Sara *fille's* wedding at, 242, 244; Mrs S.T.C.'s departure from, 243, 244
Greta, River, 129

Grimaldi, Joseph (in "Mother Goose"), 181

Hampstead, 247–257 *passim*; Herbie, "The Rose of Hampstead", 248; Downshire Place, 247, 248, 252
Hardy, Thomas (republican), 266
Hartley, David, *Observations on Man*, 38, 80
Hawkes, Thomas, of Moseley, 79
Hazlitt, William, 270
Helston, 241, 244, 247
Highgate, 224–227, 229–232, 235, 236, 247–257 *passim*
Hill, Rev. Herbert, 27, 28, 31, 72
Hucks, Joseph, 34, 36, 40
Hutchinson family, 15, 143, 269, 270
Hutchinson, Mary (*see* Wordsworth, Mary)
Hutchinson, Sarah, 15, 139, 142, 143, 158, 159; brought up in Kendal, 270; "Asra", 146–150; *Dejection Ode*, 153; attempts to break with S.T.C., 162, 195; S.T.C.'s jealousy, 178–181; her reputation damaged, 190, 191; as amanuensis, 195; walks out on S.T.C., 195; on the S.T.C.-Wordsworth quarrel, 202; "never a beauty", 220; death of, 258

Imlay, Fanny (renamed Godwin), 269
Imlay, Gilbert, 154, 269

Jackson, William, builder and landlord of Greta Hall, 127, 129, 131, 136; dislike of Wordsworths, 177; death of, 194
"Jackson's House", 194, 273
Jenner, Edward, 268

Keble, John, 228, 230, 274
Kemble, Charles (in *Town and Country*), 181
Kendal, 171
Kendal Black Drop (*see also* laudanum), 134, 175
Keswick, 15, 127, 132, 166; its favourite midwife, 156; Hartley at day school, 165; S.T.C. a great addition to Keswick society, 197; (*see also under* Coleridge *and* Southey *entries*)

Lake Country and Lakers, "Tour of the Lakes" by carriage, 165; non-stop summer cavalcades of, 168, 197
Lamb, Charles, 34, 134, 161, 170, 201, 209, 226; visits Stowey, 89; quarrels with

S.T.C., 97; with Coleridges in Buckingham St, 125, 126; help for Hartley, 216; at Highgate, 235; play, *Pride's Cure* (later called *John Woodvil*), 268
Lamb, Mary, 170, 200, 268
Laudanum, 54, 55, 65, 75, 81, 83, 84; quantities, 83; attitudes of the Wordsworths toward, 95, 96; for rheumatism, 122, 130; Kendal Black Drop, 134; with brandy, 134, 162
Lewis, Matthew Gregory ("Monk" Lewis), 96, 181, 267; *The Monk*, 267; *The Wood Demon*, 181
Lichfield, 88
Lloyd, Charles, 79, 80, 83–85, 88, 89; as troublemaker, 95–97; writing a tragedy, 268
London, 47, 124–126, 153, 161, 170–171, 180, 181, 200–210 *passim*
Longman, bookseller, 130, 200
Losh, James, 127
Lovell, Mary (née Fricker), 23, 24, 30, 37, 41, 46, 98, 183, 239, 241, 243; engagement to Robert Lovell, 31; widowed, 82; to Greta Hall, 156, 161
Lovell, Robert, 31, 37, 41, 55, 56
Lovell, Robert, Jnr, 82, 265
*Lyrical Ballads* (*see also* S.T.C. *and* Wordsworth *entries*), 91, 96, 130–132

Mackintosh, James, 184, 266
Malta, 161, 162, 164–166, 168
Montagu, Basil, 198–204, 231, 272
Montagu, Mrs Basil, née Skipper, 198, 199
Morgan, John, 186, 189, 200, 202, 204; bankruptcy of, 210; *Biog. Lit.* written at Calne, 217, 218; Morgans "good for S.T.C.", 217
Morgan, Mrs John, née Mary Brent, 186, 188, 224
*Morning Post, The*, 124, 126, 130, 131, 135, 153, 266

Nether Stowey, 44, 45, 72, 79, 82, 84–98 *passim*, 104, 120–124, 126, 127; Book Society, 58; Mrs S.T.C.'s 1807 visit, 182–186; her 1823 visit, 237; her 1830 visit, 247–248; in golden retrospect, 256
Newman, John Henry, 226, 274

Ottery St Mary, 42, 79, 122–124, 179, 180, 182–184
Oxford Movement, 227, 228

Oxford University, 27–40 *passim*, 216–231 *passim*; Colleges: Balliol, 27–29, 31–35, 40, 48, 275; Christ Church, 27, 226, 272; Corpus Christi, 273; Merton, 216, 226, 227; Oriel, 226–231; University, 34

Paine, Thomas, 56
Patteson, John, 244, 273
Peachey, Colonel William, 127
Penrith, as early home of Hutchinson sisters and Dorothy Wordsworth, 270
Percy, Thomas, *Reliques of Ancient English Poetry*, 96
Phillips, bookseller, 130
Phillips, Mrs Elizabeth, née Coleridge (half sister to S.T.C.), 128
Poole, Charlotte, 45
Poole, John, 45
Poole, Thomas, 16, 37, 44, 45, 78, 79, 82–127 *passim*, 138, 154, 204, 234, 255, 257; death of, 258; radicalism, 44, 45, 58, 72, 79; first meeting with S.T.C., 45; friendship with S.T.C., 71–73, 78, 81, 82–84, 182–186, 203, 225, 237, 247, 248, 256, 257; and with Sara, 71, 72, 87, 185, 237, 247, 248; as neighbour to the Coleridges, 84–124 *passim*, 126, 127; involvement with Berkeley tragedy, 104–117, 268; estranged from S.T.C., 123, 138, 144, 147, 180, 182; reconciled with S.T.C., 182, 185, 186, 203; Poole and the Wordsworths, first impression, 89; suspicious of, 94–97, 102, 104; tug of war for S.T.C., 126, 127; interest in Hartley, 213, 214
Potter, Stephen, 30
Pridham, Mary (*see also* Mrs Derwent Coleridge), 240, 242, 249
Priestley, Joseph, 38, 39, 46, 118
Purchas, Samuel, 96

*Quarterly Review, The*, 236, 255, 274

Racedown, 89
Regent's Park, 259
Rickman, John, 175
Roberts, Augusta, 29
Robespierre, Maximilian, 45, 263
Robinson, Henry Crabb, 190, 201
Romford, Count von, 85, 266
Roskilly, Mr, 107, 268
Rousseau, Jean Jaques, influence of, 39, 58–60, 92, 126, 267

Russell, Thomas, 169, 179
Rydal Mount, 213, 234, 240, 244, 246, 254, 258

Sandford, Mrs Henry, 65, 66, 268
Senhouse, Humphrey and family (at Derwent Water Bay), 243
Sheridan, Richard Brinsley, 87, 97
Shurton Bars (near Bridgwater), 67
Sneyd, Honora (second Mrs Richard Edgeworth), *Practical Education*, 267
Society of Friends, 24, 31, 79
Southey, Edward (brother of R.S.), 28
Southey, Henry Herbert (brother of R.S.), 218, 219
Southey, Robert, 15, 16, 17, 21, 22, 28, 29, 31, 33, 75, 81, 82, 144, 155; birth of, 23; childhood and friendship with the Fricker girls, 23, 26, 29–32; courtship of Edith: rejection of Sara, 31, 32; as "fiery democrat", 27–29, 31–34, 45, 46, 56, 57, 61, 62; and as Pantisocrat, 35–58 *passim*, 61–65); first meeting with S.T.C., 33–35; part he did *not* play in S.T.C.-Sara marriage, 52; ruptures with Coleridge, 63–67, 73, 121, 123; marriage and departure for Portugal, 72, 73, 270; return from Portugal, 81; early career and married life, 81, 82, 153, 270; to Greta Hall, 161; his generosity to Sara and her children, 212, 213, 242; as family man, 166, 218–223; relationship with Sara, 113, 120, 121, 153, 212, 213, 219–223, 242–244; advisor to her over "separation", 174, 176; as friend of Morgans, 186, 187; 210; literary lion and Laureate, 16, 168, 210, 219, 220; learns of S.T.C.'s death, 258; marriage to Caroline Bowles, 258; his senility, 259; death of Southey, 258;
Poems: *Botany Bay; Eclogues*, 40; *Fall of Robespierre, The* (with S.T.C.), 47; *Joan of Arc*, 40, 57; *Madoc*, 268. *Life and Letters of*, 16, 17, 262
Southey, Mrs Robert (*see also under* Fricker, Edith), 82, 113, 120–122, 160, 161, 168, 201, 202, 222, 238, 241–243; death of, 258; their children, Bertha, 218, 239; Cuthbert, 239, 241, 262; Edith May, 218; Herbert, 218, 219; Isobel, 218, 239, 241; Kate, 218, 239; Margaret, 156, 161
Southey, Robert Snr, 23, 28
Southey, Mrs Robert Snr, née Margaret Hill, 26, 28–30, 41, 49, 56, 72

Southey, Thomas (brother of R.S.), 41
Spedding, James (1808–1881), 262
Spedding, John (1770–1851), 127
Spedding Margaret (1774–1821), 127, 134
Spedding, Mary (1768–1825), 127, 134
Spry, Rev. Benjamin, 69
Stoddart, John, 161, 164, 165, 168, 270
Stoddart, Sara, 270
Strutt, Jedediah, 265
Stuart, Daniel, 131, 153, 266

*Tait's Edinburgh Magazine*, 16
Taylor, Henry, 16, 262
Tennyson, Alfred, Lord, 262
Thelwall, John, 89, 137
Tintern Abbey, 62–64
Tooke, John Horne, 263, 266
Trevenen, Emily, 244, 246
Tyler, Elizabeth, 26–30, 32, 47, 49

Wade, Josiah, 69, 89, 212
Wedgwood annuity of S.T.C., 97; over-
    spending of, 134; Josiah's threatened
    withdrawal of, 184, 185; withdrawn, 209,
    213
Wedgwood family, 72, 266
Wedgwood, John, 266
Wedgwood, Josiah, 97, 184, 266
Wedgwood, Thomas, 97, 156–158, 184,
    266
Westbury (Bristol), 23, 113
Westminster School, 27, 29
Whateley, Richard, 228, 229, 274
Wilkinson, Joseph, 127
Wilson, Mrs, "Wilsy", 129, 131, 134, 136
Wollstonecraft, Mary, 144, 154, 264, 265,
    269; *A Vindication of the Rights of
    Woman*, 58–61, 264

Wordsworth, Dorothy, 15–18, 89, 90–94; in
    middle age, 193, 220; early friendship
    with Mary Hutchinson, 270; distorted
    view and presentation of Mrs S.T.C.,
    15–18, 93, 94, 135, 138, 139, 152, 161,
    187; early role in the Coleridge marriage,
    91–98; role in the "separation", 139, 140,
    152, 154, 170, 171, 175, 176, 187, 189,
    190; disturbed condition, 190; friend of
    Sara Coleridge, 240, 241, 244, 258; at
    Allan Bank, 189–203; sad disillusionment
    with S.T.C., 178, 190, 194–196, 201; on
    his love for Sarah Hutchinson, 195; upset
    by Hartley, 240; helping Hartley, 244,
    253; a chronic invalid, 258
Wordsworth, William, 15, 91–98, 191, 256;
    early friendship with S.T.C. at Alfoxden,
    88–98; dismissal of Sara, 91, 93; *Lyrical
    Ballads* at Dove Cottage, 130–132; as
    sympathetic to S.T.C.'s early opium and
    complaints, 95, 96, 135, 139; at Coleorton
    with S.T.C., 178–180, 181; quarrel with
    S.T.C., 198–205; friend and counsellor
    of Sara Coleridge, 170, 171, 214, 258;
    friend and protector of Hartley, 213, 214,
    216, 233, 234, 240;
    Poems: *Lyrical Ballads*, 91, 130–132; *Ode
    to Immortality*, 153; *Poem on the Growth
    of an Individual Mind (The Prelude)*,
    178; *Tintern Abbey* ("The River Y"), 268;
    *White Doe, The*, 189
Wordsworth, Mrs William, née Mary
    Hutchinson, 15, 139, 149, 161, 191, 195;
    helping Hartley, 244, 253, 256, 270; their
    children, Catharine, 191, 195, 213, 271,
    272; Dora, 165, 192, 193; John, 243;
    Thomas, 171, 213, 272; William (Willy),
    birth of, 195